NORTH KOREA'S OPEN DOOR POLICY – THE IMPOSSIBLE DREAM?

Risks and Prospects in FDI and Trade from the Legal and Political Perspectives

by

Pilho Park

ISBN 979-8950011030

Library of Congress Control Number: 2018675309
Printed in the United States of America

For permissions, inquiries, feedback or to contact the author:
peacekor4ever@gmail.com

Seetory Inc.
Irvine, California

… for a better tomorrow …

to my granddaughter Yebin
and her generation

Contents

Preface

Humankind landed on the near side of the Moon to explore its never-before-experienced soil fifty-six years ago and rovers are moving around the surface of Mars to explore it even at this moment. We are living in an era of discovery and exploration of the solar system and beyond. But we often feel like living on a different planet from the one North Korea is located because we, the people of the rest of the world, know less about this country than we do about Mars or Jupiter, so to speak.

This book is the product of tracking North Korea's limited open door policy since 1984 and more closely from 1991 onward in order to assess to what extent this limited open door policy could be implemented within a socialism-oriented nonmarket economy. In the course of pursuit of this policy's implementation, the most curious finding is that the North Korean government has never abandoned its open door policy, especially from 1991, the second stage, although it has never opened widely.

As a host country of foreign direct investment, North Korea has never been remiss in amending and supplementing relevant laws and implementing regulations to bolster its open door policy while the United States and a number of potential investor countries have continued to impose heavier economic sanctions. Furthermore, the United Nations Security Council has also joined the ranks of those imposing harsh economic sanctions on North Korea, doing so eleven times from 2006 to 2017 and these are still in effect. North Korea might, in its own terms, take pride in having survived what it describes as the imperialists' conspiracy to suffocate it.

North Korea has placed itself into such a difficult situation by strenuously developing and testing nuclear weapons as well as launching ballistic missiles over the past three decades. At the same time, it has never abandoned the pursuit of foreign direct investment, which is hardly compatible with such a bellicose posture. No one would assume that this contradictory posture could be friendly or harmonious with an open door policy. It is a dilemma that North Korea is saddled with. It is also a conundrum for outsiders as to how North Korea might find the key to this puzzle. Could it be as if the case of the musical "Man of La Mancha – I, Don Quixote" who relentlessly pursues his own dream as portrayed in the song "The Impossible Dream"?

Acknowledgements

I wish to express my gratitude to scholars who have produced valuable academic materials about North Korea before me. The same applies to journalists who have reported news and information about North Korea. Both public and private organizations and the specialists working with them have also contributed a great deal, visibly and invisibly, to my work on North Korea. They may have faced the same difficulty in accessing necessary sources and information in the course of their work, as I have throughout the entire period of preparing this book.

It is a curious fact that North Korea has not widely publicized its open door policy, particularly since its formal declaration in 1991. Although North Korea published some printed materials in English to advertise the policy and projected special economic zones to potential investors, these were distributed to only a very limited number of places and entities around the world. It was extremely difficult to access or obtain relevant materials about the open door policy. In addition, it was also practically impossible to obtain even a single academic article from a law journal published in North Korea, let alone relevant booklets.

Up until recent years, relevant materials and information have been difficult to find in the United States, South Korea, Japan, the United Kingdom, and EU member states, despite the fact that businesses from these countries are the major potential investors and trading partners. North Korea has not even opened and maintained its own website for advertising and attracting foreign investment and trade. Such a reclusive approach is entirely at odds with an open door policy. I would strongly urge the North Korean authorities to take more active steps in publicizing the policy and the business environment of North Korea regardless of ongoing economic sanctions imposed by the United Nations Security Council, United States and other potential investor countries.

In citing the sources written in Korean, I used the *italicized* Revised Romanization of Korean which is the official Korean language romanization system of the Republic of Korea.

Chapter 1 Introduction of Foreign Investment

A. Overview

North Korea, the common name for the Democratic People's Republic of Korea, briefly opened the door to foreign direct investment in 1984 but the door was slowly closed around the time the Berlin Wall collapsed in 1989. It achieved minimal success in contrast to its neighboring former socialist countries such as China or Vietnam. North Korea again initiated the second stage of open door policy in 1991 with more preparation and wider range than the first one. While North Korea has never called or named its action as the "open door policy," in order to facilitate the second open policy, North Korea has enacted dozens of laws and made scores of implementing regulations to bolster the policy. It did so, however, without restructuring the 'socialist economy line' peculiar to North Korea, without examining whether such an economic environment could be compatible with market-oriented foreign businesses, and without considering how incoming foreign businesses could survive in North Korea's unfriendly business environment.

The initiation of the second stage was closely interlinked with the dissolution of the Soviet bloc in 1991. The second stage has had a relatively longer life than the first and has survived to the present. In the meantime the economic environment surrounding North Korea has become heavily entangled with the disordered economic planning internally and international politics externally; thus, such an environment has caused the country's economy to stagnate further.

However, North Korea has achieved only a limited number of cases and modest amounts in attracting foreign direct investment until the United Nations Security Council started to impose the harsh economic sanctions eleven times against North Korea from 2006 to 2017. From this period to the present, incoming foreign direct investment and foreign trade have dropped markedly. The United Nations' economic sanctions were triggered by North Korea's testing of nuclear weapons and launching of ballistic missiles. The United States has also imposed various and numerous economic sanctions from 1950 immediately after the Korean War broke out. In these circumstances, it is natural to say that it is extremely difficult to boost its economy through attracting foreign direct investment and trade.

There is no doubt that the comprehensive economic sanctions laid by the United Nations and the United States were the major factor to impede the flow of foreign capital to North Korea. It is also true, however, that foreign direct investment was not actively pursued even before the United Nations imposed economic sanctions, or when the United States loosened sanction measures following the conclusion of the Agreed Framework in 1994 as compared to neighboring countries like China and Vietnam. The difference between North Korea and the neighbors is the size of potential risks.

The potential risks associated with North Korea's open door policy can be broadly grouped into two categories. One set of risks emanates from the political sphere and the other from the economic sphere although they are intertwined in many areas.

The risks from the political sphere encompass both ideological identity and international politics. The major thought sustaining North Korean regime is the 'Juche' idea. It is interpreted as the idea to stand alone, that is, self-reliance rather than depending on others. It replaced Marxism-Leninism as the national ideology, as declared in the first Socialist Constitution of North Korea in 1972.[1] It created derivative sub-ideas such as independence in politics, self-sufficiency in economy, and self-defense in national defense as discussed in other subchapters below. The Juche idea is stressed in the North Korea's Constitution and the Covenant of the Workers' Party of Korea numerous times. The Juche idea has eventually evolved to create sub-ideas 'Kimilsungism and Kimjongilism' named after Kim Il Sung, the founding leader of North Korea and Kim Jong Il, son and successor of the senior Kim. In the long run, no one could deny that the idea of self-reliance has contributed to North Korea remaining a reclusive country.

As for international politics as another significant risk factor, North Korea has been afflicted for many decades by economic sanctions, particularly those imposed by the United States. In recent years, a further set of economic sanctions was imposed on this country by the United Nations Security Council. Additional sanction measures against North Korea from several economically developed countries are also underway, in addition to those countries' active compliance with United Nations measures. These countries will be huge prospective investors as well as trade partners once such

[1] *See* the Socialist Constitution of the Democratic People's Republic of Korea of 1972 art. 4.

economic sanctions are lifted. Details on economic sanctions will be discussed in Chapter VI.

Risks from economic aspects emanate from the fundamental tenets that North Korea has maintained since its founding. The current Socialist Constitution of the DPRK declares that this country relies on the 'socialist production relations' and an 'independent national economy.'[2]

The principle of the socialist production relations gave birth to the ideas of socialized ownership of production means and it has been embodied in the Socialist Constitution.[3] It further declares that the State solely owns almost all resources and services such as natural resources, railway and air transport services, post and telecommunications, factories, enterprises, ports and banks and more.[4] Foreign investors doing business in North Korea will encounter difficulties whenever they deal with North Korean counterparts or relevant government offices, as these are not service-oriented but rather bureaucratic, given that the State controls everything.

The independent national economy results in several sub-principles such as minimizing imports but relying on self-support, self-supporting energy and natural resources, and self-training engineers and technicians. This principle was rooted in the Juche idea and eventually led to North Korea's isolation from the international community, particularly in the realm of external economic relations.

In addition, North Korea is the country of the planned economy. Every sector of the economy is operated based on the nation's planning although such planning is not always accurately implemented especially in recent years. Operation of joint-ventured enterprises with foreign partners may be included as a part of nation's economic planning since such companies are considered North Korean businesses. In certain circumstances, foreign-invested enterprises may find it difficult to obtain domestically produced supplies if an unexpectedly large number of foreign investors enters North Korea, as such demand may fall outside the planned production schedule.

Another economic risk resides in the industrial infrastructure. Coupled with the historical event of the collapse of the Soviet bloc and severe natural disasters that occurred over a few years in the

---

[2] *See* the Socialist Constitution of 2023 art. 19.
[3] *See id.* art. 20.
[4] *See id.* art. 21.

1990s, North Korea's economic planning was not possible to carry out as planned. During this period which was named by the regime 'arduous marching,' the country's ration system, an important pillar of the ideological principle of independent national economy, collapsed and as a result, the famine had been rampant for several years. At the same time, private commercial transactions, though illegal but tacitly tolerated, began to emerge spontaneously in market yards called *jangmadang* nationwide. In this circumstance, North Korea was not able to maintain, construct or improve various social infrastructures, of course, including and more specifically industrial infrastructure that deteriorated as time went by.

As such, North Korea faces so many challenges that can only be resolved by North Korea itself, as long as it wishes to attract foreign capital. In this book, relevant issues that North Korea is saddled with are discussed to recognize what kind of challenges North Korea encounters and how North Korea could respond to them.

On the other hand, and particularly with regard to its potential, North Korea has many positive attributes. North Korea has a population of 26.5 million as estimated by the World Bank Group in 2024. Its land size is about 121,000 square kilometers (approx. 47,000 square miles), slightly larger than the State of Pennsylvania of the United States or a bit smaller than England of the United Kingdom.

North Korea has brilliant geographical merits. It shares borders with China along the Tumen ("*Duman*" in Korean) River and the Yalu ("*Amrok*" in Korean) River. It also shares the border with Russia along with the lower reaches of the Tumen River. The convergence point of these three borders and its surrounding areas are referred to as the 'Golden Triangle' in the context of the Greater Tumen Initiative (GTI), as discussed below. The Golden Triangle is located in the northern flank of the Rason Economic and Trade Zone (or "Rason ETZ" hereafter) which is North Korea's most developed special economic zone.

The Rason ETZ has two seaports, Rajin Port and Sonbong Port. The former is larger than the latter. They are ice-free ports in winter unlike Vladivostok, the largest seaport in the Russian Far East. Although China's territory extends to the lower reaches of the Tumen River, it ends approximately nine miles before the river's mouth at the East Sea of Korea, as that final stretch is shared by North Korea and Russia. North Korea is bordered with two provinces of China, Jilin and Liaoning. Heilongjiang province's southern border is fifty miles away from North Korea. Of these, Heilongjiang and Jilin provinces, with a combined population of sixty million, are landlocked. If they can use the ports of the Rason ETZ coupled with the Changjitu Plan[5] and the UNDP's Great Tumen Initiative (GTI), transportation costs to seaports will be greatly saved. Thus, China's provinces and Russia's eastern territories can be economic hinterlands of the Rason ETZ.

North Korea has affluent natural resources especially in minerals. The topography of North Korea is mountainous and the land contains more than 200 minerals including coal, iron ore, gold, magnesite, lead, zinc, tungsten, graphite, barite, and molybdenum, and various rare earth minerals. The estimated total value is reportedly approximately USD 10 trillion.

North Korea's human resources are, arguably more importantly, well-qualified. This country has very high rate of literacy, 100% for adults because it has compulsory schooling up to secondary education. In addition, the people of North Korea are trained from kindergarten and elementary school to memorize lengthy directives authored by the Workers' Party of Korea or its leaders, and to express verbally or in writing what they learn from them. Koreans are industrious as shown in the cases of South Koreans who share identical history, culture, language, and customs with the North Koreans. The sole difference between them is that they have lived apart for several decades due to the political environment.

North Korea has established four special economic zones at the four corners of its land in addition to more than twenty economic development zones inside the territory in order to promote foreign direct investment, trade and tourism. These will be reviewed and discussed in the chapter III. North Korea has completed or is in the process of finalizing measures to facilitate such zones by enacting relevant laws, issuing implementing regulations and administrative measures, and preparing to construct industrial infrastructure.

These special economic zones especially have wonderful economic hinterlands respectively. In the northeastern corner, the Rason ETZ has as economic hinterlands Russian cities in the east as well as Chinese cities in the northeast of China and these cities are connected with railroad and land routes. In the northwestern corner,

[5] This plan is China's economic program starting from 2009 to develop its northeastern provinces. The Changjitu stands for names of three areas: Changchun City-Jilin City-Tumen River areas (including Yanbian Korean Autonomous Prefecture).

the Hwanggumphyong and Wihwado Economic Zone (HWEZ) shares borders with Chinese cities, especially those of Liaoning Province. In the southeastern corner, the Wonsan City - Kalma Beach resorts - Mt. Kumgang belt has all of South Korea as its economic hinterland, as the belt is connected by land routes. In the southwestern corner, the Kaesong Industrial Complex (KIC), although its operations have been suspended, also has all of South Korea as its economic hinterland.

As such, North Korea has contrasting aspects like any other country but one side may overwhelm the other. This is why we must examine the details more closely, although the scope of this book is limited to the legal and political issues connected with North Korea's open door policy.

B. The Term 'Risk'

Risks should be considered in the course of making a foreign investment and operating a business. Such consideration is especially necessary when the foreign investment is to be made in a developing country or an economy in transition. Since investment and business operation are ventures by nature, various types of risks arise from the time of decision-making through to the closure of the business. The term risk frequently appears in the literature, especially in the field of business administration as well as in legal literature recently. There are a number of different types of risk in the business world.

Some risks appear in relation to business performance itself such as marketing, competition with other business, availability of inputs and so on. Other risks come from external or non-business factors such as the political environment, government policy, the legal regime of the host country, the creditworthiness of the host country's banks, and economic or political influences from the international environment. The former types of risks are typically called the customary economic risks of business, and are usually discussed in the field of business administration. The latter are classified into various categories of risk according to their nature.

Political risk is, among other things, frequently found in the legal literature in relation to foreign investment or activities of multinational corporations in a foreign country, while some other risks such as regulatory risk, country risk and legal risk are also discussed from time to time. However, definitions of the risks are not clearly delineated [6] and, in fact, demarcations among the risks are not unambiguously drawn or overlap one another in their definitions. The concept of political risk emerged against the backdrop of post-colonialism, as many developing-world governments were newly established beginning in the 1960s. The term political risk is thus discussed as an integral part of foreign investment even though its concept is somewhat vague and is therefore defined differently by different scholars. Some scholars have defined the term broadly while others have done so more narrowly.

Relatively broad definitions, among others, are: political risk is "changes" in the operating conditions of foreign enterprises that arise out of political process;[7] political risk is manifestations of instability and of a lack of security and legal protection;[8] political risk is the probability that events in the nonmarket (political, economic and social) environment of business will cause financial, strategic or personal loss to the firm;[9] political risk relates either to the stability of the host country's political system, where disruptive upheaval might bring about economic or social discontinuity detrimental to all business enterprises, or to forces that might prove detrimental only to the interests of foreign investors; [10] political risk is government interference through specific acts or events[11]; political risk is the risk

---

[6] The term political risk appears in hundreds of articles in law journals, but none of the authors appears to have attempted to clarify the definition of the term.

[7] DAVID A. JODICE, POLITICAL RISK ASSESSMENT: AN ANNOTATED BILIOGAPHY 5 (1985).

[8] HANS SIEGWART ET AL., IVO G. CAYTAS AND JULIAN I. MAHARI, GLOBAL POLITICAL RISK: DYNAMIC MANAGERIAL STRATEGIES 20 (1989).

[9] CHARLES R. KENNEDY, JR., MANAGING THE INTERNATIONAL BUSINESS ENVIRONMENT: CASES IN POLITICAL & COUNTRY RISK 1 (1991). The author supplementarily explains that "[t]his definition encompasses a broad spectrum of events, including terrorism, debt restructurings, nonpayment, demographic changes, expropriation, and the impact of a wide range of government policies ... on a country's financial and competitive position."

[10] DOLPH WARREN ZINK, THE POLITICAL RISKS FOR MULTINATIONAL ENTERPRISE IN DEVELOPING COUNTRIES: WITH A CASE STUDY OF PERU 31 (1973). The author displays examples of political risks as follows: import controls; local contract requirements; local equity requirements; personnel requirements; borrowing restrictions; profit and royalty remittance restrictions; tax discrimination; investment barriers; incentive discrimination; demand for exports; prevention of acquisitions; expropriation and nationalization.

[11] DAN HAENDEL, FOREIGN INVESTMENT AND THE MANAGEMENT OF POLITICAL RISK 71 (1979).

of changes in the rules for foreign investment;[12] political risk is events occurring in the environment, i.e., an irregular change in regime, or at the junction of environment and firm, i.e., expropriation, which are typically associated with acts of government;[13] political risk is changes prompted by political acts and decisions.[14]

Relatively narrow definitions, among others, are: political risk is a threat that a host country will interfere with the property rights of a foreign investor;[15] political risks are currency inconvertibility and transfer restrictions, expropriation, war, terrorism, civil disturbance, breach of contract, or non-honoring of financial obligations;[16] political risks are breach of contract including unavailable enforcement of a favorable arbitration award or judicial decision against the host country, currency inconvertibility and transfer restriction, expropriation including indirect (or creeping) expropriation, and war and civil disturbance including sabotage and terrorism.[17]

As shown above, the definition of political risk is not well established. In general terms, political risk is described as 'changes,' 'instability,' 'government interference,' 'governmental events,' 'probability of loss,' and so on. The common aspects among many definitions consist of two elements – impact from non-economic mechanisms of business and a certain connection with governmental actions. However, not all impacts caused by non-economic

---

[12] Lars H. Thunell, Political Risks in International Business Investment Behavior of Multinational Corporations 5 (1977).

[13] Stephen J. Korbin, Managing Political Risk Assessment: Strategic Response to Environmental Change 33 (1982).

[14] Howard L. Lax, Political Risk in the Interantional Oil and Gas Industry 9 (1983). It includes changes in tax laws or prices, shortage of foreign exchange, or an adverse balance-of-payments position, if they are triggered by governmental processes.

[15] David Frisch and Raj Bhala, Global Business Law Priciples and Practice 525 (1999).

[16] *See* 22 U.S.C. § 9621(d). This is the policy of the International Development Finance Corporation (DFC) of the United States which replaced formerly OPIC in 2018.

[17] *See* MIGA Investment Guarantee Guide available at <https://www.miga.org/sites/default/files/2023-05/MIGA%20Investment%20Guarantee%20Guide%202021%20Digital%20Version%20v3.pdf> (visited July 6, 2025). The Multilateral Investment Guarantee Agency (MIGA) is a member of the World Bank Group and the Guide is derived from the art. 11 of the MIGA Convention of 1985.

mechanisms and governmental actions relate solely to political risk. Regulatory risk, defined as a risk arising from an authority's change of laws or regulations, closely resembles political risk.[18] Country risk, used by international bankers to describe certain financial risks,[19] also overlaps with political risk in terms of its meaning. Legal risk, which encompasses all manner of legal risks that may be encountered in the host country, also shares certain commonalities with political risk.

Aside from the types of risks mentioned above, many kinds of risks have been named in relation to foreign investment such as sovereign risk, financial risk, currency risk, market risk, insolvency risk and so on. All risks — especially in the foreign investment arena — overlap or are intertwined with one another in terms of their concepts. If a broad definition of political risk is to be employed, it will encompass almost all other notions of risks and accordingly, demarcations among risks will disappear. Therefore, in this book, the narrowly delineated definition of political risk as set out by the United States' International Development Finance Corporation (DFC), established by the BUILD Act of 2018, and the World Bank's Multilateral Investment Guarantee Agency (MIGA) Convention of 1985, will be used.

---

[18] FRISCH ET AL, supra note 15 at 526. However, there is "regulatory risks arise from different legal systems, overlapping jurisdictions, and dissimilar policies that influence such conditions as the application of anti-trust law." *See* ZINK *supra* note 10 at 31. This definition is similar to that of legal risk.

[19] KENNEDY, JR, *supra* note 9 at 1. There is another definition very similar to that of political risk. That is "Country risk refers to risks or threats to property interests in an investment by the host country government." *See* FRISCH ET AL., *supra* note 15 at 530.

Chapter 2 Socialism Embedded in the Business Environment

A. Socialism and Leadership Peculiar to North Korea

The formation of the North Korean regime was a product of Cold War confrontation. Until the demise of the Soviet Union bloc in the early 1990s, North Korea's political development was shaped largely by the context of the Cold War. During World War II, there were a series of meetings among the heads of the Allied states concerning, among other matters, Korea's independence from Japanese occupation of the Korean Peninsula. These meetings were the Cairo Conference in November 1943, the Yalta Conference in February 1945, and the Potsdam Conference in July 1945.

The independence of Korea was declared in the Cairo Conference and confirmed in the Potsdam Conference which was held from July 17 to August 2, 1945. Six days after the close of the Potsdam Conference, and two days after the first atomic bomb was dropped on Hiroshima, the Soviet Union, one of the three major Allied powers at the Conference, declared war on Japan by invading Manchuria, then under Japanese occupation. It was a week before the Japanese surrender. The Soviet Union then advanced into Korea, also then under Japanese occupation. Some Soviet forces also landed separately in the northeastern part of the Korean Peninsula by sea in August 1945. In the meantime, the United States, busy with the preparation of landing on the Japanese main island, was concerned about the Soviet troops' rapid southward advance, which might lead to occupation of the entire peninsula and proposed to the Soviet Union that it not advance beyond the 38th parallel. The Soviet Union unexpectedly accepted this proposal and halted its advance at the 38th parallel. It was the background of Korea’s division. The offer by the United States was the cause of the division but in a sense, it saved a half of Korea from communization of the whole Korean territory.

Japan unconditionally surrendered on August 15, 1945. About a month after the Soviet army's advance into Manchuria and the Korean Peninsula, United States troops landed in Korea and began to administer the southern part of the peninsula. From the time, two military powers, the communist Soviet Union and the capitalist

United States, controlled each part of Korea with different political ideologies for around three years until the two Koreas each established their own separate governments in 1948.

The Workers' Party of Korea (hereinafter 'WPK' or 'Party'), the power base of the communist regime, was created in August 1946 under the banner of Marxism-Leninism. The Democratic People's Republic of Korea ("DPRK" or "North Korea" hereafter) was established in September 1948. Kim Il Sung (1912 - 1994) became the Chairman of the WPK and the Premier[20] of the government. Upon coming to power, he began to systematically purge his political rivals and opponents in order to consolidate his authority in North Korea. His consolidation of power was significantly accelerated during the three years of the Korean War (1950 - 1953) through the elimination of various factions within the Party, and he emerged as the absolute leader of the WPK by the late 1950s.

In fact, the Korean War provided Kim Il Sung with the decisive opportunity to eliminate not only anti-revolutionary landowners and former officials from the Japanese colonial period, but also communist comrades who posed as potential challengers. He has been referred to as 'Suryong'[21] qualified by the adjective 'Great' — as in 'the Great Suryong (Leader)' — since the Korean War. Since then, no one has dared to challenge his formidable authority, either during his lifetime or after his death. His words, as recorded in the Analects of Kim Il Sung, have become the supreme guidelines for the interpretation of policy, law, economy, education, and all other fields, both during his lifetime and after his death. The same pattern was inherited to his successors.

After senior Kim's death in July 1994, his son Kim Jong Il immediately succeeded to power and ruled North Korea for seventeen years until his death in December 2011. Kim Jong Un, the third son of Kim Jong Il, inherited the position of supreme leader of North Korea in his late twenties upon his father's death and has held absolute power ever since. North Korea's fundamental policies in both domestic and external affairs have not changed since the era of Kim Il Sung.

---

[20] He held the Premiership until he became President in 1972.

[21] Originally it was an official title of the chief of a town or village in the Balhae (or *Bohai* in Chinese) Dynasty (A. D. 698 – 926) which was one of Korean dynasties in Manchuria after the fall of Goguryeo Dynasty. However, its modern colloquial meaning is more awesome and charismatic than the original one.

As to the identity of the nation, the Charter of the Workers' Party of Korea prescribes that the immediate goal of the Workers' Party of Korea is to build a wealthy, powerful, and civilized socialist society in the northern part of Korea and to realize independent and democratic progress of society nationwide, while the ultimate goal is to construct a communist society in which the people's ideals are perfectly realized.[22] The phrases "to realize ... nationwide ... to construct communist society ..." mean to transform South Korea into a communist society like North Korea's own.

The regime also declares that it must expel American imperialists' military invasion, to ultimately liquidate political and military domination of the United States in South Korea ... to achieve peaceful unification of the nation at the earliest opportunity ....[23] This is the current position of North Korea toward South Korea and the United States.

B. Foreign Investment Policy in the Socialist Economy

1. Socialist Economy Lines

In March 1946, under the control of the Soviet Civil Administration, which served as the Soviet military authority in the northern part of the Korean Peninsula, the Provisional People's Committee for North Korea declared the Land Reform Decree. This Decree ordered the confiscation of all Japanese-owned land, tenanted land from a landowner, pro-Japanese Korean's land, and an excessive portion of land owned by a large landlord, in order to distribute these lands free of charge to farmers who did not own land.[24]

In the same month, after the above Decree, the Committee announced a platform declaring the nationalization of all properties owned by Japanese nationals or pro-Japanese Koreans, including commercial and manufacturing enterprises, power plants, transportation businesses, banks, mines, and cultural enterprises.[25] In

---

[22] *See* the eleventh paragraph of the Charter of the Workers' Party of Korea Preamble of 2021. This Charter is regarded as the supreme norm, above the constitution, of the regime.

[23] *See id.* the twenty-seventh paragraph.

[24] *See Bukjoseon Tojigaehyeok-e gwanhan Beopryeon* (Decree for Land Reform in North Korea of 1946) art. 1, 2, 3, 5, 6 and 11.

[25] *See 20gaejo jeonggang* (Platform of 20 Planks of 1946) plank 9; *see also Bukjoseon Imsiinminwiweonhoe-eui Saneop Gyotong Unsu Chesin deung-eu*

the same year, confiscation of the land and nationalization of industries were confirmed by the Platform of the Workers' Party of Korea[26] and later affirmed by the first Constitution of the DPRK in 1948.[27] As a result of these measures, 90% of industry was nationalized or converted to 'people's' ownership.

The next stage of socialization was the cooperative farming system. The scheme of cooperative farming in North Korea was initiated in 1953 and by 1958, when the scheme was completed, 100% of the peasants of North Korea came to belong to one of the cooperative farms. The cooperative farming system means that the collective farmers' labor and the land and other means of production are consolidated into a single production unit. As of 1992, there were three thousand cooperative farms in North Korea encompassing 90% of the total farm land. The remaining land belonged to the State.[28]

Farming, commerce and manufacturing are interdependent with one another. For this reason, the socialization of commerce and manufacturing was also carried out alongside the restructuring of farming from 1947 to 1958. As a result of socialization in these sectors, 97.5% of the entire population belonged to one of the cooperative organizations for farming, manufacturing, and related sectors in 1959.[29]

In the meantime, with aid from the Soviet Union, China, and socialist allies in Eastern Europe, North Korea initiated a series of economic development plans beginning shortly after the Korean War, from 1954 through 1993.[30] The final stages of these economic plans coincided with the collapse of the Soviet bloc. In the course of implementation of these economic plans, North Korea put great

---

Gukyuhwa-e gwanhan Beopryeong (Decree by Provisional People's Committee for Nationalization of Industry, Transportation Service, Postal and Communication Service, and Bank in North Korea of 1946).

[26] *See Joseon Rodongdang Gangryeong* (Platform of the Workers' Party of Korea of 1946) plank 3, 4, and 5.

[27] *See* Constitution of the Democratic People's Republic of Korea of 1948 art. 5 and 6.

[28] *See* KOREA INSTITUTE FOR INDUSTRIAL ECONOMIC & TRADE ("KIET" hereafter), Industry Operation and Enterprise Management System of North Korea at 112, 113 (1992).

[29] *See id.,* at 7, 8.

[30] The Three-Year Plan (1954 - 1956), the Five-Year Plan (1957 - 1961 but completed in 1960), the first Seven-Year Plan (1961 - 1967 but extended to 1970), the Six-Year Plan (1971 - 1976, extended to 1977), the second Seven-Year Plan (1978 - 1984), the third Seven-Year Plan (1987 - 1993).

weight in the military and heavy industry. As a result, the country suffered from a shortage of consumer goods and light industrial products, but the North Korean government took no meaningful action to address this imbalance between industries.

There were two reasons why North Korea maintained a policy of prioritizing heavy industry. One was to take advantage of the well-constructed heavy industry factories and equipment left by the Japanese in the northern part of the Korean Peninsula, and the other was to develop the national defense industry in preparation for what North Korea termed the liberation of South Korea from the colonial rule of the United States.

Until the 1970s, major industrial facilities were imported from the former Soviet Union, Eastern European countries, and China under grant assistance programs or loans, although most of these facilities were not backed by up-to-date technologies. However, North Korea's economy recorded steady growth through the end of the 1980s, but negative growth rates began in 1990. North Korea was seriously affected by the dissolution of the former Soviet Union bloc and the open door policy of China. The deterioration of North Korea's economy in the 1990s and beyond was primarily due to the loss of its markets in the former socialist countries. The longstanding practice of bartering and exchanging aid based on socialist solidarity and goodwill, rather than applying free market principles, is also viewed as a fundamental reason for North Korea's inability to recover its collapsed economy to this day.

Although North Korea has experienced serious economic depression since the collapse of the socialist bloc, North Korea still strongly upholds the idea of socialistic economy planning. The most recent Charter of the Workers' Party of Korea still emphasizes 'socialistic economy lines.' The Charter of the WPK ranks as a higher norm than the Constitution. The most recent constitution of North Korea also succinctly declares that the people's economy is a planned one.[31]

2. Questions on Economy in Transition

How can North Korea's economy be defined in relation to a market system? Is it a "non-market economy" or "non-market economy in transition"? Such a definition may be one of the

[31] *See* art. Socialist Constitution of DPRK of 2023 art 34.

important factors for foreign enterprises in determining whether to invest in a country. If North Korea is defined as a country of nonmarket economy, risks in foreign investment in such a country will be greater. This is because several U.S. economic sanctions on North Korea would continue as long as it remains a nonmarket economy rather than an economy in transition.

For example, it may affect trade with the United States, as goods manufactured by an investor in North Korea and exported to the United States may be subject to anti-dumping provisions. That is, in the U.S. Tariff Act of 1930 as amended, when merchandise is exported from a nonmarket country and the administering authority determines that the foreign merchandise is being sold in the United States at less than its fair value, an antidumping duty shall be imposed on such merchandise.[32]

The "market disruption" provision of the U.S. Trade Act of 1974[33] can also be applied to take an action against the "Communist" countries for exports to the United States which is a significant cause of material injury (or threat) to a United States domestic industry.[34] In this Act, the International Trade Commission, upon filing of a petition by an entity concerned or upon request of the President or other authorities, must make an investigation to determine, with respect to the imported articles from a "Communist" country, whether market disruption exists with respect to an article produced by a domestic industry.[35]

If the Commission finds that market disruption exists, it must determine the appropriate amount of the duty or other import restriction on such article which is necessary to prevent or remedy the market disruption.[36] Although a non-market economy does not necessarily mean a communist country, in defining non-market economies under antidumping laws, generally only nations with a communist-dominated government such as North Korea are identified as non-market.

---

[32] *See* 19 U.S.C. § 1677b(c) (2015); RALPF H. FOLSOM AND MICHAEL W. GORDON, INTERNATIONAL BUSINESS TRANSACTIONS, HORNBOOK SERIES 796-801 (1995)

[33] *See* 19 U.S.C. § 2436 (1999).

[34] *See* 19 U.S.C. § 2436(e) (1999).

[35] *See* 19 U.S.C. § 2436(a)(1) (1999).

[36] *See* 19 U.S.C. § 2436(a)(3) (1999).

However, there is no clear test or demarcation line to distinguish non-market from market economy. The rate of transition from non-market to market economy and the disruption to the economy caused by the process of transition vary widely from one country to the next. [37] Furthermore, a test is suggested that "when the government regulatory activity in the means of production and distribution becomes so pervasive as to substantially eliminate the market influences, that nation is usually referred to as a non-market economy."[38]

The pervasiveness test helps to explain the degree of the government's interference which goes beyond what a market economy needs. However, the pervasiveness test still does not provide a clear definition of a non-market economy.

Another test to determine whether a country is a non-market economy is found in the U.S. Tariff Act of 1930. Section 771 (18)(b)[39] of the Act provides the following criteria to determine the extent of a country's economic transition:

(1) the extent to which the currency of the foreign country is convertible into currency of other countries;
(2) the extent to which wage rates in the foreign country are determined by free bargaining between labor and management;
(3) the extent to which joint ventures or other investments by firms of other foreign countries are permitted in the foreign country;
(4) the extent of government ownership or control of the means of production;
(5) the extent of government control over the allocation of the resources and over the price and output decisions of enterprises and;
(6) such other factors as the administering authority considers appropriate.

By the Tariff Act test, if a country fully satisfies all six conditions, the country will not be a non-market economy and it will not be subject to antidumping or countervailing duties.

---

[37] *See* FOLSOM ET AL. 800 at *supra* note 32.
[38] *Id.* at 797.
[39] 19 U.S.C. § 1677(18)(B) (2020).

Applying (1) above, North Korea's Law on Foreign Investment allows foreign investors to remit their legitimate profits and other income earned from invested business or banking operations to foreign countries without restriction.[40] North Korea's Law on Foreign Currency Control also allows foreign investors' remittance of distributed profits, salaries and legally earned income.[41] However, the laws do not specify whether a foreign investor in North Korea is permitted to exchange North Korean *won* into a foreign currency or one foreign currency into another. Therefore, the first condition may not be applicable to North Korea.

Applying (2) above, North Korea does not have any mechanism to bargain wage rates between the labor and the management. The Constitution declares that the national economy of North Korea is a planned economy[42] and workers shall receive equal pay for the same work regardless of sex, age, or nationality.[43] The Government shall make a grading system of living expenses[44] and distribute the living expenses to factories and enterprises.[45] The Labour Law of the DPRK for Foreign-invested Enterprises, enacted in 2009 as the special law governing foreign-invested businesses, does not address wage bargaining, and it is natural that North Korean authorities would not permit such a mechanism. In this context, there is no room to locate the issue of wage bargaining. Therefore, North Korea does not meet the requirement of (2).

Criterion (3) provides identification as a market economy if a country fully permits joint venture or other investments by foreign countries. North Korea welcomes foreign joint ventures and investment through its laws and regulations without limiting nationality or imposing other restrictions. For this reason, North Korea fulfills the requirement of (3).

Criterion (4) is least applicable to North Korea because the means of production are owned exclusively by the State and social and cooperative organizations.[46] There is no limit to the property which the State can own in North Korea[47] and the property of social,

---

[40] *See* Law of DPRK on Foreign Investment art. 20.

[41] *See* Law of DPRK on Foreign Currency Control art. 28 and 29.

[42] *See* Socialist Constitution of DPRK of 2023 art. 34.

[43] *See* Socialist Labor Law of DPRK art. 37.

[44] *See id.* art. 38.

[45] *See id.* art. 40.

[46] *See* Socialist Constitution of DPRK of 2023 art. 20.

[47] *See id.* art. 21.

cooperative organizations is collectively owned by the working people involved in the organization concerned.[48] Therefore, it is not possible to apply this criterion.

Considering criterion (5), in North Korea, the prices of materials and products are determined by agencies of the government. Price control is defined as an absolute order in the course of price making and price application.[49] Therefore, North Korea does not satisfy criterion (5).

Reviewing the criteria with North Korea's circumstances, factors (1), (2), (4), and (5) fail to meet the requirements, whereas factor (3) barely satisfies the conditions for classification as a market economy. Therefore, as of 2025, the status of North Korea's transition to a market economy is still far away.

3. Greater Tumen Initiative

Before discussing North Korea's open door policy, it is important to review the Tumen River Area Development Programme (TRADP), which was initiated by the United Nations Development Programme (UNDP) in 1991. It was later renamed as the Greater Tumen Initiative (GTI) in 2005 with the expanded geographic coverage to the Greater Tumen Region, and six priority sectors — transport, trade and investment, tourism, energy, environment, and agriculture — have been identified for future cooperation as of 2025.

The declaration of the then Rajin-Sonbong Free Economic and Trade Zone (FETZ) as North Korea's first special economic zone in 1991 was a part of the TRADP. According to the UNDP, the Tumen River area was considered to have great potential for international trade because of the strategic location of the Tumen transport corridor, the strong complementarities within the Tumen River area, its vast natural and human resources, and its accessibility to the resources and workforce of Northeast Asia.[50]

TRADP essentially encompassed the terrain located within conceptual boundary lines drawn from Chongjin in North Korea through Yanji in China to Nakhodka in Russia and back to Chongjin.[51] The Tumen River Economic Development Area

---

[48] *See id.* art. 22.

[49] *See* Civil Law Dictionary of North Korea 1 (1997).

[50] Defunct website of the UNDP's Tumen Programme as of Aug. 21, 2002.

[51] *See* the Agreement on the Establishment of the Consultative Commission for the Development Area and Northeast Asia, Appendix 1 of the first paragraph. This

(TREDA) Programme specifically incorporated the then Rajin-Sonbong Free Economic and Trade Zone (it was later renamed as Rason Economic and Trade Zone: Rason ETZ) in North Korea, the Yanbian Korean Autonomous Prefecture in China, and Vladivostok and the Free Economic Zone of Nakhodka in Russia.[52]

The TRADP's basic concept originated at the first Northeast Asian Economic Development Conference, held in China in 1990. In the Conference, China proposed development of the Tumen River Golden Triangle.[53] The idea was formally accepted by the UNDP in 1991, and the UNDP had initiated a development plan thereafter with five member countries: China, North Korea, Russia, South Korea, and Mongolia.

One of the supporting rationales for the UNDP to initiate the plan was the political environment at the beginning of the 1990s, in which the overall trend in world politics and economics was moving toward the free market system following the stagnation experienced under socialist planned economies.

In addition, with the geographical consideration, the riparian area of the Tumen River was home to relatively active cities in both China and Russia.[54] Although the Tumen River region was engaged in relatively active economic activities, industrial infrastructure was not well prepared enough to attract foreign investment and support vigorous economic activities. The UNDP established an ambitious plan to invest US$30 billion in this region over a twenty-year period in order to construct solid infrastructure, including a UN international

---

Agreement was signed in New York on December 6, 1995 by five member countries: China, Mongolia, North Korea, Russia, and South Korea.

[52] *See id.*, the second paragraph.

[53] The Tumen (*Duman* in Korean) River is located in northeastern part of North Korea and shares national borders with China and Russia along with the natural flow of the River. Its origin is Mount *Changbaishan (Baekdu* in Korean) and flows into the East Sea of Korea. The Tumen River Golden Triangle was the connections of pivotal cities of Hunchun in China, Rajin in North Korea and Posyet in Russia consisting of 1,000 square kilometers (386 square miles).

[54] China's Yanbian Korean Autonomous Prefecture, located in the Tumen River region was one of economically leading places until it was replaced by China's special economic districts in southern China. Russia's Nakhodka and Vladivostok near the Tumen River also began to bustle with foreign trade after the reform (*Perestroika*) and open (*Glasnost*) policy in mid-1980s.

city, that would develop the three triangle cities: Rajin of North Korea; Hunchun of China; Posyet of Russia.[55]

In the meantime, North Korea established a special economic zone (SEZ) named the Rajin-Sonbong Free Economic and Trade Zone in December 1991.[56] North Korea's establishment of its first SEZ was encouraged by the UNDP's TRADP, in addition to the need to cope with economic difficulties caused by the rapid reduction of foreign aid from its former allies in Eastern Europe and the resulting failure of the third seven-year economic plan.[57]

The UNDP's implementation of TRADP can be divided into three stages since its adoption of the Program in 1991. The first stage between 1991 and 1995 can be classified as an interim period. During the first stage, TRADP was formally launched in 1993 as an international organization with the objective of creating a joint special economic zone to be built on lands leased from China, Russia and North Korea.

In this interim period, UNDP proposed an amount of some US$30 billion for infrastructure investment and construction of an international city under the idea of establishing the "Rotterdam" of Northeast Asia. The proposed idea never moved forward. In 1994, the UNDP reviewed the feasibility of its own program and abandoned the US$30 billion master plan due to legal difficulties involved in leasing sovereign territory and problems in raising the necessary financing.[58] Instead, the UNDP and member countries adopted less ambitious development programs focusing on individual free economic zones in their respective countries – China, Russia, and North Korea. In this

---

[55] In 1991, the Golden Triangle was expanded to a larger area which would connect Chongjin of North Korea, Yanji of China and Vladivostok and Nakhodka of Russia consisting of 10,000 square kilometers (3,861 square miles).

[56] It was established as the 'Rajin Free Economic and Trade Zone' in 1991 and later changed to the 'Rajin-Sonbong Free Economic and Trade Zone' by including adjacent 'Sonbong' city in 1993. In 1999, North Korea deleted "Free" from the title of the Zone. In 2002, it became the 'Rason Economic and Trade Zone' as cities of Rajin and Sonbong merged into Rason.

[57] The third seven-year economic planning was implemented from 1987 to 1993.

[58] See Hughes, Christopher W. Tumen River Area Development Programme: Frustrated Micro-Regionalism as Microcosm of Political Rivalries 19, Centre for the Study of Globalisation and Regionalisation (CSGR), University of Warwick, Coventry CV4 7AL available at <https://wrap.warwick.ac.uk/id/eprint/2068/1/WRAP_Hughes_wp5700.pdf> (visited July 22, 2025).

period, three agreements in relation to development implementation were formally signed by the countries concerned.[59]

The second stage between 1995 and 2000 was a period of enactment of the intergovernmental agreements. The TRADP Secretariat was established in Beijing, China, to facilitate the programs. In this second stage, in order to achieve development with focuses on trade, investment and environmental management, the UNDP and member countries made efforts to remedy the previous failures and to implement the intergovernmental agreements concluded during the first stage.

These agreements transformed the Tumen River Program from a local development initiative into a regional framework for cooperation. Regular meetings of the sectoral committees and boards were established to institutionalize and implement regional cooperation. In this period, trade and transit grew with the opening of border crossings and the construction of roads and railroad sections. Regular shipping services provided transit, through North Korea and Russia, from China to Japan and South Korea.

Tourists from China have visited North Korea and Russia in large numbers, and tourists from South Korea through Russia or China have also visited Mt. *Changbaishan* (or Mt. *Baekdu*) on the border between North Korea and China.

The third stage, beginning in 2000, charted a new course for the program: firstly to strengthen institutional framework to become operationally and financially sustainable; and secondly to contribute to the economic development of the region across five sectors - trade and investment, transport and communications, environment, tourism and energy.

Given the nature of infrastructure investment, which does not yield returns in the short term, private enterprises are rarely willing to invest in it. Without active involvement of international financial institutions (IFIs) such as the Asian Development Bank (AsDB) or the World Bank, financing for infrastructure construction was not practically feasible.

---

[59] Agreements signed by member countries are: the Tumen River Area Development Coordination Committee signed by three riparian countries – China, North Korea and Russia; the Tumen River Area Consultative Commission signed by five TRADP member countries; and the Memorandum of Understanding on Environmental Protection signed by five TRADP member countries.

However, both North Korea and Russia were (and are) not members of the AsDB, and by its establishing agreement, the AsDB is not available to finance non-member countries. North Korea is also not yet a member of the World Bank. To overcome such a difficult situation, the UNDP once proposed establishing an independent Northeast Asia/Tumen Investment Corporation, but this was not fully approved by the TRADP member countries.

In 2005, the TRADP was revitalized and renamed the Greater Tumen Initiative (GTI) with the extended geographical coverage ranging from the original one to the three northeastern provinces and Inner Mongolia of China, eastern part of Mongolia, eastern port cities of South Korea, and Russia's Far East region. It also enlarged its programs into five but later six priority sectors including transport, trade & investment, tourism, energy, environment and agriculture.

In 2009, North Korea withdrew from the GTI for political reasons. In 2012, GTI created the Association of GTI Export and Import Banks (or "Northeast Asia EXIM Banks Association") of member countries as a regional development financing mechanism to support future projects. As of 2025, according to the GTI, it "continues to strengthen regional cooperation through policy dialogue and the implementation of priority projects."[60]

In reviewing the GTI's implementation, the TRADP was initially launched with a grandiose scheme to establish a highly attractive free economic zone in Northeast Asia, with the added implication of fostering new political circumstances of rapprochement in the final stages of the Cold War era. However, the plan appeared to have been driven by overly simplistic assumptions that overlooked many significant factors necessary to make the region a successful economic zone. It seems that, in the words of a maxim familiar to Northeast Asians, the Program started with a dragon's head but ended with a snake's tail. Without well-constructed industrial infrastructure, including soft infrastructure such as procedures of immigration, customs clearance and other administrative services, it is practically impossible to attract foreign business entities. Sensitive political issues, such as North Korea's development of nuclear weapons and ballistic missiles, also arose and partly hindered the smooth advancement of the GTI programs.

[60] See GTI website <http://www.tumenprogramme.org/?list-1524.html> (visited June 21, 2025).

In relation to the foreign investment in North Korea, the GTI has two issues to resolve. North Korea must return to the GTI membership as soon as possible. Without active participation of North Korea as the operator of major seaports in the East Sea including the Rason Special Economic Zone, GTI's business would be much less effective. The other is to get involvement of international financial institutions (IFIs) in GTI's projects especially for the construction of infrastructure. As mentioned above, financing from IFIs is critically important to drive the implementation of GTI projects. However, this question would not be solved until North Korea has a membership of any IFI and Russia has membership of AsDB. Therefore, while North Korea remains outside the GTI, the AsDB, and the Asian Infrastructure Investment Bank (AIIB), the remaining member countries of the GTI may need to initiate infrastructure development in the parts of the Northeast Asian region covered by GTI programs, financed through IFIs. It will certainly facilitate North Korea's return to the GTI.

C. Ideology, Bureaucracy and Corruption

1. Economy in the Juche Idea

The Juche idea is the dominant ideology permeating all sectors of North Korean society. Although Marxism-Leninism served as the founding ideology at the time of the state's establishment in 1948,[61] Kim Il Sung proclaimed the Juche idea — broadly translated as "self-reliance" — in 1955. It was also deployed as an instrument for suppressing dissenting factions while advancing the plans and policies of the Workers' Party of Korea following the Korean War.

At the time, several factions shared power within the Party in the 1950s: the Soviet-oriented faction, the pro-China faction, the domestic underground faction (formed during the Japanese occupation), and Kim Il Sung's own partisan faction of anti-Japanese guerrillas. Each represented the interests of its respective background. By institutionalizing the Juche idea as the governing political doctrine, Kim successfully marginalized the leaders of rival factions and consolidated his long-term hold on the Party.

Juche is defined as "the independent stance of rejecting dependence on others and of using one's own powers, believing in

---

[61] *See* NAEWOE PRESS, *BUKHAN YONG-EO 250 SEONJIP* [Anthology of North Korea's Terminology 250] 56-8 (1992).

one's own strength and displaying the revolutionary spirit of self-reliance."[62] Its implementing principles are organized around four pillars: self-reliance in ideology; independence in politics; self-sufficiency in economy; and self-defense in national defense.[63]

Juche also occupies a central role in North Korean law. As interpreted through the principle of self-reliance, it serves as the primary standard for evaluating all phenomena arising from legal activities, assessing the legality of conduct, and guiding the evolution of law itself.[64] The word "Juche" appears twelve times in the current Constitution, as follows:

> (1) The Democratic People's Republic of Korea is the socialist State of Juche ...;[65] (2) The great *Suryong* Comrade Kim Il Sung originated the immortal Juche Idea ...;[66] (3) The great *Suryong* Comrade Kim Il Sung put forward Juche-oriented revolutionary lines ...;[67] (4) The great *Suryong* Comrade Kim Il Sung ... laid solid foundations for the prosperity of this socialist State and accomplishment of revolutionary cause of Juche;[68] (5) The great leader Comrade Kim Jong Il developed in depth and in all-round way the immortal Juche Idea ...;[69] (6) [The great leader Comrade Kim Jong Il] ... ensured the continuity of the Korean revolution by pioneering the great cause of immortalizing the *Suryong* for the first time in history and sustainably developing the revolutionary traditions of Juche ....,[70] (7) The Democratic People's

---

[62] *See* Library of Congress, North Korea – A Country Study – The Role of Chuch'e available at <http://countrystudies.us/north-korea/60.htm>.(visited June 22, 2025)

[63] *See* Kim Jong Il, *Juche sasang-eh daehayeo* (About Juche idea), Thesis presented by Kim Jong Il to the Juche idea forum held on the occasion of celebration of Kim Il Sung's 70th birthday in 1982), published by DONG-AH ILBO, *WONJARYORO BON BUKHAN* (North Korea seen through Original Resources) 355-70 (1989).

[64] *See* CHOI DAL GON and SHIN YOUNG HO, *BUKHANBEOP IPMUN* [Introduction to Law of North Korea] 17 (1998).

[65] Socialist Constitution of 2023, Preamble.

[66] *Id.*

[67] *Id.*

[68] *Id.*

[69] *Id.*

[70] *Id.*

> Republic of Korea and the people of Korea shall uphold the great *Suryong* Comrade Kim Il Sung and the great leader Comrade Kim Jong Il as the eternal leaders of Juche Korea …;[71] (8) [The Democratic People's Republic of Korea] … further complete the great mission of the Juche Revolution …;[72] (9) The Socialist Constitution of the Democratic People's Republic of Korea is the Kim Il Sung – Kim Jong Il Constitution that codifies the ideas of Juche-oriented nation building …;[73] (10) The State, keeping a tight rein on the line of building a socialist, independent national economy and accelerating the people's economy to be Juche-oriented …;[74] (11) The State … shall endeavor to turn the people's economy to the highly developed Juche-oriented economy …;[75] and (12) The State shall develop Juche-oriented and revolutionary art and literature ….[76]

The Juche idea directly gave rise to a new economic doctrine known as the 'independent national economy.' This principle has since served as the foundational precept of North Korean economic policy. The current Socialist Constitution enshrines this commitment, declaring that "[t]he Democratic People's Republic of Korea shall rely on the socialist relations of production and the foundation of an independent national economy."[77] The Socialist Constitution of North Korea also states that:

> "The independent national economy as resided in the Democratic People's Republic of Korea shall be a solid foundation for the people's happy socialist life and for the country's prosperity.
>
> The State, keeping a tight rein on the line of building a socialist, independent national economy … shall endeavor to turn the people's economy to the highly developed

[71] *Id.*
[72] *Id.*
[73] *Id.*
[74] *Id.* art. 26.
[75] *Id.*
[76] *Id.* art. 52.
[77] *Id.* art. 19.

> Juche-oriented economy and to build material and technical foundations commensurate with the a complete socialist society."[78]

The independent national economy is defined as 'the economy that independently reproduces — through self-supporting and self-procuring methods of materials, technology, and labor — the full linkage from production to consumption, without dependence on foreign countries."[79]

Construction of an independent national economy system is "to build an economy that can walk [ahead] by itself without being subordinated to others … and to exercise full sovereignty and equality politically and economically in international relations."[80] To construct the independent national economy, the people "[s]hall develop the economy in various aspects and in comprehensive ways."[81] To build a developed economy in various aspects and comprehensive ways, "[we] shall develop heavy industry in priority while [we] do also light industry and agriculture together."[82] And

> "[t]o carry out the principle of self-defense in national defense, [we] have to establish our own base of military industry … [I]t has significant meaning that a new developing country should establish its own national defense industry in the circumstances. In these days, especially Americans and their fellow imperialists are viciously maneuvering to subordinate other countries by means of offering weapons and they are earning enormous profits through sales of armament as well as plundering people in other countries."[83]

---

[78] Socialist Constitution of 2023 art. 26.

[79] BANG CHAN YOUNG, *BUKjOSEON-EUI DAEWOE GAEBANG GAEHYEOK JEONGCHAEK-GWA HAPRIJEOK DAEBUK JEONGCHAEK-EUI MOSAEK* (North Korea's Open and Reforming Policy and Seeking for Reasonable Policy on North Korea) 62 (1996). Cited from *Gyeongjesajeon* (Economics Dictionary) published by *Sahoe Gwahak Chulpansa* (North Korea Social Science Publishing) 208 (1985).

[80] Kim Jong Il, DONG-A ILBO, 359.

[81] *Id.*

[82] *Id.*

[83] *Id.* at 362,

As a consequence of the Juche idea and its implementing principles, North Korea channeled a disproportionately large share of state resources into the military and heavy industry, particularly during the 1960s and 1970s.[84]

Consequently, raw materials and energy that would otherwise have been directed toward agricultural development and infrastructure construction were diverted, in excess, to the military and heavy industry sectors. This distortion disrupted the supply chain and generated severe material shortages across the entire economy. The shortage of essential inputs, including crude oil, precipitated a serious economic contraction following the dissolution of the Soviet bloc and China's adoption of an open door policy, as imports of oil and raw materials previously supplied as economic aid were sharply curtailed or eliminated.[85] Compounding these difficulties, economic sanctions imposed by the United States since 1950 and by the United Nations Security Council from 2006 — in response to North Korea's nuclear weapons tests and ballistic missile launches — became decisive factors in entrenching the country's chronic economic depression.

The Juche idea and the independent national economy line were not, in principle, designed to preclude foreign economic engagement. North Korea has maintained economic relations with other countries, though these were largely confined to socialist allies in the Eastern bloc and selected third-world nations until the collapse of the Soviet Union. The relationship between the Juche idea and its implementing self-support principle in economy was defined that "the construction of 'independent national economy' does never mean to close our gate. It is not to deny international cooperation but to oppose to be ruled and subordinated by other countries."[86] Nevertheless, in practice, the independent national economy line significantly constrained external economic activity for many decades, further compounded by the political turbulence surrounding the Korean peninsula.

In the early 1980s, confronted with a shortage of foreign currency to service its external debts and drawing lessons from China's open

---

[84] In 1961, domestic investment in the heavy industry was 69.7% of the total industry and after steady increasing during 1960s, North Korea's investment in heavy industry reached up to 80.7% in 1970.

[85] *See* Oh Seung Ryeol et al, *Bookhan-eui Gyeongjegaehyeok-gwa Nambuk Kyeonghyeop* (North Korea's Economic Reform and South-North Korea Economic Cooperation): Research Report 95 – 22, KNIU (1995) at 22-31.

[86] Kim Jong Il, DONG-A ILBO at 360.

door policy, North Korea enacted the *Habyeongbeop* (Law on Equity Joint Ventures) in 1984, marking its first attempt to attract foreign direct investment. This initiative ultimately failed, however, because North Korea insisted on its own model of joint venture — one rooted in the 'independent national economy' policy and the imperatives of the command economy. In practice, this meant pervasive state interference in wages, recruitment, and dismissal, compounded by severely inadequate industrial infrastructure in transportation, roads, ports, and electricity supply. These factors combined to render the initial open door experiment unsuccessful.

During the decade of limited openness from 1984 to 1993, North Korea recorded a total of 140 investment contracts amounting to US$150 million, with approximately 90% of investment originating from Korean-Japanese enterprises. By comparison, Vietnam — which opened to foreign direct investment in 1988 — concluded 836 contracts worth US$7.5 billion over the same period. By 1993, all but twenty of the 140 foreign-invested enterprises in North Korea had either gone bankrupt or suspended operations.[87]

Notwithstanding the failure of its initial joint-venture policy, North Korea in 1991 took a further step toward economic opening by establishing a free economic zone in Rajin-Sonbong (now Rason), located in the northeastern part of the Korean peninsula. The government subsequently enacted the relevant enabling legislation and implementing regulations, while also revising the existing joint-venture law.[88]

A notable development during the period of foreign investment promotion was North Korea's launch of a political campaign centered on the slogan "our style socialism." In a 1988 editorial in the Rodong Shinmun — the official organ of the Workers' Party of Korea — Kim Jong Il declared that "[p]olitical tension is being escalated by South Korea and the United States' machinations of war and by the cultural-ideological infiltration of imperialists ... [W]e must

---

[87] *See* CHUN HONG TACK and OH KANG SOO, *BUKHAN-EUI WOEKUKIN TUJAJEDO-WA DAEBUKTUJA CHUJIN BANGAN* [North Korea's Foreign Investment Climate and a Proposal for Investment in North Korea] KOREA DEVELOPMENT INSTITURTE (KDI) 17, 24-7 (1995); *see also* BANG CHAN YOUNG, *supra* note 79 at 75-6.

[88] North Korea's free economic and trade zone was an imitation of China's special economic zones in southern China. However, the Chinese ones were made under the plan to adopt partial market economy whereas North Korea's was made without consideration of such a plan of adoption.

thoroughly carry out the Party's slogan of 'let us live in our style' in order to cope with current adversities and to go forward with revolution and construction."

"Our style" meant to carry on the tradition of resistant struggle during the time of Japanese occupation. That is, "we shall live, produce, and learn in the way of the anti-Japanese guerilla style."[89] The theme was recast as 'our style socialism' during the 1990s as a countermeasure to the capitalist influences that might accompany foreign capital, particularly in the context of investment promotion in the newly established free economic zone. North Korea continues to adhere strongly to the 'independent national economy line' alongside the principle of 'our style socialism,' both of which derive from the Juche idea — the ideological cornerstone of the North Korean state. The central dilemma is this: attracting foreign direct investment necessarily introduces capital and labor from market economies, yet any such investment must be structured so as not to undermine 'our style socialism,' even within a joint venture involving a North Korean and a foreign partner. How North Korea resolves this inherent tension remains an open question.

2. Bureaucracy and Corruption

Bureaucracy admits of many definitions. This subchapter focuses on its dysfunctional dimensions — rigid procedures, red tape, and inflexible rules — as they manifest in the North Korean context. While the scholarly literature generally characterizes North Korea as an inherently bureaucratic society, detailed analysis remains scarce, largely owing to the severe constraints on outside access to the country.

Bureaucracy is among the most significant factors bearing on foreign direct investment decision-making, shaping the entire business cycle from initial negotiations through to final liquidation. Its manifestations are varied: they include excessive operational oversight through frequent inspections of facilities and working conditions, undue interference in day-to-day business management, official procrastination in granting licenses, approvals, or permits, supply chain dysfunction attributable to the absence of a service orientation, and a lack of inter-agency coordination, among others.

The following anecdote illustrates how procrastination is structurally embedded in the planned economy. Upon receiving a

---

[89] *See* NAEWOE PRESS, *supra* note 61 at 59.

report of a shortage in fountain pen supply, the Prime Minister summoned the pen factory manager, who attributed the shortfall to insufficient steel deliveries. The steel factory manager, in turn, blamed a lack of iron ore from the mining enterprise; and the mine manager explained that operations had been hampered by a shortage of pit props from the woodwork industry. The episode reveals the cascading nature of supply failures under a centrally planned system with no self-correcting market mechanism.[90]

A further episode illustrates the dysfunction arising from failures of inter-agency coordination. A foreign company operating in North Korea required a technician from its equipment supplier abroad to carry out repairs. The technician's visa application was delayed for six months due to a cumbersome procedure requiring referrals between the company's supervising authority and the visa-issuing official at an overseas mission. Forced to halt production throughout this period, the company ultimately ceased operations. Comparable bureaucratic impediments remain prevalent in a number of Commonwealth of Independent States (CIS) members — the successor states that emerged from the Soviet Union in 1991.

The bureaucratic and authoritarian attitude made by government and party officials is a chronic issue in North Korea just as the same is true in many former allied countries in Soviet Russia and East Europe. No considerable improvements have been made yet in North Korea while many of its former allies have been struggling especially after transition to market economy. Rather, North Korea's bureaucracy became deteriorated coupled with economic crisis in 1990s after the collapse of the Soviet Union and further United Nations' economic sanctions from 2006 caused by test of nuclear weapons and launching of ballistic missiles.

In North Korea, where freedom of movement is not recognized as a right, government officials hold discretionary authority over internal travel permits, the distribution of rations, and the mobilization of citizens for state-assigned labor projects. Given that nearly all operative powers over daily life are vested in government offices — with private economic activity confined to the informal markets that have emerged in recent years — it is virtually inevitable

[90] *See* Kim Sung Chull, *Bukhan gwanryobupae yeonku* (Study on Government Officials' Corruption in North Korea): Research Report 94 – 01, KINU, at 54-5 (1994).

that officials and party cadres assume bureaucratic and authoritarian postures as a matter of course.

Red tape is another hallmark of bureaucratic and authoritarian governance. Government operations are structured around the convenience of the provider rather than the needs of the applicant. Government offices, banks, utility providers, and customs agencies routinely impose extensive documentation requirements on those seeking services — documentation that must frequently be resubmitted at successive offices within the same authority.

Corruption is the corollary of concentrated bureaucratic power. The adage that "power tends to corrupt, and absolute power corrupts absolutely" finds a compelling illustration in North Korean society. Corruption intensified markedly during the so-called 'Arduous March' (1994–1998), when the public distribution system collapsed under the combined pressures of sharply reduced trade and aid from former Eastern bloc partners — itself a consequence of the Soviet Union's dissolution in 1991 — and successive years of natural disasters, including droughts and floods.

Corruption is most commonly defined as the abuse of public office for private gain, and it flourishes wherever officials exercise broad discretionary authority with limited accountability. North Korea, however, exhibits a distinctive pattern that departs from this paradigm. Owing to the collectivist character of North Korean society, corruption is not confined to personal enrichment but extends to the advancement of organizational interests. This form of organizational corruption does not primarily aim at the economic benefit of individual members, though it may incidentally confer fringe benefits such as bonuses or promotions.

A study about corruption in North Korea, based on interviews with defectors from North Korea, classifies it into four categories: (1) economic corruption for the interest of an organization; (2) non-economic corruption for the interest of an organization; (3) economic corruption for the personal interest; (4) non-economic corruption for the personal interest.[91]

Organizational economic corruption arises from the structural imperatives of the planned economy. Enterprises compete with one another for scarce raw materials and components required to meet state-assigned production targets. Where supply is insufficient,

---

[91] *See id.*

enterprise executives resort to bribing procurement officials. The competitive pressure is acute: failure to meet targets set by the 'Supreme Leader' (currently Kim Jong Un) — particularly where production has military applications — carries the risk of reprimand or demotion.[92]

Foreign-invested enterprises frequently need to procure locally sourced materials in the course of their operations. North Korean foreign investment law expressly encourages in-country procurement by such enterprises. As a consequence, foreign investors engaging in local supply chains may find themselves exposed to the entrenched networks of corruption that characterize such markets.

Non-economic organizational corruption manifests primarily through nepotism and cronyism. Relatives of the North Korean elite are frequently appointed to influential positions across various organizations, and enterprises actively cultivate such connections to secure patronage and resolve operational difficulties.[93] Cronyism is deeply embedded in Korean social culture, both North and South, with informal networks organized around shared educational institutions, regional origins, and familial clans, whose members extend preferential treatment to one another across a range of contexts. Foreign investors from Western societies may find these practices unfamiliar; nonetheless, an awareness of these dynamics is a practical necessity for conducting business in North Korea.

Personal economic corruption is the most prevalent form of corruption not only in North Korea but universally. Common examples include misappropriation of public funds or materials, bribery for the issuance of travel permits, and payments to secure favorable transfers or appointments.[94] Such conduct may directly or indirectly affect foreign investors' business operations in North Korea.

Non-economic personal corruption encompasses moral misconduct, particularly in relation to sexuality. In documented cases, influential figures such as high-ranking Party members have provided material support to women in exchange for sexual relations.[95] While such conduct is not unique to North Korea, its prevalence and precise

---

[92] *See id.* at 36-7.
[93] *See id.* at 44.
[94] *See id.* at 46-52.
[95] *See id.* at 53.

scope within the country remain largely unknown to outside observers.

The foregoing analysis, derived from interviews with and firsthand accounts by North Korean defectors, warrants further scholarly scrutiny. Given that corruption has emerged as a systemic problem in China and Russia following their respective open-door policies, corruption in North Korea — particularly as it intersects with foreign investment and trade — merits careful and sustained investigation.

Moreover, North Korea's criminal law prescribes comparatively lenient penalties for bribery by imposing a maximum of ten years' correctional labor service.[96] The relevant provision stipulates that: (i) one who accepts the large amount of bribes, he or she shall be punished by disciplinary labor service; (ii) one who accepts the particularly large amount of bribes, he or she shall be punished by correctional labor service for not more than five year; and (iii) on who accepts the particularly large amount of bribes in exchange of providing illegal service or on who is in the managerial post accepts the particularly large amount of bribes shall be punished by five years or more but not more than ten years of correctional labor service, but if commission is profound, punished by more than ten years of correctional labor.[97] However, the Criminal Law does not describe what constitutes the 'large amount' of bribes, 'particularly large amount,' or 'profound commission.' Compare this to South Korean criminal law. A South Korea's statute stipulates a life sentence in prison as maximum to givers and takers of a bribe.[98]

In any society, the line between a bribe and a gift is not always clearly drawn, and this ambiguity is particularly pronounced in many Asian contexts. All jurisdictions maintain laws prohibiting bribery and other forms of corruption, and most supplement these with ethical codes and conduct regulations for public officials, though the precise scope of what is prohibited or permissible varies considerably across countries.

North Korea's Criminal Law does not provide for monetary fines as a sanction for bribery; disciplinary or correctional labor service constitutes the sole criminal penalty. Notably, the Criminal Code

---

[96] *See* Criminal Law of the DPRK art. 270.

[97] *See id.*

[98] *See* The Act on the Aggravated Punishment, etc. of Specific Economic Crimes art. 3.

criminalizes the bribe recipient but not the giver or any intermediary. It should also be noted that American citizens and corporations remain subject to prosecution under the U.S. Foreign Corrupt Practices Act of 1977 as amended for bribing North Korean officials, irrespective of North Korean domestic law.[99]

The full extent of corruption in North Korea — particularly as it relates to foreign investment — remains opaque to the outside world. North Korea ranks among the most closed societies globally, affording its citizens far fewer opportunities for contact with foreigners than virtually any other country. Transparency International (TI), a leading non-governmental organization monitoring corruption, ranked North Korea 170th out of 180 countries in its 2024 Corruption Perceptions Index.[100]

---

[99] *See* 15 U.S.C. § 78dd-1 (1998).

[100] *See* Transparency International's corruption perceptions index (CPI) 2024 available at <https://www.transparency.org/en/cpi/2024> (visited June 23, 2025).

Chapter 3 Investment in Special Economic Zones

A. Rason Economic and Trade Zone

While the Tumen River Area Development Programme was still in its formative stages, North Korea announced an ambitious plan in December 1991 to develop the Rajin-Sonbong area — subsequently renamed Rason Special City in 2000 — into a free economic and trade zone, and promulgated the Law of the Democratic People's Republic of Korea on Free Economic and Trade Zone in connection therewith.[101] The Zone encompasses 746 square kilometers (288 sq. miles) along the northeastern coast of the Korean peninsula, abutting the borders of both China and Russia.

As noted above, the establishment of the Zone was driven by a confluence of factors. First and foremost, North Korea was in pressing need of additional hard currency reserves, as the dissolution of the Soviet Union and the eastern bloc in the early 1990s had dealt a severe blow to key economic sectors. Foreign aid from its former socialist allies was curtailed sharply, and China was increasingly pressing North Korea to pay for oil supplies in hard currency.

Second, the implementation of the third seven-year economic plan (1987–1993) had begun to falter, owing both to the external reduction or elimination of allied aid and to deepening structural imbalances within the domestic economy. Those imbalances were largely the product of a long-standing policy of privileging heavy and military industry since the end of the Korean War in 1953, while systematically neglecting light industry oriented toward domestic consumption.

Third, North Korea recognized the need to reinvigorate foreign investment following the manifest failure of its earlier, narrowly conceived open door policy, most notably as embodied in the Joint Venture Law of 1984.

Fourth, North Korea was drawn by the UNDP's initiative to develop the Tumen River region, which presented the prospect of establishing an export and import hinterland proximate to the borders of China and Russia. The cities of Rajin and Sonbong possessed comparatively well-developed port facilities capable of serving as transit hubs for the northeastern Chinese provinces, which were

---

[101] As mentioned at *supra* note 56, the term "Free" was deleted in 1999.

themselves far removed from major seaports. The Rajin-Sonbong area also benefited from a concentration of established heavy industrial plant.

Fifth, the geographic remoteness of the Rajin-Sonbong area from the capital, Pyongyang, made it an attractive site from a political standpoint. North Korea was intent on shielding its population from the permeation of Western cultural influences that foreign capitalist activity would, almost inevitably, carry in its wake. In this respect, the Rajin-Sonbong area presented itself as the most suitable location for the new free economic and trade zone.

A series of legal and administrative support measures followed the declaration of the Zone's establishment. As a threshold matter, North Korea amended its constitution to provide the legal foundation for subsequent legislation and regulation governing foreign investment. The Socialist Constitution as amended in 1992 stipulates that "[t]he State shall encourage institutions, enterprises and organizations in our country to take part in joint ventures and co-operation of enterprise with foreign corporations and individuals."[102] Between 1991 and 1996, North Korea enacted or revised nearly fifty laws and regulations bearing on foreign direct investment, in support of its broader policy of attracting foreign capital.

These laws and regulations were designed to apply to the entirety of North Korean territory, and not solely to the Rason Economic and Trade Zone, unless otherwise specified. They set forth a range of benefits and incentives intended to draw foreign investors. By way of illustration, goods may be freely introduced into the Zone and may be stored, processed, manufactured, sorted, and packed for export to third countries.[103]

Among the other benefits and incentives provided under the relevant legislation are the following: transit cargoes and commodities imported for re-export are exempt from customs duties within the Zone;[104] foreign-invested enterprises and foreign individuals operating in the Zone may engage in transactions

---

[102] Socialist Constitution of 1992 art 37. This article was revised in 1998 by adding a phrase at the end of the sentence. That is "… and to establish and operate various kinds of enterprises in special economic zones." It meant that, by mentioning the special economic zones, North Korea had planned to establish more special economic zones on or before 1998.

[103] Law of the Democratic People's Republic of Korea on Rason Economic and Trade Zone ("Rason ETZ Law" hereafter) art. 76.

[104] *See id.* art. 54.

involving goods, services, and technology, and may also conduct export and import agency business;[105] designated enterprises that have operated in the Zone for more than ten years are entitled to exemption from or reduction of enterprise income tax; [106] the enterprise income tax rate in the Zone is 14% of net profit, reduced to 10% in priority sectors ,[107] compared with 25% for enterprises operating outside the Zone;[108] and income legitimately earned in the Zone — including profits, interest, dividends, rental income, service fees, and proceeds from the sale of property — may be remitted outside North Korean territory without restriction;[109]

Against the backdrop of North Korea's history, the establishment of the Rason Economic and Trade Zone carries considerable significance. From the founding of the state until the enactment of the Joint Venture Law in 1984, North Korea had in practice never embraced any capitalism-oriented economic model, operating instead under the banner of constructing a "socialist paradise" and adhering to the Juche idea, which had in practice entailed a categorical rejection of cooperation with capitalist countries.[110] The nation's long-term economic development programs were designed around the principle of "self-sufficiency in economy," a derivative of the Juche idea. During the ten years following the first joint venture law of 1984, one hundred and forty-eight cases of foreign direct investment were reportedly made by outside parties. Of these, one hundred and thirty-one cases (88.5%) were attributable to Korean-Japanese enterprises; South Korean investors were hardly permitted access to North Korea by the respective authorities. The great majority of businesses that did invest in North Korea subsequently went bankrupt or ceased operations.[111]

---

[105] *See id.* art. 66.

[106] See id. art. 68

[107] *See* id. art. 67.

[108] *See* Taxation Law for Foreign Investment-businesses and Foreign Individuals art. 10.

[109] *See* Rason ETZ Law art. 65.

[110] However, it was emphasized that Juche idea does not negate external cooperation with foreign. *See* Kim Jong Il, *Juche sasang-eh daehayo* (About Juche Idea), *in* DONG-A ILBO, *supra* note 63 at 360.

[111] KOREA TRADE-INVESTMENT PROMOTION AGENCY [KOTRA], NORTH KOREA BUSINESS FACTBOOK 20 (2001). *See* also JUN HONG TAEK ET AL, *supra* note 87 at 17, 24 – 7.

The failure of this initial experiment was attributable primarily to business interruptions engineered by the relevant authorities in matters such as workers' wages, recruitment, and dismissal, compounded by grossly inadequate industrial infrastructure. In light of this experience, the question naturally arises: what lessons, if any, did North Korea draw from the failure of the 1984 joint venture initiative?

As discussed above, the failure of the first attempt to attract foreign investment stemmed from deficiencies in both hard infrastructure — the physical facilities necessary to support commercial activity — and soft infrastructure — the services, systems, and regulatory environment that invisibly underpin such activity. The question then becomes whether, in the intervening years, North Korea remedied these infrastructural deficiencies and reoriented its services and systems to better serve the needs of foreign investors.

Telecommunications facilities and services remained far below the threshold required to sustain economic activity in the Zone. Even if a joint venture company were somehow able to independently install telephone lines and the necessary equipment, it would nonetheless encounter serious difficulties arising from unreliable electricity supply, poor road conditions, and inadequate transportation facilities. The Zone lacks an airport of any kind, whether international or domestic. As noted above, visitors to the Rason ETZ must arrive at Yanji International Airport in China, some 170 kilometers (107 miles) from the center of Rason City, and then travel overland to the China–North Korea border crossing for customs clearance, quarantine inspection, and immigration processing before entering North Korean territory. Completing all required procedures at the border post typically takes many hours. This circuitous route nevertheless remains the shortest available approach to the Zone — considerably shorter, in fact, than the overland journey from Pyongyang by car, bus, or train, given that regular domestic air services are not in operation.

The broader industrial infrastructure surrounding Rason City has seen little meaningful improvement in recent years, notwithstanding certain efforts by the North Korean authorities. Following a succession of increasingly severe economic sanctions imposed by the United Nations Security Council beginning in 2006, North Korea found itself unable to finance the construction or maintenance of the

Zone's industrial infrastructure, while its broader economic deterioration continued to deepen. This stagnant business environment reflects an intractable complex of mutually reinforcing factors — political and economic, domestic and external — as examined throughout this book.

With respect to soft infrastructure, it can be argued that such infrastructure is, in certain respects, even more consequential than its physical counterpart, in that it bears more directly on investors and their day-to-day business operations. After nearly eight decades of socialist practice — a system that provides no profit-oriented incentives to enterprises or individuals — North Korea may be characterized as among the most rigidly institutionalized societies in the world, surpassing even its former allies such as the Soviet Union and the countries of Eastern Europe.

Government officials are generally not oriented toward service delivery; on the contrary, they tend to be deeply bureaucratic. North Korean business entities are state-owned or quasi-state-run, as the establishment and operation of private enterprises is not legally permitted. They have no experience in operating within a capitalist or market-oriented framework. Whereas in a capitalist enterprise the board of directors bears responsibility for management and directors are appointed or removed by shareholders, North Korean enterprises have neither boards of directors nor shareholders, in keeping with the logic of a centrally planned socialist economy.

The governance of North Korean enterprises remains opaque. When North Korea amended its Socialist Constitution in April 2019, it introduced a new management framework designated the "responsible management system of socialist enterprises." The precise content of this system has not been made public, but it appears to vest sole managerial responsibility in the enterprise's chief executive officer. Prior to this reform, managerial authority within enterprises had resided in each enterprise's party committee, pursuant to the so-called "Taean Work System." Created by Kim Il-sung in the early 1960s, the Taean Work System had been in operation for nearly sixty years before it was formally abolished in April 2019. The system was designed to boost productivity by reinforcing top-down, directive-driven performance management. After such a prolonged history of socialist practice, a North Korean partner in a joint venture may not be as genuinely profit-oriented as market conditions require.

In practice, the overwhelming majority of joint venture companies established in the Rason ETZ since its creation in 1991 are understood to have been unsuccessful. As a consequence, North Korean authorities have moved away from encouraging the formation of joint ventures and now actively promote the establishment of wholly foreign-owned enterprises as the preferred investment vehicle.

One significant contributing factor to business failure in the Zone — apart from the management issues already discussed — has been unreasonable administrative delay in approving the establishment of joint venture companies, followed by persistent business interference through frequent inspections and supervisory oversight once companies have been established. By the terms and underlying logic of the relevant legislation, a joint venture company is treated as a component of North Korea's domestic business sector, to be operated under the ongoing supervision and control of North Korean authorities.[112]

Among the many risks associated with investment in the Rason ETZ, the most consequential is the profoundly uncertain political environment. North and South Korea have remained in a state of military and political confrontation since the peninsula's division in 1945. The Korean War, which lasted more than three years from June 1950, resulted in millions of casualties, and a formal state of hostilities has never been brought to a legal close, despite intermittent efforts by the two sides to sustain dialogue.

Through these periodic exchanges, the two sides have on occasion made measurable progress in reducing political tensions and expanding inter-Korean trade, investment, humanitarian assistance, and cultural exchanges. Yet such rapprochement has invariably proved superficial and fragile, vulnerable to collapse in the wake of a single provocative incident.

Beyond inter-Korean political dynamics, the prevailing international environment is also deeply unfavorable to North Korea's efforts to attract foreign investment and expand trade. North Korea has been the subject of eleven rounds of United Nations Security Council (UNSC) sanctions since 2006, imposed in response

---

[112] *See* the Joint Venture Law art. 6. The same provision is found in the Rason ETZ Law for the newly established enterprises in the Rason ETZ regardless of whether it is joint venture or not but it is known that the wholly-foreign owned companies are less interrupted by the North Korean authorities. *See* Rason ETZ Law art. 38.

to six nuclear weapons tests and more than one hundred ballistic missile launches carried out since that year. In addition to the UNSC regime, the United States has maintained its own extensive economic sanctions against North Korea since the outbreak of the Korean War in 1950, as discussed in a separate chapter of this book. The European Union, Canada, Japan, Australia, South Korea, and others have also enacted their own respective sanction measures.

From 2018 onward, the first Trump Administration undertook a series of diplomatic initiatives aimed at securing sanctions relief for North Korea in exchange for the dismantlement of its nuclear weapons testing and ballistic missile programs. As part of these efforts, President Trump met with North Korean leader Kim Jong Un on three occasions between 2018 and 2019, though the meetings produced no tangible outcome. Since that time, official and unofficial contacts between the two parties have continued, albeit on a minimal and intermittent basis, through to the latter part of the Biden Administration in 2024. As of the time of writing in 2025, President Trump, at the outset of his second term, has expressed a willingness to meet with Kim Jong Un, though neither the timing nor the substance of any such meeting remains certain.

Notwithstanding the foregoing, the Law of the Rason Economic and Trade Zone does contain several noteworthy provisions aimed at promoting foreign investment. The Law obliges the State to establish and maintain a series of specialized industrial parks within the Zone, organized according to industrial category. These include parks dedicated to: high-tech industry; international logistics; equipment manufacturing; primary processing; light industry; service businesses; and modern agriculture.[113] The State is further obligated to actively encourage investment in infrastructure construction, advanced science and technology, and the production of internationally competitive goods.[114] Foreign-invested enterprises operating in these priority sectors are entitled to a reduced enterprise income tax rate of 10%, down from the standard 14%, together with certain additional benefits.[115]

With respect to the protection of investors' rights, the Law provides that investors' property, lawfully earned income, and vested

[113] *See* Rason ETZ Law art. 3.

[114] *See id.* Law art. 6.

[115] *See* Tax Law of the DPRK for Foreign-invested Business and Individuals art. 16.

investment rights within the Zone are protected under applicable law, and that investors' property shall not be nationalized or expropriated.[116] However, in unavoidable reasons, an investor's property can be expropriated or used for public interest.[117] The nationalization or expropriation of an investor's property especially in a developing country is always a critical issue and risk although such a case is not a perennial concern. This issue is examined more fully in Chapter IV below.

An investor may acquire both the right to use land and ownership of buildings erected thereon. The term of land use rights extends up to fifty years and is renewable upon the expiration of the original contract period.[118]

Another provision of note concerns the employment of labor within the Zone. The Law requires foreign-invested enterprises to employ North Korean workers as their primary labor force, but permits the engagement of foreign workers upon simple notification to the Rason management authority, without the need to obtain any further approval or permit.[119] Labor-related issues are addressed more fully in Chapter IV.

The Rason ETZ was not designed, from the outset, to attract capital from South Korea, and the Rason ETZ authority has been consistently reluctant to admit investments from South Korean enterprises, notwithstanding the shared East Sea coastline. A small number of South Korean businesses and ethnic Korean enterprises based overseas have invested in the Zone, but they are reported to have ceased operations after a relatively short period. In the meantime, the emerging Arctic Sea Route — also known as the Northern Sea Route — has been developing as global warming accelerates, with the prospect of linking seaports across East Asia and Western Europe through a substantially more cost-effective corridor in terms of both distance and transit time. South Korea, too, has been monitoring this route with growing interest. Were both Koreas to cooperate in developing the Arctic Sea Route, the resulting synergies could be considerable. It is an exercise worth undertaking to model a direct sea link between two major ports — Rason City in East Asia and

---

[116] *See* Rason ETZ Law art. 7.
[117] *Id.*
[118] *Id.* Law art. 16 and 17.
[119] *See id.* art. 49.

Rotterdam in Western Europe — and to consider what such a connection might mean in the near future.

The Rason ETZ has never become the thriving commercial hub that its founders envisioned, despite the clear geographic advantages conferred by its position at the apex of the Tumen River triangle and the availability of an ice-free port. The reasons for the Zone's prolonged stagnation are deeply complex, involving a dense web of interrelated political, economic, and institutional factors — both domestic and international — as examined throughout this book. North Korea, as the host country, holds the key to resolving this impasse. A simpler and more straightforward path forward is both available and necessary.

B. Sinuiju Special Administrative Region – a mirage?

North Korea's efforts to attract foreign investment began in 1991 with the establishment of the Rason ETZ. As noted above, a series of laws and regulations was enacted to facilitate and promote foreign direct investment. From the outset, however, the majority of potential investors remained reluctant to commit to so insular a state. As a result, only a modest volume of investment materialized in the Rason ETZ over its first decade — falling well short of the ambitious aspirations behind the partial open-door policy.

Meanwhile, Kim Jong Il visited China in January 2001 and was reportedly struck by the dramatic transformation of Shanghai's Pudong District. Upon returning home and recognizing that the Rason ETZ had fallen far short of expectations, North Korea moved to establish a series of special economic zones (SEZs) across its territory in September 2002. Accordingly, the Sinuiju Special Administrative Region ("Region" or "Sinuiju SAR" hereafter) was established in the city of Sinuiju — situated in the northwestern part of North Korea, a riparian city, open port, and gateway to the lower reaches of the Amrok (Yalu in Chinese) River along the Chinese border.[120]

The next SEZ to be declared was the Mount Kumgang Special Tourism Zone in the southeastern part of the territory, immediately north of the Demilitarized Zone (DMZ). Another SEZ declared subsequently was the Kaesong Industrial Complex ("Kaesong

[120] The Sinuiju Special Administrative Region encompasses 130 square kilometers (50 square miles) and would be walled off from the rest of North Korea as was done in the Rason ETZ.

Complex" or "KIC" hereafter), located in the southwestern part of its territory, a few miles from Panmunjom, the truce village on the DMZ. By 2003, North Korea had thus established four special economic zones, one at each corner of its territory.

The Law on the Sinuiju Special Administrative Region ("Sinuiju Law" hereafter) contains a number of notably progressive provisions compared to existing foreign investment laws and regulations. The Law confers autonomous authority over the legislative, executive, and judicial branches of the Region. It ensures independence from the Cabinet, committees, ministries, and other organs of the central government, though the Region remains under the direct authority of the 'central authority' — that is, the relevant WPK department directly answerable to North Korea's supreme leader. The Region's designated lifespan as a special administrative region is fifty years; accordingly, land lease contracts will expire in 2052 unless a petition for extension is filed.

The Sinuiju Law designates the Region as a hub for international business encompassing finance, trade, commerce, manufacturing, high technology, recreation, and tourism. It further guarantees protection of private property against nationalization, as well as inheritance rights. Where property is appropriated on grounds of national security, however, compensation equivalent to its full value must be paid. The Region is authorized to establish its own financial and monetary policy and may move foreign currencies freely in and out. Tax policy also falls within the Region's purview, permitting a separate system from the prevailing tax regime of North Korea; the rates and types of taxes are determined by the Region's own authority. A preferential tariff system likewise applies, with rates set by the Region.

Development of the Sinuiju SAR came to an abrupt halt when the newly appointed Administrator — a Chinese-Dutch entrepreneur who had envisioned transforming it into a Hong Kong- or Macao-style enclave — was arrested by Chinese authorities in 2003 and sentenced to eighteen years in prison for tax evasion. The true political circumstances behind the arrest were never made public, and the North Korean government declined to comment on either the case or the SAR's future. Development plans have been effectively dormant ever since. As of 2025, neither the founding declaration nor the governing law of the Sinuiju SAR has been officially rescinded. The

Region has simply lingered in a kind of institutional limbo, its ultimate fate still unresolved.

In a parallel move, the North Korean government announced in 2006 the development of the Hwanggumphyong and Wihwado Economic Zone on two Amrok River islands near Sinuiju. During the 2010s, Kim Jong Un paid several visits to the city and commissioned the preparation of a master plan for the 'Sinuiju International Economic Zone' though the extent of any subsequent progress remains uncertain. North Korean authorities have long recognized Sinuiju's geographic advantages while simultaneously contending with the formidable obstacles that continue to hamper meaningful international engagement.

C. Defunct Mt. Kumgang Special Zone for International Tourism

North Korea promulgated the Law on Mount Kumgang Special Tourism Zone in November 2002. It overhauled this Law and made new one titled the Law on Mt. Kumgang Special Zone for International Tourism ("Mt. Kumgang Law" or "Mt. Kumgang SZIT Law" hereafter) in 2011. The Mt. Kumgang SZIT Law was reportedly abolished in December 2023. However, it is worthwhile to review this defunct law since the Mt. Kumgang zone is a good option for North Korea to reopen it to foreign investors and tourists once a favorable environment is made again. The City of Wonsan and its Kalma beach resort about forty miles away by land from the Mt. Kumgang National Park are under development. Mt. Kumgang is located in the south-eastern part of North Korea and it has been one of popular places for tourists from ancient times since its picturesque scenes have been well known to the people in East Asia.

North Korea opened Mt. Kumgang to South Korean tourists in 1998, shortly after an agreement was concluded between a South Korean private enterprise and a North Korean semi-governmental body. The initiative was designed to draw Korean visitors, with South Koreans and overseas ethnic Koreans as the primary audience. The vast majority of visitors were indeed South Korean, with arrivals from South Korea — by ship and bus alike — totaling more than 1.93

million over eleven years[121] until the tourism was banned by the South Korean government in July 2008. A small number of non-Korean foreign visitors also came during this period.

The ban followed a fatal incident in which a South Korean tourist was shot dead by a North Korean sentry after allegedly straying beyond the Zone's boundary into a militarily restricted area.

Although the Zone was conceived primarily as a tourist destination, North Korea also encouraged foreign investment there and offered a range of incentives.[122] According to the defunct Mt. Kumgang SZIT Law, foreign investors may, either on their own account or jointly with others, invest in various forms of business — including the construction of infrastructure facilities for the development of the SZIT and businesses concerning travel, accommodation, restaurants, casinos, golf, amusement, and welfare services.[123] Branches, representative offices, and agencies of foreign investors may be established in the SZIT.[124] Enterprises and individuals may open accounts with a North Korean bank or a foreign bank operating in the SZIT.[125] Within the SZIT, investors and tourists are permitted to use convertible foreign currency only.[126]

Foreign investors may freely bring currencies into or take them out of the SZIT and may remit profits and lawfully earned income. Businesses and individuals operating within the SZIT are subject to tax under the relevant laws, though those active in priority sectors — including airports, railways, roads, ports, and power stations — qualify for tax exemptions or reductions.[127] A preferential tariff regime also applies: customs duties are waived on materials imported for the development and operation of the SZIT, as well as on office supplies and personal necessities up to prescribed limits.[128] Duties are

---

[121] Statistics from the Ministry of Unification of the Republic of Korea available at <https://www.data.go.kr/data/15106609/fileData.do≥ (visited May 2, 2025).

[122] Defunct Law of the Democratic People's Republic of Korea on the Mt. Kumgang Special Zone for International Tourism (Mt. Kumgang Law hereafter) art. 4.

[123] *Id.* art. 24.

[124] *Id.* art. 28.

[125] *Id.* art. 29.

[126] *Id.* art. 34.

[127] *Id.* art. 36.

[128] *Id.* art. 38.

nonetheless imposed if duty-exempt goods are sold outside the SZIT or if state-controlled materials enter without authorization.[129]

One notable departure from the general investment framework concerns labor. Businesses in the SZIT are permitted to hire South Korean nationals and overseas ethnic Koreans alongside North Korean workers.[130] Under the standard rules governing foreign-invested enterprises, investors are typically required to hire North Korean labor through state-run labor exchanges.[131] While investors may decline a placement if the assigned worker is deemed unqualified,[132] they have limited recourse in practice given the absence of a free labor market. The Mt. Kumgang SZIT Law thus represents a notable exception, permitting the engagement of South Korean and diaspora workers. The rationale is straightforward: broadening the available labor pool was intended to attract greater investment from South Korea and abroad.

Since South Korea imposed its tourism ban in 2008, the prospect of the SZIT's reopening has remained an open question. From 2006 onward, successive UN Security Council sanctions have further constrained financial flows to North Korea. Recent reports indicate, however, that North Korean authorities have been actively developing tourism infrastructure at Mt. Kumgang and the adjacent Wonsan-Kalma coastal area, following the designation of this region as a tourism special zone in 2014. Mt. Kumgang's inscription as a UNESCO World Heritage Site in July 2025 may yet generate renewed international interest. In a striking diplomatic episode that same month, Russian Foreign Minister Sergey Lavrov spent three days at the Wonsan resort and met with Kim Jong Un. While sanctions continue to cast a long shadow over investment and tourism, the successor project — the Wonsan-Kalma Coastal Tourism Zone — may open its doors before long to international tourists. For Russians in particular, it could yet become the Antalya of the Far East.

D. Kaesong Industrial Complex

North Korea enacted the Law on the Kaesong Industrial Complex ("Kaesong Law" or "KIC Law" hereafter) in November 2002, just

---

[129] *Id.*
[130] *Id.* art. 33.
[131] Labor Law for Foreign-Invested Enterprises art. 12.
[132] *Id.*

days after the Mount Kumgang Law came into effect. Under the Kaesong Law, the Kaesong Industrial Complex ("KIC" or "Complex") is designated as a site for international business in industry, foreign trade, commerce, finance, and tourism.[133] The Complex is open to South Koreans, overseas ethnic Koreans, and non-Korean foreign nationals alike.[134] Kaesong is situated in the southwestern part of North Korea, adjacent to the South Korean border, with the Complex positioned a few hundred yards north of the Korean Demilitarized Zone (DMZ).

The Kaesong Industrial Complex falls under the authority of the central body responsible for industrial complexes,[135] whereas other special economic zones — including the Rason ETZ, the Hwanggumphyong- Wihwado Economic Zone, and the Economic Development Zones — are overseen by the central guidance organ for special economic zones. This arrangement effectively places the KIC under direct central authority, meaning under the office of the State's leader. With respect to property protection, the Kaesong Law guarantees investors' rights and interests, including inheritance rights.[136] Invested properties are in principle not subject to nationalization; however, where an investor's property must be taken for reasons of public interest, the investor is entitled to prior consultation and full compensation for the value of the property.[137]

To facilitate investor access, North Korea permits visa-free entry to the Complex via the designated route from South Korea.[138] Commodities moving to and from the Complex are exempt from tariffs,[139] though taxes arising from business activities are not.[140] The corporate income tax rate is 14% of net profit, reduced to 10% for infrastructure construction or high-technology businesses.[141]
Designated convertible hard currencies, supplemented by credit cards, may circulate within the Complex,[142] and foreign currencies —

---

[133] Law of the Democratic People's Republic of Korea on Kaesong Industrial Complex ('Kaesong Law' hereafter) art. 1.

[134] *Id.* art. 3.

[135] *Id.* art. 5.

[136] *Id.* art. 7.

[137] *Id.*

[138] *Id.* art. 28.

[139] *Id.* art. 33.

[140] *Id.* art. 43.

[141] *Id.*

[142] *Id.* art. 41

including those earned through business activities — may be freely brought in or taken out.[143] In practice, however, credit card use was not available in the Complex prior to its closure in 2016. Designated convertible hard currency encompasses: (i) convertible foreign currency in cash; (ii) securities such as bonds and stocks, denominated in convertible foreign currencies; (iii) means of payment such as notes, checks and certificate of deposits, denominated in convertible foreign currencies; and (iv) precious metals such as gold, silver, platinum, osmium and iridium, excluding ornaments.[144]

Foreign investors can lease a plot of land in the Complex for up to fifty years but the leased land can be extended upon application at the end of the term.[145]

The Kaesong Complex is not an autonomous region. The general laws and regulations of North Korea apply in full, as do existing foreign investment laws and regulations, except where the KIC Law provides otherwise. In several respects, the KIC Law offers foreign investors stronger protections than other North Korean investment statutes.

In its taking clause, for example, the KIC Law requires the relevant authority to consult with the private property owner before proceeding, and limits the grounds for taking to public interest, with full compensation for the value of the property.[146] While the power of eminent domain is inherent in sovereignty and prior consultation is not typically a procedural requirement, North Korea's inclusion of this requirement signals a positive disposition toward investor protection. The public interest limitation provides an additional safeguard.

That said, the compensation standard — defined simply as the "value" of the taken property — remains as vague here as in other North Korean statutes. It is unclear to outside observers whether North Korea has accredited assessors or established standards and formulae for property valuation. The government maintains price-fixing agencies for general commodities, but since land is not transacted between individuals or business entities, the basis on which land value would be assessed is uncertain.

---

[143] *Id.* art. 44.

[144] See Regulations on Control of Foreign Currency for Kaesong Industrial Complex of 2004 art. 4.

[145] *Id.* art. 12.

[146] *Id.* art. 7.

For disputes arising from business activities in the KIC, the Law provides first for resolution through consultation between the parties. If that fails, the parties may turn to one of three mechanisms: the Agreement between South and North Korea on Procedure for Business Dispute Settlement,[147] arbitration, or the court of law of North Korea.[148] The first option appears to anticipate that the overwhelming majority of investors in the Complex would be South Korean. However, the inter-Korean Agreement concluded in 2000 is not functional in practice, having never been applied due to a number of structural deficiencies[149] — a situation analogous to that under the Mt. Kumgang SZIT Law, both zones having been developed primarily to attract South Korean investors and tourists.

Should a dispute proceed to litigation, the appellate court of Kaesong Municipality, which falls directly under central authority, has original jurisdiction over matters involving foreigners and foreign business entities.[150] North Korea's judicial structure differs markedly from that of majority countries: in both criminal and civil proceedings, two non-lawyer "people's assessors" sit alongside a judge, participate in proceedings, and vote on the judgment — an arrangement reminiscent of the Chinese court system and the former Soviet model.

The independence of North Korea's judiciary cannot be taken for granted in cases where a foreign party's interests conflict with those of a North Korean entity, particularly where guidance from a higher or politically influential authority may be brought to bear. This aspect of the legal system is likely to raise concerns among foreign investors about the prospect of a fair hearing.

The Kaesong Industrial Complex has been shut down since February 2016, when the South Korean government ordered the suspension of operations and further investment by South Korean enterprises in response to North Korea's nuclear weapons tests and ballistic missile launches. In retaliation, the North Korean government expelled all South Korean personnel from the Complex. South Korean-invested enterprises had been operating and producing goods there from 2005 until the closure.

---

[147] The Agreement between South and North Korea on Procedure for Business Dispute Settlement was concluded in 2000.

[148] *Id.* art. 46.

[149] *See* Pilho Park, *Structural Flaws in the Dispute Settlement Mechanism between North and South Korea*, Dankook Law Journal, January 2010

[150] Law of DPRK on Civil Procedure of 2022 art. 18.

At the time of closure, 165 South Korean enterprises were operating in the Complex. The total value of industrial output in 2015 had reached USD 563.3 million, and approximately 55,000 North Korean workers were employed by South Korean companies when the Complex was shut down.

Since the closure, North Korean authorities have repeatedly called for South Korean businesses to return. However, any such resumption would likely constitute a violation of UN Security Council sanctions imposed from 2006 onward — notwithstanding that South Korean enterprises operated there until 2016. Additional U.S. sanctions may also serve as a further impediment. For now, the prospect of South Korean or other foreign investors re-entering the Complex appears remote. The path forward depends ultimately on the broader trajectory of international politics.

E. Hwanggumphyong and Wihwado Economic Zone

The Law of the Democratic People's Republic of Korea on the Hwanggumphyong and Wihwado Economic Zone ("HWEZ Law" hereafter) was enacted in December 2011, nine years after the Kaesong Industrial Complex Law. The Hwanggumphyong and Wihwado Economic Zone ("HWEZ" hereafter) is a visa-free zone for foreign nationals and their vehicles, accessible through a designated entry route.[151] Those entering the HWEZ from other parts of North Korea, or departing the Zone for other parts of the country, are required to follow separately prescribed procedures.[152]

The Hwanggumphyong is a strip of North Korean riparian land effectively adjoining the Chinese side of the Amrok (Yalu) River. It lies southwest of Sinuiju City, at the river's estuary, and is contiguous with Dandong City in China. Once an island, it gradually merged with the mainland through natural sedimentation and has since been used for agriculture. The Wihwado is an island in the Amrok River between North Korea and China, located northeast of Sinuiju City. The two sites are approximately nineteen kilometers (roughly twelve miles) apart along the river.

The HWEZ is a special economic zone operating under preferential economic policies.[153] The Hwanggumphyong area is

---

[151] *See* HWEZ Law art. 67.

[152] *Id.*

[153] *See id.* art. 2.

designated for priority development in information technology, light industry, agriculture, commerce, and tourism, while the Wihwado area is to be developed separately under its own development plan.[154] The Zone is open to investment by foreign corporations, individuals, and economic organizations, as well as by ethnic Koreans residing outside North Korea.[155]

North Korea undertakes to extend preferential treatment to investors in areas including land use, labor employment, taxation, and market access.[156] Investment is particularly encouraged in the construction of infrastructure facilities, state-of-the-art science and technology, and production of internationally competitive goods.[157] Investment and business operations that are detrimental to national security, public health, social and moral welfare, or the environment, or that involve economically or technically obsolete projects, are prohibited.[158]

The State undertakes not to nationalize or expropriate investors' property in the Zone. Where expropriation or temporary use for public interest is nonetheless required, the investor must be notified in advance, the prescribed legal procedures must be followed, and sufficient and effective compensation must be paid on a non-discriminatory basis.[159]

This taking clause represents a step forward compared to earlier statutes such as the Foreign Investment Law and the Kaesong Industrial Complex Law. The HWEZ Law explicitly addresses both "expropriation" and "nationalization" as grounds for taking, adds the standard of "sufficient and effective compensation," and includes the qualification "without any discrimination" — all provisions designed to reassure prospective investors.

Foreign currency may be freely brought into or taken out of the HWEZ, and legitimate profits and other income may be remitted abroad without restriction.[160] Property brought into or acquired within the HWEZ may likewise be removed from the Zone freely.[161] Enterprises in the Zone may also sell their products outside the

---

[154] *See id.* art. 3.
[155] *See id.* art. 4.
[156] *See id.* art. 5.
[157] *See id.* art. 6.
[158] *Id.*
[159] *See id.* art. 8.
[160] *See id.* art. 47.
[161] *Id.*

Zone.[162] Land use rights are granted for fifty years from the date of issuance of a land use certificate, consistent with the terms applicable in other special economic zones.[163]

Enterprises in the Zone are subject to tax in accordance with applicable law. The enterprise income tax rate is 14% of net profit, with a reduced rate of 10% for enterprises in priority sectors,[164] consistent with the rates in other special economic zones. Designated enterprises that have operated in the Zone for more than ten years are eligible for exemptions or reductions in enterprise income tax.[165]

Where an enterprise reinvests dividends within the Zone to increase its registered capital, or operates a newly established business for more than five years, it is entitled to a refund of 50% of the enterprise income tax paid on the reinvested amount.[166] Where the investment is directed toward infrastructure construction, a full refund of enterprise income tax on the reinvested amount is available.[167]

Customs duties are waived on materials brought into the Zone for processing, transit trade, and barter trade; on imports required for the production and operation of enterprises; on goods produced for export; on office supplies and personal necessities for investors; on materials needed for the construction of the Zone; and on other designated items.[168]

The establishment of a new special economic zone is, in principle, a promising signal that North Korea is seeking to benefit from foreign investment. In practice, however, the provisions of the HWEZ Law are likely to have limited effect for as long as the economic sanctions imposed by the United Nations, the United States, and other countries remain in force. Beyond sanctions, the absence of adequate hard and soft infrastructure represents a further obstacle that North Korea must address if its efforts to attract foreign investment are to bear fruit.

F. Economic Development Zones

---

[162] *See id.* art. 38.
[163] *See id.* art. 16.
[164] *See id.* art. 43.
[165] *See id.* art. 62.
[166] *See id.* art. 64.
[167] *Id.*
[168] *See id.* art. 68.

The Law of the Democratic People's Republic of Korea on Economic Development Zones ("EDZs Law" hereafter) was enacted in May 2013. The legislation was designed to govern multiple economic development zones spread across every province of North Korea as part of a broader economic promotion strategy — even as UN and U.S. sanctions were tightening. At the outset, thirteen EDZs were designated, roughly one per province. By the end of 2019, nine additional zones had been added, bringing the total to twenty-two. North Korea thus now operates four major special economic zones — Rason, Mt. Kumgang, Kaesong, and Hwanggumphyong-Wihwado — alongside twenty-two smaller zones designated as economic development zones.[169]

EDZs are categorized into two tiers – central government-level and provincial (or city directly under central government) government-level.[170] By the end of 2021, North Korea had set four special economic zones controlled by the central government, four central-level economic development zones and eighteen provincial-level economic development zones.

The EDZs are also categorized, depending on business environment of the location, as industrial development zones, agricultural development zones, tourism development zones, export-processing zones and high-technology development zones.[171] Foreign enterprises and/or individuals can invest in EDZs and also establish a company, branch or liaison office there.[172] The State actively encourages investment in infrastructure construction, advanced science and technology, and the manufacture of goods competitive in international markets.[173]

The EDZs Law provides that the State will not nationalize or expropriate investors' property; however, where expropriation or

---

169 *See* North Korea Information Portal of the Ministry of Unification of Rep. of Korea available at <https://nkinfo.unikorea.go.kr/nkp/knwldg/view/knwldg.do?menuId=NK_KNWLDG_DICARY&knwldgNo=59> (visited May 10, 2025). Also see Korea Trade-Investment Promotion Agency (KOTRA) website available at <http://news.kotra.or.kr/user/globalBbs/kotranews/786/globalBbsDataView.do?setIdx=247&dataIdx=164210> (visited May 10, 2025).

170 *See* Law of the DPRK on the Economic Development Zones (EDZ Law) art. 3.

171 *See* EDZ Law art. 6.

172 *See id.* art. 5.

173 *See id.* art. 7.

temporary use for public interest is required, the investor must be notified in advance and sufficient compensation for the value of the property must be paid.[174] This taking clause is an improvement over earlier general foreign investment statutes, though it is marginally less explicit than the HWEZ Law provision, omitting the terms "effective" (in relation to compensation) and "without any discrimination.'

Land use rights are granted for fifty years, consistent with other special economic zones, and are renewable upon expiration of the contract.[175] Enterprises may sell, sublet, gift, inherit, or mortgage their land use rights.[176] The EDZs Law also specifically encourages foreign direct investment in the construction of economic development zones, whether jointly with North Korean entities or by a foreign investor acting alone.[177]

The enterprise income tax rate is 14% of net profit, with a reduced rate of 10% for enterprises in priority sectors.[178] The EDZs Law replicates the tax incentives available under the HWEZ Law: enterprises operating in an EDZ for more than ten years are eligible for enterprise income tax exemptions or reductions.[179] Notably, while the HWEZ Law reserves this benefit for "designated" enterprises, the EDZs Law extends it to all qualifying enterprises. Where an enterprise reinvests dividends to increase its registered capital, or operates a newly established business for more than five years, a 50% refund of enterprise income tax on the reinvested amount is available.[180] If an investment is made in the construction of infrastructure facilities, the whole enterprise income tax that has been paid on the reinvested amount is refunded.[181] Customs duty incentives on materials for processing, export, import, and investor necessities are identical to those under the HWEZ Law.[182] Foreign currencies may be freely brought into and out of the EDZs, and

---

[174] *See id.* art. 8.
[175] *See id.* art. 25.
[176] *See id.* art. 29.
[177] *See id.* art. 20 and 26.
[178] *See id.* art. 45.
[179] *See id.* art. 53.
[180] *See id.* art. 54.
[181] *Id.*
[182] *See id.* art. 56. *See* also HWEZ Law art. 68.

legally earned profits and income may be remitted abroad without restriction.[183]

As of the end of 2025, twenty-two economic development zones have been designated across the country. Whether any foreign direct investment has actually been made in any of them remains unknown. Under the weight of UN Security Council and U.S. sanctions, among others, few foreign investors are likely to venture capital into so uncertain an environment.

G. Questions on Country of Origin

One of the most important considerations for foreign direct investors in North Korea is the question of country of origin, particularly where the investment involves manufacturing, processing, assembling, or other forms of goods production. If such products are exported to another country, investors must carefully determine whether any restrictions or disadvantages apply to North Korean-origin goods in the destination market. Discriminatory tariffs may be imposed on such products, as discussed below, and import restrictions may already be in effect. Investors operating manufacturing businesses, other businesses mentioned above, in North Korea must therefore weigh these potential risks carefully. This subchapter examines country of origin issues; other restrictions arising from economic sanctions are addressed in a separate chapter.

There is no universally established or clear-cut standard for determining the country of origin of a particular product, especially when its components, elements, or ingredients come from multiple countries. Where an article is produced entirely within a North Korean facility using North Korean materials and labor, its country of origin is unambiguously North Korea, and it will be marked accordingly under the applicable marking statute.[184] The reason this issue deserves particular attention is that North Korea maintains an unusual trade relationship with several countries — most notably the United States.

With respect to the definition of rules of origin, the World Trade Organization (WTO) Agreement on Rules of Origin stipulates that such rules "shall be defined as those laws, regulations and administrative determinations of general application applied by any

---

[183] *See id.* art. 47.

[184] For the case of the United States, *see* 19 U.S.C. § 1304 (2020).

Member (state) to determine the country of origin of goods."[185] The Agreement also incorporates an implementation principle of 'last substantial transformation' in cases where more than one country is involved in the production of a good.[186] Contracting parties to the Agreement are accordingly required to establish their own rules of origin along these lines.

In the United States, country of origin must be marked under the provisions of Section 304 of the Tariff Act of 1930, as amended by the Customs Administrative Act of 1938, which provides as follows:

> [E]very article of foreign origin ... imported into the United States shall be marked in a conspicuous place as legibly, indelibly, and permanently as the nature of the article (or container) will permit in such manner as to indicate to an ultimate purchaser in the United States the English name of the country of origin of the article.[187]

Country of origin is defined in the United States as "[t]he country of manufacture, production, or growth of any article of foreign origin entering the United States."[188] And then "[f]urther work or material added to an article in another country must effect a substantial transformation in order to render such other country the 'country of origin' within the meaning of this part [of the law] ...."[189] A question thus arises: if an American investor operating a manufacturing business in North Korea exports a partly processed product to a third country — South Korea, for example — to complete it there, what degree of manufacturing would constitute "substantial transformation" sufficient to avoid a "made in North Korea" marking when the finished product is subsequently imported into the United States? Several cases have interpreted the substantial transformation standard as applied under country of origin regulations.

Before turning to substantial transformation, it is useful to consider the definition of "manufacture." The Supreme Court addressed this in 1908 as follows:

---

[185] WTO Agreement on Rules of Origin art. 1.

[186] *Id.* art. 9.

[187] 19 U.S.C. § 1304(a) (2020).

[188] 19 C.F.R. § 134.1(b)(2021)

[189] *Id.*

> [M]anufacture implies a change, but every change is not manufacture, and yet every change in an article is the result of treatment, labor and manipulation. But something more is necessary …. [T]here must be transformation; a new and different article must emerge, "having a distinctive name, character or use."[190]

This interpretation was adopted as the substantial transformation test in the *Gibson–Thompson* case in 1940, which held that substantial transformation occurred when articles lost their identity and became new articles with a new name, character, or use.[191] Thereafter, to determine if substantial transformation occurred or not, it is important to know whether significant value or costs are incurred by the process.[192] Following *Gibson–Thompson*, the *John E. Murray, Jr.* case further clarified that 'transformation' means 'fundamental change' and 'substantial' means 'more than fundamental.'[193] Because it is still vague to verify in individual cases if a specific article has been substantially transformed or not, the standard of country of origin varies depending on the value added or degree of process of the goods involved.

In *Torrington Co. v. United States*, a sewing machine needle produced in a beneficiary developing country (BDC) from wire manufactured in a non-BDC was found to have undergone substantial transformation after more than 35% in value or costs had been added. The 35% threshold was the minimum required for BDC treatment and duty-free status.[194] The court determined that a substantial transformation occurred since the sewing machine needles were produced from imported wire through the process of swaging, striking, boring, carving, pointing, cleaning, hardening, etc. This process satisfied the 35% BDC content prerequisite[195] since it was substantially transformed.

---

[190] *Anheuser-Busch Brewing Association v. United States*, 207 U.S. 556, 562 (1908).

[191] *United States v. Gibson-Thomsen Co., Inc.*, 27 C.C.P.A., 267, 273 (1940).

[192] *See United States v. John E. Murray, Jr.*, 621 F.2d 1163, 1169 (1980). In this case, the court defines the terms as follows: "substantial" means "a very great change in the articles' real worth value" and "transformation" means "a fundamental change in the form, appearance, nature, or character of an article."

[193] *See United States v. John E. Murray, Jr.*, 621 F.2d 1163, 1169 (1980).

[194] 19 C.F.R. §10.176(a)(1) (2000).

[195] *Torrington Company v. United States*, 764 F.2nd 1563, 1567, 1572 (1985).

In *Ferrostaal Metals Corp. v. United States*, the court likewise affirmed a substantial transformation where Japanese steel was imported into the United States after processing in New Zealand. The steel had been annealed and galvanized by a process known as "continuous hot-dip galvanizing" applied to full hard cold-rolled steel sheet from Japan, and the value of the processed sheet increased from US$ 350 per ton to US$ 550–630 per ton. The New Zealand processing thus constituted a substantial transformation, changing the country of origin from Japan to New Zealand.[196]

By contrast, in Superior Wire v. United States, the court denied a finding of substantial transformation where only minor value was added in the process of drawing wire from wire rod. A Canadian supplier of wire mesh had imported wire rod from Spain and added approximately fifteen percent in value to draw wire from the rod before selling it to an importer in Michigan. The court held that no transformation from producers' goods to consumers' goods had taken place, as the processing was neither complicated nor costly and the value added was relatively small. Since both parties agreed that the value change was 15%, the country of origin of the wire was held to be Spain rather than Canada.[197]

A further example of a denied substantial transformation arises in *F.F. Zuniga a/c Refractarios Monterrey, S.A. v. United States*, where the plaintiffs-appellants claimed duty-free status under the Generalized System of Preferences (GSP) for kiln furniture imported from Mexico, a GSP beneficiary country. The United States classified that the kiln furniture casting slip was subject to a custom duty. The kiln furniture is a shaped refractory article that holds ceramicware during firing, and the casting slip is an essential part of the kiln furniture. The kiln furniture was produced by dry ingredients such as kaolin, clay, sierralite talc, etc. All ingredients were imported from the United States which was not entitled to a GSP status for its own exported articles if they were not substantially transformed. In the production process, these ingredients were mixed with additional materials to produce casting slip, which was then poured into molds. The court found that producing the casting slip required only a simple addition of water and dispersing agents to the imported dry

---

[196] *See Ferrostaal Metals Corp. v. United States*, 664 F. Supp 535, 540 (1987).

[197] *See Superior Wire, a Division of Superior Products Co., a Michigan Corp. v. United States*, 669 F. Supp. 472, 490 (1987). *See* also same case 867 F.2d 1409 (1989).

ingredients, and that the slip therefore did not lose the identifying characteristics of its dry components. The casting slip was accordingly held to remain clearly recognizable as a simple blend of those ingredients and had not undergone substantial transformation sufficient to change the country of origin.[198]

As the foregoing cases illustrate, customs duties are assessed on the basis of the actual country of origin rather than nominal origin. Most disputes concerning country of origin have arisen in the context of attempts to circumvent quotas assigned to a specific country or to qualify for duty-free treatment as a BDC under the GSP.

North Korea is neither a BDC nor a country with an assigned quota in trade with the United States. It is not a member of the WTO. Far from qualifying as a BDC, North Korea — as a nonmarket economy — is ineligible for nondiscriminatory treatment (normal trade relations) because it denies its citizens the right or opportunity to emigrate, as required under the Trade Act of 1974, as amended. The Trade Act of 1974 is intended to reinforce the United States' commitment to fundamental human rights. A country that falls within this category

> [s]hall not participate in any program of the Government of the United States which extends credit or credit guarantees or investment guarantees, directly or indirectly, and the President of the United States shall not conclude any commercial agreement with any such country, during the period beginning with date on which the President determines that such country: (1) denies its citizens the right or opportunity to emigrate ….[199]

As a consequence, products of North Korean origin receive discriminatory treatment when imported into the United States. They are classified under column 2 duty rates in the Harmonized Tariff Schedule of the United States, resulting in substantially elevated customs duties. Under the 2025 Harmonized Tariff Schedule, for example, ski boots and snowboard boots from North Korea are subject to a 35% duty, whereas the same goods from column 1 (general) countries enter duty-free. Column 2 rates across all product categories

---

[198] *See F.F. Zuniga a/c Refractarios Monterrey, S.A. v. United States*, 996 F.2d 1203, 1207 (1993).

[199] *See* 19 U.S.C. § 2432 (a) (1998).

are similarly elevated.[200] As of 2025, North Korea is one of only four column 2 states, alongside Cuba, Belarus, and Russia.[201]

Despite its column 2 status, North Korea continues to seek foreign investment under its various investment laws. In practice, however, foreign direct investors operating manufacturing businesses in a North Korean special economic zone face a stark reality: exporting North Korean-origin products to the United States is effectively foreclosed by prohibitive customs duties, compounded by UN Security Council sanctions and additional U.S. import restrictions.

On the country-of-origin question vis-à-vis the United States, so long as North Korea declines to reform its policies and institutions in ways that would satisfy American requirements, potential investors seeking to produce goods for the U.S. market will have strong reasons to look elsewhere.

---

[200] *See* Harmonized Tariff Schedule of the United States Revision 11 (2025) Chapter 64, Heading/subheading 6402.12.00.

[201] *See* Harmonized Tariff Schedule of the United States Rev. 11 (2025), General Notes 3(b). The column 2 rate is applied to products of four countries whether they are imported directly or indirectly.

Chapter 4 Itemized Legal Issues in Foreign Direct Investment

In April 1992, North Korea amended its Socialist Constitution of 1972 to adapt to the new political environment following the collapse of the Soviet bloc. Among the revisions was the insertion of a provision stating that "[t]he State shall encourage its own institutions, enterprises and organizations in our country to create equity and contractual joint ventures with foreign corporations and individuals."[202]

Building on this constitutional foundation, North Korea enacted the Law of the Democratic People's Republic of Korea on Foreign Investment ("Foreign Investment Law" hereafter) in October 1992 — its first legislation specifically governing foreign investment. A series of further laws and regulations followed, including: revisions to the Equity Joint Venture Law of 1984 and its implementing regulations; the Law on Contractual Joint Venture and its regulations; the Law on Foreign Enterprise and its regulations; the Law on Foreign Investment Bank and its regulations; the Labor Regulations for Foreign-Invested Business; the Law on Foreign Investment Enterprise and Foreign Individual Tax and its regulations; and the Law on Leasing of Land and its regulations, among others. Additional legislation followed in subsequent years. North Korea now has approximately one hundred laws and implementing regulations relating to the introduction of foreign investment.

North Koreans had little familiarity with profit-oriented foreign business practices, having had only limited exposure during the first open door policy period in 1984. The knowledge and experience needed to engage effectively with foreign investors and private capital were largely absent. It appears that North Korea modeled much of its early investment legislation on Chinese law or the laws of other transitional economies, adapting them as best it could to its own circumstances. The initial body of laws and regulations contained

[202] *See* Socialist Constitution of DPRK of 1992 art. 37. In 1998, a phrase "as well as the establishment and operation of a variety of enterprise in special economic zones" was added to the sentence of the art. 37 in order to give constitutional ground for the operation of a special economic zone in the Rajin-Sonbong area from 1992 and more SEZs in the future.

numerous flaws and internal contradictions that the authorities likely did not recognize at the outset. Over time, however, these deficiencies were identified and addressed incrementally. North Korea's ongoing efforts to improve its statutes and implementing regulations have yielded some progress, though the socialist legal and economic framework, combined with limited experience in modern commercial operations, continues to present significant constraints. In this respect, North Korea still has considerable ground to cover in modernizing the legal architecture governing foreign direct investment. The following sections examine North Korea's foreign investment laws and regulations on an issue-by-issue basis.

A. Currency and Foreign Exchange Control

Currency is one of the essential elements of foreign investment. In the foreign investment context, currency control takes various forms — governing access to borrowing, the transfer of dividends, the payment of royalties for the use of intellectual property, the repatriation of capital, and more. Currency risk also arises from government intervention in exchange rates, as well as from inflation and indexation in the host country. Political instability and economic crises in the host country create additional risks.

North Korea's principal regulatory instruments for foreign currency are the Law of the Democratic People's Republic of Korea on Foreign Currency Control ("Foreign Currency Control Law" hereafter) and the Regulations for Implementation of the Law on Foreign Exchange Control ("Foreign Exchange Control Regulations" hereafter). Certain currency-related provisions also appear in other legislation, including the Law on Foreign Investment and the Law on Rason Economic and Trade Zone.

North Korea's legal tender is the North Korean *won*, and no foreign currencies are permitted to circulate within its territory.[203] All currencies other than the North Korean *won* constitute foreign exchange, as do all claims denominated in foreign currencies and precious metals.[204] Foreign exchange encompasses both convertible and inconvertible foreign currencies.

Convertible foreign exchange includes the banknotes and coins of countries whose currencies are freely convertible, together with all

---

[203] *See* Foreign Currency Control Law of 2020 art. 4.

[204] *See id.* Law art. 2.

securities and foreign exchange instruments denominated in those currencies. Such instruments include government bonds, debentures, bills, checks, bank cards, negotiable certificates of deposit, gold, silver, and platinum other than decorative articles, gold and silver coins traded on international financial markets, and other precious metals.[205]

A question is raised if a foreign investor is allowed to borrow money from a domestic financial institution in North Korea. There is no straight stipulation to limit foreigners' access to borrowings of local or foreign currency from domestic financial institutions. The Equity Joint Venture Law only stipulates that an equity joint venture enterprise may borrow 'money' needed for its business activities either from a DPRK bank or a bank of a foreign country.[206] And its implementing regulations of 2005 stipulate that a joint venture enterprise may be granted a loan needed for its business activities from a bank either in North Korea or in a foreign country.[207]

Under the Foreign Investment Law, foreign-invested enterprises in sectors that the State actively promotes — such as those requiring advanced technology, producing internationally competitive goods, or developing natural resources — are entitled to preferential access to bank loans.[208] No other legislation specifically addresses foreign investors' access to domestic financial institutions for borrowing. Reading the relevant provisions in context, loans in both domestic and foreign currency appear to be permitted, as neither "loans" nor "money" is expressly limited to foreign currency. In practice, however, the situation may be quite different: it is doubtful whether North Korea holds sufficient foreign exchange reserves to lend to foreign investors, and excessive collateral requirements cannot be ruled out. Access to domestic financing may become available in time, but is unlikely in the near term.

If foreign investors can access domestic financial institutions for borrowing, what degree of accessibility could they have? Will they be treated same as domestic entities? There is no direct answer to this question but in socialist economies with centrally controlled banking systems, foreign entities generally do not enjoy the same borrowing eligibility as domestic ones. This reflects the State's overriding

---

[205] *See id.* art. 2.

[206] *See* Equity Joint Venture Law of 2014 art. 29.

[207] *See* Equity Joint Venture Regulations of 2005 art. 103.

[208] Foreign Investment Law of 2020 art. 7 and 8.

priority of using the banking system to channel production funds to domestic entities and to facilitate the smooth circulation of currency among economic actors in support of national economic plans.[209] Foreign investors' access to local currency borrowing, if permitted at all, would likely be constrained by this principle. The position is unlikely to change until North Korea dismantles centralized economic planning and embraces market economy principles.

Collateral is generally required when a foreign investor applies for a loan, even though the relevant laws and regulations do not expressly say so. Acceptable collateral takes the form of personal guarantees, material goods, or mortgages.[210]

The transferability of foreign currency is, in many respects, the most fundamental consideration in foreign direct investment. The need to transfer currency holdings abroad arises in a variety of circumstances: repatriation of capital or profits, payment of interest on foreign borrowings, payment for goods or technology, and personal remittances by foreign employees. Some foreign businesses operate for decades; others for shorter periods. In either case, foreign personnel will eventually return home and need to transfer funds. All of North Korea's foreign investment laws and regulations permit foreign investors to remit abroad the profits earned from business activities and to take out assets originally brought in when the business term expires.[211] Within North Korea, including its special economic zones, there is no prescribed ceiling on the remittance of profits or the transfer of capital.[212]

The foreign exchange rate regime is another important consideration for investors. Exchange rates are generally set by government action, market forces, or a combination of the two. In North Korea, the rate is determined by the central financial guidance organ,[213] leaving no room for autonomous market mechanisms.

North Korea operates a fixed exchange rate system. The rate of the Korean *won* against foreign currencies is set by the central

---

[209] *See* JUN HONG TAEK ET AL. at 176; *see also* Civil Law Dictionary at 174.

[210] *See* Civil Law Dictionary at 155 and 174.

[211] *See* Foreign Currency Control Law art. 29; Rason ETZ Law art. 65; Equity Joint Venture Law art. 42; Foreign Investment Law art. 20; Wholly Foreign-owned Enterprise Law art. 21; Foreign-Invested Bank Law art. 33; Contractual Joint Venture Law art. 16; HWEZ Law art. 47; EDZ Law art. 47; and Kaesong Law art. 44.

[212] *See* Foreign Currency Control Law art. 29.

[213] *See id.* art. 7.

financial guidance organ, which is the Ministry of Finance of the Cabinet. The Foreign Trade Bank of the Democratic People's Republic of Korea (also known as the Korea Trade Bank or Joson Trade Bank) is the principal foreign exchange bank and specializes in foreign currency transactions. It determines the procedures and methods for foreign exchange dealings and foreign business transactions,[214] and, on the basis of the Ministry of Finance's fixed rate, sets both the exchange rate for foreign cash and the transaction rate against the North Korean *won*.[215]

As of 2021, one U.S. dollar was equivalent to 105.90 North Korean *won*. Statistical data show that the official exchange rate has remained relatively stable since 2006, when it stood at 141.00 *won* per dollar — the year UN Security Council sanctions were first imposed.[216] Given the profound changes in North Korea's economic environment over this period, the stability of the official rate is striking and suggests that the *won* may not reflect its true value against foreign currencies, particularly the U.S. dollar, given that the rate is set by the government itself. Meanwhile, the black market rate has diverged dramatically: according to the Ministry of Unification of the Republic of Korea, one U.S. dollar was trading at around 8,000 North Korean *won* on the informal market in 2022.[217] The possibility of a sharp devaluation of the *won* at some future point cannot be discounted.

A foreign-invested enterprise must obtain approval from the central financial guidance organ before opening a bank account in a foreign country,[218] and is required to submit documents on foreign exchange revenue and expenditure to the foreign exchange control authority within thirty days after the end of each quarter.[219]

---

[214] *See* Foreign Exchange Regulations of 2004 art. 5. *See* also *Bukhan Jeongbo* Portal (Information Portal on North Korea) of the Ministry of Unification of the Republic of Korea updated in July 2023 < https://nkinfo.unikorea.go.kr/nkp/pge/view.do;jsessionid=qZMaqlR3R5n23TGAGgPK5puyOxylMEWi73ZQoDTa.ins22?menuId=EC209> (visited May 11, 2025).

[215] *Id.* art. 9.

[216] *See Bukhan Jeongbo* Portal (Information Portal on North Korea) of the Ministry of Unification of the Republic of Korea updated in July 2023. < https://nkinfo.unikorea.go.kr/nkp/pge/view.do;jsessionid=qZMaqlR3R5n23TGAGgPK5puyOxylMEWi73ZQoDTa.ins22?menuId=EC209> (visited May 11, 2025)

[217] *See id.* website.

[218] *See* Foreign Currency Control Law art. 8.

[219] *See* Foreign Exchange Regulations of 2004 art. 73.

B. Banking system

The basic framework of North Korea's banking system was first set out in the '20 Platforms' announced by the Provisional People's Committee of North Korea in March 1946, seven months after Korea's liberation from Japanese colonial rule. The 20 Platforms declared that all banks in the northern part of the peninsula, along with other sectors of industry, would be nationalized.[220] The banks then operating in Korea had been established either by Japanese colonial authorities or by Korean nationals, and included branches of major Japanese financial institutions.

Subsequently, in April 1946, the Provisional People's Committee of North Korea promulgated a decree creating the Farmer's Bank of North Korea.[221] This was the first bank of North Korea after the liberation established by Korean nationals who controlled northern part of Korea under the Soviet supervision. Nationalization of the northern banking sector was reaffirmed on two further occasions in 1946: by a decree of the Provisional People's Committee[222] and by a platform of the Workers' Party of Korea.[223] The Central Bank of North Korea was established under the Regulations on Establishment of the Central Bank of North Korea issued by the Provisional People's Committee in October 1946.[224] Nationalization was subsequently enshrined in the first North Korean Constitution of 1948 and has remained a constitutional principle ever since.

However, in spite of such consistent policy on state-owned banking system, a change occurred when North Korea initiated the limited open door policy in the 1980s. From 1987, several banks were established with foreign private investment, structured as joint

---

[220] *See* Platform of 20 Planks para. 9.

[221] Decree on the Establishment of the Farmers Bank (decision No. 3 of the Provisional People's Committee of North Korea on April 1. 1946).

[222] *See* Decree by the Provisional People's Committee on Nationalization of Industry, Transportation, Traffic, Communications and Bank declared on August 10, 1946.

[223] Platform of the Workers Party of Korea para. 5 declared on August 29. 1946.

[224] Decision about the Central Bank (decision No. 103 of the Provisional People's Committee of North Korea on Oct. 29, 1946). By the Decision, all assets of then-existing banks including formerly Japanese-owned banks located in northern part of Korean peninsula were merged into the newly established Central Bank.

ventures or foreign-invested banks. This development sits in some tension with the constitutional provision — then as now — declaring that "[b]anks shall be owned solely by the State."[225]

As of 2019, thirty-four financial institutions were known to be operating in connection with foreign investment, trade, and business transactions, in addition to the Central Bank. Of these, six were joint ventures with foreign entities and five were non-bank financial institutions dealing in insurance, investment, and related activities.[226]

While there had not been any statute regulating the Central Bank of North Korea[227] or general banking business, North Korea enacted the Law of the DPRK on Foreign-invested Banks ("Foreign-invested Bank Law" hereafter) in 1993 followed by the Implementing Regulations for the Law on Foreign-invested Bank in 1994.[228] The Law states that its purpose is to develop and expand cooperation with different countries in the area of financing.[229] Foreign-invested banks are defined to include joint venture banks, wholly foreign-owned banks and branch offices of foreign banks.[230]

A joint venture bank is a bank, which is jointly established and operated within the territory of the DPRK by contribution from both a bank or any financial institution of North Korea and a foreign investor in order to share profits or losses according to their portion of contribution.[231] A wholly foreign-owned bank is the one that is solely established and operated by a foreign investor with his sole contribution only in the special economic zones.[232]

A branch office of a foreign bank is also established and operated in the special economic zones by a head bank of another country.[233] As a result, business of a foreign bank and a branch of a foreign bank is geographically confined to the special economic zones. In order to

---

[225] *Id.*; *see* also the Socialist Constitution of 2023 art. 21.

[226] *See* KOREA DEVELOPMENT BANK (KDB), *BUKHAN-EUI SANEOP I*, PDF (Industry of North Korea vol. I) (2020) at 378-9 available at <https://nkinfo.unikorea.go.kr/nkp/pblictn/view.do;jsessionid=7mjPZ6w_kvi_kk27nIwOSecl4gOYVoc3QoHoTb2V.ins22?menuId=OC0002&pblictnNo=200> (visited May 11, 2025).

[227] North Korea's Law on Central Bank was enacted in 2004.

[228] Implementing Regulations for the Law on Foreign-invested Bank ("Foreign-invested Bank Regulations" hereafter).

[229] Foreign-invested Bank Law art. 1.

[230] *Id.* art. 2.

[231] *See* Foreign-invested Bank Regulations of 2002 art. 3.

[232] Foreign-invested Bank Law art. 3.

[233] *Id.*

mitigate such a negative effect and to facilitate the business activities of foreign-invested banks, the Foreign-invested Bank Law and its Regulations declare that foreign-invested banks have ownership of their banking property including the right to use and dispose of their banking property and they are independent in their management.[234] These are, however, guarantees of what ought to go without saying.

Foreign-invested banks are supervised and controlled by the Central Bank of North Korea and the central tax guidance organ.[235] The Central Bank reviews and approves the establishment, dissolution, and scope of business of foreign-invested banks, formulates the rules under which they operate, and oversees compliance.[236] Foreign exchange transactions of foreign-invested banks are separately approved, monitored, and controlled by the foreign exchange control authority.[237]

A foreign investor wishing to establish a foreign-invested bank must file an application with the Central Bank.[238] In the case of a joint venture bank, the application is filed by the North Korean partner alone rather than jointly.[239] That partner must be a financial institution; there is no equivalent requirement for the foreign partner.[240] It means that foreign partner should not be necessarily a financial institution. Instead, The application is evaluated on the basis of accompanying documents including a copy of the joint-venture contract, the articles of association, feasibility study report, a copy of the investor's business license, investor's balance sheet for three years audited and verified at the foreign investor's country, and résumés of the foreign investor and the president of the bank.[241]

The application for establishment of a wholly foreign-owned bank should be applied by the foreign investor.[242] The required applying documents are the same as the case of a joint venture bank mentioned above except for a joint venture contract.[243]

---

[234] *See id.* art. 4 and Foreign-invested Bank Regulations of 2002 art. 6 .
[235] *See* id. Law art. 7
[236] *See* Foreign-invested Bank Regulations of 2002 art. 9.
[237] *Id.*
[238] Foreign-invested Bank Law art. 9; *id.* Regulations of 2002 art. 10.
[239] *Id.* Law art.10.
[240] *Id.*
[241] *Id.*
[242] *Id.* Law art. 11.
[243] *Id.*

In case of establishment of a branch of a foreign bank, the application should be made by the head office of the foreign bank. The applying documents are the articles of association, feasibility study report, a copy of the investor's business license, investor's balance sheet for three years audited and verified at the foreign investor's country, and résumés of the foreign investor and the president of the bank.[244]

The Central Bank of North Korea will conduct an examination over the documents of application and decide whether to approve or reject within thirty days from receipt.[245] If decision is made within thirty days as prescribed by the law without procrastination, it looks quite speedy. Once application is approved, a certain period is given for preparation of banking operations.[246] If a foreign-invested bank does not complete the preparation for operations until the first day of the business term as indicated on the approval notice, the Central Bank has to cancel the approval of the establishment, retrieve the approval notice and notify relevant institutions of such measures taken by it.[247] There are a number of required things to prepare for operation of banking business as demonstrated in the article 15 of the Foreign-invested Bank Law.[248]

The next step is to apply for approval for business operation. This application must be accompanied by a set of documents including the approval notice of the bank establishment, internal guidance of work, registration certificate of address, registration certificate of tax, verification report for performed investment, confirmation letter for opening a deposit account, deposit certificate of bank reserves and the like.[249]

The final step is the issuance of a banking business license. That is, the Central Bank, upon receiving an application for approval for business operation of a foreign-invested bank, shall decide, after conducting an examination, whether to approve or reject the application based on on-the-spot inspection for the preparedness of

---

[244] *Id.* Law art. 12.
[245] *Id.* Law art. 13.
[246] *Id.* Law art. 14.
[247] *Id.*
[248] *Id.* Law art. 15.
[249] *Id.* Law art. 16.

business operations within 30 days of receipt thereof. In case of approval, a banking business license shall be issued.[250]

The process of establishing a foreign-invested bank is notably complex. From the first application for approval for establishment to the final application for business operation license, it takes quite a long time. The process is as follows: application for establishment with about 6 or 9 required documents → 30 days for decision to approve or reject → if approved, prescribed preparation period as indicated on the approval notice (preparation list is stipulated in the article 15 of the Law) → another application for business operation license with 7 different documents → approved or rejected within 30 days. The overall timeline is considerable. Whether there is scope to streamline the process or reduce the documentation burden is a question worth asking.

Once the license is issued, the business term of a foreign-invested bank is twenty years and it can be extended upon application for extension but the Law does not mention if it can be extended the same term as the first license.[251]

Foreign-invested banks can open 'bank offices' in North Korea under their control to handle such businesses as economic survey, data collection or external affairs upon approval of the Central Bank. But the foreign-invested banks cannot open a branch or sub-branch office that offers banking services, nor are bank offices above allowed to deal with business transactions.[252] While the restriction on bank offices handling transactions is understandable since their functions are prescribed by the Law to be limited as such, the blanket prohibition on opening branches or sub-branches within North Korea seems unduly restrictive. It may be an excessive regulation of banking activities for foreign-invested banks. An investor establishing a bank in the Rason ETZ, for example, would reasonably expect to be able to operate branches not only within that zone — which is larger than New York City and divided into several specialized districts — but potentially in other special economic zones or economic development zones as well. It is quite unreasonable not to set up a bank branch of a foreign-invested bank even within the same ETZ.

Another notable thing is about a prerequisite to obtain an approval from the Central Bank of North Korea when a

[250] *Id.* Law art. 17.
[251] *Id.* Law art. 18.
[252] *Id.* Law art. 19.

foreign-invested bank is going to newly appoint the president or a vice-president of its bank. The Law of Foreign-invested Bank states that if a foreign-invested bank wishes to do such works as revision of articles of association, merger or division of business, making changes in the registered capital, or replacing the president or a vice president of the bank, an application for approval to that effect should be filed with the Central Bank and the particulars of the change must be registered upon approval.[253]

It may make a sense for the case of a joint-venture bank since it has mixed capital from both North Korean side and foreign counterpart. The relevant law in fact states that an equity joint-venture enterprise should be a corporate body of the DPRK from the date of its registration with the investment management organ.[254] However, in the case of a wholly foreign-owned bank, whose capital derives entirely from a market economy, the appointment of a president or vice-president would ordinarily be a matter for shareholders or the board of directors, without government intervention. Pre-approval requirements for the appointment of banking executives fall outside normal regulatory practice and may give pause to prospective foreign investors.

In view of international standard, the Core Principles for the Effective Banking Supervision made by the Basel Committee on Banking Supervision[255] suggests that the licensing authority evaluate any bank's proposed senior management as to expertise and integrity, any potential for conflicts of interest. Such evaluation may include skills and experience in banking business and record of criminal activities or adverse regulatory judgements that make a person unfit to uphold important position in a bank.[256] But it never suggests banking authority's pre-approval for appointment of top managements of a private bank. North Korean authorities may consider revising this clause.

---

[253] *Id.* Law art. 20.

[254] *See* the Equity Joint-venture Law art. 6.

[255] The Committee was organized by the Bank for International Settlement (BIS) in 1974.

[256] See the Core Principles for Effective Banking Supervision (2012) principle 5 para. 7.

As noted, the business term of a foreign-invested bank is twenty years, extendable upon application to the Central Bank, with the duration of any extension left unspecified by the Law.[257]

On the question of capital adequacy, the 2011 version of the Foreign-invested Bank Law required banks to maintain their own capital at no less than 5% of their security funds against debts, or of total liabilities.[258] China, by comparison, applies a general capital adequacy ratio of no less than 8% for all commercial banks.[259] The revised 2020 Law is silent on capital adequacy, and it is unclear whether the implementing regulations address the point. Given that the BIS minimum standard is 8%, North Korea would do well to consider bringing its requirements into alignment with that benchmark.

The next issue is about national treatment. National treatment is generally known as treatment of foreign investors and investments no less favorable than treatment of domestic investors and investment in given circumstances, with respect to the establishment, acquisition, expansion, operation, management, maintenance, use, enjoyment and sale or other disposition of investment.[260] It is, in essence, foreign investors' enjoyment of equal treatment in the host country as domestic investors and investors from any other country.

While national treatment is a well-established principle in international trade law, its counterpart in international investment law is less developed — partly because cross-border investment has historically been more the concern of economically developed countries, whereas international trade involves virtually all states.

However, even though there are no commonly recognized norms of national treatment in international investment, OECD's (Organization for Economic Co-operation Development) defunct draft of the Multilateral Agreement on Investment (MAI) can play an important role in establishing a practice standard of national treatment

---

257 Foreign-invested Bank Law of 2020 art. 18.

258 *Id.* Law of 2011 art. 20; *id.* Regulations of 2002 art. 39.

259 *See* Law of the People's Republic of China on Commercial Banks of 2003 art. 39.

260 *See* Multinational Agreement on Investment (MAI) para. III, OECD. The MAI had been under negotiations among OECD member countries from 1995 but the negotiations were discontinued in 1998. *See* also OECD Declaration on International Investment and Multinational Enterprises of 1976 ["OECD Declaration of 1976" hereafter] para. II; *See* also OECD Declaration of 2023 amendment para. V.

together with the OECD Declaration and Decisions in International Investment and Multinational Enterprises ("OECD Declaration" hereafter) that declares national treatment in international investment.[261] Assessed against these standards, North Korea's practice of extending preferential treatment to domestic business entities over foreign-invested ones is difficult to reconcile with the national treatment principle.

The Foreign-invested Bank Law exempts foreign-invested banks from enterprise income tax on interest earned from loans made on favorable terms to North Korean banks and enterprises.[262] Where a foreign-invested bank extends to a North Korean bank or enterprise either a loan at a rate below LIBOR or a long-term loan with a maturity exceeding ten years, it is also exempted from turnover tax on the interest income from that loan.[263]

The practical effect of these provisions is that domestic entities receive preferential tax treatment compared with foreign-invested ones. As mentioned above, even though there is no well-established standard for national treatment in international investment and North Korea is not directly related to the OECD Declaration, granting favors to its domestic business entities will, to some degree, discourage prospective foreign investors' intention to invest. It can give a negative effect on consideration of investment in North Korea as long as it is seen as an investment risk.

A final issue concerns whether foreign-invested banks may engage in local currency transactions. The Foreign-invested Bank Law permits foreign-invested banks to conduct transactions between foreign-invested enterprises and foreigners.[264] They may also extend loans in foreign currency to — and conduct investment business with — North Korean institutions, enterprises, and organizations (though not individual citizens), but in those cases may not carry on any other business, aside from foreign currency loans and investment business, with such entities.[265] No mechanism exists for foreign-invested banks to apply for a license to handle local currency business. This restriction does not necessarily constitute discrimination; it is a matter of banking policy. However, the ability to conduct local currency

---

[261] *See id.* OECD Declaration of 1976 para. II.

[262] *See* Foreign-invested Bank Law art. 33.

[263] *See* Foreign-invested Bank Regulations of 2002 art. 59 para. 2.

[264] See Foreign-invested Bank Law art. 26.

[265] See *id.* Law art. 27.

transactions would make North Korea a significantly more attractive destination for foreign banking investment.

China similarly restricted foreign banks from local currency business in the past, but has permitted it since 1996 under its Regulations on Foreign Financial Institutions, subject to various conditions relating to business location and lines of activity.[266] North Korea could consider offering foreign-invested banks a comparable pathway to local currency business through appropriate legislative reform.

Overall, the risks surrounding North Korea's banking framework for foreign direct investment stem largely from the limited experience of its authorities in operating a banking system that meets global standards. It is important that North Korean policymakers engage seriously with international benchmarks and best practices in banking regulation — and design their framework accordingly.

C. Transfer of Technology

Technology is the systematic knowledge required for the manufacture of a product, for the application of a process or for the rendering of a service and does not extend to the transactions involving the mere sales or lease of a good.[267] It includes not only the knowledge or methods that are necessary to carry on or improve existing production and distribution of goods and services but also entrepreneurial expertise and professional know-how.[268] Technology transfer is the process by which commercial technology is disseminated.

The Draft International Code of Conduct on the Transfer of Technology (1985)[269] listed various types of transfer transactions:[270]

---

[266] *See* Regulations of the Peoples Republic of China on Administration of Foreign-funded Financial Institutions art. 18-20; *See* also the Tentative Administrative Measures for the Pilot Operation of *Renminbi* Business by Foreign Financial Institutions in the Shanghai Pudong Area cited from WANG GUIGUO AND JOHN MO, CHINESE LAW 363 (1999).

[267] *See* the Draft International Code of Conduct on the Transfer of Technology (1985) Chapter 1, Section 1.2.

[268] Cited by Peter Muchlinski in MULTINATIONAL ENTERPRISES AND THE LAW, Blackwell, Oxford, 1999 426.

[269] Under the auspices of UNCTAD, Least Developing Countries (LDCs) have sought the adoption of an international code on technology transfer by initiating discussion from 1976. The United Nations General Assembly convened a UN Conference in 1977 to negotiate a final draft and to make all the necessary decisions.

(a) The assignment, sale and licensing of all forms of industrial property,[271] except for trademarks, service marks and trade names when they are not part of transfer of technology transactions;
(b) The provision of know-how and technical expertise in the form of feasibility studies, plans, diagrams, models, instructions, guides, formulae, basic or detailed engineering designs, specifications and equipment for training, services involving technical advisory and managerial personnel, personal training;
(c) The provision of technological knowledge necessary for installation, operation and functioning of plant and equipment, for a turnkey project;
(d) The provision of technological knowledge necessary to acquire, install, and use machinery, equipment, intermediate goods and/or raw materials which have been acquired by purchase, lease or other means;
(e) The provision of technological contents of industrial and technical cooperation arrangements.

The list does not include non-commercial technology transfers, such as those found in international cooperation agreements between developed and developing countries.[272]

There are two principal methods of technology transfer. The first is to license the technology to an independent licensee or to a joint

---

The Conference held six sessions between 1978 and 1985. However, no further sessions have taken place because of disagreement between the developed and the developing countries in some areas such as restrictive business practices in technology transfer agreement and applicable law and settlement of disputes. The Code is still pending.

[270] *See id.* Chapter 1, Section 1.3.

[271] In its article 1(2), the Paris Convention for the Protection of Industrial Property (Paris Convention) defines that industrial property includes patents, utility models, industrial designs, trademarks, trade names, indications of source or appellation of origin etc. And in its article 1(3), the Paris Convention states that an industrial property also applies to agricultural and extractive industries and to all manufactured or natural products etc.

[272] *See* PETER MUCHLINSKI, MULTINATIONAL ENTERPRISES AND LAW 426 (1995).

venture with a local partner. The second is to transfer the technology internally to a subsidiary.[273]

North Korea defines that the TOT is an activity in foreign trade, moving technology from one country to another by a contract or economic interactions. It classifies the TOT into two categories: (1) one which is protected by industrial property law such as patent, trade mark, design etc.; and (2) one which is non-industrial property and is protected by a contract of parties such as diagrams, plans, instructions, guides, etc.[274] North Korea does not have laws regulating transfer of technology while they have some provisions on the transfer of technology.

North Korea's laws on foreign-investment permit foreigners to invest in the form of industrial property rights and technical know-how for the various forms of investment by means of transfer to an independent licensee,[275] to a joint venture, or to a subsidiary.[276] North Korea's laws and regulations provide various tax incentives for foreign-invested enterprises if they introduce high-technology.

North Korea's emphasis is clearly on securing the most advanced technology available. A wholly foreign-owned enterprise — such as a subsidiary of a multinational corporation — may not be established unless it meets at least one of the following conditions: (1) it is equipped with high-technology, modern production facilities; (2) it is capable of producing internationally competitive goods; or (3) it is capable of raising product quality to international standards.[277]

Establishment of a wholly foreign-owned enterprise is, moreover, prohibited in the following cases: (1) in case it may endanger or hinder the security of North Korea; (2) in case it may have an adverse effect on public health, landscape and resources of the country; (3) in case it uses equipment and production processes which are outdated economically and technologically; (4) in case products it makes have no or small demand locally and internationally; or (5) in case the type of business and mode of management of the enterprise do not

---

[273] *See id.* at 431; *see also* FOLSOM ET AL., *supra* note 32, at 464 – 65.

[274] *See* Civil Law Dictionary of North Korea at 110

[275] *See* Foreign Investment Law art. 12; Wholly Foreign-owned Enterprises Regulations of 2005 art. 18; Technology Introduction Regulations for Foreign-invested Enterprises of 2005 art. 2; and Tax Regulations for Foreign-invested Enterprises and Foreign Individuals of 2002 art. 20.

[276] *See* Equity Joint Venture Law art. 11; Equity Joint Venture Regulations of 2005 art. 32 and 35.

[277] *See* Wholly Foreign-owned Enterprises Regulations of 2005 art. 10.

conform with or may have a negative impact on the sound ideological emotions of the people and mode of life.[278]

As a general matter, the more restrictive the regulatory framework, the less technology transfer takes place; and the greater the degree of government control or intervention in technology transfer agreements, the weaker the incentive to produce and share technology. North Kore's laws and regulations provide no clear guidelines or standards for applying the restrictions they impose. It is far from obvious, for example, what "international standard" means for these purposes, or what would constitute a negative impact on the "sound ideological emotions" of the people.

Many countries dismantled restrictive technology transfer laws during the 1980s, either by formal repeal, replacement with more transfer-friendly and intellectually property-protective legislation, or through a more relaxed interpretive approach and broad automatic approval of terms agreed between transferor and transferee.[279] This liberalizing trend continued through the 1990s, as countries increasingly paired the removal of restrictive technology transfer rules with the adoption of stronger intellectual property protection, including for know-how.[280]

The protection of invested technology is a further concern in North Korea. In the absence of dedicated legislation, contractual arrangements between the parties to a foreign investment agreement must carry the main burden of protection. Where technology is contributed within the framework of a joint venture, the agreement should be explicit about the extent of the local partner's access to sensitive technologies, since foreign investors typically wish to maintain control over such access.[281] In practice, however, contractual protections do not always function as intended, as a well-known episode from India illustrates.

> (The Government of) India demanded that Coca-Cola Company alter its structure from a wholly foreign-owned investment to a joint venture. While the Indian government did not expressly state that the foreign parent

---

[278] *Id.* art. 11.

[279] *See* FOLSOM, RALPH H. ET AL. INTERNATIONAL BUSINESS TRANSACTIONS (2001) 466.

[280] *See* FOLSOM ET AL., at 466 – 67.

[281] *See id.* at 469.

> would have to share the secret formula, the government did say that such sharing would be the natural consequence of the partnership sense of the joint venture. Coca-Cola would not disclose the technology, and withdrew its business from India, not to return until the 1990s when India had relaxed its previously strict foreign investment rules.[282]

The Foreign Investment Law provides that "the State shall protect, by law, the managerial secrets of foreign invested enterprises and shall not disclose them without prior agreement with the foreign investor."[283] This is the only provision in North Korean law directly addressing the protection of invested technology. It is not clear whether the "managerial secrets" include invested technology and know-how. Beyond this single provision, no dedicated legislation for the protection of invested technology had been enacted as of 2025.

North Korea has been a party to the Paris Convention for the Protection of Industrial Property of 1883 since 1974. The Convention provides a number of important protections. At present, it constitutes the only verifiable — though not directly enforceable domestically — mechanism for the protection of technology transferred to North Korea.

D. Labor

Labor is a subject of particular significance in North Korea, a state founded under Soviet auspices on the principle of the dictatorship of the proletariat as the path toward a communist world order. The ruling party is, tellingly, the Workers' Party of Korea. North Korea enacted the Socialist Labor Law in 1978, thirty years after the establishment of the government. The Labor Regulations for Foreign-Invested Business ("Foreign-invested Labor Regulations" hereafter) were introduced in 1993 alongside a number of other foreign investment laws and regulations. North Korea subsequently enacted the Labor Law for Foreign-invested Enterprises ("Foreign-invested Enterprises Labor Law" hereafter) in 2009 as a special statute applicable to foreign-invested businesses. Supplementary zone-specific regulations followed: the Labor Regulations for the

---

[282] *Id.*

[283] *See* Foreign Investment Law art. 21.

Kaesong Industrial Complex (2003), the Labor Regulations for the Mt. Kumgang Special Zone for International Tourism (2012), the Labor Regulations for the Rason Economic and Trade Zone (2013), and the Labor Regulations for the Economic Development Zones (2013). North Korea thus now has two labor laws — governing general labor matters and foreign-invested business labor matters respectively — together with five sets of regulations applicable to four special economic zones and to foreign-invested businesses generally. The complexity of this regulatory landscape reflects the deliberate policy of calibrating labor arrangements by location: the Kaesong and Mt. Kumgang regulations offer additional incentives to South Korean investors that are not available to foreign investors in other special economic zones.

In most non-socialist societies, labor law is structured around three parties: government, workers, and employers. The Socialist Labor Law of North Korea departs fundamentally from this model, reflecting socialist ideology. North Korea's conception of the labor relationship is encapsulated in the maxim "one for all, all for one"[284] — the idea that workers help and guide one another in a spirit of collectivism.

North Korea characterizes the labor law of bourgeois societies as no more than a hypocritical declaration designed to deceive the working class and to legitimize exploitation and oppression.[285] The Socialist Labor Law accordingly cannot be mapped onto the tripartite framework that most countries have adopted. It is not designed around an employer–employee relationship arising organically from a labor market.

The Socialist Labor Law articulates the duties of the State and of workers, but makes no mention of workers' rights as such.[286] Labor supply and demand are managed through the State's labor plan, itself a component of the national economic plan; workers may be reassigned, for example from agriculture to industry, to meet plan targets or State priorities.[287] Rights of association, collective

[284] *See* Socialist Labor Law art. 3.

[285] *See* CHOI JONG KO, *BUKHANBEOP* (Laws of North Korea) 316 (1996) as cited from Dictionary in the Politics of North Korea 327 (1973).

[286] Articles from 62-66 of the Socialist Labor Law mention only about workers' right of leave and rest. They are all about workers' rights mentioned in the Socialist Labor Law. The same is true for the Labor Law for the Foreign-invested Enterprises.

[287] *See* Socialist Labor Law art. 25 and 27.

bargaining, and kindred workers' rights are wholly incompatible with this framework.

Although North Korea has now another labor law for foreign-invested enterprises and five labor regulations for foreign-invested entities, general provisions of the Socialist Labor Law, as a general principle of law, are applied to the areas not covered by the later promulgated law and regulations.

The Labor Law for Foreign-invested Enterprises and its five regulations are far from the framework of the Tripartite Declaration of Principles concerning the Multinational Enterprises and Social Policy ("MNE Declaration" hereafter) of the International Labor Organization (ILO) adopted in 1978.[288] The MNE Declaration is an ILO instrument that "provides direct guidance to enterprises on social policy and inclusive, responsible and sustainable workplace practices."[289] Since North Korea does not have a tripartite party structure, it is so difficult to apply even some portions of the MNE Declaration directly to North Korea's labor system. This ideological incompatibility with international labor norms is a significant disadvantage for North Korea in attracting foreign direct investment.

The MNE Declaration states that governments should declare and pursue, as a major goal, an active policy designed to promote full, productive and freely chosen employment.[290] This part is not applicable to North Korea because the Socialist Labor Law declares that unemployment has permanently disappeared in North Korea and that all workers shall be provided with stable working positions and conditions by the State.[291] As a result, multinational enterprises as foreign direct investors in North Korea do not need to endeavor to increase employment opportunities and standards in the manner envisaged by the MNE Declaration.[292]

What a multinational enterprise as a foreign investor in North Korea can do by itself is to determine the number of employees needed for its operation, conclude a contract of employment with the

---

[288] North Korea is not a member country of ILO along with a few countries in the world. However, the Declaration can be used as a good standard in analysis of labor issues in relation to foreign direct investment.

[289] *See* ILO website < https://www.ilo.org/publications/tripartite-declaration-principles-concerning-multinational-enterprises-and-3> (visited 05/16/2025)

[290] *See* MNE Declaration (Fifth edition 2017) para. 13.

[291] *See* Socialist Labor Law art. 5

[292] *See* MNE Declaration para. 16.

labor administration institution, not with individual employees, and deploy the labor provided under that contract.[293] The labor administration institution also called the labor exchange, governmental agency, is located in the same city or province where the foreign- invested business seats.

A foreign-invested business is required to use the labor of North Korea for business activities. In case foreign nationals are recruited as managerial staff, or technicians and skilled workers of special job classifications, prior consent should first be secured from the central organ of the DPRK.[294] This employment priority policy for nationals is consistent with the Declaration.[295] If so, can a foreign investor reject manpower provided by the labor administration institution of North Korea? It is allowed by the Labor Law for Foreign-invested Enterprises.[296] However, the difficulty arises afterwards: in the absence of a labor market, there is no alternative channel through which to source replacement workers without going back through the labor exchange. This structural constraint is a further deterrent to foreign investment.

By contrast, Vietnam permits foreign investors to recruit local workers at their own discretion, including through open advertisement in the media. China similarly states in its investment guidelines that a joint venture determines its own hiring, and no one may compulsorily assign workers to it.[297]

Concerning termination of employment, the MNE Declaration states that "in considering changes in operations, including those resulting from mergers, take-overs and transfers of production, which would have major employment effects, multinational enterprises should provide reasonable notice of such changes to the appropriate government authorities and representatives of the workers ..."[298] This

---

[293] *See* Labor Law for Foreign-invested Enterprises art. 9 and 12; Labor Regulations for Foreign-invested Enterprises of 2005 art. 10. Other labor regulations for individual special economic zones have same stipulations.

[294] *See id.* Regulations art. 3.

[295] *See* MNE Declaration para. 18.

[296] See Labor Law for Foreign-invested Enterprises art. 12.

[297] *See* Je Sung Ho, *Bookhan woeja yoochi bupryong-eui moonjejum* (Issues on North Korea's Foreign Investment Laws): Research Report 98 – 05, KNIU, 55 (footnote 87) (1998), at 49.

[298] *See* Tripartite Declaration para. 34.

is particularly important in the case of the closure of an (business) entity involving collective lay-offs or dismissals.[299]

However, in North Korea, in case a foreign-invested enterprise wishes to terminate employment, the Labor Law for Foreign-invested Enterprises requires a foreign investor to have a consultation with the trade union and the labor exchange concerned, instead of providing a notice as stated in the Declaration.[300] The Law specifically stipulates dismissal reasons before the expiry of the term of employment in situations where: (i) due to illness or injury, an employee cannot continue to work at the present position or other one; (ii) any redundancy of labor is caused due to the changes in production management and technical conditions; (iii) an employee has made serious accident in violation of labor discipline; (iv) due to lack of technical skills, an employee is unable to perform assigned work; or (v) an employee has caused serious damage to the property of the enterprises.[301] However, in the article 44 of the Labour Law for Foreign-invested Enterprises, a foreign-invested enterprise is required to have "consultation" with the trade union concerned before actual dismissal.[302] This clause makes readers of the Law confused because, on the contrary, in the article 46 of the same law, a foreign-invested enterprise is required to have an "agreement" with the trade union before dismissal of an employee. It should be clarified. Anyhow, the requirement of the agreement can be used in North Korea as a somewhat curbing measure in cases of dismissals or lay-offs while the reasonable notice suffices according to the MNE Declaration. It is totally North Korea's option although such requirement is not attractive to foreign investors.

The Law also prohibits dismissal of an employee who is receiving medical treatment for an occupational disease or a work-related injury and has been on sick leave for up to six months, or who is a female employee, married, pregnant, on maternity leave, or breastfeeding.[303]

The Labor Regulations for Foreign-invested Enterprises further stipulate that a foreign-invested business shall give subsidy to the dismissed employee at a rate decided on the basis of the years of his or her services if the foreign-invested business dismisses an employee

[299] *Id.*
[300] *See* Labor Law for Foreign-invested Enterprises art. 44.
[301] *See* Labor Law for Foreign-invested Enterprises of 2005 art. 45.
[302] *See id.* Law art. 44.
[303] *See id.* art. 47.

not by his or her own fault but for some other reasons.[304] This is, in general, consistent with the Declaration which states that governments, in cooperation with multinational as well as national enterprises, should provide some form of income protection for workers whose employment has been terminated.[305]

With regard to worker's rights that should have been stipulated in the Labour Law or Regulations for foreign-invested enterprises, none of them has any provisions related to a workers' right to freedom of association, right to collective bargaining and so on. As noted, a foreign-invested enterprise is required to conclude a labor contract with the trade union,[306] to have consultation or agreement with the union before dismissing an employee[307] and when it pays a bonus to well-performing employee.[308] The foreign-invested enterprises also must be supervised by the upper-level trade union with respect to the payment of social insurance premiums, expenditures of the insurance fund.[309]

How are North Korean workers protected or how do they insist on their rights without such worker's rights as the right to freedom of association or collective bargaining when they want to improve working conditions or increase salaries? The relevant laws and regulations do not have a single sentence regarding the self-protective measures for employees/workers. According to the current Labor Law for Foreign-invested Enterprises and the Labor Regulations for Foreign-invested Enterprises of 2005, the central labor administration organ shall supervise and control in a unified way all the matters concerning labor organization and working conditions in the foreign-invested business.[310]

North Korea's trade unions are not voluntary organizations formed by workers. The absence of recognized workers' rights in the relevant legislation might, paradoxically, be read as offering implicit incentives to foreign investors who prefer to minimize confrontation with workers — though the MNE Declaration specifically cautions

---

[304] *See* Labor Regulations for Foreign-invested Enterprises of 2005 art. 17.

[305] *See* MNE Declaration para. 36.

[306] *See* Labour Law for Foreign-invested Enterprises art. 14; Labour Regulations for Foreign-invested Enterprises of 2005 art. 8.

[307] *See id.* Law art. 46; *id.* Regulations art. 15.

[308] *See id.* Regulations art. 30.

[309] *See id.* art. 41.

[310] *See* Labour Law for Foreign-invested Enterprises art. 7; *id.* Regulations art. 9.

that any special incentives offered by host countries to attract foreign investment should not include the limitation of workers' freedom of association or collective bargaining rights.[311] In a strict technical sense, North Korea does not "limit" these rights in its labor legislation; it simply never acknowledges them.

How could the trade union exist without workers' right? The Socialist Labor Law does not mention trade unions at all. It frames workers as agents of production whose interests are served by raising labor productivity and advancing economic construction. It also declares, as noted, that unemployment has been permanently eliminated and that the State guarantees all workers stable employment.[312] And working people are the masters of everything including the social system of North Korea.[313] Therefore, in this environment, employer-employee relationship in working places is conceptually redundant.

Under the Socialist Labor Law, the State formulates and implements detailed labor plans.[314] State organs and enterprises are prohibited from dismissing surplus workers; instead, excess labor is to be transferred to other factories, enterprises, or cooperative farms.[315] All the workers are paid the same amount of remuneration for the same kind of labor regardless of sex, age, and nationality.[316] The State should provide workers with houses and accommodations free of charge, food at a low price, compulsory education, and free medical services.[317] In this environment, there is no occasion or mechanism for workers to negotiate with management over living standards or working conditions — the State provides for everything by design.

There are some workers' unions peculiar to North Korea. They are: the General Union of Occupation; the Farm-workers Union; the Socialist Union for Junior Workers; and the Democratic Women's Union of North Korea. They are all known as peripheral or satellite organizations of the Workers' Party of Korea. These unions, of course, are not workers' voluntary organizations. Their mission is to mobilize

---

[311] *See* MNE Declaration para. 52.
[312] *See* Socialist Labor Law art. 5.
[313] *See* Socialist Constitution of 2023 art. 8.
[314] *See* Socialist Labor Law art. 27.
[315] *See id.* art. 34.
[316] *See id.* art. 37.
[317] *See id.* art. 69, 70, 72 and 79.

the work force and supervise labor practice in work places throughout the country.[318]

The General Union of Occupation of North Korea consists of all the workers, laborers, technicians, and clerical workers whose ages are over thirty and who do not belong to other unions in North Korea. The Union has sub-organizations in provinces, cities, and counties and has nine branches according to the line of industrial sectors such as metal-chemical industry, electricity and coal mining industry, forestry, fishery, transportation and so on. The Unions' mission is, among others, to provide for training and education of communism, of technology and culture for members, mobilization of the workforce for the purpose of successful achievement of production goals as planned, increasing efficiency in work, and supervising implementation of labor regulations.[319]

The function of unions in North Korea as discussed above is much different from other countries. Prospective local workers at a foreign-invested enterprise must be members of one of the above unions, and members of a trade union at a foreign-invested enterprise may not be familiar with voluntary activities or negotiations with foreign management. Instead, members may act or negotiate as instructed by the upper union from the city, provincial or central level. As a whole, it is a question for foreign investors how they will cope with various problems arising from labor related issues since union members in their enterprises do not have discretion or independent power to negotiate with the management of the enterprise they belong to.

E. Tax

Taxation is an integral consideration at every stage of foreign investment — from the initial decision whether to invest through to the ongoing operation of a business. Constitutionally, North Korea is a state without taxation. The 1948 Constitution provided that citizens should pay tax according to their economic means.[320] Under that framework, North Korea operated a relatively straightforward tax

---

[318] *See* Sun Han Seung, *Nambookhan nodongjedo-eui bigyo-wa nodongjeongchaek yonkoo* (Comparative Study of Labor Systems of South-North Koreas and Labor Policy), Korea Labor Research Institute, 31 (1998).

[319] *See* NAEWOE PRESS, *supra* note 83, at 50-1.

[320] *See* Constitution of 1948 art. 29.

system encompassing levies on enterprise income, individual income, the acquisition and registration of real estate, motor vehicles, and similar matters.

The first Socialist Constitution of 1972, however, declared that the State should completely abolish taxation as a relic of the old society.[321] This was followed by an official proclamation in 1974 that Kim Il Sung had taken "on March 21, 1974, the Great Leader Comrade Kim Il Sung takes a historical measure on complete abolition of taxation systems based on scientific analysis of current circumstances of the State which has developed a socialist economy and has firm self-reliance in its national economy."[322] Despite this declaration, North Korea enacted the income tax law applicable to joint venture enterprises and foreign individuals in 1985, in connection with the first joint venture law of 1984, which was primarily directed at attracting Korean-Japanese capital as mentioned earlier.

From the 1972 Socialist Constitution to the current 2023 Constitution, North Korea has amended its constitution ten times, each time maintaining the position that that "[t]he increasing material wealth of society in our country, where tax has been abolished, is used entirely to promote the well-being of the working people."[323] However, after the declaration of the second stage of the open door policy in 1991, North Korea created an exception by stating that "the Great *Suryong* [Kim Il Sung] together with the Great Leader Comrade Kim Jong Il took a wise action to apply the taxation system within the Rajin-Sonbong Free Economic and Trade Zone to the foreign enterprises and foreigners."[324]

In 1993, the Tax Law for Foreign-invested Businesses and Foreign Individuals ("Foreign-invested Tax Law" hereafter) was enacted to ensure the impartial and accurate assessment and payment of tax by foreign-invested businesses and foreign individuals.[325] Tax Regulations for Foreign-invested Enterprises and Foreign Individuals in 2002, as well as zone-specific Tax Regulations for the Kaesong Industrial Complex in 2003 and for the Mt. Kumgang Special Zone for International Tourism in 2012 followed. Further, while North

[321] *See* Socialist Constitution of 1972 art. 33.
[322] Civil Law Dictionary at 437.
[323] Socialist Constitution of 2023 art. 25.
[324] Civil Law Dictionary, at 438.
[325] *See* Foreign-invested Tax Law art. 1.

Korea does not have enough experience in tax administration due to its socialist economy, it offers tax incentives especially to foreign-invested enterprises in special these economic zones, in construction of infrastructure as well as in sectors of high technology.

North Korea's business entities are allowed to establish and operate, within the territory of North Korea, an equity joint venture with corporations or individuals of foreign countries.[326] Once a joint venture is established, it becomes a corporate body, which is a legal person, of North Korea on the day from the registration.[327] 'Legal person' is a legally qualified institution, enterprise, or organization which is able to act independently as a party in civil law relations[328] and that has the capacity to enjoy the same civil rights as a citizen.[329]

A legal person created by the law of North Korea is treated as a person of North Korea.[330] North Korea has abolished taxes as the Socialist Constitution states but levies taxes on its own corporations, that is, legal persons. How can this discrepancy be explained? How can an inferior tax law to the Constitution stipulate about taxation contrary to the superior law? Even though the Constitutional provision is inspirational and declaratory, and therefore not directly enforceable, the logical inconsistency persists.

Nine categories of tax apply to foreign-invested businesses in North Korea: (i) enterprise income tax; (ii) individual income tax; (iii) property tax; (iv) inheritance tax; (v) turnover tax; (vi) business tax; (vii) resource tax; (viii) city management tax; and (ix) vehicle tax.

Enterprise income tax is levied on its earnings derived from business activities in the territory of North Korea as well as on other incomes earned in North Korea, including interest, income from dividends, proceeds from the lease or sale of fixed assets, proceeds from the transfer of assets, royalties on industrial properties and know-how and management fees. A foreign-invested enterprise must also pay enterprise income taxes on incomes earned through its branches, agencies, or subsidiaries established outside the territory of the DPRK.[331]

---

[326] *See* Equity Joint Venture Law art. 2.

[327] *See id.* art. 6.

[328] Civil Law Dictionary at 261.

[329] *Id.* at 263

[330] *See id.* at 262.

[331] *See* Foreign-invested Tax Law art. 9.

The taxation of foreign-source income raises the issue of double taxation, since both North Korea and the country where the income arises may claim taxing jurisdiction over the same profits. Double taxation can be addressed through unilateral or bilateral measures. The most common bilateral approach is a tax treaty between the relevant countries, usually called 'double taxation avoidance agreement.'

The common unilateral measure is to adopt either the tax credit system or the tax exemption method. The tax credit system is to offset the taxes paid by its subsidiaries, branches or representative offices in the foreign country they seat against its tax liability to North Korea on its remitted profits. For instance, if a foreign residing subsidiary of a North Korea's foreign-invested enterprise has paid 20% of profit as an income tax to the foreign country and then remitted the remaining 80% to the parent company in North Korea, the tax authority of North Korea may need only to assess the difference of 5% on the total profit since its enterprise income tax rate is 25%. If the subsidiary has already paid 30% in the foreign country, North Korea must not further assess any tax on it.

The tax exemption method is to exempt taxes on the profits of a foreign subsidiary, branch, or agent from domestic enterprise income taxation when the profits are remitted to the parent company in North Korea but the North Korean tax authority may assess a tax only when the parent company distributes those remitted profits as a dividend to its shareholders.

North Korea adopted the tax credit system in the Tax Regulations to prevent the possibility of evasion of enterprise income tax by foreign-invested businesses imposed on its foreign subsidiary.[332] The paid amount of enterprise income tax in a foreign country may be deducted from the North Korean assessment if it is equivalent to or less than the sum calculated on the basis of the tax rates of North Korea. However, a greater portion of payment than the amount calculated by North Korea's rate is not deducted.[333] This method seems quite reasonable.

Any foreigner who earns income inside the territory of North Korea must pay individual income tax.[334] Any foreigner must also

---

[332] *See* Foreign-invested Tax Regulations of 2002 art. 28.

[333] *See id.*

[334] *See* Foreign-invested Tax Law art. 20; *id.* Regulations art. 35.

pay the tax on earnings from outside the territory of North Korea if he or she stays or resides for more than one year in North Korea.[335]

In case the foreigner has already paid income tax outside the territory of North Korea, he or she can apply for a deduction against the income tax already paid abroad provided that the deduction is limited to the amount of income tax calculated and payable under the North Korean Tax Regulations as shown in the tax credit system of the above paragraphs. The application shall be accompanied by original tax documents issued by the tax administration body of the country in question.[336]

Taxable individual incomes or earnings are from: (i) remuneration for work; (ii) interest payments; (iii) dividends; (iv) lease and rent of real property; (v) sale of assets; (vi) royalties for intellectual property and technological know-how: (vii) provision of management-related service; and (viii) earnings from gift.[337] The scope of taxation is accordingly broad: a foreigner's income from a patent registered abroad, bank interest, or rental income in the home country is all taxable once that person has resided in North Korea for more than a year, regardless of whether those amounts are ever remitted.

North Korea's tax assessment range is broad even if consideration is given that North Korea could have taxing jurisdiction over any individual who is legally residing in North Korea for a long-term period. For example, under such rule, a foreign individual who has rented out her own house in her home country while working in North Korea must report and pay 20% of her rental income as the Foreign-invested Tax Law stipulates so. Violation of reporting and/or payment requirement is subject to fine or penal liability.[338]

Such rules may not be practicable. In contrast, in China, only foreign individuals who resided in China more than 183 days or six months are subject to tax payment over incomes earned in China, according to China's current Individual Income Tax Law. In this case, to be exempted from the tax payment, they must file with the tax bureau in charge. And also tax exemption for foreign incomes goes to until residency reaches to six years. Foreigners who resided more than six years in China are subject to individual income tax payment over

---

[335] *See id.* Law art 20; *id.* Regulations art. 35.
[336] *See id.* Regulations art. 41.
[337] *See* Foreign-invested Tax Law art. 21.
[338] *See id.* art. 71 and 72.

incomes earned both inside and outside China. The Chinese rule looks more reasonable and practicable.

A question about impracticability is also raised by the issue of tax on inheritance whether it is by will or the intestacy statute. A foreign individual can own properties in North Korea such as buildings,[339] vessels, or aircraft, and must pay the related taxes.[340] Accordingly, if such property in North Korea is inherited to a foreign inheritor, he or she is obliged to pay inheritance tax in North Korea. It may be taken for granted. However, a foreign individual resident in North Korea must also pay inheritance tax on any property that he inherited outside the territory of North Korea.[341] North Korean authority concerned may consider the case of China's law that gives foreign individual residents six years of levying suspension.

Taxable inherited properties include such properties and property rights as personal property and real estate, cash, securities, deposits, savings, insurance money, intellectual property rights, and claims.[342] The tax base for the inheritance tax is the remaining value of the inherited property, after all outstanding debts relating to it are settled.[343] Any foreign inheritor regardless of residency must report and pay the inheritance tax on the inherited property, whether or not the property in question is located in North Korea, to the tax authority of North Korea within three months of the date of inheritance.[344]

Imposing taxation on resident foreigner's inherited property in a foreign country looks impracticable. Further, North Korea's tax authority does not have device to look into or detect such inheritance in a foreign country unless the heir voluntarily reports to pay the tax. If it is practiced, the issue of double taxation cannot be avoided. By this stipulation, a resident foreign investor, who steadily operates a business in North Korea, can automatically be a status of non-compliance or in violation of the North Korean Tax Law once he inherits properties in his own country until he reports and pays the tax to North Korean tax office.

F. Customs

---

339 The building includes houses and residential flats, villa and attached buildings. *See* Foreign-invested Tax Regulations of 2002 art. 43.

340 *See* Foreign-invested Tax Law art. 29.

341 *See id* art. 35.

342 *See* Foreign-invested Tax Regulations of 2002 art. 54.

343 *See* Foreign-invested Tax Law art. 36.

344 *See id.* art. 40.

North Korea enacted its first customs law in 1983, the Customs Law of the Democratic People's Republic of Korea ("Customs Law" hereafter), having previously relied on the simple Regulations on Export and Import Taxes of 1948 adopted immediately after the state's foundation. The 1948 Regulations remained in force until replaced by the 1983 Customs Law, which was introduced in preparation for the country's first, narrowly scoped open door policy permitting joint ventures with foreign partners from 1984. The Law has since been amended seventeen times, most recently in 2021. Through successive revisions it has evolved into a more functional general customs statute, supplemented by three specialized implementing regulations covering the special economic zones of Rason (2000), Mt. Kumgang (2001), and Kaesong (2003). It remains unclear whether general implementing regulations applicable to the nation's open ports, international airports, and border posts — apart from those three SEZ-specific instruments — have been adopted.

According to the Customs Law of North Korea, its mission is to provide "strict guidelines for cross-border cargoes for export and import, goods temporarily brought in or taken out, transports, international postal matter, personal effects and other articles, thereby contributing to safeguarding national security, protecting the independent national economy and promoting external economic relations."[345]

For the principle of imposition of customs duties, the North Korean government levies low or zero tariff rates on materials whose import and export are encouraged and in the same context, high tariff rates on materials whose import and export are discouraged in order to protect the independent national economy.[346] The Customs Law applies to all the institutions, enterprises, organizations and individuals that bring in or take out cargoes for exports and imports, goods temporarily brought in or taken out, means of transport, international postal matter, personal effects and other articles across the border of the DPRK.[347]

Institutions, enterprises, organizations and individuals include the foreign-invested businesses, foreign-invested banks, and the representative missions of foreign countries and international organizations, foreign corporate bodies and foreign individuals in the

---

[345] Customs Law art. 1.
[346] *Id.* art. 8.
[347] *Id.* art. 12.

territory of North Korea.[348] Enterprise and individuals mentioned above include foreign-invested enterprises and foreign individuals.[349]

The Law further provides that customs procedures in special economic zones are to be set by separate instruments;[350] this provision served as the basis for the three zone-specific implementing customs regulations covering the Rason ETZ, the Mt. Kumgang SZIT (whose legal status lapsed in 2023), and the Kaesong Industrial Complex (operations ceased in 2016). Equivalent regulations for the Hwanggumphyong-Wihwado Economic Zone and the economic development zones may follow in due course.

Customs inspection covers all cargoes, commodities, international mail, personal effects, and means of transport brought into or taken out of North Korea.[351] The Law repeatedly emphasizes that controlled goods and contraband must not be brought in or taken out by any means, including through international postal items.[352] Notably, however, neither the Customs Law nor the SEZ-specific regulations specifies or defines what goods are controlled or classified as contraband.

With regard to the standard price for customs duties for levying on export and import cargoes, it should be based on the contract price concluded with a foreign trade counterpart but within the price range approved by the central foreign trade organ which may be referred to the price fixing institution according to the Law on Price of North Korea[353] that can usually be enacted in socialist countries. For the international postal matters and personal effects and belongings, customs duties are imposed on the portion of prices that exceed prescribed standards.[354] The imposing base is the retail price.[355] But it is unknown to the public what amounts in individual items are price limit to be free from customs duties.

Customs duties are not be levied on the four categories of following items: (i) materials brought in according to the measures taken by the State; (ii) designated duty-free or duty-reduced cargoes and articles according to the treaty, convention or agreement

---

[348] *Id.*
[349] *Id.*
[350] *Id.*
[351] *Id.* art. 24.
[352] *Id.* art. 43.
[353] *Id.* art. 47.
[354] *Id.* and *id.* Law art 50
[355] *Id.*

concluded between the DPRK and a foreign country; (iii) goods temporarily brought in or taken out, duty-free commodities or other items; and (iv) international postal matter or individual luggage within the prescribed limit.[356]

The Customs Law further stipulates that in case a foreign-invested business or foreign-invested bank sells within the territory of the DPRK equipment and materials imported for the purpose of production and operation, customs duties are not exempted from customs duties.[357] On the other hand, in its article 56 of the current Customs Law, it displays items exempted from customs duties as mentioned above; but it does not include imported foreign investor's equipment and materials necessary for establishing, production and/or operation of business. In the article 57 of the current Customs Law, it vaguely hints that such equipment and materials would not be exempted if they are sold in North Korea. However, the Customs Law of 2012 explicitly stipulated that "[m]aterials brought in by foreign-invested businesses for the production and management, goods that they produced for the purpose of export ...." are exempted from customs duties.[358] After the 2012 amendment, the Customs Law has been revised four times until the current Law of 2021; therefore, the incentive provision for prospective foreign direct investors might have been altered in between. The incentive provision should be clarified by direct mentioning in the next amendment.

The Customs Law provides that export and import duties are to be assigned by reference to a tariff line.[359] It means that North Korea's tariff line may classify exported and imported items according to designated categories and designate duty rates item by item and sub-item by sub-item. The tariff line is generally called harmonized tariff schedule. However, in North Korea, there is no tariff schedule open to the public. It is unknown whether North Korea has a well-classified tariff schedule that can be used by exporters and importers. The tariff schedule is significant information for business entities engaged in foreign trade. The World Customs Organization (WCO) having 186 member states as of 2025 recommends the 'Harmonized Commodity Description and Coding System' (also simply called 'Harmonized System') for the tariff line. The

---

[356] *Id.* art. 56.

[357] *Id.* art. 57.

[358] *See* Customs Law of 2012 art. 49.

[359] See Customs Law art. 49.

Harmonized System is used by over 200 countries regardless of WCO membership. As a non-member of WCO, North Korea may have to consider joining it or at least receptive to its recommendation.

Nonetheless, real risks may lie in the conception of customs duty since North Korea has dual standards on the customs. According to the North Korea's conception, the customs duty in capitalist countries is explained as a means of exploiting working class people. It is said that imperialists led by the United States impose high customs duty on imported goods; thus, allowing monopolizing businesses to make high profits through monopolized prices.[360] It is also said that they, imperialists, force developing countries to import goods with a low tariff in order to dominate in the importer's market.

With such ideas and circumstances on customs duty, how many foreigners would be interested in investing in and trading with North Korea?

G. Immigration Procedure and Residence

North Korea enacted the Immigration Law of the Democratic People's Republic of Korea ("Immigration Law" hereafter) in 1996, revising it three times through 2013. It was not known to outside what kind of law or regulations functioned as immigration law until the current law was enacted. Rather than issuing general implementing regulations under the parent law, North Korea produced three zone-specific implementing regulations: for the Rason ETZ (2000), the Kaesong Industrial Complex (2003), and the Mt. Kumgang SZIT (2011).[361] It is unknown to the public if they have been revised or not since then. Equivalent regulations for other special economic zones, such as the Hwanggumphyong-Wihwado Economic Zone and the economic development zones, have not been issued, presumably because those zones have not been operationally active.

In these three immigration regulations, North Korea created new types of simplified entry procedures or entry permit system aside from existing regular entry visa system. The new types of entry procedures or entry permit are applied for visitors or tourists to three respective special economic zones above. For example, in the Rason ETZ, a visitor can directly enter the zone from a foreign country with

---

[360] *See* Civil Law Dictionary at 134.

[361] Immigration regulations in relation to the Mt. Kumgang might be defunct since the parent law has been reportedly abolished since 2023.

an invitation (letter or format) issued by North Korea's inviting party such as institution, enterprise, organization or a foreign-invested enterprise if the inviting party arranges it with relevant authorities in advance by submitting name(s) of visitor(s).[362] In the KIC, either a visitor or inviting party can apply for such an entry permit[363] and in the Mt. Kumgang SZIT, a visitor, inviting party or travel agency can do for such a permit.[364]

Depending on the purpose of entry, a foreigner may stay or reside in North Korea.[365] Stay is categorized into short-term for up to 90 days or long-term for more than 90 days.[366] The Immigration Law itself sets no minimum duration for residency, but the KIC and Mt. Kumgang implementing regulations require a foreigner who wishes to remain for more than one year to apply for residency status.[367] The Rason ETZ regulations require the application for a residence card without specifying a qualifying duration.[368]

Foreigners may stay, reside or tour in North Korea depending on the purpose of the entry as mentioned above. In the Rason ETZ, foreigners must stay at a hotel or motel designated by the Rason ETZ authority and they register for stay within the next day of arrival.[369] It must be overly kind that the authority designates a specific hotel or motel for foreigners to stay. However, foreigners visiting KIC may not need to register if they leave KIC within seven days; otherwise, they must register their stay within 48 hours.[370] If foreigners stay in a place other than their destination for more than 48 hours, they must have their stay registered with the local immigration administration organ.[371]

---

[362] *See* Regulations on Entry, Exit and Stay in the Rason ETZ of 2000 ("Rason Immigration Regulations of 2000" hereafter) art. 7.

[363] *See* Regulations on Entry, Exit, Stay and Residence in the Mt. Kumgang of SZIT of 2011 ("Mt. Kumgang Immigration Regulations" hereafter) art. 4.

[364] *See* Regulations for Immigration, Stay and Residence in the KIC of 2003 ("KIC Regulations" hereafter) art. 4.

[365] *See* Immigration Law art. 42 and 51.

[366] *See id.* art. 43.

[367] *See* Regulations for Immigration, Stay and Residence for KIC of 2003 art. 17 and Regulations for Immigration, Stay and Residence for Mt. Kumgang SZIT of 2011 art. 18.

[368] *See* Regulations for Immigration and Stay in the Rason ETZ of 2000 art. 24.

[369] *See* Rason Immigration Regulations art. 19 and 22.

[370] *See* KIC Immigration Regulations art. 15 and 16; Mt. Kumgang Immigration Regulations art. 17.

[371] *See* Immigration Law art. 45.

On the other hand, following foreigners are exempted from registration of their stay: (i) members of parliament, government or other high-level delegations of a foreign country; (ii) members of diplomatic or consular representative offices of foreign countries or international organizations in North Korea; (iii) foreigners who enter North Korea to leave on the same day without lodging; (iv) crewmen of foreign ships, airplanes and railway trains that entered the port, airport or railway station; (v) foreigners designated by the competent organ of North Korea;[372] and for the cases of KIC specifically, (vi) foreigners who are to return within seven days from arrival in the KIC; (vii) members of international organizations and representatives of foreign countries residing in South Korea; (viii) tourists entering from South Korea; (ix) visitors who are exempted from registration by pre-arrangement.[373]

The Rason ETZ Regulations contain comparatively detailed provisions on resident representative offices of foreign businesses. A resident representative office of a foreign business can be opened and operated in the Rason ETZ.[374] The term of residence of the representative office is up to three years and it is extendable.[375] The constituent numbers of the representative office must not exceed five.[376] The officers (of the representative office) include the senior representative and other representatives but exclude administrative and technical staff such as interpreters, typewriters, bookkeepers and accounting clerk, and service personnel such as drivers and guards.[377] It would be better to lift limiting the number of officers since prospective large-scaled enterprises may need more than five officers in their representative offices. Where a foreign business opens a representative office, it must apply to the central economic cooperation and management organ of North Korea through the Rason ETZ authority.[378] In the case of a foreign financial institution, the application should be submitted to the Central Bank of North Korea through the Rason ETZ authority.[379] The central economic

---

[372] *See id.* art. 48 for (i) – (v) items.

[373] *See* KIC immigration Regulations art. 16 for (vi) – (ix) items.

[374] *See* Regulations on Resident Representative Office in the Rason ETZ of 2005 ("Rason Representative Office Regulations" hereafter) art. 1.

[375] *Id.* art. 4 and 21. The term of residence is for the office itself.

[376] *Id.* art. 4.

[377] *Id.*

[378] *Id.* art. 9.

[379] *Id.*

cooperation and management organ should notify approval or disapproval of the application within 30 days from the date of its receipt of the application.[380]

Representative offices are encouraged to open accounts with the Foreign Trade Bank of North Korea or other banks authorized to handle foreign exchange transactions.[381] Their permitted activities encompass liaison, consultation, and the dissemination of economic and technical information relevant to transactions of the parent business.[382] A representative office also may engage, if necessary, in agent activities by entering into contracts with clients and by making payments and deliveries of goods as authorized by the parent business.[383] In this case, the representative office is required to submit a letter of authorization signed by the parent business to the Rason ETZ authority.[384] However, it is not allowed to engage in profit making activities such as importing goods for intermediary trade or entrusted sale, or exporting goods obtained in North Korea if those activities are not authorized by the parent business and unless otherwise agreed between North Korea and the country of the business concerned.[385]

In case of renting a building, a representative office should enter into a contract with the property management organ of North Korea.[386] Where the representative office needs to employ a citizen of North Korea, it must also enter into a contract with the labor exchange organ in charge of the Rason ETZ as mentioned in the labor subchapter above.[387] The screening organ and the Rason ETZ authority are authorized to inspect and examine activities of the representative office. In this case, the representative office is obliged to comply with the inspector's requirements and to provide access to any documents and information requested.[388] Where a representative office closes — whether at the expiry of its authorized term or earlier — it must give written notice to both the External Economic

[380] *Id.* art. 10.
[381] *Id.* art. 18.
[382] *Id.* art. 5.
[383] *Id.*
[384] *Id.*
[385] *Id.* art. 6.
[386] *Id.* art. 23.
[387] *Id.*
[388] *Id.* art. 27.

Commission and the zone authority, and must settle all outstanding tax, claims, and liabilities within thirty days prior to closure.[389]

Several aspects of the immigration and residence framework give cause for concern. One is the penalty for loss of immigration documents. If a foreigner loses any document issued by the immigration office — such as an entry-exit permit, tourist certificate, visa, travel certificate, automobile pass, certificate of stay, or certificate of residence — reissuance is subject to a charge of ten times the standard fee.[390] This appears to be a punitive measure rather than a straightforward administrative fee, and a tenfold surcharge for an innocent loss seems disproportionate regardless of what the underlying fee may be.

North Korea does not currently permit foreign businesses to establish resident representative offices outside the special economic zones. Allowing such offices in Pyongyang and other major cities would be a meaningful step toward making North Korea more accessible to foreign investors.

The inspection and examination powers conferred on North Korean authorities under the Rason Representative Office Regulations are also a source of concern. The language of those provisions appears broad enough to extend to external communications between a representative office and its headquarters or business counterparts, both within and outside North Korea. For foreign investors with proprietary business information, trade secrets, or know-how, this creates a significant exposure that is difficult to mitigate. The ground or rationale to conduct such a broad power to inspect and examine business activities of a representative office may not be justified nonetheless.

As such there are a number of issues that possibly risk foreign direct investment. North Korea must review to address risky items for better attraction of foreign direct investment.

H. Land Tenure

Land was one of the most politically and economically charged subjects in North Korea. The first land reform was initiated by the Decree of Land Reform in March 1946, six months after liberation from Japanese rule and during the period of Soviet military

---

[389] *Id.* art. 25.
[390] *Id.* art. 33.

administration. Under the Decree promulgated by the Provisional People's Committee, most arable land owned by Japanese nationals, pro-Japanese Koreans, and wealthy landlords was confiscated without compensation. Title was transferred to the Provisional People's Committee for free redistribution to members of the working class who were neither pro-Japanese nor from landlord families.[391] The reform was to be completed within one year of the Decree's promulgation.[392]

The confiscation and free redistribution of land was reaffirmed in the Platform of 20 Planks issued by the same Provisional People's Committee in the same month.[393] In August 1946, the Platform of the Workers' Party of Korea confirmed the confiscation of land owned by Japanese and pro-Japanese nationals and its free distribution to 720,000 peasant families who owned little or no farmland.[394] The nation's first Constitution of 1948 reconfirmed the confiscation of all land owned by the Japanese state, Japanese nationals, and Korean landlords, declared the permanent abolition of the tenant farming system, and prohibited ownership by absentee landlords.[395] It also declared the permanent abolition of the tenant farming system, and prohibited ownership by absentee landlords.[396]

As to the size of the land ownership, individual families were allowed to own between 5 *jeongbo* (12 acres) and 20 *jeongbo* (49 acres) depending on the location or fertility of the land while state and cooperative farms faced no upper limit.[397] Despite these constitutional provisions, the collectivization of farmland was resolved by the 6th Central Committee of the Workers' Party of Korea in August 1953 — just nine days after the Korean Armistice Agreement — and implementation began immediately. Collectivization was completed nationwide by 1958, bringing 100 percent of the peasantry into cooperative farms.

The first Socialist Constitution of 1972 declared that all means of production were owned either by the State or by cooperative

---

[391] *See* Decree of Land Reform in North Korea of 1946 art. 2, 3, 5, 6, 12, 13, 14, and 15.

[392] *Id.* art. 17.

[393] *See* Platform of 20 Planks plank 9.

[394] *See* Platform of the Korea Workers Party of 1946 plank 3.

[395] *See* the Constitution of 1948 art. 6.

[396] *Id.*

[397] *Id.*

organizations.[398] It defined that the State ownership meant ownership of whole people.[399] Ownership of a cooperative organization was a collective ownership of workers who belonged to the cooperative account.[400] Thus they had to work collectively with the system of their products being distributed. While all the peasants of North Korea became members of any one of the cooperative farms, the collective organs to which they belonged, they have been allowed to own and dispose limited personal property rights on products from the kitchen garden.[401] The allowed size of the kitchen garden per family varies depending on the cooperative farm they belong to but it must be between 20 *pyeong* (712 square feet) and 30 *pyeong* (1067 square feet).[402]

In the meantime, nationalization of all industrial sectors had also been accomplished by 1958 and thus private ownership in industrial sectors has been abolished since then. In 1977, North Korea enacted the Law of the DPRK on Land ("Land Law" hereafter) in order to regulate comprehensive land use in the territory according to what the law said. In this law, North Korea declared that land in North Korea belonged to the State or cooperative organizations and thus no one was allowed to buy, sell or privatize it.[403] This was because land was considered a valuable prize of the socialist revolution.[404]

In 1991, soon after the then-Rajin-Sonbong Free Economic and Trade Zone was declared and the Socialist Constitution was again amended in 1992, North Korea subsequently encouraged its economic organs to have a joint venture with foreign partners. To support such open door policy, a series of laws as supported by implementing regulations were enacted thereafter. The first law mentioning land tenure was the Law of the DPRK on Foreign Investment (or "Foreign Investment Law" hereafter) in 1992. This law stipulated that the State was obliged to lease the land as required

---

[398] *See* the Socialist Constitution of 1972 art. 18. This clause has been carried over to the further amendments until the last version of Socialist Constitution of 2023.

[399] *See* the Socialist Constitution of 1972 art. 19 and 20.

[400] *See id.* art. 20.

[401] *See id.* art. 22. This provision is still effective by the article 24 of the Socialist Constitution as amended in September 2023.

[402] Law of the DPRK on Land ("Land Law" hereafter) art. 13.

[403] Land Law art. 9.

[404] *See id.* art. 1.

to foreign investors for a maximum period of 50 years.[405] It maintains the same position up until now. Rights on the leased land could further be transferred or inherited within the terms of the lease contract subject to the approval of the relevant authority.[406] Although it was applied to a few foreign direct investment cases, this was the first legal recognition of a land lease to a private party, transfer or inheritance of rights on land since nationalization of production means including land in 1950s and official confirmation of it by the first Socialist Constitution of 1972.

In 1993, the Law of the Democratic People's Republic of Korea on Land Lease ("Land Lease Law" hereafter) was enacted as the general law to establish land leasing orders in relation to foreign investment in North Korea. A lessee has the 'right to use' the land leased.[407] By the Land Lease Law, foreign corporate bodies or individuals may lease and use land in North Korea.[408] For the implementing regulations of the Land Lease Law, it was adopted in 1994 but abolished some time later. Instead, North Korea made the Implementing Regulations on Real Estate in the Kaesong Industrial Complex ("KIC Real Estate Regulations" hereafter) in 2004 and Implementing Regulations on Real Estate in the Rason Economic and Trade Zone ("Rason ETZ Real Estate Regulations" hereafter) in 2014. General implementing regulations for the Land Lease Law applicable nationwide have not been enacted as of 2025.

North Korean business entities are allowed to use their 'land use right' as their equity share when they establish a contractual or equity joint venture company with foreign investors upon approval obtained from the authority that controls the land in question.[409]

The land use right has been recognized as a property right[410] of a private party for the first time since all lands were nationalized or socialized in 1950s although it is limited to foreign investment cases while ownership of the leased land remains exclusively with the State. As a property right, the land use right can, therefore, be invested, transferred or mortgaged to a third party. However, the land use right

[405] Foreign Investment Law of 1992 art. 15.

[406] *Id. See* also Land Lease Law of 1993 art. 6 and Land Lease Law of 2011 (current) art. 15.

[407] *See* Land Lease Law art. 3

[408] *Id.* art. 2.

[409] *Id.* art. 5.

[410] *Id.* art. 7.

does not cover natural resources and deposits in the land in question since these belong to the State.[411]

Land leases require approval from the central land and environmental protection guidance organ. The lease contract itself is concluded by the land and environment protection department of the relevant provincial people's committee (or the people's committee of a municipality directly under central authority, such as Pyongyang or Rason).[412] Leases are generally conducted through consultation[413] though tender and auction are also available in the special economic zones.[414] The lease period is determined by the parties by agreement, having regard to the intended use of the land and the nature of the investment, subject to a maximum of fifty years.[415]

Four types of land use rights are created as private property by the Land Lease Law in addition to the right to mortgage.[416] These include the right to sale, sublease, gift and inheritance of the leased land. These four rights are transferable, a part or the whole of the land leased, to a third party subject to the approval of the lessor authority.[417] The term of any transfer or mortgage may not exceed the remaining period under the original lease contract.[418] On a transfer of the land use right, the rights and obligations relating to use of the land, together with any structures, fixtures, and attachments on it, pass to the transferee.[419]

As mentioned above, there are three ways to lease the land: consultation (that is, negotiation); tender; and auction. Consultation is a generally acknowledged method anywhere whereas tender and auction can be practiced only in the special economic zones in addition to the consultation.[420]

To sell the land use right, the vendor and purchaser must first conclude a contract, obtain notarial attestation, and then submit an application for approval to the lessor authority together with a copy of

---

411 *Id.* art. 3.

412 *Id.* art. 4.

413 However, its North Korean wording is 'negotiation' rather than consultation

414 *See* Land Lease Law art. 9.

415 *Id.* art. 6.

416 *Id.* art. 15 and 21.

417 *Id.* art. 15.

418 *Id.*

419 *Id.* art. 17.

420 *Id.* art. 9.

the contract.[421] The lessor authority retains a right of pre-emption: where a lessee offers the land use right for sale, the lessor authority may purchase it in preference to any other prospective buyer.[422]

Sublease of the land is an act of transfer from the lessee who holds the land use right. The lessee must file an application for sublease approval[423] and, if approved, both parties must go to the land registration office for registration of the sublease. The contract of sublease comes into force from the moment when the registration is through. By the nature of sublease, however, the right and obligation of the lessee (sublessor) stipulated in the original land lease contract in relation to the land use is not transferred to the sublessee. The sublessor retains right to collect the rated rent for the sublease.

The lessee can make a gift of the land use right of the leased land to a third party.[424] The gift means such an act of transfer that the lessee gives the right to a donee without consideration. The third party donee is not limited to a natural or legal person of a foreign country or to an institution, enterprise, or organization of North Korea. However, a natural person of North Korea is excluded from the status of a donee beneficiary of the gift as North Korea's Socialist Constitution prohibits individual's ownership of production means including land and derivative rights. The donation of the gift is subject to approval from the lessor authority[425] and the registration of the land use right is the prerequisite of validity of the donation. The certificate of the gift tax payment must be submitted at the time of the registration.

The land use right can also be passed at the lessee's death to his devisee or heirs by law or under a will or by the judgment of the court of law.[426] The heir must re-register the new name of the holder of the right with the municipal or county land administration. In this case, the payment of inheritance tax is a prerequisite for the re-registration. Upon completion of the re-registration, the whole rights and

---

[421] *Id.* art. 18.

[422] *Id.* art. 19.

[423] *Id*, art. 20. The Land Lease Law in its article 20 states the sublease as 're-lease' and it sounds like an assignment but the re-lease does not mean transfer of original lessee's rights and duties to the re-leased person. Rather, it is a form of 'sublease upon approval' and thus the sublessor maintains original contractual relationship with the lessor authority.

[424] *Id.* art. 15.

[425] *Id.*

[426] *Id.*

obligations of the lessee contained in the land lease contract is automatically taken over by the devisee or heir.

The lessee is allowed to mortgage the land use right.[427] Mortgage of the land use right on a specific land is lessee's act to put the said right as guarantee for any loan to be drawn from a bank or any other financial organization. In case of mortgaging the said right, the structure and other fixtures in the land are mortgaged all together.[428] The 'structure' encompasses building for the use of residence, office, commerce or storage and the 'fixture' means any article attached to the land or building.

In North Korea, building is categorized as one of real properties differently from land, along with other kind of real properties such as natural resources, forests, rivers, and creeks, roads, sea ports, territorial waters, factory buildings, parks, resort places, among others.[429] However, with regard to the land use right in relation to foreign direct investment, North Korea altered the conception of building from independent real property to a part of land. Therefore, a building on land is not mortgaged separately from the land as far as it is concerned with land use right in the foreign direct investment case. Both mortgagor and mortgagee of the land use right must register with the lessor authority within 10 days from the conclusion of the mortgage contract.[430] The registration is the precondition of the mortgage to come into force.

Upon consultation with the mortgagee, the mortgagor can transfer the land use right.[431] The mortgagee is entitled to dispose of the land use right on the mortgaged land in the following cases where: (i) the mortgagor fails to redeem debts by the expiry of the mortgage; (ii) mortgagor's business is dissolved or goes bankrupt during the term of the mortgage contract;[432] and (iii) no successor in title is available at the time of death of the mortgagor during the period of mortgage.[433] The disposal of the mortgaged land use right is subject to approval from the lessor authority.[434] As such, the mortgaged right

[427] *Id.*

[428] *Id.* art. 21.

[429] *See* Civil Law Dictionary at 297.

[430] Land Lease Law art. 23.

[431] *Id.* art. 26.

[432] *Id.* art. 24.

[433] *See* Rason SEZ Real Estate Regulations of 2014 art. 38 and KIC Real Estate Regulations of 2005 art. 52.

[434] *See* Land Lease Law art. 15.

can be disposed of by auction or in the case of several mortgages, in such a way as multiple mortgagees consult and agree upon one another. The mortgagee is compensated prior to other creditors with proceeds from the sale of the mortgaged right. Priorities among mortgagees on the same right are determined by chronological order of registration with the land registration office.

The mortgage on the land use right is terminated or withdrawn in the cases where: (i) the mortgagor clears his liability; (ii) the mortgagee voluntarily waives the mortgage; and (iii) the mortgagee and the mortgagor agree and settle the liability of mortgage by means of substitution.[435]

With regard to the payment in relation to land use right, there are three types: (i) rental charge; (ii) cost of land development; and (iii) annual land use fee.[436] The rental charge is the price of the 'right of use' of the land in question. It is payable to the lessor which is the leasing authority.[437] The 'rental charge' should be paid by the lessee who is a foreign-invested enterprise or foreign-invested bank in total amount within 90 days of conclusion of the land lease contract.[438] The 'cost of land development' is the costs of land realignment, road construction, water supply and drainage, telecommunications, electricity and heating system as constructed by the leasing authority.[439] The cost is charged to the user (lessee) of the newly developed land and payable to the leasing authority. This cost is not separately charged as it is included in the rental charge.[440] The 'land use fee' is a payment for the usage of the State-owned land. The land use fee is paid every year by the lessee who is a foreign-invested enterprise or foreign-invested bank and payable to a financial institution located in the land user's domicile in North Korea.[441]

The land use right is automatically returned to the lessor authority at the expiry of the period of the lease as stipulated in the contract.[442] The structure and fixtures in the land should also be returned without

[435] *See* Land Lease Law art. 27; Rason ETZ Real Estate Regulations of 2014 art. 37; KIC Real Estate Regulations of 2005 art. 51.

[436] Land Lease Law art. 28, 29 and 33.

[437] *Id.* art. 28.

[438] *Id.* art. 30.

[439] *Id.* art. 29.

[440] *Id.*

[441] *Id.* art. 33.

[442] *Id.* art. 34.

compensation.[443] However, if the land has been leased for more than 40 years, compensation may be paid against the residual value of the main buildings that have been built in the last ten years before the expiry of the lease.[444] The lessee must return the certificate of land use to the issuing authority and cancel the registration of the right to land use.[445]

Extension of the lease period may be granted upon submission of an application to and approval of the lessor authority six months prior to the expiration of the lease.[446] When the lessor authority does not want to take over any of the structure and fixtures, warehouses, open storage yards, private sidings and other auxiliary facilities, the lessee should, at his own expenses, demolish and remove them and restore the land.[447]

In principle, the land use right may not be revoked during the lease term.[448] However, the right can be cancelled during the period of the lease by the lessor authority if unavoidable circumstances demand the withdrawal of the land use right during the term of lease. In this case, the lessor should obtain consent from the lessee six months in advance and offer the lessee other land in the same conditions or pay appropriate indemnity.[449]

There are several sanctions on violation of the Land Lease Law and its implementing regulations. Where a lessee illegally uses land without the certificate of land use, or changes the purpose of use of land, or transfers or mortgages the land use right without approval, the lessee will be fined, or have the facilities on land confiscated or be required to restore the land to original state, and the contract of transfer or mortgage will be declared null and void.[450]

With regard to the settlement of disputes, any disagreements arising out of leasing land, transferring or mortgaging leased land to a third party should be settled through consultation between the parties

---

[443] *Id.*
[444] *Id.*
[445] *Id.* art. 35.
[446] *Id.* art. 36.
[447] *Id.* art. 37.
[448] *Id.* art. 38.
[449] *Id.*
[450] *Id.* art. 39.

concerned.[451] Disputes should also be settled through mediation, arbitration or judicial procedures.[452]

In reviewing the land use right, there are several problems and risks for foreign investors. First of all, there is a question about price. Who and how can decide the rental charges and land use fees stipulated in the Land Lease Law? As mentioned above, a foreign investor who leased land must pay rental charges for the price of the right to use of land within 90 days from the date of the conclusion of the lease contract in addition to annual land use fees.[453] However, it is unknown to outsiders whether the system of fair assessment is operative by certified and impartial land appraisers of North Korea together with well-established standard and neutrality. In North Korea, land price including rentals is not decided by the market mechanism but by the price fixing authorities of central and provincial governments.

North Korean entities are permitted to contribute land use rights as their equity share to the equity or contractual joint venture when they make investment in kind.[454] Foreign parties may not know if the price of North Korean party's contribution or the rental charge is fair enough. The same question will come up when the land use right is transferred by sale, gift, inheritance or sublease or is mortgaged. This is one of foreign investment risks.

In China, for each appraisal case, two certified and registered appraisers examine the documents provided by the applicants and then conduct a site inspection. The appraisers are required, by the regulations concerned, to make a report which contains a description of the property, its nature and quality in detail including zoning and future prospects of the property. The report must also discuss the impact of the market on the value of the property.[455] Keeping in mind the China's case, North Korea should make guidelines on how to appraise land. They should also establish a system for training certified or qualified appraisers.

The other potential risk for a foreign investor is about the question of freedom of contract and wide discretion of the lessor

---

[451] *Id.* art. 42.

[452] *Id.*

[453] *See* art. 30 and 33.

[454] *See* Land Leasing Law art. 5.

[455] *See* PATRICK A. RANDOLPH JR. ET AL., CHINESE REAL ESTATE LAW 177-78 (2000).

authority of North Korea. Every single transaction including gifts and mortgage is subject to approval from the lessor authority. If an unapproved transfer of the land use right is made by sale, gift or sublease, or unapproved mortgage or unapproved disposal of the mortgage is made by the mortgagor, such transactions are declared null and void as mentioned above. It is too harsh administrative action. In addition, the land use right or the mortgage may further be deprived of, depending on the degree of violation.[456] As all transactions are required approval from the North Korean authority, its discretional power becomes stronger and transacting parties' freedom of conducting economic activities will become more shrunk. In addition, the lessor authority has a preemptive right to buy the right of use of the land in the case the lessee offers to sell it.[457] These facts give the lessor authority great power and wide discretion whereas the freedom of contract for foreign-investors is shrunk by a great margin. It is necessary to ease the power of the authority while promote freedom of contract of foreign-investors. Foreign investors do not come to North Korea to bite the bullet.

With regard to mortgage foreclosure, there is no device to protect the mortgagor's rights. According to the implementing regulations for the KIC and the Rason ETZ, the mortgage on the land use right is disposed in cases of mortgagor's default, business dissolution, bankruptcy, or mortgagor's death without a successor.[458] Thus, the mortgagee is entitled to dispose the mortgaged land use right to recover its loan. To dispose of the mortgaged right, the required procedure for the mortgagee is just to file an application with the lessor authority. The lessor authority reviews and decides whether to approve or reject the application before sending a notice to the applicant, the mortgagee. In the meantime, the mortgagor does not have any recourse to defend himself and can only wait for his property to be taken to an auction if the mortgagee's application is approved. Is it fair enough for the mortgagor?

In the same context, the next question is about the fairness of the executing authority. The lessor authority, an administrative agency, functions as a judicial court for the foreclosure action disregarding

---

[456] *See* Land Lease Law art. 26; Rason ETZ Real Property Regulations of 2014 chapter 6.

[457] *See id.* Law art. 19.

[458] *See id.* Law art. 24; KIC Real Property Regulations art. 52; Rason ETZ Real Property Regulations art. 38.

giving the mortgagor any opportunity to defend himself before being foreclosed. Further, it is not clear which agency is responsible for conducting the auction after the lessor authority approves the mortgagee's application for disposal. In case of judgment in North Korea, execution of the judgment is conducted by a bailiff[459] but an administrative decision approving a foreclosure application is not a court judgment, and it is uncertain how execution is effected in practice.

A further dimension concerns the mortgagor's right of redemption. In equity, redemption allows a mortgagor to recover mortgaged property by paying the outstanding debt at any time before foreclosure sale. In many U.S. states, statute additionally confers a right of redemption for a prescribed period even after the foreclosure sale has taken place — so-called statutory redemption. Redemption is not generally recognized in civil law systems, but the complete absence of any equivalent mechanism leaves the mortgagor in a particularly vulnerable position. Since foreign investors are invariably potential mortgagors, North Korea would do well to consider introducing some form of mortgagor protection.

The introduction of a land leasing system represents a notable concession for a state whose foundational ideology regards private land rights as instruments of capitalist exploitation. North Korea has historically prohibited not only private ownership of land but also the leasing of land by private parties — viewing the landowner-as-lessor as a class enemy who extracts wealth from the proletariat. By adopting a land lease law to attract foreign investment, North Korea has had to modify this foundational position, introducing the concept of the land use right, which is recognizably a product of market-economy thinking. The tension is not merely rhetorical: the North Korean state now occupies the position of lessor — the very role its official doctrine has long characterized as exploitative. Whether this ideological accommodation will prove durable, and what it signals about North Korea's broader orientation toward market-based reform, remains an open question.

I. Expropriation

[459] Law of the DPRK on Civil Procedure ("Civil Procedure Law" hereafter) art. 297. In the USA, a responsible officer executing judgment is sheriff, court officer or bailiff, etc. and it differs state by state.

Among the most significant risks in foreign direct investment is the taking of property by the host state, whether denominated as expropriation, nationalization, or confiscation. Such takings have occurred with some frequency in modern times, in both economically developed and developing countries, including non-market economies.[460] They take a variety of forms: intervention, nationalization, expropriation, and confiscation on the one hand, and de facto takings such as creeping expropriation and severe administrative interference on the other.

Intervention typically describes a situation in which a government assumes temporary control of a business to achieve a particular objective, intending to return the enterprise to its owners once that objective has been met. As long as the taking remains interventionary in character, the property is not permanently appropriated.[461]

Nationalization refers to a host country government's taking of property as part of a broader plan to assume control of an entire sector or industry, generally with the aim of effecting wider economic or social change.[462] The terms nationalization and expropriation are often times used interchangeably since in fact their borderline is not succinct. Both actions involve the taking of property which was not expected when investment was made. Nationalization might sound softer term than expropriation but practice has often shown differently from such conjecture. There has also been talk of compensation for nationalization often times, although the compensation plan may be illusory in many cases often in developing countries and raise questions on international law standards of proper compensation as shown many cases internationally and historically.[463]

Expropriation seems to have harsher tones than nationalization, perhaps defining an angry taking of property owned by a foreign investor located in the host country where political conflict is involved, such as Cuba after the 1959 revolution. A taking without

---

[460] A series of expropriation was done in France after the socialist government came into power in 1982.

[461] *See* FOLSOM ET AL. at 639 – 40.

[462] *See* DAVID FRISCH AND RAJ BHALA, GLOBAL BUSINESS LAW: PRINCIPLES AND PRACTICE 532 (1999).

[463] *See* FOLSOM at 640.

any compensation shades into confiscation.[464] The term expropriation is often used as a general term for any types of takings.

Confiscation is defined as a taking without compensation with or without judicial procedure.

> At the time of foreign investment is taken over by the host nation government, it is not always clear what to call it. That is because it is not clear whether the taking is (1) merely to be temporary and actually constitute an intervention, or (2) to be or become permanent and be followed by compensation and thus be a nationalization or expropriation, or (3) to be permanent but not be followed by proper compensation and thus be a confiscation. If the Cuban takings are properly called confiscation in 1993, since by that time more than 30 years have passed without compensation, will they ultimately be called nationalization or expropriation, assuming there is some final settlement? If a property taken in 1960 is returned in 1995, should it be called an intervention?[465]

While the demarcation among different types of taking is not always clear, the same ambiguity is true in North Korea's taking provisions. North Korea had only a single taking clause, in the Foreign Investment Law, until the mid-2000s; it now has taking clauses in several statutes: the Foreign Investment Law,[466] the Rason ETZ Law,[467] the KIC Law,[468] the Hwanggumphyong and Wihwado Economic Zone Law[469] and the Economic Development Zones Law.[470]

Taking clauses of North Korean laws unequivocally state that the State would not nationalize or seize foreign-invested properties unless unavoidable circumstance makes it necessary for the public interest. It is unclear whether the wording "nationalize" is used in a broad sense of nationalization that includes expropriation or in a narrow sense that

---

[464] *See id.* at 640.
[465] *Id.* at 641.
[466] *See* Foreign Investment Law art. 19.
[467] *See* Rason ETZ Law art. 7.
[468] *See* KIC Law art. 7.
[469] *See* HWEZ Law art. 8.
[470] *See* EDZs Law art. 8.

does not. China's joint venture law, for example, distinguishes one from another, stipulating that "[t]he State shall not nationalize or requisition any equity joint venture."[471] In Vietnam, its Constitution mentions the term 'nationalization' as a taking measure,[472] while 'nationalization' and 'confiscation' as assuring measures not to take invested assets through them are stipulated in the Law on Investment of Vietnam.[473]

North Korea's term "seizure (as used in North Korean law in the sense of "not to seize")" is similarly ambiguous: by the logic of the Korean language it is closer to confiscation, but since it appears alongside a compensation provision, it is better read as expropriation. The phrase "unavoidable circumstances" as both a precondition and a justifying ground for taking is equally vague. The accepted international standard requires that expropriation serve a public purpose, but the content of that requirement remains contested. China's joint venture law uses "social public interest" as the operative test.[474] North Korea's foreign investment laws use "public interests" as the test of taking.

As to the compensation standard, North Korea's foreign investment laws offer either "sufficient" compensation or "sufficient and effective" one. In the practice of expropriation, there are some different kinds of compensation standards such as "fair,"[475] "just,"[476] "appropriate,"[477] or "prompt, adequate, and effective"[478] compensation. International law generally holds that a lawful expropriation must serve a public purpose, be non-discriminatory, and

---

[471] *See* Law of the People's Republic of China on Chinese-Foreign Equity Joint Ventures of 2005 ("Chinese Equity Joint Venture Law" hereafter) art. 2.

[472] *See* Constitution of the Socialist Republic of Vietnam of 2013 art. 51.

[473] *See* Law on Investment of Vietnam of 2020 art. 10.

[474] *See* Chinese Equity Joint Venture Law art. 2.

[475] Chorzow Factory decision, 1928 P.C.I.J. (Ser. A) No. 17.

[476] U.S. CONST. amend. V; Section 712 of the Restatement (Third) on the Foreign Relations Law of the United States.

[477] the Restatement (Third) on the Foreign Relations Law of the United States.; The United Nations resolution 3281 on the Charter of Economic Rights and Duties of States (1975); *Texas Overseas Petroleum Co/California Asiatic Oil Co. v. Government of Libyan Arab Republic*, 17 Int'l Legal Mat. 3, 29 (1978); Arbitration between Kuwait and American Independent Oil Co. (AMINOIL), 21 Int'l Legal Mat. 976 (1982). The last two cases are cited from FOLSOM ET AL., *supra* at 665, footnote § 24.14.

[478] The standard of the United States government since 1938.

be accompanied by compensation — but no single universally accepted formula for calculating that compensation exists.

A sovereign country has full and permanent sovereignty over its natural resources and economic activities. It is clearly stated in the United Nations Resolution on Permanent Sovereignty over Natural Resources.[479] The sovereignty gives a country the right to take privately owned property regardless of whether the property is owned by its own nationals or foreigners. Of course, such taking is not allowed for any reason. There are limitations under customary international law. It must be for a public purpose.[480] However, as noted above the definition of public purpose has never had a very clear explanation. It is often expressed in such broad words as "improvement of social welfare or economic betterment of the nation."[481] International law does not contain its own definition of it but leaves it to the taking country to judge what it considers useful for the welfare of its people.[482]

Therefore, it is not generally in issue whether an expropriation is undertaken for a public purpose or not. The taking country may enjoy relatively wide discretion in this respect. However, there is a minimum limitation in conducting such discretionary power. It must not be for the purpose of private gain at least. If the property is seized in the course of committing crimes against humanity, genocide, or other violations of human rights, of course, the taking would be contrary to the public purpose. In the same context, if the taking is motivated by political concerns that are not directly relevant to the country's economic policy, and are not justified by exceptional circumstances, it may be unlawful.[483]

The recent international trend is that the question of lawfulness of an expropriation tends to flow to whether the expropriation was in pursuit of an appropriate public policy purpose, and that question should be answered by the host country's government. International law nonetheless requires that the host state offer at least some minimum justification for its action.

---

[479] *See* Preamble of the General Assembly resolution 1803 (XVII) of 14 December 1962, "Permanent sovereignty over natural resources."

[480] These are grounds or reasons of public utility, security or the national interest which are recognized as overriding purely individual or private interests. *See id.* para. 4.

[481] FOLSOM ET AL., at 661.

[482] *See* FRISCH ET AL., at 535.

[483] *See* MUCHLINSKI, at 504 – 05.

On the other hand, the question of discriminatory taking requires a comparison between the treatment of the investor in question and that of other foreign investors in the same or analogous sectors. Discriminatory treatment that cannot be justified by reference to the host state's economic policy is considered illegitimate under international law. A taking motivated by extraneous political considerations — such as retaliatory action against an investor from a hostile state — falls outside the bounds of acceptable conduct.[484]

As discussed above, to be lawful, an act of expropriation requires compensation. On the other hand, however, there is no agreed framework or formula as to how the compensation should be measured and there is no single universal standard for calculating compensation.

The United States government's long established compensation standard for a taken property in its foreign investment is that it is required under international law, and it must be prompt, adequate and effective. In the U.S. Model Bilateral Investment Treaty, expropriation and compensation should be made: (1) for a public purpose; (2) in a non-discriminatory manner; (3) on payment of prompt, adequate and effective compensation; and (4) in accordance with due process of law and minimum standard treatment that includes fair and equitable treatment and full protection of security as stipulated in the article 5 of the Treaty.[485] The "prompt, adequate and effective" compensation standard became the firm policy of the government after it was used by Secretary of State Hull in 1938, in his note to the Mexican government claiming compensation for expropriated agrarian lands owned by U.S. nationals.[486]

However, courts of the United States have taken different position from this standard as it was shown in the *Banco National de Cuba v. Chase Manhattan Bank* decision in 1981. The Court instead suggested that the consensus of nations was to apply an "appropriate" standard in place of the government standard of 'prompt, adequate and

---

[484] *See* MUCHLINSKI, at 505.

[485] *See* 2012 U.S. Model Bilateral Investment Treaty art. 5 and 6.

[486] *See* FOLSOM ET AL. at 663. S*ee also* Oscar Schacther, Comment, *Compensation for expropriation*, AM. J. INT'L L. 121 (1984) cited in DAVID FRISCH at 536. This note if found at website of the Office of the Historian of the Department of State available at <https://history.state.gov/historicaldocuments/frus1938v05/d662> (visited Aug. 18, 2025>

effective.' [487] However, the U.S. government's standard is still effectively used when the U.S. government negotiates a treaty with another country with regard to foreign investment.

The "appropriate" compensation standard was first suggested by the United Nations Resolution 1083 of 1962. It was subsequently suggested in the *Banco National* decision in the United States, as noted above, and in two important international arbitrations – the *Texas Overseas Petroleum Co/California Asiatic Oil Co. v. Government of the Libyan Arab Republic* (TOPCO/CALASIATIC) in 1978 and the *Arbitration between Kuwait and the American Independent Oil Co.* (AMINOIL) in 1982.[488] If an investor receives 'appropriate' compensation for an expropriation, it seems to be the closest standard reflecting what international law requires. And if this standard reflects the consensus, then perhaps it is because 'appropriate' is so vague that it can be interpreted consistently with most, if not all, of other standards.[489]

The "just" compensation standard in the Fifth Amendment to the United States Constitution was adopted by the Restatement (Third) of the Foreign Relations Law of the United States in the Section 712 to replace the term 'appropriate.' This was done largely to avoid the possible inclusion of host country's demanded deductions under the 'appropriate' standard. Several host countries had calculated compensation by taking the company's value of the property and deducting so-called excess profits or improper pricing of resources to make a conclusion that either no compensation was due, or that the company actually owed the expropriating host country.[490]

The "fair" compensation standard was first referred to in the 1928 *Chorzow Factory* decision of the Permanent Court of International Justice. Questions have branched out from this decision as to whether it must be the 'fair actual value,' as some international arbitrators and judges have said, or the 'fair market value,' as was stated in Article 1110 of Chapter 11 of the defunct North American Free Trade Agreement (NAFTA).[491] Although this Agreement has been replaced by the United States-Mexico-Canada Agreement (USMCA) since

---

[487] *See Banco Nacional de Cuba v. Chase Manhattan Bank*, 658 F.2d 875, 888 – 890 (2d Cir. 1981).

[488] *See* FOLSOM ET AL. at 665; *See also* § 24.14, footnote 2 in the same page.

[489] *See* FRISCH ET AL. at 536.

[490] *See* FOLSOM ET AL. at 665.

[491] FRISCH ET AL. at 536.

July 2020, the "fair market value" remains the compensation standard for expropriation.[492] However, either the actual value or the fair market value has not been generally accepted as a proper standard of compensation, nor has it become an accepted norm in international law.[493]

Aside from the discussed standards of compensation, 'equitable' compensation and 'speedy' compensation were also suggested by other cases, but neither of these has been strongly supported in international society. Nor do they have a clear-cut meaning or interpretation.

North Korea has adopted the "sufficient" compensation or "sufficient and effective" compensations standard. This standard is still vague as it is not clear what constitutes sufficiency and/or effectiveness. It may be better to adopt 'appropriate' compensation standard since it is more recognized in international society than other standards although no compensation standard offers clear definition as discussed above.

Further questions arise as to how expropriated property would actually be valued in North Korea. In the absence of a stock market or any independent mechanism for appraising foreign-invested assets, the prospect of a foreign investor receiving genuinely sufficient compensation is uncertain. Additional open questions include whether future profitability should be factored into the compensation assessment, in what form and on what timetable payment would be made, and who would adjudicate any dispute. The most effective safeguard available to a prospective investor is likely the conclusion of a bilateral investment treaty between North Korea and the investor's home state, which would give more concrete content to the standards currently left vague in North Korea's domestic law.

Three doctrinal defenses are available to a taking state when sued in connection with an expropriation: the Act of State doctrine, sovereign immunity, and the Calvo doctrine. The Act of State doctrine originated from the 1674 English case of *Blad v. Bamfield* and the doctrine was formed in the United States in the *Underhill v. Hernandez* case in 1897.[494] The doctrine was reaffirmed in the *Banco*

---

[492] See United States-Mexico-Canada Agreement art. 14.8.

[493] *See* FOLSOM ET AL. at 665.

[494] *See* FOLSOM ET AL. at 685.

Nacional de Cuba v. Sabbatino case in 1964[495] which also began the contemporary history of the Act of State doctrine.

In this case, the Act of State doctrine precluded the court from invalidating the Cuban government's title to a quantity of sugar in issue which was previously an American company's property and which was nationalized by the Cuban government. Congress subsequently reacted to the *Sabbatino* decision and passed the Second Hickenlooper Amendment[496] of the Title 22 Foreign Relations and Intercourse stating that:

> [N]o court in the United States shall decline on the ground of federal act of state doctrine to make a determination on the merits giving effect to the principles of international law in a case in which a claim of title or other right to property is asserted by any party including a foreign state (or party claiming through such state) based upon (or traced through) a confiscation or other taking … by an act of that state in violations of the principles of international law, including principles of compensation and other standards set out in the subsection: Provided, That this subparagraph shall not be applicable (1) …, or (2) in any case with respect to which the President determines that application of the act of state doctrine is required in that particular case by the foreign policy interest of the United States and a suggestion to this effect is filed on his behalf in that case with the court.[497]

In application of this Amendment to North Korea's taking provision and in the absence of the bilateral treaty, if an expropriation by the North Korean government is executed based on: (1) the principles of international law such as a taking for the purpose of public use; (2) non-discriminatory measures; and (3) the principles of compensation – even though a clear standard was not suggested by the Amendment, and if (4) the following lucky fact that the President of the United States determines to apply the Act of State doctrine for the foreign interests of the United States is added, North Korea may

[495] *See* 11 L.Ed.2d 804, 376 U.S. 398, 418, 84 S.Ct. 923, 935 (U.S.N.Y. 1964).
[496] 22 U.S.C. § 2370(e)(2) (2021).
[497] *Id.*

assert the act of state doctrine as a defense in the courts of law of the United States.

The second defense of a taking country is the doctrine of Sovereign Immunity. Sovereignty is the power to do anything within a state without accountability – to make laws, to execute and apply them, to impose and collect taxes, to levy contributions, to make war or peace, to form treaties of alliance or of commerce with foreign countries, and the like.[498] Sovereign Immunity is a judicial doctrine which precludes bringing suit against a government without its consent.[499] The foreign Sovereign Immunity is to preclude a state from the jurisdiction of domestic courts of another state.[500]

Two theories regarding foreign Sovereign Immunity, the absolute and restrictive ones, have developed and the United States generally accepted the absolute theory of immunity until 1952. Now, a limited scope of state immunity, which is termed the restrictive theory, is that of the United States.[501] Based on the restrictive theory, the United States codified the Foreign Sovereign Immunity Act (FSIA) of 1976. In fact, the main purpose of the FSIA is to categorize actions for which foreign states are not entitled to claim state immunity in the courts of the United States.[502] Three of the main exceptions to the state immunity stipulated in the FSIA occur in any case where: (1) the foreign state has waived its immunity either explicitly or by implication; (2) the action is based upon a commercial activity; or (3) rights in property taken in violation of international law are in issue.[503] Therefore, aside from the exceptions in the FSIA, any foreign state including North Korea may assert the sovereign immunity in U.S. courts as a defense to an expropriation carried out by its sovereign power.

The third defense is the Calvo doctrine. This doctrine, named after an Argentine jurist, is that a government is not bound to indemnify aliens for losses and injuries sustained by them in consequence of domestic disturbances or civil war where the state is not at fault. Therefore, foreign states are not justified in intervening,

---

[498] *See* BLACK'S LAW DICTIONARY (sixth ed.) at 1396.

[499] *See id.*

[500] *See* BARRY E. CARTER AND PHILIP R. TRIMBLE, INTERNATIONAL LAW 549 (1991).

[501] *See id.* at 550 – 51.

[502] *See* 28 U.S.C. § 1602, 1605 (2016).

[503] 28 U.S.C. § 1605(a)(1) – (3) (2016); *see also* FRISCH ET AL. at 539.

by force or otherwise, to secure the settlement of claims of their citizens on account of such losses or injuries.[504] The purpose of the Calvo doctrine is to prevent a state from bringing a claim on behalf of one of its nationals based on another state's responsibility at international law, because of an alleged waiver of such rights by the national.[505] The doctrine is sometimes expressed in an agreement signed by a foreign investor that he/she will not be entitled treatment different from domestic investors – national treatment – and recourse to one's own diplomatic channels such as diplomatic intervention will result in a forfeiture of the property.[506] If the purpose of a Calvo clause is merely to enforce the obligation to resort to the domestic remedy as national treatment before an international claim is sought, it is unobjectionable. But if the clause purports to go beyond the national treatment and to exclude diplomatic protection altogether, its validity is open to doubt.[507] North Korea's position on the Calvo doctrine has not been publicly articulated, but given its general rejection of private entities as subjects of international law, its insistence on national law as the governing framework for foreign nationals' rights, and its historic hostility to diplomatic intervention, it is reasonable to expect North Korea to be sympathetic to the doctrine.

North Korea has ever carried out a huge size of nationalization or socialization of private properties from the dawn of national foundation and further until the time it accomplished taking of the country's whole land and industry in 1958. Since then, no cases have been reported that North Korea has officially nationalized or expropriated any foreign-invested property.

However, somewhat uncommon type of taking took place when North Korea froze 165 South Korean enterprises and their assets and facilities in the Kaesong Industrial Complex in February 2016. It happened one day after the South Korean government declared cease and desist of operation of all South Korean businesses in the Complex and evacuated all South Korean personnel from there. It was a consequence of exchanges of tit for tat several times since 2010 as both sides clashed over the military and political issues including North Korea's testing nuclear weapons and launching ballistic missiles. A freezing action is not a common type of taking but it can

[504] *See* BLACK'S LAW DICTIONARY at 205.
[505] *See* MARTIN DIXON, TEXTBOOK ON INTERNATIONAL LAW 212 – 13 (1990).
[506] *See* FOLSON ET AL. at 668.
[507] *See* DIXON at 213.

be a kind of creeping expropriation by the lapse of time. Further, in June 2020, North Korea has angrily demolished a four-story building built and owned by the South Korean government having used for the purpose of liaison and consular affairs in the Complex. Since then, no further progress for this issue has been made between the two as of August 2025.

North Korea has taking clauses in foreign investment laws and their standards to take foreign-invested properties. Its standard for compensation is not literally far from the international practice according to their law provisions. However, practice may be different from what the laws say. When an actual taking takes place over the property of foreign investors, considering the socialist legal environment peculiar to North Korea, many questions lie ahead until the time transparent and fair procedures are guaranteed by system and practice in the court of law of North Korea.

J. Political Risk Insurance

Risk is an inherent companion of investment. They exist markets both in and outside country but there seems to be no sophisticated mechanism to insure various risks, especially in the markets out of home country. A number of investment guarantee schemes exist in the United States, in other economically developed countries, and in international organizations. This section examines two prominent schemes — those of the United States and the World Bank — together with the private insurance market, and assesses their applicability to foreign direct investment in North Korea.

1. DFC

The United States International Development Finance Corporation ("DFC" hereafter) was established by the BUILD Act of 2018[508] by merging the Overseas Private Investment Corporation (OPIC), which was established by the Foreign Assistance Act of 1969, with the Development Credit Authority (DCA).[509] Its stated purpose is to mobilize and facilitate the participation of private sector capital and skills in the economic development of less developed countries

[508] Better Utilization of Investments Leading to Development Act of 2018. *See* 22 U.S.C. § 9601 notes.

[509] Development Credit Authority was a part of the United States Agency for International Development(USAID).

and countries in transition from nonmarket to market economies.[510] DFC is "building on the need for increased private sector investment in emerging markets, enhancing U.S. global economic markets" and it "partners with the private sector to mobilize capital for strategic investment around the world."[511]

For the U.S. businesses to invest in developing countries, the DFC offers: (1) debt financing through direct loans and guaranties up to 1 billion USD with the tenor between 5 and 15 years; (2) direct equity investment that can provide critical support to companies committed to creating developmental impact; (3) investment funds to support for emerging market private equity funds to help address the shortfall of investment capital; (4) feasibility studies to support for the analysis of potential DFC project; (5) political risk insurance to cover up to $1 billion against losses due to currency inconvertibility, government interference, and political violence including terrorism in addition to offering reinsurance to increase underwriting capacity; and (6) technical assistance to support to increase the developmental impact or commercial sustainability of existing DFC projects or develop potential DFC projects.[512]

As to the political risk insurance program above (5), the BUILD Act displays coverage of political risks as follows: (a) currency inconvertibility and transfer restrictions; (b) expropriation; (c) war; (d) terrorism; (e) civil disturbance; (f) breach of contract; or (g) nonhonoring of financial obligations.[513]

The currency inconvertibility and transfer restriction covers: (i) new or more restrictive foreign exchange regulations; (ii) failure by an exchange control authority to approve of – or simply to act on – an application for hard currency; (iii) an unlawful effort by the host government to block funds for repatriation; and (iv) discriminatory host government actions resulting in an inability to convert and transfer local earnings. However, this coverage does not protect against the devaluation of a country's currency.[514]

---

[510] *See* 22 U.S.C. § 9612(b).

[511] See DFC "About Us" < https://www.dfc.gov/about-us> (visited May 31, 2025).

[512] *See* DFC "Our Products" <https://www.dfc.gov/what-we-offer/our-products> (visited May 31, 2025).

[513] *See* 22 U.S.C. § 9621(d) (2019) or BUILD Act Sec. 1421(d).

[514] *See* DFC "Political Risk Insurance." <https://www.dfc.gov/what-we-offer-our-products/political-risk-insurance> (visited May 31, 2025).

Applying this coverage to foreign direct investment in North Korea raises several questions. North Korea's laws and regulations do formally guarantee investors the right to transfer income earned from business operations and to repatriate invested assets upon liquidation; foreign employees and individuals are similarly permitted to remit legally earned income. In practice, however, bureaucratic delays or political considerations in the approval process, or a shortage of hard currency reserves, could impede the transfer of funds. A further uncertainty is that North Korea's laws are silent on whether foreign investors may convert local currency into hard currency. North Korea should clarify whether it prohibits such conversion as a matter of policy.

As to the expropriation coverage, DFC displays detailed items including nationalization, confiscation and creeping expropriations,[515] abrogation, repudiation or impairment of contract including forced re-negation of contract terms, imposing of confiscatory taxes, confiscation of funds and/or tangible assets, and outright nationalization of a project.[516] This policy is enough to cover North Korea's possible direct or indirect nationalization, expropriation or confiscation since it includes not only direct takings but indirect takings such as creeping expropriations, abrogation, and impairment of contract, among others.

The remaining coverage categories — war, terrorism, and civil disturbance — are standard political risk insurance items, carrying forward OPIC's established policy. DFC's political violence coverage protects against assets and income losses caused by: declared or undeclared war, hostile actions by national or international forces, revolution, insurrection and civil strife, and terrorism and sabotage. Further, investors may optionally purchase insurance for assets, business income, or both. In addition, DFC can provide coverage for evacuation expenses, income losses resulting from temporary abandonment of a project caused by political violence and income

---

[515] Creeping expropriation is a series of illegal government actions that cumulatively deprive an investor of the financial interest in his investment. *See* Paul Comeaux and Kinsella N. Stephan, *Reducing Political Risk in Developing Countries: Bilateral Investment Treaties, Stabilization Clauses, and MIGA & OPIC Investment Insurance*, 15 N.Y.L. Sch. J. Int'l & Comp. L. 1, (1994) at 35.

[516] *See* DFC website "Political Insurance." <https://www.dfc.gov/what-we-offer-our-products/political-risk-insurance> (visited May 31, 2025).

losses resulting from damage to specific sites outside the insured facility, such as a critical railway spur, power station, or supplier.[517]

One question raised at this point is about the requirement of exhaustion of local remedy before DFC is obligated to pay any claim especially for the cases of taking including nationalization, expropriation and confiscation. In general, political risk insurance policy contract includes provisions that the insurance claimant must exhaust local remedies, including administrative and judicial claims, to prevent or contest the challenged action by the host government. It was an OPIC's policy and the DFC would be the same as OPIC.[518]

As to local remedies in North Korea, it is unknown which government body is responsible for dispute settlement or hearing on an expropriation or nationalization case. A government body, the Arbitration Committee for International Trade Affairs of the Democratic People's Republic of Korea, handles disputes in relation to joint venture, trade and services related to international businesses between business entities in North Korea but the Arbitration Committee does not handle any case related to a State's act such as expropriation or currency inconvertibility.[519] The only possible way to exhaust local remedy is to bring the case to a local court. In general and with the socialist's conception, North Korea does not allow a private entity to sue the State. Even if a private party is allowed to sue, it is hardly expected that a court can reverse a government action in favor of a foreign investor because, according to North Korea's civil law conception, the court and a judge must advocate and protect the policy of their ruling political party which is implemented by the government. Therefore, it is hard to apply the exhaustion of local remedy principle to the cases of North Korea.

To apply the DFC political risk insurance programs to the foreign direct investment in North Korea, there are several prerequisites stipulated in the BUILD Act and other legislation. The DFC is "to mobilize and facilitate the participation of private sector capital and skills in the economic development of less developed countries ... and countries in transition from nonmarket to market economies

---

[517] Id.

[518] Exhaustion of local remedies was usually included in the contract between an investor and OPIC.

[519] *See* Law of the DPRK on Arbitration for External Economic Affairs ("Arbitration Law" hereafter) art. 4.

…."[520] However, since North Korea is not be classified as a 'country in transition from a non-market to market economy' as discussed earlier, this prerequisite is not satisfied.

Regardless of applicability of the BUILD Act, a number of statutes and administrative regulations function to restrict investment in or trade with North Korea. In addition, dozens of economic sanctions initiated by the United States and imposed by the United Nations Security Council prohibit foreigners' investment in North Korea. They will be examined in Chapter VI below.

2. MIGA

The Multilateral Investment Guarantee Agency (MIGA) is a member of the World Bank Group. It was established in 1988 with the main objective of encouraging the flow of investments for productive purposes among its member countries and in particular to its developing member countries.[521] Member countries of MIGA are 182 as of 2025.[522] Since its inception in 1988, MIGA has issued more than $84.5 billion of guarantees, in support of over 1,030 projects in 123 host countries until June 2024.[523]

According to the Convention establishing the Multilateral Investment Guarantee Agency ("MIGA Convention" hereafter) of 1985 as amended in 2010, any natural person and any juridical person are eligible to receive the Agency's guarantee if: (1) such natural person is a national of a member nation other than the host country; (2) (i) such juridical person is incorporated and has its principal place of business in a member or (ii) the majority of its capital is owned by a member or members or nationals thereof, provided that such member is not the host country; and (3) such juridical person, whether or not it is privately owned, operates on a commercial basis.[524] In other words, a national or corporation of a non-member country is not eligible to apply the MIGA's investment guarantee program.

---

[520] 22 U.S.C. § 9612(b) (2019).

[521] *See* Convention establishing the Multilateral Investment Guarantee Agency ("MIGA Convention" hereafter) art. 2.

[522] Among them, 154 are developing countries.

[523] *See* MIGA, Management's Discussion & Analysis and Financial Statements at 2. <https://www.miga.org/sites/default/files/2024-08/MIGA%20MD%20%26A%20and%20Financial%20Statement%20June%2030%202024.pdf> (visited May 31, 2025).

[524] MIGA Convention art. 13.

Four types of political risks are covered by the MIGA program: currency transfer; expropriation and similar measures; breach of contract; and war and civil disturbance.[525]

Currency transfer restriction coverage in general protects losses arising from an investor's inability to convert local currency (capital, interest, principal, profit, royalties, and other remittances) into foreign exchange for transfer outside the host country. MIGA's currency transfer covers a loss resulting from any introduction attributable to the host government of restrictions on the transfer outside the host country of its currency into a freely usable currency or another currency acceptable to the holder of the guarantee, including a failure of the host government to act within a reasonable period of time on an application by such holder for such transfer.[526] Currency devaluation is not covered, similar to the DFC policy.

Expropriation coverage protects against loss resulting from any legislative action or administrative action or omission attributable to the host government which has the effect of depriving the holder of a guarantee of his ownership or control of, or a substantial benefit from, his investment.[527]

> It would encompass measures attributable to the host government such as nationalization, confiscation, sequestration, seizure, attachment and freezing of assets. The phrase "any legislative or administration action" in the provision includes measures by the executive, but not measures taken by judicial bodies in the exercise of their functions. Measures normally taken by governments to regulate their economic activities such as taxation, environmental and labor legislation as well as normal measures for the maintenance of public safety, are not intended to be covered by this provision unless they discriminate against the holder of the guarantee.[528]

Breach of contract coverage protects against losses arising from the host government's breach or repudiation of a contract with the

[525] *See id.* art. 11.
[526] *See id.*
[527] *See id.*
[528] *See* Commentary on the Convention Establishing the Multilateral Investment Guarantee Agency [hereafter "Commentary"] para. 14.

investor. Indemnification is available only when an investor has no forum to pursue the contractual claim against the government or when recourse to such a forum is hampered by an unreasonable delay or when, after obtaining a final decision in his favor, the investor is unable to enforce it.[529]

War and civil disturbance coverage is intended to include revolutions, insurrections, coups d'état and similar political events which are typically outside the control of the host government. Acts of terrorists and similar activities which are specifically directed against the holder of the guarantee are, however, not intended to be covered by this provision but may be covered under the approval of the Board, by special majority. In any case, the risk of devaluation or depreciation of currency is not covered.[530]

With regard to applicability, North Korea is not eligible to be a host country of an investment guaranteed by MIGA. The MIGA Convention states that "[i]nvestments shall be guaranteed … if they are to be made in the territory of a developing member country."[531] As discussed above, as of 2025, 182 countries are members of MIGA and among them, 154 countries are classified as developing countries. North Korea is neither a member nor a signatory of the MIGA Convention. All other neighboring countries such as China, Russia, Vietnam, and Mongolia are members and enjoy membership status as eligible host countries.

3. Other Multilateral and Private Political Risk Insurance

Beyond the DFC and MIGA, the political risk insurance (PRI) market encompasses national providers, multilateral agencies, private insurers, and reinsurers. On the public side, many countries maintain their own PRI agencies for the benefit of their nationals investing abroad, comparable to the DFC. Multilateral PRI providers include the African Trade Insurance Agency, the Asian Development Bank, the Inter-American Development Bank, the Arab Investment and Export Credit Guarantee Corporation (Dhaman), the Islamic Corporation for the Insurance of Investment and Export Credit, and MIGA.[532] However, policies of these PRIs may not be eligible for the

---

[529] *See id.* para. 15

[530] *See* MIGA Convention art. 11 and Complementary para. 16.

[531] MIGA Convention art. 14.

[532] *See* MIGA, The Political Risk Insurance Industry, WIPR Report 2010 at 55 available at <https://www.miga.org/documents/WIPR10ebookchap3.pdf> (visited May 31, 2025).

investment in North Korea since North Korea is not a member or signatory of such organizations.

On the other hand, the private market's PRI falls into two main categories: (i) political risk activities similar to that of the public insurers as discussed in DFC and MIGA that covers investments in developing countries against expropriation, political violence, and so on; and (ii) developing-country nonpayment risk insurance that covers contract frustration and default by governments.[533] OECD provided some information about PRI providers from both public and private sectors.[534] The private market includes about twenty Lloyd's syndicates and about eight private insurance companies mainly based in London, Bermuda and the United States. These private insurance companies are known as: American International Group Inc. (AIG); Zurich Insurance Group; AXA Group; Atradius; Liberty Specialty Markets; Marsh; and Willis Towers Watson Plc (WTW), among others. Some of the top reinsurers include Munich Re and Hannover Re of Germany, Swiss Re of Switzerland, and Berkshire Hathaway/General Re of the United States.[535]

---

[533] *See id.*

[534] *See* OECD, Investment Policy Perspectives (2008) at 111 and further pages available at <https://www.oecd.org/content/dam/oecd/en/publications/reports/2009/01/oecd-investment-policy-perspectives-2008_g1gha04d/ipp-2008-en.pdf> (visited May 31, 2025).

[535] *See* MIGA, The Political Risk Insurance Industry, WIPR Report 2010 at 55 available at <https://www.miga.org/documents/WIPR10ebookchap3.pdf> (visited May 31, 2025).

[illegible] medical [illegible] insurance companies mainly based in London, Germany and the United States. These private insurance companies are known as American International Group (AIG), Zurich Insurance Group, AXA Group, [illegible] Liberty Mutual, [illegible] and Willis Towers Watson, [illegible] among others. Some of the top names include Munich Re and Hannover Re of Germany, Swiss Re of Switzerland and Berkshire Hathaway/General Re of the United States.

Chapter 5 Risks in Dispute Settlement Mechanism

A. Legal System of North Korea

In view of comparative legal taxonomy, it is not easy to classify the category to which the North Korean legal system belongs. Scholars have proposed various frameworks for categorizing legal systems by culture, geography, and history, but all legal systems — however classified — have been shaped by multiple external influences over in the course of evolution and transformation. Roman law, for example, was itself influenced by Greek philosophy and Christianity; the laws of England and Germany alike bear the imprint of Roman legal thought. Most national legal systems are, in this sense, hybrid and composite. North Korea's law and legal system is no different.

In order to understand current laws and legal system of North Korea, it may be helpful to note following four interrelated factors. First, by using a dichotomous approach[536] that distinguishes common law from civil law, North Korea's law and legal system falls within the civil law family in that it does not recognize precedent judgments and decrees of courts as a source of enforceable law.[537] Instead, all the individual laws are intensively codified although precedent cases are never ignored in the course conducting a trial or practice of law. Moreover, all laws should be interpreted within the ideas written in analects of national leaders, Kim Il Sung, Kim Jong Il and incumbent leader Kim Jong Un.

Second, North Korea's law is also a member of the socialist law family. The socialist law is independent in the classification of legal system. As shown in the laws of the Soviet Union, it is distinguished by: (i) the influence of state ownership of the principal means of production; (ii) the special role that the communist party plays in the legal system; (iii) the close relationship between the legal system and national economic plan; (iv) the denial of distinction between public and private law; and (v) a conception of the role of law as an instrument for restructuring society, shaping the new order and

---

[536] The Black Law Dictionary seems to follow this approach. *See* THE BLACK'S LAW DICTIONARY 246 (6th ed. 1991).

[537] The Soviet Union, influencing North Korean legal system partly, recognized the judgment as a supplementary source of law.

dismantling the old.[538] Laws of North Korea have all of above distinctions.

Third, North Korea's law is also Korean law influenced by Japanese law. The traditional Korean law and legal system, applying to all parts of Korea, had been sustained for one thousand years through two dynasties. It was officially abolished by the Japanese annexation of Korea in 1910. Instead, Japanese law and legal system which were introduced mainly from Germany in the latter part of the 19th century were practiced until the time Korean was liberated from the Japanese rule in August 1945. In November 1945, the Provisional People's Committee of North Korea that governed the northern part of the 38th parallel of the Korean Peninsula promulgated a decree that invalidated Japanese laws and instead initiated making its own laws and regulations. However, newly enacted laws were within the boundary of German-Japanese legal context while adding a distinctly socialist coloration.

Fourth, the laws of North Korea are Juche-oriented ones peculiar to North Korea. The idea of Juche (self-reliance) has been the leading idea in every aspect of national activities including legislation, administrative actions and judgment of law, as earlier described in Chapter II above. As Juche idea is the dominant philosophy in interpreting North Korea's law, analects and instructions of the author of the idea, Kim Il Sung, his son Kim Jong Il and his grandson and current ruler Kim Jong Un, are the ground of studying, enforcing and judging laws. In this aspect, North Korea's law is similar to religious laws such as canon law or sharia.

B. Judicial System in North Korea

In North Korea, justice is administered by the Central Court, the court of the province (or city directly under the central authority such as Pyongyang or Rason), the people's court of the city (or district in a big city) or county, and special courts.[539] Verdicts are delivered under the names of the Democratic People's Republic of Korea.[540] The Central Court is the apex court and supervises the judicial activities of

---

[538] THE NEW ENCYCLOPAEDIA BRITANICA, MACROPAEDIA VOL. 22 939 (15th ed. 1989).

[539] *See* Socialist Constitution of 2023 art. 159.

[540] *Id.*

all other courts.[541] The Central Court is accountable to the Supreme People's Assembly and to the Presidium of the Supreme People's Assembly when the Assembly is not in session.[542]

The provincial court functions as the appellate court except for some cases where by law it acts as a trial court. The people's court is the trial court and is established in cities (not specially authorized to have districts), counties, and urban districts. There are two types of special courts: the military court and the railroad court.[543] Judges of the military court and the railroad court are appointed by the Central Court.[544]

The mission of the Central Court, among others, is to: (1) protect through judicial procedure the State's power and the socialist system established in the DPRK, the property of the State and social/ cooperative organizations, personal rights as guaranteed by the Constitution, lives and property of citizens; (2) ensure that all institutions, enterprises, organizations and citizens abide strictly by the State laws and staunchly combat class enemies and all law-breakers; (3) execute judgement and decisions with regard to property and conduct notarial work,[545] and (4) oversees and control activities of all courts in North Korea.[546]

Subject matter jurisdiction of the Central Court in a civil case is divided into four categories: (1) an extraordinary appeal by the reason of violation of law;[547] (2) a re-trial by the reason of discovery of new evidence after judgment of lower courts;[548] (3) an appeal for the judgment and decisions rendered by provincial courts or special courts,[549] and (4) any case that the Central Court decides to conduct a trial regardless of whether its original jurisdiction belongs to the people's court of county (or city or district) or provincial court.[550]

For cases of a re-trial and an appeal for a decision made by courts other than the Central Court, a three-justice panel of the Central Court

---

[541] See *id.* art. 167; Organizational Law of Courts art. 18.
[542] *See id.* Constitution art. 168.
[543] *See* Organizational Law of Courts art. 3.
[544] *See* Socialist Constitution of 2023 art. 161; *id.* Law art. 5.
[545] *See* Socialist Constitution of 2023 art. 162.
[546] *See* Organizational Law of Courts art. 18.
[547] *See* id. art. 15; Civil Procedure Law art. 263.
[548] *See* Organizational Law of Courts art. 15; Civil Procedure Law art. 279.
[549] *See* Civil Procedure Law art. 19.
[550] *Id.*

conducts a hearing.[551] However, for an extraordinary appeal by the reason of violation of law from a decision by the three-justice panel of the Central Court, an *en banc* court (full court) of the Central Court conducts re-hearings and renders a decision.[552]

The full court for re-hearing consists of all justices of the court including the Chief, the Deputy of the Central Court. [553] The Prosecutor General of the Central Public Prosecutors Office attends the full court hearing without a right to vote.[554] Quorum of the full court hearing is two-thirds of the Central Court justices and the majority vote makes a decision.[555] And an extraordinary appeal to the Central Court by the reason of violation of law can be filed only by the Chief of the Central Court or the Prosecutor General.[556] On the other hand, there is no publication of precedent cases in public. It is unknown to outsiders how the Central Court internally compiles precedent cases and how they are used internally and externally.

The original jurisdiction of a civil trial court varies. If (i) one of parties is an institution (government body), enterprise (public corporation) or organization (cooperative farm or various social organizations) that belongs to the county (or city or urban district) or (ii) parties between citizens of North Korea, people's court of the county (or city or urban district) is the trial court.[557]

The subject matter jurisdiction of a provincial court is: if (i) any case that one of parties is an institution, enterprise or organization that belongs to a province or city directly under the central authority; (ii) any case that a party is a foreigner including foreign legal person, (iii) any case that a party is an institution or enterprise for military supply or special sectors; (iv) an appellate case that comes from a people's court in the province concerned; or (v) any case that the provincial court wishes to conduct it as a trial court.[558] Any appellate case from provincial courts and special courts such as the military court or the railway one is tried by the Central Court [559] in addition an

---

551 *See* Civil Procedure Law art. 267 and 284.

552 *Id.* art. 267. No laws or regulations of North Korea set the number of justices of the Central Court.

553 *See id.* art. 268.

554 *See id.* art. 269.

555 *See id.* art. 268.

556 *See id.* art. 263.

557 *See id.* art. 17.

558 See *id.* art 18.

559 *See id.* art. 19.

extraordinary appeal by the reason of violation of law or re-trial by the discovery of new evidence. However, upper courts (provincial courts and the Central Court respectively) have a power to try by themselves any case originally allocated to their lower courts or to re-allocate any case to other lower courts.[560]

The trial court consists of a judge and two people's assessors.[561] In addition, a public prosecutor, an executor, parities of the suit and the third party who has an interest to the case participate in a trial as responsible members of the court.[562] The judge as chief of the court conducts hearing[563] and casts a vote for judgment along with the two assessors.[564] Judgment is made by the majority vote cast by the judge and the assessors.[565] People's assessors are not necessarily lawyers[566] and they are elected by the people's assembly corresponding level to the court in question.[567] People's assessors conduct inquiries at a hearing along with the judge.[568] The public prosecutor participating in a civil trial can conduct inquiries upon approval of the judge.[569]

The office of public prosecutors (*i.e.* equivalent office of the district attorney in the United State) is established in corresponding jurisdictions to the courts. A public prosecutor's mission is, among other things, to: (1) ensure strict observance of State laws; (2) ensure that decisions and directives of State bodies conform to the Constitution, laws, ordinances, decisions and decrees of various organs; (3) institute legal proceedings against criminals and offenders.[570]

Investigations and prosecutions are conducted under the unified direction of the Central Public Prosecutors' Office. All public prosecutors' offices are subordinate to their higher prosecutors' offices as well as the Central Public Prosecutors' Office.[571] In a civil

---

[560] *See id.* art. 18 and 19.

[561] *See* Socialist Constitution of 2023 art. 163, Organizational Law of Courts art. 9 and Civil Procedure Law art. 177.

[562] *See* Civil Procedure Law art. 38.

[563] *See id.* art. 177.

[564] *See id.* art. 214.

[565] *See id* art. 218.

[566] *See* Organizational Law of Courts art. 6.

[567] *See id.* art. 4.

[568] *See* Civil Procedure Law art. 194.

[569] *See id.*

[570] *See* Socialist Constitution of 2023 art. 156.

[571] *See id.* art. 157.

litigation, a public prosecutor participates in the hearing procedure along with a judge and people's assessors.[572] The prosecutor is required to participate in the important proceedings and he has power to submit his opinion if he finds errors in the proceeding.[573] However, the court can conduct proceedings even if a prosecutor is not appeared at the trial.[574] The prosecutor can conduct an examination to parties after getting an approval from the judge.[575]

Private practice by a licensed-lawyer in North Korea is not as usual as seen in the majority of other countries. Due to the nature of socialism peculiar to North Korea, there is no private practice in law by licensed lawyers. All lawyers must work under the supervision of the committee that he or she belongs to in geography or by the sector.[576] The respective committee as the standing organization under the Central Lawyers Committee is established at the central, provincial (or city directly under the central government) and county (or city) level respectively as well as at necessary sectors.[577] The mission of lawyers is to advocate State's laws and legal system, to abide positively themselves to laws and regulations and ensure client's legal rights and interests.[578]

In practice, however, potential clients' access to licensed lawyers is limited when they are in need of legal services since names or addresses of practicing lawyers are not open to the public. The lawyers' committee only assigns requested legal services to individual lawyers and collects service fees on their behalf.

C. Socialist's Civil Law Conception

Since the establishment of North Korea's socialist government after World War II, new legal conceptions have been developed on socialist foundations. The impetus was partly ideological: the new state needed to repudiate both the class-oriented legal heritage of pre-modern Korea and the capitalist legal framework that Japan had imposed. North Korea maintained that its liberation from Japanese rule was the product of a great revolutionary struggle, one that freed

[572] *See* Civil Procedure Law art 38, 167, 180 and 248.
[573] *See id.* art. 167.
[574] *See id.* art. 180.
[575] *See id.* art 194.
[576] *See* Law for Lawyers 2023 art. 7 and 8.
[577] *See id.* art. 7, 8, 9, 10 and 11.
[578] *See id.* art. 23.

workers and peasants from bourgeois suppression. That narrative required a corresponding rejection of the legal conceptions Japan had introduced and their replacement with a distinctly socialist legal order.

Furthermore, after the Juche idea was articulated, it has been positioned at the apex of interpretation and definition of legal terminology in North Korea. The "Analects of Kim Il Sung" has also been used as the basic instrument for explaining terminology. In these days, the analects of Kim Jong Il and Kim Jong Un have been added for interpretation and study of law. The Kims' analects are the anthology of instructions, expressions and quotations of the Kims produced in the course of ruling the country. These include their ideas about legal conception and guidelines for implementation of laws. According to the Civil Law Dictionary of North Korea, which embodies the analects of the Kims', 'law' is simply defined as one of means to achieve the socialist revolution.[579]

The law of transactions, for example, is explained as an instrument of guaranty to secure bourgeois' transactions. In addition, a stock exchange market is the place where fraud and swindle prevails.[580] A more serious question in interpretation of legal terminology is that in the Civil Law Dictionary, there are often two yardsticks for a term. In explanation of arbitration, for instance, there is not much difference in function, procedure, standing, and so on from any other countries' practice and recognition of arbitration. However, the explanation of arbitration further recognizes other societies' arbitration as very different from its own, defining that bourgeoisie arbitration functions to protect private ownership and monopolized capitalism.[581] Much of the legal terminology has such dual standards. This obviously raises troublesome questions; for example, is it likely that North Korean authority would admit an award of foreign arbitration under its conception?

The following are excerpts from selected entries in the *Minsabeop Sajeon* [Civil Law Dictionary] published by the Press of the Ministry of Social Security of the Democratic People's Republic of Korea in relation to foreign investment.

---

[579] *See* Civil Law Dictionary at 257.
[580] *See id.* at 26.
[581] *See id.* at 532.

(i) Contract: Contract does not exist without an agreement of parties ….. In an order-obedience relationship, contract cannot be formed even though there is an agreement …. The agreement should be to bring out certain legal effect and the effect should be about the matter of property …. Depending on whether or not the contract is based on the project of people's economy plan, there are two types of contract - planned contract and general contract …. The contract system guarantees successful achievement of people's economic plan and it actively contributes to promote workers' materialistic and cultural life.[582]

(ii) Planned Contract: The contract based on people's economy plan between institutions, enterprises, and organizations …. The "planned contract" includes material supply contracts, commodity supply contracts, agricultural product purchase contracts, construction contracts, and cargo transportation contract.[583]

(iii) Contract not based on Plan: Contract that is formed based on two parties' agreement.

(iv) Freedom of Contract: a fraudulent principle in the bourgeois civil law suggesting that an individual can conclude free contract based on one's own will while the State should not interfere with the contract as possible as it can …. This principle, in fact, is … an expression of fraudulent slogan advocated by capitalists to carry out capitalistic exploitation against workers …. Such freedom contributes to only rich capitalists in the society that is economically unequal and dominated by exploitation, suppression …. Freedom is, in practice, the freedom to limitlessly exploit empty-handed workers as shown in employment contracts …. In the stage of imperialism, monopolistic capitalists threw away the fraudulent non-interference policy to overcome escalating contradictions of capitalism and instead have made various "controlling laws" to go forward to fascistization.[584]

---

[582] *See id.* at 126.
[583] *See id.* at 125.
[584] *See id.* at 128 - 29.

(v) Principle of "Agreements of the Parties must be Observed" (*pacta sunt servanda*): A slogan that once concluded contract must be performed. It is bourgeois terminology .... The bourgeois practice this principle on one hand, and they offer contrary principle of "the principle of change of contractual circumstances" (*clausula rebus sic stantibus*) on the other hand .... The latter principle is not to observe the contract once it becomes to be disadvantageous to land owners and capitalists .... This is a reactive (against communism) and anti-people slogan to consolidate capitalists' exploitation by subordinating workers to them and by embellishing this principle through a nominal catch phrase of anti-feudal system.[585]

(vi) Merchant: A class who merchandizes (goods) to make profits .... No social wealth is created by the merchant's activities .... Merchants who own trading capital, with professional skills and knowledge in commerce, conduct business to buy goods from producers at a low price and sell them to consumers in a high price by way of fraud, deceit, and spoils .... Merchants do not exist anymore by the time of completion of socialist revolution.[586]

(vii) Tax: Taxation was born at the same time of appearance of nations and has been serving as a tool for a nation to exploit working class people for thousands of years ... (and) bourgeois countries rake up taxes by way of menace through laws of taxation passed by the parliament that represents interests of the exploiting class .... Capitalist countries superficially assess taxes to the exploiting classes such as capitalists but in practice the taxes are transferred to workers by various legal and illegal ways .... The Great *Suryong* ... took a historical action to have completely abolished taxation system on March 21, 1974 .... The Great *Suryong* and the Great Leader Comrade Kim Jong Il took a wise action to apply taxes to

[585] *See id.* at 130. Parentheses and Latin terms are added by the Author.
[586] *See id.* at 367.

foreign-invested enterprises and foreign individuals in the Rajin-Sonbong Free Economic and Trade Zone.[587]

(viii) Principle of Equality of Trial Parties: It is an introduction of fraudulent slogan in the bourgeois procedural law that everyone must be in equal before law …. But in the capitalist society where everything is done by money, the equality of parties in a civil procedure is severely trampled and destroyed …. This principle is a fraudulent system of procedural law to make working class people obedient to the bourgeois court.[588]

(ix) Lawyer (Attorney at Law): The lawyer in this country, by the Party's judicial policy, assists institutions, enterprises, organizations and people, and contributes to the achievement of people's democratic dictatorship through helping the court's activities …. In capitalist countries, lawyers, as the ones who are used for the disguise of a fair trial, protect interests of, and rationalize delinquency of the capitalist class by maneuvering all possible sly tactics.[589]

(x) Court of Law: The court is the place of hearing and solving cases brought in, and the place for educating people to obey the law …. Courts in bourgeois countries are used as a place to legitimatize exploitation of exploiters such as landowners and capitalists against working class people.[590]

(xi) Judge: A worker who is specialized in presiding over trials …. A judge must advocate and safeguard the Party and the *Suryong*, put into practice the Party's judicial policy, and protect people's life, property and socialist gains from all the criminal invasions …. A judge must take the great Juche idea as a guideline in judicial activities and guarantee accuracy and impartiality in adjudication based on the Party's judicial policy and State's law …. Judges in bourgeois countries are reactionaries who warrant interests of the exploiting class as servants of such class.[591]

---

[587] *See id.* at 437-38. However, in fact, applying tax is made to not only foreign-investment businesses in the Rajin-Sonbong ETZ (presently Rason ETZ) but all foreign-invested businesses in North Korea.

[588] *See id.* at 158.

[589] *See id.* at 269.

[590] *See id.* at 604.

[591] *See id.* at 666.

D. Dispute Settlement by North Korean Law

If a dispute arises between a foreign investor and a North Korean party, various types of mechanisms to settle the dispute can be considered. Aside from litigation, widely recognized mechanisms for dispute settlement in relation to foreign investments are mediation, conciliation and arbitration. Other types of dispute settlement can also be agreed upon bilaterally. Many of North Korean laws for attraction of foreign investment suggest alternative dispute settlements such as arbitration, mediation, consultation or negotiation in addition to litigation where a disagreement or dispute arises in connection with foreign investments between a foreign investor and a North Korean party.[592] Consultation or negotiation is in some cases a prerequisite before a party may proceed to arbitration or litigation, though neither is a formal process in the sense of involving a neutral third party or referee. While North Korea's foreign investment laws repeatedly invoke the need for consultation or negotiation, they provide no procedural rules or guidelines to formalize it. Where the consultation or negotiation is required as a precondition before a dispute is brought to arbitration or litigation, the absence of any type of formality to prove that such a consultation or negotiation has been made but failed could be a source of difficulty.

Arbitration is suggested as a method of dispute settlement in most foreign investment laws of North Korea. Arbitration is often used where making an agreement through consultation or negotiation fails.[593] There are two types of arbitration in North Korea: State arbitration and external economy arbitration. The former is a part of judicial activities that resolve disputes between North Korean entities arisen in the course of implementing the national economy plan as stipulated in the "Arbitration Law" of North Korea.[594] The latter deals with disputes arising out of external economic activities as stipulated in the "Law of External Economy Arbitration" of North Korea.[595]

The External Economy Arbitration Law stipulates rules and procedures to settle disputes in relation to foreign investment, trade,

---

[592] *See* Foreign Investment Law art. 22; Equity Joint Venture Law art. 46; Contractual Joint Venture Law art. 23; Foreign Enterprise Law art. 30; Rason ETZ Law art. 81, 82 and 83; and Foreign Invested-Bank Law art. 42, among others.

[593] *See id.*

[594] *See* Arbitration Law art. 6.

[595] *See* External Economy Arbitration Law art. 1 and 2.

service, maritime, and computer software.[596] However, one thing to note is about enforcement of rendered arbitration award. According to the External Economy Arbitration Law, if a property as a subject matter to be enforced by the arbitration award is located in a foreign country, the award creditor may request a judicial authority of the foreign country for the enforcement of the rendered arbitration award.[597] For a rendered award to be effective in a foreign country, there must be a bilateral or multilateral agreement unless the foreign country in question concedes unilaterally. There is a multilateral agreement in recognition and enforcement of arbitration award rendered in a foreign country.

It is the 1958 Convention on the Recognition and Enforcement of Foreign Arbitral Awards ("New York Convention" hereafter) initiated by the United Nations Commission on International Trade Law (UNCITRAL). By the participation of the New York Convention, enforcement of a rendered arbitration award in North Korea can be assured in other countries.[598]

However, North Korea is not a contracting state of the Convention while 172 states have joined this Convention as of 2025. Accordingly, as long as North Korea stays outside the Convention, the award creditor holding an award rendered by a North Korean arbitral tribunal has no reliable mechanism for securing enforcement abroad. This is the same as an international arbitration case, as discussed below.

All foreign investment laws of North Korea permit litigation as a type of dispute settlement. It is taken for granted that a party can bring in a lawsuit against the other party for the purpose of enforcing a right or seeking a remedy. The Law of Civil Procedure of North Korea ("Civil Procedure Law" hereafter) is, of course, the foundational instrument governing this process. Whether it is well suited to accommodate a foreign investor as a litigating party in internationally connected disputes is, however, a genuine question.

The Civil Procedure Law was designed primarily to adjudicate disputes among domestic institutions, enterprises, organizations, and citizens, though it states that it is applicable to foreign-invested enterprises and foreigners.[599] The Civil Procedure Law says that the

---

[596] *See id.* art. 3.
[597] *See id.* art. 63.
[598] See New York Convention art. I and III.
[599] *See* Civil Procedure Law art. 6.

State should conduct trial activities based on (the interest of) people (the mass)[600] — a concept that raises an immediate question: who are "the people" in this context, and does the term include foreigners? If not, litigation before North Korean courts may be structurally weighted in favor of North Korean parties as a matter of principle. Combined with the unusual Soviet-style trial structure discussed earlier in this work, foreign investors cannot reasonably expect a neutral hearing if a dispute requires adjudication within North Korea.

North Korea enacted the Civil Law on External Relations in 1995. It is the North Korean version of private international law or law of conflicts since it is the law of reference or choice applicable to North Korean legal persons or citizens and foreign legal persons or foreigners with respect to civil disputes related to property or family matters.[601]

Some notable provisions are: (1) if one of the parties is North Korean, the domicile law is the law of North Korea;[602] (2) where intellectual property is the subject matter, North Korea's law is primarily applied;[603] (3) in property transactions such as sale of goods, transportation contracts and insurance contracts, the applicable law is that of a country's agreed upon by the parties;[604] (4) in tort cases, the place of commission of tort is the applicable law;[605] (5) North Korean law is applied in a special economic zone with regard to the property related matters such as establishment of foreign investment enterprises.[606]

E. Dispute Settlement in a Foreign Jurisdiction

A dispute may be taken to an arbitration agency in a third country *i.e.*, neutral party,[607] for settlement if a foreign investor in North Korea needs to solve a problem with a North Korean counterpart.[608]

---

[600] *See id.* art. 4.

[601] *See* Civil Law on External Relations art. 2.

[602] *See id.* art. 7. para. 1.

[603] *See id.* art. 23.

[604] *See id.* art. 24.

[605] *See id.* art. 31

[606] *See id.* art. 27.

[607] The neutral party mentioned here includes an international arbitration tribunal held in the territory of DPRK.

[608] *See* Rason ETZ Law art. Art. 82; Law on Economic Development Zone art. 61; Law on Hwanggumphyong and Wihwado Economic Zone art. 73, etc.

This approach can be applied to all contract cases with North Korean parties in relation to trade, investment and service if the parties agree to submit disputes to arbitration in an agency of the third country as permitted in the Law on External Economic Contract ("External Economic Contract Law" hereafter) of North Korea.[609] In practice, the majority of foreign investment comes from economically developed countries, and those countries generally have a neutral arbitration system or agencies to solve foreign investment disputes. However, filing arbitration in an investor's home country can raise a question of neutrality from North Korea's perspective. Such speculation is supported by North Korea's general conception of distrusting capitalists or so-called bourgeois countries as discussed above.

An international arbitration agency may be preferable to both parties, as it is likely to command greater credibility than a domestic institution. Two international arbitration bodies are the most widely accepted across the world: the International Centre for Settlement of Investment Disputes (ICSID) and the International Court of Arbitration of the International Chamber of Commerce (ICC Court).

ICSID, an agency of the World Bank Group, was established by the Convention on the Settlement of Investment Disputes between States and Nationals of Other States ("ICSID Convention" or "Washington Convention" hereafter) in 1966. As of 2025, it had 158 contracting parties. Based on the Convention, rules for arbitration and conciliation were respectively made in 1967.

Mutual consent by the parties to submit such disputes to arbitration constitutes a binding agreement which requires that any arbitral award be complied with.[610] While ICSID provides facilities for the arbitration (or conciliation) of disputes, the tribunal consists of a sole arbitrator or any uneven number of arbitrators appointed as the parties agree.[611] The majority of the arbitrators should not be nationals of either party except when it occurs because the sole arbitrator or arbitrators are appointed by agreement of the parties.[612]

However, the ICSID Convention is only applicable to disputes between contracting States and nationals of other contracting

[609] *See* Law on External Economic Contract art. 2.
[610] *See* Washington Convention the sixth paragraph of the preamble..
[611] *See id.* art. 37(2)(a).
[612] *See id.* art. 39.

States,[613] and North Korea is not a contracting State as of 2025. Accordingly, any party who needs an arbitral award in relation to foreign investment in North Korea does not have an opportunity to bring disputes to the most well-known international arbitration agency.

The ICC Court, established in 1923, is a non-governmental arbitration agency to deal with disputes arising from international trade and investment. The ICC Court is a widely recognized arbitration agency with a high reputation based on factors such as neutrality, speed and economy, and confidentiality. The ICC Court has its own Rules of both arbitration and conciliation and clauses of the Rules have been used in international investment agreements.[614] Under the Rules of Arbitration of International Chamber of Commerce ("ICC Rules" hereafter) of 2021, the Court does not itself settle disputes but it functions to ensure application of the Rules.[615] Any party — whether private or a state — can file arbitration with the ICC Court regardless of a membership of the ICC but parties must submit an agreement to the arbitration. Arbitration is initiated by the submittal of a request by one party and an answer by the other party.[616] Disputes will be decided by a sole arbitrator or by three arbitrators appointed by the Court unless the parties agree to appoint respectively an arbitrator or jointly the president of the arbitral tribunal.[617]

The Chamber of Commerce of North Korea was established in 2004 and enacted the Law on the Chamber of Commerce in 2010 to give the Chamber and its sub-organizations legal grounds for their activities. The Chamber of Commerce of North Korea has not yet joined ICC as of 2025 though ICC membership is in any event not a prerequisite for participation in ICC arbitration.

The ICC Rules state, like other arbitration rules, that every award is binding on the parties. Where a prevailing party against a North Korean party wishes to enforce the rendered award, it must file a petition with the relevant court of North Korea based on the agreement of both parties submitted to the ICC Court as required. However, if the North Korean court rejects the petition — on grounds

---

613 *See id.* art. 1(2)

614 *See* MUCHLINSKI, *supra* at 539.

615 See the ICC Rules art. 1 para. 2.

616 *See id.* art. 4-5.

617 *See id.* art. 12.

of procedural deficiency, national policy, or otherwise — or the losing party mounts a challenge on some other basis, the award creditor has no effective means of securing enforcement. In the absence of a relevant bilateral or multilateral treaty between the countries of both parties, risks for unavailability to secure enforcement are greater.

One of the generally accepted means to secure such a rendered award in the international society is to resort to the 1958 New York Convention which was initiated by the UNCITRAL as discussed above. The New York Convention declares that:

> [T]his Convention shall apply to the recognition and enforcement of arbitral awards made in the territory of a State other than the State where the recognition and enforcement of such awards are sought .... It shall also apply to arbitral awards not considered as domestic awards in the State where their recognition and enforcement are sought.[618]

Arbitration Rules of the ICC Court are relatively flexible in selection of a forum. Therefore, the tribunal can be held in any place including North Korea if the parties agree.[619] An award by such arbitration is not considered a domestic one as the Convention embraces flexibility.

However, North Korea was not a signatory of the New York Convention as of 2025 as mentioned above. Accordingly, any arbitration agreement between a North Korean party and a foreign investor has no means to secure enforcement of rendered awards unless North Korea voluntarily accepts the awards and abides itself. As long as North Korea remains outside the Convention, arbitration clauses in North Korean foreign investment laws offer considerably less protection than they might appear to.

Beyond the ICC Court, other non-governmental international arbitration institutions capable of handling disputes between a foreign investor and a North Korean party include the Australian Centre for International Commercial Arbitration, the Hong Kong International Arbitration Centre, the Singapore International Arbitration Centre, and the London Court of International Arbitration, among others. Aside from them, North Korea may join as a signatory the Permanent

---

[618] New York Convention art. 1.

[619] *See* ICC Rules art. 18.

Court of Arbitration at Hague and the Regional Arbitration Centres of the Asian-African Legal Consultative Committee at Kuala Lumpur as they are serving member states. Separately, disputes could be submitted to the Korean Commercial Arbitration Board (KCAB) in Seoul, which is an impartial and neutral institution. The KCAB handles disputes between parties from the third countries if they agree on the place of arbitration as Seoul or Republic of Korea.

In summary, North Korea's continued exclusion from the principal international dispute settlement frameworks imposes a measurable cost on its ability to attract foreign investment. The most immediate and practical step would be accession to the New York Convention, which would at once give meaning to the arbitration clauses already present in North Korea's own foreign investment laws.

Chapter 6 Risks in the Context of International Politics

Since North Korea's formation, there has been no meaningful economic relationship between North Korea and the Western world, and in particular the United States. A body of U.S. law and regulation governs various forms of economic intercourse with North Korea, reflecting a political confrontation that has continued since the outbreak of the Korean War in 1950. Under the rubric of economic sanctions and embargoes, U.S. laws and regulations prohibit or restrict American citizens, corporations, businesses, and financial institutions from trading with, investing in, or otherwise assisting North Korea.

A. Economic Sanctions by the United States

1. Background of Economic Sanctions on North Korea

The first economic sanction on North Korea was imposed by the United States in June 28, 1950 three days after the Korean War broke out. It was an export embargo to suspend all export licenses to sell commodities to North Korea based on the Export Control Act of 1949.[620] This was the genesis of dozens of various economic sanctions further imposed by the United States against North Korea up until these days. In December 1950, President Truman proclaimed the existence of a national emergency caused by communist aggression, invoking authority granted by the Trading with the Enemy Act (TWEA) of 1917.[621] Since then Comprehensive sanctions measures against North Korea derived from this "national emergency authority" of the TWEA. Although this authority was replaced in 1977 by the International Emergency Economic Power Act (IEEPA),[622] the sanction measures have been continued through the Presidential Determination of yearly extensions of the authority in the national interest of the United States.

---

[620] *See* Federal Register vol. 15, number 126 (15 F.R § 4189, published on June 30, 1950).

[621] *See* Presidential Proclamation 2914 on December 16, 1950 available at <https://www.trumanlibrary.gov/library/public-papers/304/proclamation-2914-proclaiming-existence-national-emergency> (visited June 5, 2025).

[622] 50 U.S.C. § 1701 – 1706.

In June 1951, by the section 5 of the Trade Agreement Extension Act of 1951, the United States suspended the most favored nation (MFN) status to all imports from the Soviet Union and other communist nations or communist controlled areas.[623] In August, President Truman issued a proclamation to implement above Act effective September 1, 1951[624] and he included "any part of Korea which may be under communist domination or control" as a suspended MFN status nation or area in his letter to the Secretary of Treasury the same date as the issuance of the proclamation.[625] This provision had been carried over to the newly enacted Tariff Schedules of the United States (TSUS) of 1962 as stipulated in the 3(d) of the General Headnotes and Rules of Interpretation as "Korea (any part which may be under communist domination or control)."[626] This status continues until now as North Korea was classified as a "Column Two" state by the current Harmonized Tariff Schedule (HTS) as discussed below.[627]

In August 1955, the United States (Department of State) issued the International Traffic in Arms Regulations (ITAR) which denied exports and imports of defense articles and defense services destined or originating in certain countries including North Korea.[628] These regulations are still effective as of September 2025.

In September 1961, the Foreign Assistance Act was enacted in order to promote United States' foreign policy, security and general

---

[623] *See* Trade Agreement Extension Act of 1951 sec. 5. The term MFN was changed to "(Permanent) Normal Trade Relations (PNTR or NTR)" in 1998 but these terms are often used interchangeably.

[624] *See* Presidential Proclamation 2935 on August 1, 1951 available at <https://www.govinfo.gov/content/pkg/STATUTE-65/pdf/STATUTE-65-PgC23.pdf > (visited June 6, 2025).

[625] *See* Code of Regulations, Title III – the President, 1949-1953 Compilation at 1043 published by the National Archives and Records Service, General Service Administration, Washington D.C. (1958).

[626] *See* General Headnotes and Rules of Interpretation, Tariff Schedule of the United States of 1963, available at <https://www.gpo.gov/fdsys/pkg/STATUTE-77/pdf/STATUTE-77A-PgI.pdf> (visited June 6, 2025).

[627] *See* Harmonized Tariff Schedule of the United States Rev. 11 (2025), General Notes 3(b) available at < file:///C:/Users/User/Downloads/General%20Note%203%20(2).pdf> (visited June 6, 2025). As of June 2025, only four states are classified as "Column Two" and the others are Cuba, Belarus, and Russia.

[628] *See* 22 C.F.R § 126.1.

welfare by assisting peoples of the third world for their economic and social development. However, this law prohibits any assistance to communist countries including North Korea except for assistance to schools, libraries and hospitals founded or sponsored by United States citizens.[629] This provision is still effective as of September 2025.

In October 1968, the Foreign Military Sales Act which was later renamed as the Arms Export Control Act (AECA) in 1976 was enacted in order to support the United States government to sell defense services and military articles to benevolent countries. The AECA prohibits transactions with countries supporting international terrorism.[630] North Korea was automatically included when it was designated as a state-sponsor of terrorism in January 1988.

In January 1988, pursuant to the Export Administration Act of 1979, the United States designated North Korea as a state sponsor of international terrorism following the destruction of Korean Air Flight 858 over the Indian Ocean in November 1987, an attack by North Korean agents that killed 115 people. U.S. persons were accordingly restricted from trading in goods or conducting financial transactions with North Korea or its nationals.

North Korea was also barred from receiving U.S. foreign assistance except for solely humanitarian purposes under the Foreign Assistance Act of 1961.[631] The prohibition clause of the FAA has included wide range of bans or restrictions about various foreign assistance stipulated in the Food for Peace Act,[632] the Peace Corps Act,[633] the Export-Import Bank Act of 1945.[634]

In October 1994, the United States and North Korea concluded the so-called "Agreed Framework"[635] which provided, among other things, for the replacement of North Korea's graphite-moderated nuclear reactors with light-water reactor power plants considered less susceptible to weapons proliferation, and for movement toward full normalization of political and economic relations. In February 1995

[629] *See* 22 U.S.C. § 2370(f) (2021) and 22 U.S.C.§ 2174(a) and (b) (1985).

[630] *See* 22 U.S.C. § 2780 (2014).

[631] *See* 22 U.S.C. § 9673 (2018) and 22 U.S.C. § 2371 (2008).

[632] *See* 7 U.S.C. § 1691 (2008) and 1691a (2008).

[633] *See* 22 U.S.C. § 2501 (1985) *et seq.*

[634] *See* 12 U.S.C. § 635 (2015) *et seq.* Especially the Direct Loan Program of the Export-Import Bank is closely related to the foreign direct investment of U.S. businesses in foreign countries.

[635] Its full title was the "Agreed Framework between the United States of America and the Democratic People's Republic of Korea." It broke down in 2003.

as a follow-up action, the United States amended the Trading with the Enemy Act and relevant federal regulations to ease a large portion of economic sanctions in order to begin reducing barriers in trade and investment. The United States: (i) authorized U.S. dollar transactions with North Korean parties through the banking system; (ii) authorized transactions related to operation of diplomatic missions; (iii) allowed U.S. persons travel to North Korea in addition to removal of 200 U.S. dollar limit of travel expenditure; (iv) allowed import of North Korean-origin magnesite and magnesia; (v) allowed establishing offices of news organizations in each country; and (vi) allowed exports or imports of information or information materials if not prohibited by national security, antiterrorism or nonproliferation, among other things.[636]

In May 1996, the United States imposed sanctions on North Korea and Iran based on the Arms Export Control Act and the Export Administration Act of 1979. By these sanctions, the United States prohibited exports to North Korea and contracts with North Korean government as well as Changgwang Sinyong Corporation as known as Korea Mining Development Trading Bureau (KOMID), North Korea's main missile exporter, for missile equipment or technology covered by the Missile Technology Control Regime (MTCR).[637]

In April 1998, under the same statutory authority, the United States imposed further sanctions on Changgwang Sinyong Corp., prohibiting U.S. persons from trading with or contracting with the entity, in response to North Korea's missile proliferation activities involving Pakistan.[638] This company and its successors and subsidiaries were sanctioned more than a dozen additional times through the 2010s in connection with weapons of mass destruction (WMD) proliferation activities conducted with counterparts in Iran, Yemen, China, Russia, Sudan, Syria, and elsewhere.

---

[636] *See* 31 C.F.R. § 510 (1995) published on the Federal Register Vol. 60. No. 32 on February 16, 1995 at 8933-5 available at <https://www.govinfo.gov/content/pkg/FR-1995-02-16/pdf/FR-1995-02-16.pdf> (visited June 6, 2025).

[637] *See* Public Notice 2404 of the Bureau of Political-Military Affairs of the Department of State published on the Federal Register Vol. 61, No. 114 on June 12, 1996 at 29785 available at <https://www.gpo.gov/fdsys/pkg/FR-1996-06-12/pdf/96-14826.pdf> (visited June 6, 2025).

[638] *See* Federal Register Vol. 63 No. 85 on May 4, 1998 at 24585.

In September 1999, as North Korea pledged to freeze its long-range missile tests, President Clinton announced his decision to ease economic sanctions against North Korea. In June 2000, the United States authorized U.S. persons to have transactions involving property with North Korea or its nationals. Newly authorized transactions included exports to, investment in and brokering with North Korea or its nationals.

By this action, U.S. citizens were allowed to travel to North Korea without permission. But an import notification to and approval from the authority, Office of Foreign Assets Control (OFAC), was required for all imports from North Korea in order to screen if statutorily prohibited articles would be included. And property of North Korea previously blocked pursuant to the TWEA remained blocked as of June 16, 2000 and further continued blocked.[639]

In January 2002 four month after the September 11 attacks in New York and Washington D.C., President Bush labeled North Korea as part of the "Axis of Evil" that threatened the peace of the world. In January 2003, North Korea declared its withdrawal from the Nuclear Nonproliferation Treaty (NPT). In August of the same year, the first round of the multilateral six-party talks comprised of representatives from the United States, South Korea, Japan, China, Russia and North Korea was held with a view to resolving the issues of development of North Korea's nuclear weapons and long-range missiles.

In June 2005, while the six-party talks were stalled, the United States has listed three North Korean business entities to prohibit transactions with U.S. citizens as they were designated as responsible entities for the WMD and missile programs. Their assets in the United States were also frozen.[640]

In September 2005, the Unites States designated Banco Delta Asia (BDA), a Macau bank, as a "primary money laundering concern" under the section 311 of the USA Patriot Act[641] because it represented an unacceptable risk of money laundering and other financial crimes

---

[639] *See* Federal Register Vol. 65 No. 118 on June 19, 2000 at 38165-6 available at <https://www.gpo.gov/fdsys/pkg/FR-2000-06-19/pdf/00-15390.pdf> (visited Jan. 23, 2026).

[640] *See* Executive Order 13382 of June 28, 2005 available at <https://ofac.treasury.gov/media/8581/download?inline>. *See* also OFAC available at <https://ofac.treasury.gov/sanctions-programs-and-country-information/north-korea-sanctions> (visited June 6, 2025).

[641] *See* 31 U.S.C. § 5318A (2006).

for North Korea.[642] The United States subsequently froze about 25 million US dollars of North Korean funds until it was released in June 2007.

In May 2006, the United Sates prohibited persons subject to the U.S. jurisdiction from owning, leasing, operating, or insuring any vessel flagged by North Korea.[643] In October 2006, in order to comply with the resolution 1695 (July 15, 2006) of the United Nations Security Council, the United States amended the Iran and Syria Nonproliferation Act by adding "North Korea" after "Iran" to further impose sanctions along with two other countries.[644]

Just four days before that amendment was finalized, North Korea conducted an underground nuclear test at Punggye-ri in the northeast of the Korean Peninsula. The UN Security Council responded immediately by adopting Resolution 1718, imposing economic sanctions on North Korea.

In December 2006, the United States also imposed sanctions on North Korea according to the section 102(b) (2) of the Arms Export Control Act as amended[645] and the section 129 of the Atomic Energy Act[646] to prohibit assistance except for humanitarian one followed by additional measures for prohibiting persons subject to the U.S. jurisdiction from registering vessels in North Korea in February 2007.[647]

In February 2007, at the last session of the fifth round six-party talks, the United States agreed to begin the process of removing North Korea from its designation as a state sponsor of terrorism — a status

---

[642] *See* Press Release from the Department of Treasury dated September 15, 2005.

[643] *See* Federal Register Vol. 71, No. 66 / Thursday, April 6, 2006 at 17346 available at <https://ofac.treasury.gov/media/4746/download?inline> (visited June 6, 2025).

[644] *See* Iran, North Korea and Syria Nonproliferation Act (INKSNA). 50 U.S.C.A. § 1701 Notes.

[645] *See* 22 U.S.C. § 2799aa-1(b) (2014).

[646] *See* 42 U.S.C. § 2158 (2008). *See* also Presidential Determination on Sanctions against North Korea for Detonation of a Nuclear Explosive Device (Presidential Determination No. 2007-7 of December 7, 2006) available at <https://www.govinfo.gov/content/pkg/FR-2007-01-16/pdf/07-133.pdf> (visited June 7, 2025).

[647] *See* Federal Register / Vol. 72, No. 22 / Friday, February 2, 2007 at 4960 available at <https://www.govinfo.gov/content/pkg/FR-2007-02-02/pdf/E7-1702.pdf> (visited June 7, 2025).

North Korea had held since 1988 — and to cease applying the Trading with the Enemy Act (TWEA). In June 2007, North Korea confirmed that the North Korean funds frozen at the Banco Delta Asia were transferred to North Korea's foreign accounts.

In June 2008, upon North Korea's delivery of a declaration disclosing its plutonium-based nuclear programs to China, chair-state of the six-party talks, President George W. Bush issued a proclamation stating that continuation of exercising his authority given by the TWEA with respect to North Korea is no longer in the national interest of the United States.[648]

At the same time he also issued a memorandum to rescind North Korea's designation as a state-sponsor of terrorism by stating that:

(i) the Government of North Korea has not provided any support for international terrorism during the preceding 6-month period; and
(ii) the Government of North Korea has provided assurances that it will not support acts of international terrorism in the future.[649]

However, at the same time, he issued an executive order declaring a national emergency to deal with the threat triggered by proliferation of weapon-usable fissile material on the Korean Peninsula; thus, he would continue certain restrictions on blocked property in the United States, prohibition of registration of vessel in North Korea and exporting sensitive materials to North Korea, among others, as authorized by the TWEA and IEEPA.[650]

---

[648] *See* "Presidential Proclamation 8271 – Termination of the Exercise of Authorities Under the Trading With the Enemy Act With Respect to North Korea" on June 26, 2008 available at <https://www.gpo.gov/fdsys/pkg/WCPD-2008-06-30/pdf/WCPD-2008-06-30-Pg911-2.pdf> (visited June 9, 2025).

[649] *See* "Memorandum on Certification of Rescission of North Korea's Designation as a State Sponsor of Terrorism" on June 26, 2008 available at <https://www.gpo.gov/fdsys/pkg/WCPD-2008-06-30/pdf/WCPD-2008-06-30-Pg912.pdf> (visited June 9, 2025).

[650] *See* Executive Order 13466 – Continuing Certain Restrictions With Respect to North Korea and North Korean Nationals on June 26, 2008 available at *id.* website.

In August 2010, President Obama issued an executive order imposing sanctions against North Korea in response to its unprovoked attack on a South Korean naval vessel, nuclear device testing, ballistic missile launches, procurement of luxury goods in violation of UN Security Council resolutions, and illicit activities including money laundering, counterfeiting, and narcotics trafficking. By this order, the United States blocked all North Korean property and property interests within U.S. jurisdiction and prohibited trading in arms or related materials and luxury goods, engaging in financial transactions, money laundering, counterfeiting, bulk cash smuggling, narcotics trafficking, and other illicit economic activities.[651]

In April 2011, President Obama issued a further executive order prohibiting certain transactions with North Korea, including restrictions on the import of goods, services, and technologies of North Korean origin.[652]

In January 2015, President Obama issued an executive order for additional sanctions against North Korea due to provocative, destabilizing and repressive actions and policies of North Korea including its destructive, coercive cyber-related actions in 2014 in violations of UN Security Councils resolutions. By this executive order, all property and interests in the property in the U.S. jurisdictions of an agency, instrumentality, or controlled entity, officials of the North Korean government or the Workers' Party of Korea were blocked and restricted to trade or transact in addition to suspending such related North Korean to enter the United States.[653]

In April 2015, President Obama again issued an executive order for blocking the property of certain persons engaging in significant malicious cyber-enabled activities that certainly include North Korea's illicit cyber activities.[654]

In February 2016 after North Korea's fourth nuclear test, the United States enacted the North Korea Sanctions and Policy Enhancement Act (NKSPEA) of 2016 that provided comprehensive and more stringent sanctions to address North Korea's nuclear and

---

[651] *See* Executive Order 13551 of August 30, 2010 on the Federal Register Vol. 75 No. 169 at 53837-9.

[652] *See* Executive Order 13570 of April 18, 2011 on the Federal Register Vol 76 No. 76 at 22291-2.

[653] *See* Executive Order 13687 of January 2, 2015 on Federal Register Vol. 80 No. 3 at 819-20.

[654] *See* Executive Order 13694 of April 1, 2015 on Federal Register Vol. 80 No. 63 at 18077-9.

missile development programs, human rights abuses, illicit financial activities, and cyber operations.[655]

In March 2016, President Obama issued another executive order blocking property of the government of North Korea, and prohibiting transactions with respect to North Korea in response to its launching ballistic missile in February and conducting nuclear test in January of the same year. In this executive order, he reaffirmed previous sanctions and expanded range of sanctions based on the International Emergency Act, United Nations Participation Act of 1945, North Korea Sanctions and Policy Enhancement Act of 2016, Immigration and Nationality Act of 1952 and in view of the United Nations Security Council Resolution 2270 of March 2, 2016.[656] The order added two individuals, fifteen public and semi-public entities — including the Propaganda and Agitation Department of the Workers' Party of Korea — and twenty North Korean or North Korea-related vessels to the sanctions list.[657]

In July 2016, the United States designated additional eleven individuals and five entities to the specially designated nationals list including North Korea's leader Kim Jong Un and North Korea's power base the Organization and Guidance Department of the Workers' Party of Korea.[658]

In December 2016, President Obama issued the Executive Order 13757 that amended the previous E.O. 13694. In this E.O., the President added five Russian entities and four Russian individuals as specially designated nationals (SDN) in relation to the cyber activities. Their properties in the United States are blocked and might not be transferred, paid, exported, withdrawn, or otherwise dealt in. It also added to the E.O. 13694 another prohibited cyber activity of "tampering with, altering or causing a misappropriation of information with the purpose or effect of interfering with or undermining

[655] *See* 22 U.S.C. § 9201 *et seq.*

[656] *See* Executive Order 13722 of March 15, 2016 on Federal Register Vol. 81 No. 53 at 14943-5.

[657] The list of these specially designated nationals is available at OFAC's website at <https://home.treasury.gov/policy-issues/financial-sanctions/recent-actions/20160316> (visited June 7. 2025).

[658] *See* the specially designated nationals list available at OFAC's website at <https://home.treasury.gov/policy-issues/financial-sanctions/recent-actions/20160706 > (visited Jan. 24, 2022).

election process or institutions."[659] This applies to the case of North Korean cyber activities.

In June 2017, the United States added to the Specially Designated Nationals List (SDNL) five individuals and ten entities including the State Affairs Commission of North Korea, chaired by Kim Jong Un, and the Korean People's Army, among others.

In September 2017, President Trump issued the Executive Order 13810 imposing additional sanctions which were deep and wide against North Korea since sanctions were first imposed during the Korean War.[660] This Executive Order clarified a wide range of trade-related activities to be sanctioned if North Korean individuals or entities acted as prescribed in the Executive Order. That is, all property and interests in property subject to either personal or subject-matter jurisdiction of the United States are blocked and may not be transferred, paid, exported, withdrawn or otherwise dealt in.[661] It also contained that funds in the U.S. jurisdiction were blocked and were not allowed to be transferred, paid, withdrawn, etc. in addition to prohibiting U.S. persons from transacting with sanctioned individuals or entities.[662] Foreign financial institutions could be also sanctioned if they conducted prescribed activities, such as significant transactions with specially designated persons or entities, the Government of North Korea or the Workers' Party of Korea including their officials, as stipulated in the Order.[663]

This measure is called a type of secondary boycott. Included targets for the sanction are: (i) an aircraft in which a foreign person has an interest that has landed at a place in North Korea may not land at a place in the United States within 180 days after departure from North Korea; (ii) any vessel in which a foreign person has an interest that has called at a port in North Korea within the previous 180 days may not call at a port in the United States; and (iii) any vessel in which a foreign person has an interest that has engaged in a ship-to-ship transfer with such a vessel within previous 180 days may also not call at a port in the United States.[664]

---

[659] *See* Executive Order 13757 of December 28, 2016 on the Federal Register Vol. 82 No. 1 at 18077-9.

[660] *See* Executive Order 13810 of September 25, 2017 on the Federal Register Vol. 82 No. 184 at 47705-9.

[661] *See id.* Section 1. *See* also 31 C.F.R. § 510.201(a).

[662] *See id.* Section 3. *See* also 31 C.F.R. § 510.201(d).

[663] *See id.* Section 4. *See* also 31 C.F.R. § 510.201(a) and 31 C.F.R. § 510.210.

[664] *See id.* Section 2. *See* also 31 C.F.R. § 510.208 and 31 C.F.R. § 510.518.

In November 2017, President Trump announced that North Korea would be re-designated a 'state sponsor of terrorism' nine years after the U.S. government rescinded North Korea's designation as a state-sponsor of terrorism in 2008. In the next day, the Department of Treasury of the United States (OFAC) announced a list of specially designated nationals (SDNs) including one individual, thirteen entities and twenty vessels.[665]

As of September 2025, property and interests in property of designated persons and entities of North Korea including the Government of North Korea and the Workers' Party of Korea have been blocked based on wide range of possible activities that could be conducted by individuals, entities including instrumentalities, agencies or internal organs of North Korean government and/or the Workers' Party of Korea.

Pursuant to the Executive Order 13570 (April 18, 2011), importing from North Korea into the United States has not been allowed unless obtaining license or exemption from the Department of Treasury. This prohibition applies to goods, services and technology that are used as components of finished products of a third country or substantially transformed in a third country.[666]

Pursuant to the Executive Order 13722 (March 16, 2016), exporting or re-exporting goods, services and technology to North Korea from the United States or by a U.S. person wherever located directly or indirectly is not allowed. The Bureau of Industry and Security of the Department of Commerce maintains authority to license exports of goods and technology in general.[667]

Pursuant to the Executive Order 13722, new investment in North Korea by U.S. persons without a license from OFAC or applicable exemption is prohibited.[668] As to the travel by ordinary citizens of the United States to North Korea, according to the Travel Advisory of the Department of State, North Korea is classified as a travel advisory "Level 4: Do Not Travel" as of August 27, 2025 due to the

---

[665] See OFAC website available at <https://home.treasury.gov/policy-issues/financial-sanctions/recent-actions/20171121> (visited June 7, 2025).

[666] *See* North Korea Sanctions Program, OFAC, Department of the Treasury, available at <https://ofac.treasury.gov/sanctions-programs-and-country-information/north-korea-sanctions> (visited June 7, 2025).

[667] *See* id.

[668] *See* id.

"continuing serious risk of arrest, long-term detention, and the threat of wrongful detention of U.S. citizens."[669]

As of the time of writing, sanctions against North Korea are implemented under at least twenty-two U.S. statutes and justified on more than twenty distinct grounds, including proliferation of weapons of mass destruction, U.S. national security, communism, non-market economy status, terrorism, cybersecurity, human rights, counterfeiting, money laundering, and narcotics trafficking, etc.

2. United States Statutes of Economic Sanctions on North Korea[670]

The United States has enacted at least twenty-two statutes bearing on economic sanctions against North Korea. Some classify North Korea as a communist country or a supporter of international terrorism. Others regulate the conduct of North Korean natural or legal persons engaged in prohibited or restricted activities. Still others impose affirmative obligations on the U.S. government and its agencies in furtherance of legislative and policy objectives.

The North Korea Sanctions and Policy Enhancement Act (NKSPEA) of 2016 is the most comprehensive law that sanctions against North Korea's illicit activities. Grounds of sanctions in this Act include development and proliferation of weapons of mass destruction, violation of United Nations' resolutions, censorship, cybersecurity, money laundering, counterfeit, supporting terrorism, and abusing human rights including forced and indentured labor, among others. The NKSPEA focuses on sanctioning North Korea's economic activities through blocking its assets and properties in the United States or within its jurisdiction, controlling export via license and transactions of defense articles and services, seizure and

---

[669] *See* website of the Department of State available at <https://travel.state.gov/en/international-travel/travel-advisories/north-korea.html> (visited August 27, 2025).

[670] Economic sanctions by the United States against North Korea are so deep and wide that it may not be available to contain all details in this sub-subchapter. For comprehensive information on this issue, readers may refer to an official report titled "North Korea: Legislative Basis for U.S. Economic Sanctions" appreciatively conducted and updated by the Congressional Research Service (CRS) of the United States. As of June 2025, the most recent report (updated May 31, 2023) can be found at <https://sgp.fas.org/crs/row/R41438.pdf> (visited June 7, 2025).

forfeiture of a vessel, aircraft, or conveyance used to facilitate illicit activities, and denying visas to sanctioned persons, among others.

The Iran, North Korea, and Syria Nonproliferation Act (INKSNA) of 2006 as amended is to sanction against North Korea for its nonproliferation activities.

The International Emergency Economic Powers Act (IEEPA) of 1977 as amended authorizes the U.S. President to investigate, regulate or prohibit any transactions in foreign exchange, transfers of credit or payment between, by, through, or to any banking institution, block during the pendency of an investigation, regulate, direct and compel, nullify, void, prevent or prohibit, any acquisition, holding, withholding, use, transfer, withdrawal, transportation, importation or exportation, among many other things.[671] The IEEPA grants the president wide range of powers to intercept any financial transactions of hostile countries such as North Korea.

The Arms Export Control Act (AECA) of 1976 as amended through its sections 35,[672] 40,[673] 40A,[674] 73,[675] 101[676] and 102[677] authorizes the president to control the import and the export of defense articles and services in the Munitions List with certain countries such as North Korea by the reasons of supporting terrorism, and proliferation of weapons of mass destruction, among others.

The Bretton Woods Agreement Act (BWAA) of 1945 as amended in its section 43 authorizes the Secretary of the Treasury to instruct the United States Executive Director of the Fund to actively oppose any facility involving use of the International Monetary Fund (IMF) credit by any Communist dictatorship like North Korea.[678] This statute also authorizes the Secretary of Treasury to instruct the Executive Director of the United States to the IMF to work in opposition to any extension of financial or technical assistance to any country that: (i) permits entry into the territory of such country to any person who has committed an act of international terrorism, including any act of aircraft hijacking, or otherwise supports, encourages, or harbors such person; or (ii) fails to take appropriate measures to

[671] *See* 50 U.S.C. § 1702 (2001).
[672] *See* 22 U.S.C. § 2778 (2014); 22 C.F.R. § 126.1; and 27 C.F.R. § 447.52.
[673] *See* 22 U.S.C. § 2780 (2014).
[674] *See* 22 U.S.C. § 2781.
[675] *See* 22 U.S.C. § 2797b (2014).
[676] *See* 22 U.S.C. § 2799aa (2014).
[677] *See* 22 U.S.C. § 2799aa-1 (2014).
[678] *See* 22 U.S.C. § 286aa (1993).

prevent any such person from committing any such act outside the territory of such country. North Korea is included in this category. The BWEE has operated as a gatekeeper preventing North Korea from membership in international financial institutions, with the result that North Korea is unable to access financial support from bodies such as the World Bank, the IMF, and the Asian Development Bank (AsDB). Probably, the only IFI that North Korea can be a member may be the Asian Infrastructure Investment Bank (AIIB) led by China but has not joined it yet. .

The Foreign Assistance Act of 1961 as amended stipulates that any funds for foreign assistance should not be used for North Korea as it is a communist country and a country to repeatedly support for acts of international terrorism.[679]

The Trade Act of 1974 as amended sanctions North Korea with the grounds of communist country, nonmarket economy, prohibition of emigration, market disruption, among others. By this statute, North Korea is classified as a column 2 country of the harmonized tariff schedule and is denied as a permanent normal trade relations (PNTR) status. As a result, North Korean products imported to the United States are charged with high rate of customs duty.[680]

Additional sanction measures against North Korea are embedded in the Export-Import Bank Act of 1945 as amended, the Immigration and Nationality Act of 1952 as amended, the International Financial Institutions Act of 1977 as amended, the International Security and Development Cooperation Act of 1945 as amended, the National Emergency Act of 1976 as amended, the Ports and Waterways Safety Act 1972 as amended, the State Department Basic Authorities Act of 1956 as amended, the Trade Sanctions Reform and Export Enhancement Act of 2000, the Trafficking Victims Protection Act of 2000, the United Nations Participation Act of 1945 as amended, and the USA Patriot Act of 2001, and as of 2021, the most recent legislation is the Otto Warmbier North Korea Nuclear Sanctions Act of 2019.

Dozens of administrative regulations further extend and elaborate these statutory sanctions. The path out of this comprehensive sanctions regime requires North Korea to transform its fundamental political and economic character: from a communist,

---

[679] *See* 22 U.S.C. § 2227 (2007), 2370(f) (2008), 2370(t) (2008), and 2371 (2008).

[680] *See* 19 U.S.C. § 2431, 2432 (1998), 2436 (1999) and 2439.

centrally planned, and militarized system to one that is democracy, economy-in-transition, and committed to peace. At this point, a raised question is: "Is North Korea ready to do so?"

B. Economic Sanctions by the United Nations

As far as economic sanctions against North Korea is concerned, the year 2006 is the heraldic turning point since the United Nations Security Council (UNSC) imposed direct economic sanctions against North Korea and enjoined all member states of the United Nations to the row of economic sanctions. Before 2006, some resolutions made by the UNSC were to express concerns for North Korea's threatening regional security rather than take direct measures to sanction this country. Such resolutions were, for example, for concerns such as nonproliferation of weapons of mass destruction, terrorism and six-party talks, among some others. The UNSC has adopted total eleven resolutions for economic sanctions from July 2006 to December 2017.

(1) UNSC's first round of direct sanctions against North Korea was adopted by the Resolution 1695 of July 15, 2006 ten days after North Korea launched a ballistic missile. The Resolution 1695 condemns North Korea's missile launching and demands North Korea to suspend all activities related to missile launching program. It also mandates all UN member states to prevent their missile and missile-related items, materials, goods and technology from being transferred to North Korea's missile or weapons of mass destruction (WMD) programs. The UNSC also mandates all member states to prevent the procurement of missiles or missile related-items, materials, goods and technology from North Korea and the transfer of any financial resources in relation to North Korea's missile or WMD programs, among others.[681]

(2) UNSC's second round of direct sanctions against North Korea was adopted by the Resolution 1718 of October 14, 2006 five days after North Korea conducted its first nuclear test. The Resolution 1718 prohibits all United Nations member states from the direct or indirect supply, sale or transfer to North Korea of any battle tanks, armored combat vehicles, large caliber artillery systems, combat aircraft, attack helicopters, warships, missiles or missile systems, all

---

[681] *See* United Nations Security Council Resolution 1695 (S/RES/1695 (2006)).

kinds of nuclear material, equipment and technology, missile or chemical abstract-related materials, chemical weapon-related materials and technology, and luxury goods, among others. The Resolution 1718 also requires United Nations member states to freeze North Korea's funds, other financial assets and 'economic resources' on their territories except for some humanitarian and basic human necessities. In this Resolution, UNSC establishes a UN Security Council Sanctions Committee on North Korea (a/k/a 1718 Committee) in order to effectively implement and oversee sanctions measures laid by the UNSC.[682]

(3) UNSC's third round of economic sanctions against North Korea was adopted by the Resolution 1874 on June 12, 2009, following North Korea's second nuclear test in May of that year. The Resolution 1874 reminds that North Korea could not have status of a nuclear-weapon state in accordance with the Nonproliferation Treaty (NPT) and reaffirms sanctions measures as declared by the previous resolutions. In addition, the Resolution 1874 imposes new sanctions requiring all member states (and international financial institutions where applicable) to: (i) inspect all cargo to and from North Korea in their seaports and airports; (ii) inspect vessels on the high sea if member states have reasonable grounds to believe that such vessels have such prohibited items as shown previous resolutions; (iii) prohibit the provision of fuel or supplies or other servicing of vessels to North Korean vessels if they have information that provides reasonable grounds to believe they are carrying prohibited items unless provision of such services is necessary for humanitarian purposes; (iv) prevent provision of financial services or transfer of financial assets or resources that could contribute to the North Korea's nuclear-related, ballistic-related, or other weapons of mass destruction-related programs by freezing financial asset or resources located in member states' territory; (v) not enter into new commitment for grants, financial assistance or concessional loans to North Korea; and (vi) not provide public financial support for trade with North Korea. And the Resolution also urged North Korea to join the Comprehensive Nuclear Test Ban Treaty as soon as possible.[683]

---

[682] *See* United Nations Security Council Resolution 1718 (S/RES/1718 (2006)).

[683] *See* United Nations Security Council Resolution 1874 ((S/RES/1874 (2009)).

(4) UNSC's fourth round of economic sanctions against North Korea was adopted by the Resolution 2087 on January 22, 2013 after North Korea's launching ballistic missile in December 2012.[684] In this Resolution, the UNSC recalls and reaffirms previous sanctions measures and especially calls upon member states to exercise enhanced vigilance monitoring activities of their own financial institutions and other entities with those of North Koreans'. The UNSC also directs its 1718 Committee to issue an Implementation Assistance Notice for the situations where a vessel has refused to allow an inspection after such an inspection has been authorized by the vessel's flag state or any North Korea-flagged vessel has refused to be inspected. It also deplores the violations of sanctions measures imposed by previous resolutions including the use of bulk cash to evade sanctions, underscores its concern over the supply, sale or transfer to or from the DPRK or through member states' territories of any prohibited items, and calls on member states to exercise vigilance and restraint regarding the entry into or transit through their territories of individuals working on behalf of or at the direction of a designated individual or entity. It announces the lists of five North Korean individuals subject to travel ban as well as asset freeze and six entities subject to asset freeze.[685]

(5) UNSC's fifth round of economic sanctions against North Korea was adopted by the Resolution 2094 on March 7, 2013 caused by North Korea's third nuclear test done in February of that year. In this Resolution, the UNSC expresses the gravest concern at the nuclear test conducted in February 2013 in violation of previous resolutions and at North Korea's ongoing nuclear and ballistic missile-related activities that could generate increased tension in the region and beyond. It also concerns about North Korea's abusing diplomatic privileges and immunities. The UNSC's further actions are, among others, to: (i) demand North Korea to return to the Nonproliferation Treaty regime; (ii) reaffirm its previous decisions for North Korea to abandon all nuclear weapons and existing nuclear programs in complete, verifiable and irreversible manner as well as all weapons of mass destruction and ballistic missile programs; (iii) decide for member states to expel the individuals from their territories

[684] However, North Korea's Central News Agency (KCNA) announced that North Korea launched a rocket carrying a satellite for peaceful purposes.

[685] *See* United Nations Security Council Resolution 2087 (S/RES/2087 (2013)).

if a North Korean acted in violation of UNSC's resolutions; (iv) prevent the provision of financial services or the transfer of any financial or other assets or resources including bulk cash that could contribute to the North Korea's nuclear or ballistic missile programs or other activities prohibited by resolutions including freezing any financial or other assets/resources in the member states' jurisdiction that were associated with the programs or activities above; (v) take appropriate measures to prohibit in member states' territory the opening of branches or relevant offices of North Korean banks and also prohibit North Korean banks' from establishing new joint venture with member states' counterparts if these activities could contribute to North Korea's nuclear or ballistic missile programs; (vi) take also appropriate measure to prohibit member states' financial institutions from opening of banking accounts in North Korean banks if such actions would possibly contribute to nuclear or missile programs; (vii) prohibit public financial support for trade with North Korea if such support could contribute to North Korea's activities in violation of UNSC resolutions; (viii) inspect all cargo within or transiting member states' territory that has originated in North Korea, or destined to North Korea, or have been brokered or facilitated by North Korea or its nationals or entities; (ix) deny North Korean or North Korean-flagged vessels to enter member states' ports if those vessels refused to allow inspection; (x) deny permission to any aircraft to take off from or land in or overfly member states' territory if such aircraft contained prohibited items in violation of UNSC resolutions; and (xi) exercise enhanced vigilance over North Korean diplomats so as to prevent them from contributing to North Korea's nuclear or ballistic missile programs. The Resolution also adds prohibited items, materials, equipment, goods and technology for nuclear, missile and chemical weapons development programs in its Annex III and a list of luxury goods in its Annex IV.[686]

(6) UNSC's sixth round of economic sanctions against North Korea was adopted by the Resolution 2270 on March 6, 2016 after North Korea's fourth nuclear test which was allegedly a hydrogen bomb test and another round of missile launching which was allegedly a satellite launching conducted in January and February of that year respectively. In the Resolution, the UNSC, first of all, condemns North Korea's nuclear test and missile launching in

[686] See United Nations Security Council Resolution 2094 (S/RES/2094 (2013)).

violation and disregard of UNSC's resolutions and demands North Korea not to repeat such violations by abandonment of existing programs of nuclear, missile and weapons of mass destruction. The UNSC requests all member states or decides by itself, among others, to: (i) prevent any transfers to North Korea of technical training, advice, services or assistance related to the provision, manufacture, maintenance or use of nuclear-related, ballistic missile-related or other weapons of mass destruction-related items, materials, equipment, goods and technology; (ii) prohibit again the procurement from North Korea of technical training, advice, services or assistance related to the provision, manufacture, maintenance or use of arms and related material as well as hosting of trainers, advisors, or other officials for the purpose of military-, paramilitary- or police-related training; (iii) freeze funds and assets of individuals and entities listed in the previous resolutions; (iv) prohibit entry into and transit through the territory of member states for North Korea's weapons of mass destruction-related individuals as listed in this Resolution with the same matter as in previous resolutions; (v) affirm that the "economic resources" as referred to the Resolution 1718 (2006) include assets of every kind which potentially may be used to obtain funds, goods or service, such as vessels including maritime ones; (vi) expel from the member state's territory an individual if the individual is a diplomat, governmental representative or other North Korean national acting in governmental capacity who is working on behalf or at the direction of designated individual or entity or assisting in the evasion of sanctions in violation of previous and this resolutions; (vii) identify by the 1718 Committee individuals and entities engaging in North Korea's practice of using front companies, shell companies, joint ventures and complex, opaque ownership structures for the purpose of violating measures imposed in resolutions; (viii) inspect cargo within or transiting through member states' territory, including airports, seaports and free trade zones, originated in North Korea or destined for North Korea or brokered or facilitated by North Korea or its nationals; (ix) prohibit nationals of member states and anyone in their jurisdiction from leasing or chartering their flagged vessels or aircraft or providing crew services to North Korea; (x) prohibit nationals of member states and anyone in their jurisdiction from registering vessels in North Korea, obtaining authorization for a vessel to use the North Korean flag, and from owning, leasing, operating, providing any vessel classification, certification or associated service, or insuring any vessel flagged by North Korea; (xi) deny permission to any aircraft to take off from, land in or overfly, unless under the condition of landing for inspection, their territory if they have information that provides reasonable grounds to believe that the aircraft contains items prohibited by resolutions; and (xii) prohibit the entry into member states' ports of any vessel if the member state had information that the vessel is involved activities in violation of resolutions. The UNSC also decides to: (xiii) demand North Korea to abandon all chemical and biological weapons and weapons-related programs; (xiv) prohibit North Korea from supplying, selling, or transferring coal, iron, iron ore, gold, titanium ore, vanadium ore, and rare earth minerals, and prohibit member states from procurement of such materials from North Korea; (xv) apply asset freeze as imposed by the Resolution 1718 (2006) to all funds, other financial assets and economic resources outside of North Korea that are owned or controlled by entities of government of North Korea or the Workers Party of Korea or by their agents; and (xvi) add prohibited luxury goods such as luxury watches, aquatic recreational vehicles, snowmobiles over $2000, items of lead crystal, etc. as shown in the Annex IV of this Resolution.[687] This Resolution also adds sixteen individuals for travel ban, twelve entities for asset freeze, and thirty-one vessels controlled or operated by the Ocean Maritime Management (OMM), a North Korean firm.[688]

(7) The UNSC's seventh round of sanctions against North Korea was adopted by the Resolution 2321 on November 30, 2016 after North Korea conducted fifth nuclear test in September of that year. In this Resolution, the UNSC strongly condemns the nuclear test conducted by North Korea in September 2016 in violation of its resolutions and demands again not to conduct any further nuclear test and ballistic missile launching. While many of previously decided sanctions measures are reaffirmed, the UNSC mandates, among others, member states to: (i) suspend scientific and technical cooperation involving persons or group officially sponsored by or representing North Korea if such activities would contribute to prohibited activities by resolutions; (ii) clarify as "cargo" the personal luggage and checked baggage of individuals entering into or departing from North Korea as they may be used to transport items as prohibited by UNSC resolutions; (iii) reduce the number of staff at

[687] *See* United Nations Security Council Resolution 2270 (S/RES/2270 (2016).
[688] *See id.* Annex I, II and III.

North Korea's diplomatic and consular missions in member states; (iv) take steps to restrict the entry into or transit through member states' territory the members of North Korean government, officials of the government and members of North Korean armed forces if they are associated with any activities prohibited by UNSC resolutions; (v) take steps to limit the number of bank accounts opened by North Korea's diplomatic and consular missions as well as opened by their officers at banks in member states; (vi) prohibit North Korean diplomatic agents' practice for personal profit or commercial activities in order for North Koreans to comply with the Vienna Convention on Diplomatic Relations of 1961; (vii) inspect the cargo transported to and from North Korea by rail and by road when it is within or transiting through the territory of member states as prohibited items may be transported by rail and by road; (viii) prohibit member states and their nationals from procuring North Korea's copper, nickel, silver, zinc and statues, and prevent member states the supply, sale or transfer of new helicopters and vessels to North Korea; (ix) prohibit member states and their nationals from public and private financial support for trade with North Korea; (x) expel an individual from member states' territories if he is working for North Korea's bank or financial institution; (xi) vigil that North Korea nationals are sent to work in other states for the purpose of earning hard currency that North Korea uses for its nuclear and ballistic missile programs; (xii) prohibit member states' nationals and entities from providing insurance or re-insurance services to North Korea-owned or -controlled vessels; (xiii) prohibit member states' nationals and entities from procuring vessel and aircraft crewing services from North Korea; and (xiv) de-register any vessel owned, controlled, or operated by North Korea and prohibit member states from registering any vessel that has been already de-registered by another member state.[689] This Resolution also adds eleven individuals for travel ban, ten entities for freeze asset, fifteen prohibited nuclear- and/or missile-usable items, three prohibited chemical/biological weapons- usable items, and some luxury goods in its Annex I, II, III and IV.

(8) UNSC's eighth round of sanctions against North Korea was adopted by the Resolution 2356 on June 2, 2017 after North Korea conducted a series of launching ballistic missiles especially from

[689] *See* United Nations Security Council Resolution 2321 (S/RES/2321 (2016)).

April to May 2017. In this Resolution, the UNSC strongly condemns the nuclear weapons and ballistic missile development activities including a series of ballistic missile launches and other activities conducted by North Korea since September 9, 2016 and urges North Korea to abandon such programs. The UNSC also reminds all member states of sanctions measures imposed by previous resolutions and decided to impose sanctions of freezing funds and assets on fourteen travel-banned individuals and four asset-frozen entities which are newly added in its Annex I and II.[690]

(9) UNSC's ninth round of sanctions against North Korea was adopted by the Resolution 2371 on August 5, 2017 after North Korea launched intercontinental ballistic missiles in two occasions on July 3 and July 28, 2017 respectively in violations of previous resolutions. In this resolution, the UNSC strongly condemns North Korea's launches of intercontinental ballistic missiles in disregard of UNSC's resolutions and demands North Korea not to conduct any further launches and abandon all existing nuclear programs in complete, verifiable and irreversible manner. It also adds prohibited items to the existing list such as North Korea's coal, iron and iron ore, lead, lead ore and various kinds of seafood that all member states must not procure them. It also expresses concerns about North Korean workers who work in other states for the purpose of generating foreign export earnings that North Korea uses to support development of prohibited nuclear and ballistic missile programs. The UNSC prohibits North Korea's deployment or use of chemical weapons and demands North Korea to accede to the Convention on the Prohibition of the Development, Production, Stockpiling and Use of Chemical Weapons and Their Destruction. The UNSC also mandates member states to: (i) prohibit the opening of new joint ventures or cooperative entities with North Korea or its nationals and entities as well as expansion of existing joint ventures through additional investments; and (ii) seize or dispose of items the supply, sale, transfer, or export of which is prohibited by resolutions that are identified in inspection, in a manner that is not inconsistent with their obligations under applicable resolutions. It also clarifies that companies performing financial services commensurate with banks as described in previous resolutions are considered financial institutions for the purpose of sanctions. This Resolution adds nine North Korean individuals for

---

[690] *See* United Nations Security Council Resolution 2356 (S/RES/2346 (2017)).

travel ban and asset freeze and four entities for asset freeze in its Annex I and II. It also requests the Interpol to issue Special Notice with respect to designated individuals in order to alert member states' law enforcement authorities that may apply sanctioned measures such as freezing assets, banning travel and/or arms embargo over designated North Korean individuals, among others.[691]

(10) UNSC's tenth round sanctions against North Korea was adopted by the Resolution 2375 on September 11, 2017 after North Korea conducted sixth nuclear test in the same month in violation of previous UN resolutions. In this Resolution, the UNSC strongly condemns North Korea's nuclear test conducted on September 2, 2017 in violation and disregard of previous resolutions and at the same time demands North Korea not to conduct further missile launches and to abandon all nuclear weapons and such programs. The Resolution also requests all member states to inspect vessels with the consent of the flag state, on the high seas, if the cargo of such vessels contained prohibited items for the supply, sale, transfer or export as prescribed by previous and present resolutions. It also asks all member states to cooperate with inspections of vessels through the way the resolution prescribed and affirms that such inspections should be carried out by warships and other ships or aircraft clearly marked and identifiable as being government service and authorized to that effect. At the same time, it clarifies that sovereign immunity rule under the international law would not be applicable to the inspected vessels. The Resolution also prohibits member states from supplying, selling or transferring to North Korea: (i) all condensates and natural gas liquids; (ii) all refined petroleum products except for in the amount of up to a half million barrels in the rest of 2017 and up to two million barrels during the year of 2018; (iii) an amount of crude oil that is in excess of the amount that the member state supplied, sold or transferred in the period of twelve months prior to adoption of this Resolution; and (iv) procurement of textiles including fabrics and partially or completed apparel products. It again prohibits member states' nationals, persons or entities in their jurisdiction from facilitating or engaging in ship-to-ship transfers to or from North Korea-flagged vessels of any goods or items that are being supplied, sold or transferred to or from North Korea. It also prohibits member states from providing work authorization for North Korean nationals in their

---

[691] See United Nations Security Council Resolution 2371 (S/RES/2371 (2017)).

jurisdiction in connection with admission to their territories unless the Committee determines otherwise. This Resolution also prohibits member states from the opening, maintenance, and operation of all joint ventures or cooperative entities, new and existing, with North Korean entities or individuals unless such joint ventures or cooperative ventures have been approved by the Committee. This Resolution in its Annex I and II also adds on the sanctions list an individual for travel ban and asset freeze and three entities for asset freeze. The three entities are power bases and core organs of the Workers' Party of Korea whose names are: (i) the Central Military Commission; (ii) the Organization and Guidance Department; and (iii) the Propaganda and Agitation Department of the Workers' Party of Korea.[692]

(11) UNSC's eleventh round of sanctions against North Korea was adopted by the Resolution 2397 on December 22, 2017 after North Korea launched ballistic missile on November 28 of that year in violation of previous UN resolutions. In this Resolution, first of all, the UNSC strongly criticizes North Korea's launching ballistic missile in addition to North Korea's nuclear weapons and missile programs contributed by the proceeds generated from the trade of sectoral goods including coal, iron, iron ore, lead, lead ore, textiles, seafood, gold, silver, rare earth minerals and other prohibited metals as well as by the revenue generated from North Korean overseas workers. The UNSC also prohibits all member states including their nationals and entities from supplying, selling, or transferring, directly or indirectly, to North Korea: (i) all crude oil; (ii) all refined petroleum products; (iii) industrial machinery, transportation vehicles, and iron, steel, and other metals except for spare parts needed to maintain the safe operation of North Korea's commercial passenger aircraft; (iv) an new or used vessels; (v) providing insurance and re-insurance services to vessels that may be involved in activities, or the transport of items prohibited by resolutions; and (vi) providing classification services of insurance for North Korean vessels. The UNSC also prohibits North Korea from supplying, selling or transferring food and agricultural products, machinery, electrical equipment, earth and stone including magnesite and magnesia, wood, and vessels and at the same time it also prohibits all member states from procuring above items. This Resolution also expresses concerns that North Korean nationals continue to work in other states for the

---

[692] *See* United Nations Security Council Resolution 2375 (S/RES/2375 (2017)).

purpose of generating foreign export earning that North Korea used to support its prohibited nuclear and ballistic missile programs and requires all member states to repatriate to North Korea all North Korean nationals earning income in that member states together with North Korean government safety oversight attachés who are monitoring North Korean workers abroad. This Resolution also notes with great concern that North Korea is illicitly exporting coal and other prohibited items through deceptive maritime practices and obtaining petroleum illegally through ship-to-ship transfers and requires member states to seize, inspect and freeze any vessel in their ports and in their territorial waters if the vessel involves prohibited activities. This Resolution in its Annex I and II also adds on the sanction list sixteen individual for travel ban and asset freeze and an entity for asset freeze which is the Ministry of Armed Forces of North Korea.[693]

The sanctions imposed by the UNSC against North Korea through December 2017 encompass twenty-one distinct categories of measures in broad classification; the detailed action items required by the resolutions number more than sixty.

The principal measures include: arms and related material embargo, non-proliferation of weapons of mass destruction including nuclear, ballistic missiles and other WMDs, interdiction measures on transportation means such as inspecting cargoes on the high seas and prohibition of leasing or chartering vessels or aircrafts to North Korea, freezing assets of North Korean government and the Workers' Party of Korea, banning travel for designated individuals, prohibition of financial transactions or services including bulk cash, prohibition of procurement of coal, iron, gold, and other minerals, seafood, luxury goods, and textiles from North Korea, prohibition of supply, sale or transfer of condensates, natural gas, refined petroleum products and crude oil to North Korea, repatriation of North Korean workers in member states, among many others.

However, a number of articles prohibited by the UNSC resolutions have been included in North Korea's foreign trade with its partners since 2006. If all UN member states except for North Korea itself had complied with the resolutions, could North Korea have continued to develop WMDs? No one could easily answer this question because North Korea is the goal-oriented country through

---

693 *See* United Nations Security Council Resolution 2397 (S/RES/2397 (2017)).

the planned economy prior to the quality of people's life. Probably North Korea might have never ceased the WMDs development programs but possibly implementing speed might have been adjusted.

Contrary to the UNSC's embargoes, North Korea's foreign trade volume, far from declining under UNSC sanctions, increased by 85 percent between 2006 — the year of the first UNSC resolution — and 2017, the year of the eleventh. During this period, North Korea's foreign trade volume went up to 85%. North Korea's major foreign trade partner has been China. North Korea's trade volume with China was 57% (out of total volume of USD 3 billion) in 2006 but 95% (of USD 5.5 billion) in 2017 and 98% (of USD 2.8 billion) in 2023.[694] It looks as if North Korea would have been extremely difficult to survive without China's trade partnership.

The UNSC sanctions remain in force and will continue until the Council rescinds them or North Korea verifiably abandons and dismantles its nuclear weapons and ballistic missile programs. UNSC's Economic sanctions on North Korea were initiated to deter North Korea's development of WMDs that could threaten peace of not only the East Asian region but the United States and beyond. However, while sanctions have been imposed eleven times during eleven years, North Korea has never stopped developing technologies for nuclear weapons and ballistic missiles. North Korea has eventually declared itself a nuclear state in September 2022. The same is stated in the Socialist Constitution as amended in 2023.[695]

The United Nations Security Council might have used up all kinds of measures to economically sanction North Korea as if a large department store displays every kind of goods in windows for shopping. But only a few items might have been picked up by the customers, its member states. What should the international society do with this matter?

C. Recent Political Development

---

[694] All these statistical numbers were extracted from the "*Bukhan-eui daewoe muyeok donghyang* (Trends of North Korea's Foreign Trade)" yearly published in Korean by the Korea Trade-Investment Promotion Agency (KOTRA). It is also available for downloading at <https://kosis.kr/bukhan/extrlPblictn/selectExtrnlCmmrcTrend.do?menuId=M_03_02_01_05> (visited September 1, 2025)

[695] *See* Socialist Constitution of 2023 art. 58.

It may not be easy to achieve eventual peace in the Korean Peninsula since the two sides, North Korea and its allies as one side and South Korea, the United States and their allies as the other, hostilely encountered each other from the breakout of the Korean War in June 1950. They have had so many confrontations politically and militarily during the last seven decades.

In March 1993 during the Clinton administration, North Korea announced its intention to withdraw membership from the Non-proliferation of Nuclear Weapons Treaty (NPT) [696] after the International Atomic Energy Agency's (IAEA) visit to North Korea to inspect the suspected nuclear development site, Yongbyon, in northwestern North Korea.

In October 21, 1994 in Geneva, after having a series of meetings between North Korea and the United States, the two countries concluded the "Agreed Framework between the United States and the Democratic People's Republic of Korea ("Agreed Framework" hereafter)" that resulted in a freeze of North Korea's graphite-moderated reactors in exchange for U.S. provision and construction of light-water reactors. The Agreed Framework also contained an agreement of the full normalization of political and economic relations between the two countries.

Since then, each side demanded to implement the other's obligation as agreed while holding talks and laying economic sanctions were repeated several times. Largely speaking, demands from the United States were to stop development of test-launching ballistic missiles and testing nuclear weapons whereas those from North Korea were to lift economic sanctions, normalize diplomatic relations as agreed upon and compensate for the opportunity cost that could be incurred by halting missile exports to third countries.

In the meantime in October 1999, the North Korea Policy Review led by former Secretary of Defense William Perry was disclosed after one year work. It recommended a two-path strategy. The primary approach was to involve comprehensive and integrated approach through diplomatic efforts to halt North Korea's development of nuclear weapons and long-range missiles. The alternative approach was that if North Korea was not willing to take the first approach, the U.S. and its allies would contain North Korea with maximum pressure. The former was called the engagement policy and the latter

[696] Its full name is the "Treaty on the Non-Proliferation of Nuclear Weapons (NPT) of 1968."

the containment one. This recommendation was not put into practice effectively until the Clinton administration ended in January 2001.

The diplomatic effort collapsed in January 2002, for multiple reasons but most immediately because President George W. Bush designated North Korea as part of an "Axis of Evil." In December 2002, the United States halted shipment of fuel oil to North Korea as agreed under the Agreed Framework. North Korea announced its withdrawal of membership from the NPT in January 2003 and the withdrawal was effectuated in April 2003. North Korea became the first state to withdraw the membership from the NPT.

In August 2003, the Six-Party Talks, joined by two Koreas, United States, China, Japan and Russia, began in order to draw a conclusion on many issues including development of weapons of mass destruction, missile development, among others. The Six Parties held meetings more than a dozen times and survived until April 2009 when North Korea declared that it would not further take part in the Talks due to the United Nations Security Council's condemnation for North Korea's launching ICBM missile and the Council's will to expand economic sanctions, which were already imposed twice, against North Korea. The Six-Party Talks ended without meaningful outcomes and the participants of the meeting could not further develop visible progress although some trials to revive the meeting have been made thereafter.

The Obama administration, which took office in 2009, adopted a policy of "strategic patience" that ultimately proved permissive of North Korea's continued weapons development throughout the two terms of the presidency. In Obama's term for eight years from 2009 to 2017, North Korea launched successive improved versions of its missiles at least twelve times and conducted three nuclear weapons tests. Economic sanctions imposed by both the United States and the UN Security Council grew in proportion to North Korea's provocations.

After taking office in January 2017, President Donald Trump began to take belligerent posture against North Korea during the first year. However, he, brokered by South Korean President Moon Jae In in part, abruptly turned his posture into diplomatic one from January 2018 and held a summit meeting with North Korea's leader Kim Jong Un in Singapore in June 2018 for the first time as the President of the United States. The two leaders issued a joint statement that included North Korea's commitment "to work toward complete denuclearization of the Korean Peninsula" which could be read as the withdrawal of the U.S. troops from South Korea as well as termination of the Mutual Defense Agreement between the United States and the Republic of Korea of 1953 since South Korea was under the nuclear umbrella of the United States.

The leaders from both sides had another round of summit in Hanoi, Vietnam, in February 2019 but the meeting ended without any outcome due to different expectations on the core issues such as measures and timing for scrapping development of nuclear weapons and ballistic missiles as well as those for easing economic sanctions in connection with the progress of denuclearization, among other things. The two leaders briefly met again in the DMZ of the Korean Peninsula in June 2019 on President Trump's way back home from Japan and expressed to resume talks but it was a political event rather than an arranged meeting for negotiation. Since then, the summit meeting was never pursued until President Trump's first term ended.

During the President Trump's first term, North Korea test-fired twenty ballistic missiles out of total twenty-seven times. Among them, eleven were fired after United States' turning posture to diplomacy. At the same period, the sixth nuclear test known as a hydro bomb was tested in September 2017. Soon after the test, economic sanctions through a few executive orders during the period of President Trump's first term were imposed. One of them was the executive order No. 13810 in September 2017 which included secondary sanctions. Later another secondary measure was taken by legislation named the Otto Warmbier North Korea Nuclear Sanctions Act of 2019 named after Mr. Otto F. Warmbier, a college student, who was arrested in January 2016 in Pyongyang, convicted for stealing a propaganda poster and sentenced to 15 years of imprisonment. He was freed from the prison in a comatose state in June 2017 after 17 months' detention. He died a few days after arrival in the United States at the age of 22.

After the Biden administration's launching in January 2021, United States' policy toward North Korea has not taken vivid stance. In April 2021, President Biden in his address at a joint session of Congress said that he would be working on (Iran and) North Korea's nuclear programs through "diplomacy as well as stern deterrence."[697]

---

[697] *See* Remarks by President Biden in Address to a Joint Session of Congress on April 28, 2021 available at <https://bidenwhitehouse.archives.gov/briefing-room/speeches-remarks/2021/04/2

Since then, the Secretary of State and other diplomats of the Biden administration have emphasized 'diplomatic engagement' whenever the security questions in connection with North Korea's nuclear tests and ballistic missile launches were raised. During the four years of the Biden administration, from January 2021 to January 2025, North Korea launched various missiles, from short-, and long-ranged missiles to cruise missiles, ICBMs, SLBMs and further up to reconnaissance satellite, at least 111 times in total. Among them, approximately 90 of which occurred in 2022 coinciding with Russia's full-scale invasion of Ukraine. No nuclear weapons tests were conducted during this period, the times of so-called 'strategic patience.'

After the second Trump administration was launched from January 2025, President Trump in some occasions expressed the hope of meeting with North Korean leader Kim Jong Un who he had met three times during his first term. While President Trump remained receptive to correspondence with Kim, he wrote a letter to Kim; however, it was reported in June 2025 that the delivery of letter to the North Korea's mission in the United Nations was rebuffed.[698] Assuming that it was true, North Korea might not be prepared to resume talks with the United States since it was deeply involved with the war in Ukraine by siding Russia and sending thousands of soldiers to the frontline of the war.

Meanwhile, Kim Jong Un, on his way to China by train, visited the factory producing a next-generation ICBM named Hwasong-20 that can be an immediate threat to the mainland of the United States. And the day after tomorrow in the morning, he was standing side by side with Xi of China and Putin of Russia at the center of the row of jum2025 to commemorate the 80th anniversary of the victory of war against Japan. Perhaps these actions may be interpreted as Kim's wish to up the ante in the game with the United States in the expectation of extracting greater concessions.

9/remarks-by-president-biden-in-address-to-a-joint-session-of-congress/> (visited June 16, 2025>

[698] See a news report from NK Daily available at <https://www.nknews.org/2025/06/north-korea-refusing-to-accept-trump-letter-aimed-at-restarting-dialogue-source/> (visited June 17, 2025). President Trump also expressed the same wish to meet Kim of North Korea when he had a meeting with South Korean President Lee Jae Myung in the Oval Office in August 2025.

However, material concessions may not be Kim's only objective. His regime has consistently sought international recognition of North Korea as a legitimate nuclear-armed state, entitled to treatment commensurate with that accorded to other nuclear powers. If so, what is North Korea going to do with the limited open door policy? Can it chase two rabbits and catch them all?

Chapter 7 Prospects of North Korea's Open Door Policy

North Korea aspires to be a strong country both militarily and economically. The first ambition has been substantially realized through the development of nuclear weapons and ballistic missiles and the maintenance of an army exceeding one million soldiers. The second has not. As of 2025, North Korea cannot credibly claim to have achieved economic strength. For this, North Korea may ascribe its prolonged economic stagnation to external environment such as economic sanctions mainly imposed by the United States for many decades and the U.S.-led United Nations Security Council in recent years because North Korea has casually insisted that American imperialists try to suffocate it to death. However, regardless of whether such allegation is true or not, North Korea should have to answer following questions. If sanctions were lifted and North Korea were free of external economic pressure, would foreign direct investment flow in? Can its foreign trade be galvanized thereafter? Thus, could North Korea become an economically strong country in any reasonable timeframe?

Let us assume that economic sanctions are lifted all at once someday and foreign investors rush into North Korea. If so, is North Korean regime simply happy with this situation and ready to enjoy influx of foreign capital? The answer is 'no.' Because North Korea is afraid of the situation that if they open the door more widely without screening measures, bourgeoisie's decadent culture will be accompanied by foreign capital at the same time. The regime believes such imperialist's culture surely damages country's socialistic identity and destroys people's sound life. In order to overcome this situation, North Korea made a theory that it will set up a mosquito net to welcome cool air but will not allow infiltration of mosquitoes. With keeping in mind this idea, North Korea established special economic zones at the manner that practically segregates general people from the zones by constructing fences or limiting access.

After all, North Korea can have two different economic systems under its sovereign jurisdiction. Inside the fence of a special economic zone, practicing free-market principle is allowed while outside the fence, functioning as hinterland, socialist's planning economy controls everything. Can the two different mechanisms work in tandem harmoniously or supplement one thing with the other? Foreign investors operating business in an SEZ need to hire, of course, North Korean workers. Where some investors need skilled or experienced manpower in electronics, for example, and some other investors need skilled manpower in chemical product, can North Korea's bureaucratic labor exchange meet the unplanned demands from investors while there is no free labor market? It may be able to do so in a small number of cases, but almost certainly not at the scale required to serve hundreds of foreign investors.

Consider the supply chain requirements of producing a laptop computer, which requires the assembly of at least fifty finished components, many of which would need to be sourced from various suppliers inside and outside the SEZ. Some parts would have to be supplied by North Korean manufacturers. Yet the production plan of a foreign-invested enterprise cannot realistically be incorporated into the national economic plan, even if the enterprise is required to submit an annual production projection. It is because individual foreign-invested enterprises operating in an SEZ cannot only forecast relatively accurate demand for every single part of a laptop computer but also rely on domestically produced parts if they could be manufactured and delivered on time. As a matter of fact, quality or compatibility of the product is the next concern. The production of a motorcycle or motor vehicle involves thousands of parts and would be correspondingly more complex.

In the planned economy, goods are produced as planned based on planned demand and supply. Supply chain of raw materials and parts are supplied as planned. Enterprises in this mechanism can only produce goods within the planned limit and manufactured goods are distributed to someone or somewhere as planned. In this environment, foreign-invested enterprises in SEZs cannot rely on fixed demand and supply chain of North Korea for their production because much more flexible choices in price, quality and quantity are waiting in the markets outside North Korea. Therefore, as far as sticking to the planned economy mechanism, what North Korea can do with opening SEZs is to lease land, provide energy services, supply workforce while potential investors keep their eyes on the host country's endeavors for betterment. North Korea can enjoy collecting relevant fees and taxes only from limited number of residing investors but it is far from achieving greater progress in economy. To move beyond this

— to build an economy capable of technological progress and genuine growth — North Korea must take the kind of bold step that China and Vietnam took at the outset of their open-door policies – moving to the 'economy-in-transition' stage. The key to that transition is the privatization of State-owned small and medium enterprises, particularly in light industry, to allow private business activity and market-based competition.

North Korea desires to preserve its distinctive ideological identity and culture no matter what environment it is situated. The former is represented by the Juche idea and the Kimilsungism-Kimjongilism, the principle of independent national economy, the principle of a planned economy, the principle of collective ownership, and nationalization or socialization of production means, if not more. The culture North Korea wishes to maintain may refer to the principles to carry out revolutionary culture, to establish socialist lifestyle, to promote Juche-oriented revolutionary art and literature on the one hand and to reject imperialist's cultural infiltration on the other hand. All these are enshrined in the Socialist Constitution and the Covenant of the Workers' Party of Korea as principles and guidelines for every North Korean people to keep in mind and put into practice.

Nothing in the world remains static. The conceptions we take to be permanent truths are always subject to reinterpretation as times and circumstances change. Marxism-Leninism evolved, in the North Korean context, into 'our-style socialism.' The Juche idea gave rise to Kimilsungism and Kimjongilism as new ideological formulations, justified as serving the interests of the North Korean nation and people. The author of the Kimjongilism, Kim Jong Il, clarified in his thesis 'About the Juche Idea' far earlier in 1982 that the Juche idea is not to reject economic cooperation with foreign countries but to oppose to be economically subordinated to them. Socialist countries like China or Vietnam actively opened door and fostered operation of domestic private businesses in order to meet the needs from foreign-invested businesses in SEZs in respective countries. They eventually have made great progress in economy without being subordinated to imperialists and in the case of China, it is now competing for the number one status with the United States in gross product and military power. North Korea's per capita potentiality in natural and human resources is considered superior to those of China.

Although foreign culture came into China or Vietnam, for example, with foreign capital and their people have spontaneously changed a certain degree of life style, they always love their country and keep their own value across the generations. These people still revere their nation founders Mao Zedong in China and Ho Chi Minh in Vietnam respectively, and will continue so generation after generation. They also love and respect their current and former leaders of their own countries. The capacity to absorb foreign engagement without surrendering national identity is not unique to those countries. Who is afraid of taking a giant leap for progress?

North Korea, in a sense, can be compared to a creature that has protective spines and quills that can be equated to nuclear weapons and ballistic missiles. Even the king of savannah, the lion, cannot eat a porcupine because of its sharp quills. It has survived and will do with such a mechanism for multimillion years; however, without positive will to transform itself, it cannot evolve to the largest and strongest creature like the Lion King or a T. Rex dinosaur.

The most urgent and necessary approach to effectively operate the SEZs is to adopt privatization even in limited sectors. Without privatization of State-owned small and medium enterprises as well as introduction of free market idea in the domestic market, North Korea cannot achieve the goal of 'economically strong country.' It may be as if 'Man of La Mancha' named Don Quixote wished to dream the impossible dream and reach the unreachable star. That is why people called his wishes "the Impossible Dream." However, North Korea's wish to be an economically strong country is not an impossible dream once it decides to transform itself. It can reach the unreachable star once it takes a giant stride forward.

Appendix

Constitution and Statutes of North Korea relevant to the Open Door Policy

- Socialist Constitution of the Democratic People's Republic of Korea
- Law of the Democratic People's Republic of Korea on Foreign Investment Law
- Law of the Democratic People's Republic of Korea on Wholly Foreign-owned Enterprises
- Law of the Democratic People's Republic of Korea on Equity Joint Venture
- Law of the Democratic People's Republic of Korea on Contractual Joint Venture
- Law of the Democratic People's Republic of Korea on the Rason Economic and Trade Zone
- Defunct Law of the Democratic People's Republic of Korea on the Mt. Kumgang Special Zone for International Tourism
- Law of the Democratic People's Republic of Korea on the Kaesong Industrial Complex
- Law of the Democratic People's Republic of Korea on the Hwanggumphyong and Wihwado Economic Zone
- Law of the Democratic People's Republic of Korea on the Economic Development Zones
- Law of the Democratic People's Republic of Korea on Foreign Currency Control
- Law of the Democratic People's Republic of Korea on Foreign-invested Banks
- Labour Law of the Democratic People's Republic of Korea for Foreign-invested Enterprises
- Taxation Law of the Democratic People's Republic of Korea for Foreign-invested Businesses and Foreign Individuals
- Customs Law of the Democratic People's Republic of Korea
- Immigration Law of the Democratic People's Republic of Korea
- Law of the Democratic People's Republic of Korea on Land Lease

▪ SOCIALIST CONSTITUTION OF THE DEMOCRATIC PEOPLE'S REPUBLIC OF KOREA

Adopted on December 27, 1972, at the First Session of the Fifth Supreme People's Assembly, amended and supplemented on April 9, 1992, at the Third Session of the Ninth Supreme People's Assembly, amended and supplemented on September 5, 1998, at the First Session of the Tenth Supreme People's Assembly, amended and supplemented on April 9, 2009, at the First Session of the Twelfth Supreme People's Assembly, amended on April 9, 2010, at the Second Session of the Twelfth Supreme People's Assembly, amended and supplemented on April 13, 2012, at the Fifth Session of the Twelfth Supreme People's Assembly, amended and supplemented on April 1, 2013, at the Seventh Session of the Twelfth Supreme People's Assembly, amended and supplemented on June 29, 2016, at the Fourth Session of the Thirteenth Supreme People's Assembly, amended and supplemented on April 11, 2019, at the First Session of the Fourteenth Supreme People's Assembly, amended and supplemented on August 29, 2019, at the Second Session of the Fourteenth Supreme People's Assembly, and amended and supplemented on September 26 and 27, 2023 at the Ninth Session of the Fourteenth Supreme People's Assembly

Preamble

The Democratic People's Republic of Korea is the socialist State of Juche where the ideas and achievement of the great *Suryong* Comrade Kim Il Sung and the great leader Comrade Kim Jong Il on State building are realized.

The great *Suryong* Comrade Kim Il Sung is the founder of the Democratic People's Republic of Korea and the progenitor of socialist Korea.

The great *Suryong* Comrade Kim Il Sung originated the immortal Juche Idea and, by organizing and leading the anti-Japanese revolutionary struggle under the banner of it, invented the glorious revolutionary traditions, achieved the historic cause of national liberation, and founded the Democratic People's Republic of Korea based on solid foundation for building of an independent and sovereign state on the political, economic, cultural and military fields.

The great *Suryong* Comrade Kim Il Sung, by putting forward Juche-oriented revolutionary lines and wisely leading various stages of social revolution and construction work, strengthened and developed the Democratic People's Republic of Korea into a mass-centered socialist state and into a socialist state of independence, self-sufficiency and self-defense.

The great *Suryong* Comrade Kim Il Sung elucidated the fundamental principles in nation building and activities of the State, firmly established the most outstanding state and social system, mode of politics, and social management system and method, and laid solid foundations for the prosperity of this socialist State and accomplishment of revolutionary cause of Juche.

The great leader Comrade Kim Jong Il was the matchless patriot and defender of socialist Korea who, revering the ideas and cause of the great *Suryong* Comrade Kim Il Sung, intensely developed this Republic to the State of Comrade Kim Il Sung and elevated the dignity and power of the nation to the highest level.

The great leader Comrade Kim Jong Il developed in depth and in all-round way the immortal Juche Idea originated by the great *Suryong* Comrade Kim Il Sung, created a new history of miracles and changes in all fields of the construction of socialism under the banner of modelling the whole society on Kimilsungism, and firmly ensured the continuity of the Korean revolution by pioneering the great cause of immortalizing the *Suryong* for the first time in history and sustainably developing the revolutionary traditions of Juche with purity.

The great leader Comrade Kim Jong Il honorably safeguarded the trophies of socialism which were the precious legacy of the great *Suryong* Comrade Kim Il sung by administering military-first policy, turned the DPRK into an unbeatable politico-ideological power, a nuclear power and an invincible military power, and opened a bright and broad passage to build a powerful socialist state in the midst of the collapse of the world-wide socialist system and vicious anti-DPRK campaigns as initiated by the allied imperialists.

The great *Suryong* Comrade Kim Il Sung and the great leader Comrade Kim Jong Il, by taking 《*Imin Wichŏn* (The people are my God)》 as their motto, always mixed with the people, devoted their whole lives to the people, led and took care of the people through lofty and benevolent politics, and turned all the society into a large family with the united mind.

Guided by the great *Suryong* Comrade Kim Il Sung and the great leader Comrade Kim Jong Il, the DPRK, as the unique State which successfully accomplished the fundamental and core tasks for building a wealthy, powerful and independent state, was able to shine its brilliance.

The great *Suryong* Comrade Kim Il Sung and the great leader Comrade Kim Jong Il are eternal saviors of the nation who performed immortal achievements for the national unification. The great *Suryong* Comrade Kim Il Sung and the great leader Comrade Kim Jong Il proposed the unification of the nation as the people's utmost task and devoted all their efforts and heart and soul for its realization.

The great *Suryong* Comrade Kim Il Sung and the great leader Comrade Kim Jong Il, while solidifying the DPRK as a powerful bastion for the national unification, pioneered the way to accomplish a great feat of national unification through all people's united power, by the way of setting out fundamental principles and methods for the national unification as well as evolving the national unification campaign into the all-ethnic movement.

The great *Suryong* Comrade Kim Il Sung and the great leader Comrade Kim Jong Il clarified the basic idea of foreign policy of the DPRK, on the basis of it, expanded the State's foreign relations, and ensured to exalt the international prestige of the DPRK. The great *Suryong* Comrade Kim Il Sung and the great leader Comrade Kim Jong Il opened a new era of self-reliance as doyens of world politics, carried out energetic activities for strengthening and developing the socialist movement and the non-aligned movement and for world peace and friendship among peoples, and made an imperishable contribution to the cause of mankind's self-reliance.

The great *Suryong* Comrade Kim Il Sung and the great leader Comrade Kim Jong Il were the geniuses in ideology theories and leadership arts, the invincible and iron-willed brilliant commanders, the great revolutionaries and statesmen, and the great human-beings.

The great ideas and accomplishments of the great *Suryong* Comrade Kim Il Sung and the great leader Comrade Kim Jong Il are the everlasting treasures of the Korean revolution and the basic guarantee for the prosperity of the DPRK, and the *Kumsusan* Palace of the Sun where the great *Suryong* Comrade Kim Il Sung and the great leader Comrade Kim Jong Il rest in their lifetime appearance is a grand monument to their immortality, a symbol of the dignity and an eternal shrine of the entire Korean people.

The Democratic People's Republic of Korea and its people shall highly commemorate the great *Suryong* Comrade Kim Il Sung and the great leader Comrade Kim Jong Il as the eternal leaders of Juche Korea, uphold their ideas and achievements as led by the Workers' Party of Korea, sustainably develop them, and further complete the great mission of the Juche Revolution.

The Socialist Constitution of the Democratic People's Republic of Korea is the Kim Il Sung – Kim Jong Il Constitution that codifies the idea of Juche-oriented nation building and the achievements of nation building as made by the great *Suryong* Comrade Kim Il Sung and the great leader Comrade Kim Jong Il.

Chapter 1 Politics

Article 1 The Democratic People's Republic of Korea shall be the independent socialist State representing the interests of all the Korean people.

Article 2 The Democratic People's Republic of Korea shall be a revolutionary state which has inherited the brilliant traditions achieved from the glorious revolutionary struggle in order to realize liberation of the homeland and freedom and happiness of the people while against the imperial aggressors.

Article 3 The Democratic People's Republic of Korea shall take the Kimilsungism-Kimjongilism as the unique guidance for the nation building and activities.

Article 4 The sovereignty of the Democratic People's Republic of Korea shall reside in the workers, peasants, soldiers, intellectuals and all other working people.

The working people shall exercise the sovereignty through their own representing organs which are the Supreme People's Assembly and all levels of local people's assemblies.

Article 5 All State organs of the Democratic People's Republic of Korea shall be formed and function on the principle of democratic centralism.

Article 6 All levels of State's sovereign organs, from a county people's assembly to the Supreme People's Assembly, shall be elected on the principle of universal, equal and direct suffrage by secret ballot.

Article 7 Deputies of the sovereign organs shall have close ties with their constituents and be accountable to the constituents for their work.

The electors may recall at any time the deputies they have elected if the latter lose the trust of the former.

Article 8 The social system of the Democratic People's Republic of Korea shall be a people-centered system under which the working people are the masters of everything and everything in society serves them.

The State shall defend the interests of the workers, peasants, soldiers, intellectuals and all other working people who have been freed from exploitation and oppression and become the masters of the State and society, and respect and protect human rights.

Article 9 The Democratic People's Republic of Korea shall strive to achieve the complete victory of socialism in the northern half of Korea by strengthening the people's power and vigorously performing the three revolutions – ideological, technological and cultural – and to unify the nation on the principle of independence, peaceful unification and great national unity.

Article 10 The Democratic People's Republic of Korea shall be underpinned by the politico-ideological unity of all the people based on the worker-peasant alliance led by the working class.

The State shall revolutionize all the members of society, and assimilate them to the working class by intensifying the ideological revolution, and shall turn the whole of society into a collective that is united in a comradely way.

Article 11 The Democratic People's Republic of Korea shall conduct all activities under the leadership of the Worker's Party of Korea.

Article 12 The State shall adhere to the class line and strengthen the dictatorship of the people's democracy so as to firmly defend the people's sovereign power and socialist system against all subversive acts of hostile elements at home and abroad.

Article 13 The State shall substantiate the mass line, find a way to solve problems by going among the masses, and hold fast the revolutionary work method that raises high the spiritual strength and creativity of the masses by putting ahead political work and work with people.

Article 14 The State shall vehemently conduct the Three-Revolution Red Flag Movement and other mass movements so as to fully accelerate the building of socialism.

Article 15 The Democratic People's Republic of Korea shall champion the democratic national rights of overseas ethnic Koreans and their legitimate rights and interests as recognized by international law.

Article 16 The Democratic People's Republic of Korea shall guarantee the legitimate rights and interests of foreigners in its territory.

Article 17 Independence, peace and friendship shall be the basic ideals of the foreign policy and the principles of the external activities of the Democratic People's Republic of Korea.

The State shall establish diplomatic or political, economic and cultural relations with friendly countries on the principles of complete equality, independence, mutual respect, non-interference in each other's affairs and mutual benefit.

The State shall promote unity with people all over the world who defend their independence, and resolutely support and encourage the struggles of all people who oppose all forms of aggression and interference and fight for their countries' independence, and national and class liberation.

Article 18 The law of the Democratic People's Republic of Korea shall reflect the wishes and interests of the working people and be a basic instrument for State administration.

Respect for the law and strict adherence to and execution of it shall be the duty of all institutions, enterprises, organizations and citizens.

The State shall perfect the system of socialist law and promote the socialist law-abiding life.

Chapter 2 Economy

Article 19 The Democratic People's Republic of Korea shall rely on the foundations of socialist production relations and an independent national economy.

Article 20 In the Democratic People's Republic of Korea, the means of production shall be owned by the State and social, cooperative organizations.

Article 21 The ownership of the State shall be that of the entire people.

There shall be no limit to the property which the State can own.

The State shall solely own all natural resources, railways, air transport service, post and telecommunications establishments, major factories, enterprises, ports and banks of the country.

The State shall protect and enhance on a preferential basis the State property which plays the leading role in the economic development of the country.

Article 22 The property of social, cooperative organizations shall be collectively owned by the working people involved in the organizations concerned.

Land, farm machinery, ships, small and medium-sized factories, enterprises and the like may be owned by the social, cooperative organizations.

The State shall protect the ownership of social, cooperative organizations.

Article 23 The State shall enhance the ideological consciousness and the technical and cultural level of the peasants, in the direction of promoting the leading role of the all-people's ownership over the cooperative ownership, organically consolidate the two ownerships, solidly develop the socialist cooperative management system, and gradually transform the ownership of the cooperative organizations into the all-people's ownership in accordance with the voluntary will of all members of the cooperative organizations.

Article 24 The private ownership shall be the one for the purpose of personal use and consumption of individual citizens.

The private ownership shall be derived from the socialist distribution according to performed labor and supplementary benefits of the State and society.

The products of individual sideline activities including those from kitchen gardens and the personal incomes earned from other legitimate economic activities shall also be private property.

The State shall protect private property and guarantee by law the right to inherit it.

Article 25 The Democratic People's Republic of Korea shall regard the steady improvement of the material and cultural life of the people as the supreme principle of its activities.

Where taxes have been abolished in this country, the increasing material wealth of society shall be used entirely to promote the well-being of the working people.

The State shall provide all the working people with every condition for obtaining food, clothing and housing.

Article 26 The independent national economy as resided in the Democratic People's Republic of Korea shall be a solid foundation for the people's happy socialist life and for the country's prosperity.

The State, keeping a tight rein on the line of building a socialist, independent national economy and accelerating the people's economy to be Juche-oriented, modernized, informatized and scientific, shall endeavor to turn the people's economy to the highly developed Juche-oriented economy and to build material and technical foundations commensurate with the a complete socialist society.

Article 27 The technological revolution shall be a basic link for developing the socialist economy and the scientific and technological strength shall be the most important strategic resource of the State.

The State shall enhance the leading role of science and technology in all economic activities, integrate science and technology with production, and accelerate economic construction by vigorously promoting the mass technical innovation movement.

Article 28 The State shall industrialize and modernize agriculture through expediting the technical revolution in agriculture, improve the role of the county, and strengthen the guidance and assistance to rural areas in order to eliminate the difference between the city and the rural community as well as the class distinction between industrial workers and peasants.

The State shall undertake at its own expense the building of production facilities for cooperative farms and modern houses in the rural community.

Article 29 Socialism shall be built by the creative labor of the working people.

Labor in the Democratic People's Republic of Korea shall be independent and creative labor of the working people who are freed from the exploitation and oppression.

The State shall create an environment that the labor of its working people, while unemployment is unknown to them, becomes more joyful and worthwhile as they work for the society, the collective community and themselves together with conscious enthusiasm and creativeness.

Article 30 The work hours shall not exceed eight hours a day.

The State shall set the shorter working hours than eight hours a day depending on the harshness of labor and peculiar conditions of work.

The State shall guarantee that the working hours are fully utilized through proper organization of labor and enforcement of labor discipline.

Article 31 In the Democratic People's Republic of Korea, the minimum working age shall be 16 years old. The State shall prohibit the employment of those under the minimum working age.

Article 32 The State shall properly combine, in the guidance and management toward the socialist economy, the political guidance with economic and technical guidance, the unified guidance of the State with creativeness of each unit, the unitary direction with democracy, the political and moral incentive with material incentive, and firmly adhere to the principle of guaranteeing practical gains (derived from such combinations).* *( ) is added by the translator.

Article 33 The State shall manage and operate the economy scientifically and rationally on the basis of the collective wisdom and strength of the producer masses, and decisively enhance the role of the Cabinet.

The State shall enforce the responsibility-oriented management system of socialist enterprises in economic management, and properly utilize such economic levers as cost, pricing and profitability.

Article 34 The national economy of the Democratic People's Republic of Korea shall be a planned economy.

The State shall draw up and implement the plans for the development of the national economy in accordance with the laws of socialist economic development so that the balance between accumulation and consumption can be maintained correctly, the economic construction can be accelerated, the people's standard of living can steadily be raised and the nation's defense capabilities can be strengthened.
The State shall ensure a high rate of growth in production and a balanced development of the national economy by implementing unified and detailed planning.
Article 35 The Democratic People's Republic of Korea shall compile and execute the State budget according to the national economic development plan.
The State shall intensify the campaign for production increase and frugality in all sectors, systemically increase national accumulations by strictly implementing financial control, expand and develop the socialist ownership.
Article 36 In the Democratic People's Republic of Korea, foreign trade shall be conducted by the State organs and enterprises, and social, cooperative organizations.
The State shall maintain credit-worthiness in foreign trade, improve trade structure, expand and develop external economic relations on the principle of equality and mutual benefit.
Article 37 The State shall encourage institutions, enterprises and organizations in our country to conduct equity or contractual joint ventures with foreign corporations or individuals, and to establish and operate various kinds of enterprises in special economic zones.
Article 38 The State shall pursue a tariff policy to protect the independent national economy.

Chapter 3 Culture

Article 39 Socialist culture flourishing and developing in the Democratic People's Republic of Korea shall contribute to improving the creative ability of the working people and to meeting their sound cultural and emotional demands.
Article 40 The Democratic People's Republic of Korea shall, by carrying out a thorough cultural revolution, train all the people to the builders of socialism equipped with a good understanding of nature and society and a high level of culture and technology, and thus accelerate all people's competency in science and technology.

Article 41 The Democratic People's Republic of Korea shall develop truly people-oriented, revolutionary culture which serves the socialist working people.

In building a socialist national culture, the State shall oppose the cultural infiltration of imperialism, protect its national cultural heritage on the principle of establishing the Juche orientation, the principle of historicism and the principle of scientific accuracy, and sustainably develop the heritage consistent with the existing socialist situation.

Article 42 The State shall eliminate the way of life inherent from the outmoded society and establish a new socialist way of life in every sphere.

Article 43 Through substantiating the principles of socialist pedagogy, the State shall train the rising generation to be true patriots who will fight for the society and the collective and for the country and people, and to be pivotal workers who will build the socialism in the possession of sound knowledge, morals and body.

Article 44 The State shall give precedence to the public education for people and the training of nationalistic cadres and closely combine general education with technological education, and education with productive labor.

Article 45 The State shall develop universal compulsory twelve-year education which includes compulsory one-year preschool education at a high level to meet the trend of modern science and technology and the practical requirements of socialist construction.

Article 46 The State shall train competent scientific and technical talents by enhancing the regular educational system as well as different forms of studying while working, and by constantly improving the contents, methods, conditions and environment of education.

Article 47 The State shall provide free education to all students and grant scholarships to students at universities and colleges.

Article 48 The State shall strengthen social education and provide the working people with all the necessary conditions for study.

Article 49 The State shall look after all children of preschool age in crèches and kindergartens at State and public expenses.

Article 50 The State shall establish the Juche orientation in scientific research, introduce advanced science and technology in every possible way, increase State's investment in the sectors of scientific research, pioneer new areas of science and technology, and raise the country's science and technology to the world level.

Article 51 The State shall elaborate a correct plan to develop science and technology, set up strict discipline to implement it, and strengthen creative cooperation between scientists, technicians and producers.

Article 52 The State shall develop Juche-oriented and revolutionary art and literature that contains socialist contents in the of form of nationalism..

The State shall encourage creative workers and artists to produce works of high ideological and artistic value, and the broad sections of the masses to participate in the literary and artistic activities.

Article 53 The State shall provide sufficient modern cultural facilities to meet the demands of the people who want to continually improve themselves, both mentally and physically , so that the working people enjoy a full socialist cultured, aesthetic life.

Article 54 The State shall safeguard its language from all attempts to obliterate it and develop it to meet present-day needs.

Article 55 The State shall thoroughly prepare all the people for work and national defense by popularizing physical culture and sport and making it their daily regime, and augment sporting skills to meet the country's reality and the trend in modern sporting skills.

Article 56 The State shall protect the people's lives and improve the working people's health by consolidating and developing the system of universal free medical service, strengthening the responsible district doctor system and the system of preventive medicine, and improving the endorsed supply chain to the public health sector.

Article 57 The State shall adopt measures to protect the environment, giving it preference over production, preserve and promote the natural environment, and prevent environmental pollution so as to provide the people with a hygienic living environment and working conditions.

Chapter 4 National Defense

Article 58 The Democratic People's Republic of Korea shall be based on the all-people and nationwide defense system.

As an accountable state of nuclear power, the Democratic People's Republic of Korea shall highly promote development of nuclear weapons in order to secure the State's right to existence and progress, deter war, and uphold peace and stability of the region and world.

Article 59 The mission of the armed forces of the Democratic People's Republic of Korea shall be to advocate for the sovereignty of the State, the recovery of the whole territory of the State, and the rights and interests of people, defend to the death the socialist system and revolutionary gains from all kinds of threats, and secure peace and prosperity of the homeland by means of the strong military power.

Article 60 The State shall carry out the self-defense military line whose basic contents are to train all military members to be a cadre, modernize the military forces, arm all the people and fortify every corner of the country on the basis of equipping the people and military personnel of the Korean People's Army politically and ideologically.

Article 61 The State shall establish a revolutionary command system and military spirit, strengthen disciplines of the military and the mass, and exalt the noble traditional traits of unity between a commander and the ranks, combination of the military and political affairs and unity between the military and the people.

Chapter 5 Fundamental Rights and Duties of Citizens

Article 62 The requirements for becoming a citizen of the Democratic People's Republic of Korea shall be defined by the Law on Nationality.

A citizen shall be under the protection of the Democratic People's Republic of Korea regardless of domicile.

Article 63 In the Democratic People's Republic of Korea, the rights and duties of citizens shall be based on the collectivist principle《One for all and all for one》.

Article 64 The State shall effectively guarantee the genuine democratic rights and freedom as well as the material and cultural well-being of all its citizens.

In the Democratic People's Republic of Korea, the rights and freedoms of citizens shall be amplified with the consolidation and development of the socialist system.

Article 65 Citizens shall enjoy equal rights in all spheres of State and social activities.

Article 66 All citizens who have reached the age of 17 shall have the right to elect and to be elected, irrespective of sex, race, occupation, length of residence, property status, education, party affiliation, political views or religious belief.

Citizens serving in the armed forces shall also have the right to elect and to be elected.

A person who has been disenfranchised by a Court decision and a person legally certified insane shall not have the right to elect or to be elected.

Article 67 Citizens shall be guaranteed freedom of speech, the press, assembly, demonstration and association.

The State shall guarantee the conditions for the free activities of democratic political parties and social organizations.

Article 68 Citizens shall have freedom of religious belief.

This right shall be ensured through the way to approve the construction of religious buildings, the holding of religious ceremonies and the like.

Religion shall not be used as a pretext for calling in foreign powers or for harming the State or social order.

Article 69 Citizens shall be entitled to submit complaints and petitions.

The State shall deliberate and deal with complaints and petitions impartially as stipulated by law.

Article 70 Citizens shall have the right to work.

All able-bodied citizens shall choose occupations in accordance with their wishes and skills and be provided with stable jobs and working conditions.

Citizens shall work according to their abilities and be remunerated in accordance with the quantity and quality of their work.

Article 71 Citizens shall have the right to relaxation.

This right shall be ensured by the establishment of working hours, and the provision of holidays, paid leave, taking recuperative vacations at State's expenses and the steady increase of a variety of cultural facilities.

Article 72 Citizens shall be entitled to free medical care, and persons who are no longer able to work because of old age, illness or physical disability and seniors and minors who have no means of support shall be all entitled to material assistance.

The right shall be ensured by free medical care, an expanding network of hospitals, medical facilities including sanatoria, State's social insurance and other social security systems.

Article 73 Citizens shall have the right to education.

This right shall be ensured by an advanced educational system and by the educational policy measures of the State for the benefit of the people.

Article 74 Citizens shall be free to engage in scientific, literary and artistic pursuits.

The State shall grant benefits to inventors and innovators.

Copyrights, inventions and patents shall be protected by law.

Article 75 Citizens shall have freedom of residence and travel.

Article 76 Revolutionary fighters, the families of revolutionary and patriotic martyrs, the families of soldiers of the People's Army and soldiers disabled on duty shall enjoy the special protection of the State and the society.

Article 77 Women shall be accorded equal social status and rights with men.

The State shall afford special protection to mothers and children by providing maternity leave, reduced working hours for mothers with children, expanded networks of maternity hospitals, creches, kindergartens in addition to other measures.

The State shall provide all conditions for women to play their roles in society.

Article 78 Marriage and family shall be protected by the State.

The State shall pay great attention to consolidating the family, the basic unit of social life.

Article 79 Citizens shall be guaranteed inviolability of the person and the home, and privacy of correspondence.

No citizen shall be placed under control or arrest nor shall a citizen's home be searched without a legal warrant.

Article 80 The Democratic People's Republic of Korea shall grant the right of asylum to foreign nationals persecuted for struggling for peace and democracy, national independence and socialism or for the freedom of scientific and cultural pursuit.

Article 81 Citizens shall firmly safeguard the political and ideological unity and solidarity of the people.

Citizens shall cherish their organization and collective, and exalt the spirit of working devotedly for the society and the people.

Article 82 Citizens shall observe the laws of the State and the norms of socialist way of life, and defend their honor and dignity as citizens of the Democratic People's Republic of Korea.

Article 83 Labor shall be the noble duty and honor of the citizen.

Citizens shall earnestly participate in work with self-awareness and strictly observe labor disciplines and working hours.

Article 84 Citizens shall take good care of the property of the State and social, cooperative organizations, combat all forms of misappropriation and waste, and manage the nation's economy diligently as the masters.

The property of the State and social, cooperative organizations shall be absolutely inviolable.

Article 85 Citizens shall constantly increase their revolutionary vigilance and devotedly fight for the security of the State.

Article 86 National defense shall be the supreme duty and honor of the citizen.

Citizens shall defend the country and serve in the armed forces as required by law.

Chapter 6 State Organs

Section 1 The Supreme People's Assembly

Article 87 The Supreme People's Assembly shall be the highest organ of State power in the Democratic People's Republic of Korea.

Article 88 The Supreme People's Assembly shall exercise its legislative power. The Presidium of the Supreme People's Assembly may also exercise the legislative power when the Supreme People's Assembly is not in session.

Article 89 The Supreme People's Assembly shall be composed of deputies elected on the principle of universal, equal and direct suffrage by secret ballot.

Article 90 Supreme People's Assembly shall be elected for a term of five years.

A new Supreme People's Assembly shall be elected according to a decision of the Presidium of the Supreme People's Assembly before the expiration of the incumbent's term.

When avoidable circumstances render an election impossible, the term of office of the Supreme People's Assembly shall be prolonged until an election can be held.

Article 91 The Supreme People's Assembly shall have the authority to:

1. amend or supplement the Constitution;
2. adopt, amend or supplement laws;
3. approve the major laws adopted by the Presidium of the Supreme People's Assembly when the Supreme People's Assembly is not in session;
4. establish the basic principles of the State's domestic and foreign policies;
5. elect or recall the Chairman of the State Affairs Commission of the Democratic People's Republic of Korea;
6. elect or recall the President of the Presidium of the Supreme People's Assembly;
7. elect or recall the First Vice-Chairperson, Vice-Chairpersons and members of the State Affairs Commission on the

recommendation of the Chairman of the State Affairs Commission of the Democratic Republic of Korea;

8. elect or recall the Vice-Presidents, Secretary General and members of the Presidium of the Supreme People's Assembly;
9. elect or recall the Premier of the Cabinet;
10. appoint the Vice-Premiers, Chairpersons, Ministers and other members of the Cabinet on the recommendation of the Premier of the Cabinet;
11. appoint or remove the Prosecutor General of the Central Public Prosecutors Office;
12. elect or recall the President of the Central Court;
13. elect or recall the chairperson, vice-chairpersons and members of the sectoral committees of the Supreme People's Assembly;
14. deliberate and approve the State plan for the development of the national economy and the report on its implementation;
15. deliberate and approve the State budget and the report on its implementation;
16. hear a report on the work of the Cabinet and the central bodies when necessary, and adopt relevant measures; and
17. decide on ratification or recession of treaties suggested to the Supreme People's Assembly.

Article 92 The Supreme People's Assembly shall hold regular and extraordinary sessions.

Regular sessions shall be convened once or twice a year by the Presidium of the Supreme People's Assembly.

Extraordinary sessions shall be convened when the Presidium of the Supreme People's Assembly deems them necessary, or at the request of one-third or more of the total number of deputies.

Article 93 The Supreme People's Assembly shall require a quorum of two-thirds or more of the total number of deputies in order to meet.

Article 94 The Supreme People's Assembly shall elect its Speaker and Deputy Speaker.

The Speaker shall preside over the session.

Article 95 Items to be deliberated at the Supreme People's Assembly shall be submitted by the Chairman of the State Affairs Commission, the State Affairs Commission, the Presidium of the Supreme People's Assembly, the Cabinet, and the sectoral committees of the Supreme People's Assembly of the Democratic People's Republic of Korea.

Items may also be presented by deputies.

Article 96 The first session of each Supreme People's Assembly shall elect the Credentials Committee and, on hearing the Committee's report, adopt a decision on confirmation of the credentials of deputies.
Article 97 The Supreme People's Assembly shall lay laws, ordinances and decisions on the table.
Laws, ordinances and decisions laid by the Supreme People's Assembly shall be adopted when a half or more of attending deputies consent by a show of hands.
The Constitution shall be amended or supplemented with the approval of two-thirds or more of the total number of deputies to the Supreme People's Assembly.
Article 98 The Supreme People's Assembly shall have such sectoral committees as the Legislation Committee, the Budget Committee, the Foreign Affairs Committee and the like.
A sectoral committee of the Supreme People's Assembly shall consist of the chairperson, vice-chairperson and members.
The sectoral committees of the Supreme People's Assembly shall draft or deliberate policies and bills of the State, and take measures for their implementation in the manner of assisting the work of the Supreme People's Assembly.
The sectoral committees of the Supreme People's Assembly shall work under the guidance of the Presidium of the Supreme People's Assembly when the Supreme People's Assembly is not in session.
Article 99 Deputies to the Supreme People's Assembly shall be guaranteed inviolability.
No deputy to the Supreme People's Assembly may be arrested or punished without the consent of the Supreme People's Assembly or, when it is not in session, without the consent of the Presidium of the Supreme People's Assembly, unless the deputy in question is caught in the act.

Section 2 The Chairman of the State Affairs Commission of the Democratic People's Republic of Korea

Article 100 The Chairman of the State Affairs Commission of the Democratic People's Republic of Korea shall be the supreme leader of the Democratic People's Republic of Korea, who represents the State.
Article 101 The Chairman of the State Affairs Commission of the Democratic People's Republic of Korea shall be elected at the Supreme People's Assembly according to the unanimous will of all the Korean people.

The Chairman of the State Affairs Commission of the Democratic People's Republic of Korea shall not be elected as a deputy to the Supreme People's Assembly.

Article 102 The term of office of the Chairman of the State Affairs Commission of the Democratic People's Republic of Korea shall be the same as that of the Supreme People's Assembly.

Article 103 The Chairman of the State Affairs Commission of the Democratic People's Republic of Korea shall be the commander-in-chief of the armed forces of the Democratic People's Republic of Korea and command and direct all the armed forces of the State.

Article 104 The Chairman of the State Affairs Commission of the Democratic People' Republic of Korea shall have the following duties and authority to:

1. direct the overall affairs of the State;
2. guide the work of the State Affairs Commission by himself;
3. make public laws and regulations of the Supreme People's Assembly and the major decrees and decisions of the State Affairs Commission;
4. appoint and remove key cadres of the State;
5. appoint or recall the diplomatic representatives residing in other countries;
6. ratify or rescind major treaties concluded with other countries;
7. exercise the power of granting special pardon;
8. proclaim a state of emergency, state of war and mobilization order within the country; and
9. organize and direct the National Defense Committee in wartime.

Article 105 The Chairman of the State Affairs Commission of the Democratic People's Republic of Korea shall issue orders.

Article 106 The Chairman of the State Affairs Commission of the Democratic People's Republic of Korea shall be accountable to the Supreme People's Assembly.

Section 3 The State Affairs Commission

Article 107 The State Affairs Commission shall be the supreme policy-oriented leadership body of State power.

Article 108 The State Affairs Commission shall consist of the Chairman, First Vice-Chairperson, Vice-Chairpersons and members.

Article 109 The term of office of the State Affairs Commission shall be the same as that of the Supreme People's Assembly.

Article 110 The State Affairs Commission shall have the following duties and authority to:

1. discuss and decide important policies of the State;
2. exercise supervision over the fulfilment of the orders of the Chairman of the State Affairs Commission of the Democratic People's Republic of Korea, and decrees, decisions and directives of the State Affairs Commission, and take measures for their fulfillment;
3. abrogate decisions and directives of State organs which run counter to the orders of the Chairman of the State Affairs Commission of the Democratic People's Republic of Korea and the decrees, decisions and directives of the State Affairs Commission; and
4. appoint or remove vice-Premiers, chairpersons, ministers and other members of the Cabinet on the recommendation of the Premier of the Cabinet when the Supreme People's Assembly is not in session.

Article 111 The State Affairs Commission shall issue decrees, decisions and directives.

Article 112 The State Affairs Commission shall be accountable to the Supreme People's Assembly.

Section 4 The Presidium of the Supreme People's Assembly

Article 113 The Presidium of the Supreme People's Assembly shall be the highest organ of State power when the Supreme People's Assembly is not in session.

Article 114 The Presidium of the Supreme People's Assembly shall consist of the President, Vice-Presidents, Secretary General and members.

Article 115 The term of office of the Presidium of the Supreme People's Assembly shall be the same as that of Supreme People's Assembly.

The Presidium of the Supreme People's Assembly shall continue its work until a new Presidium is elected, even after the term of the Supreme People's Assembly expires.

Article 116 The Presidium of the Supreme People's Assembly has the following duties and authority to:

1. convene sessions of the Supreme People's Assembly;
2. deliberate and adopt new draft bills and regulations, and amendments and supplements to the current laws and regulations raised in the intervals between sessions of the

Supreme People's Assembly, and obtain the approval of the next session of the Supreme People's Assembly for major laws which are adopted and enforced;

3. deliberate and approve the State plan for the development of the national economy, the State budget, and plans for their adjustment raised for unavoidable reasons in the intervals between sessions of the Supreme People's Assembly;
4. interpret the Constitution, current laws and regulations;
5. supervise law observance and enforcement by the State organs and take relevant measures;
6. rescind the decisions and directives of State bodies which run counter to the Constitution , orders of the Chairman of the State Affairs Commission of the Democratic People's Republic of Korea, laws, regulations and decisions of the Supreme People's Assembly, decrees, decisions and directives of the State Affairs Commission, and the decree, decisions and directives of the Presidium of the Supreme People's Assembly, and suspend the implementation of unwarranted decisions of local people's assemblies;
7. conduct the election of deputies to the Supreme People's Assembly and organize the elections of deputies to the local people's assemblies;
8. work with the deputies to the Supreme People's Assembly;
9. work with the sectoral committees of the Supreme People's Assembly;
10. create or abolish commissions and ministries of the Cabinet;
11. appoint or remove members of sectoral committees of the Presidium of the Supreme People's Assembly;
12. elect or recall the judges and people's assessors of the Central Court;
13. ratify or abrogate treaties concluded with other countries;
14. institute decorations, medals, honorary titles and diplomatic ranks, and confer decorations, medals and honorary titles;
15. grant general amnesties;
16. establish or alter administrative units and districts; and
17. conduct external activities including contacts with foreign parliaments and inter-parliamentary organizations.

Article 117 The President of the Presidium of the Supreme People's Assembly shall organize and guide the work of the Presidium.

The President of the Presidium of the Supreme People's Assembly, in the name of the State, shall receive the credentials and letters of recall of accredited diplomatic representatives of foreign countries.

Article 118 The Presidium of the Supreme People's Assembly shall convene the Plenary Meeting and the Meeting of the Permanent Committee.

The Plenary Meeting shall consist of all the members and the Meeting of the Permanent Committee shall consist of the President, Vice-Presidents and Secretary General.

Article 119 The Plenary Meeting of the Presidium of the Supreme People's Assembly shall deliberate and decide on important matters arising in fulfilling the duties of the Presidium and the exercising its authority.

The Meeting of the Permanent Committee shall deliberate and decide on matters entrusted to it by the Plenary Meeting.

Article 120 The Presidium of the Supreme People's Assembly shall issue decrees, decisions and directives.

Article 121 The Presidium of the Supreme People's Assembly may set up sectoral committees to assist it in its work.

Article 122 The Presidium of the Supreme People's Assembly shall be accountable to the Supreme People's Assembly.

Section 5 The Cabinet

Article 123 The Cabinet shall be the administrative and executive body of State power and organ of overall State administration.

Article 124 The Cabinet shall consist of the Premier, vice-premiers, chairpersons, ministers and other members as required.

The term of office of the Cabinet shall be the same as that of the Supreme People's Assembly.

Article 125 The Cabinet shall have following duties and authorities to:

1. adopt measures for the implementation of State policies;
2. adopt, amend or supplement the regulations on State administration on the basis of the Constitution and the laws;
3. direct the work of the commissions and ministries of the Cabinet, organs directly under its authority and local people's committees;
4. establish or abolish organs directly under its authority, major administrative and economic bodies, and enterprises, and adopt measures for improving State administration bodies;
5. draft the State plan for the development of the national

economy and adopt measures to put it into implementation;

6. complete the State budget and adopt measures to implement it;
7. organize and execute the work of industry, agriculture, construction, transport, post and telecommunications, commerce, foreign trade, land administration, municipal administration, education, science, culture, health service, physical culture and sport, labor administration, protection of environment, tourism and other sectors;
8. adopt measures to strengthen the monetary and banking system;
9. inspect and control the establishment of order in State administration;
10. adopt measures to maintain public order, protect the property and interests of the State and social, cooperative organizations, and safeguard the rights of citizens;
11. conclude treaties with foreign countries and conduct external affairs; and
12. rescind the decisions and directives of administrative and economic bodies which run counter to the decisions and directives of the Cabinet.

Article 126 The Premier of the Cabinet shall organize and guide the work of the Cabinet.

The Premier of the Cabinet shall represent the Government of the Democratic People's Republic of Korea.

Article 127 The Cabinet shall convene the Plenary Meeting and the Meeting of the Permanent Committee.

The Plenary Meeting of the Cabinet shall consist of all members of the Cabinet and the Meeting of the Permanent Committee shall consist of the Premier, vice-premiers and other members of the Cabinet appointed by the Premier.

Article 128 The Plenary Meeting of the Cabinet shall deliberate and decide on new and important administrative and economic matters.

The Meeting of the Permanent Committee shall deliberate and decide on matters entrusted to it by the Plenary Meeting of the Cabinet.

Article 129 The Cabinet shall issue decisions and directives.

Article 130 The Cabinet may have non-permanent sectoral committees to assist it in its work.

Article 131 The Cabinet is accountable to the Supreme People's Assembly and to the Presidium of the Supreme People's Assembly when the Supreme People's Assembly is not in session.

Article 132 The newly elected Premier of the Cabinet shall take an oath of allegiance on behalf of the members of the Cabinet at the Supreme People's Assembly.

Article 133 The commissions and ministries of the Cabinet shall be departmental executive bodies of the Cabinet and central departmental bodies of administration.

Article 134 The commissions and ministries of the Cabinet shall supervise and guide the work of the sectors concerned in a uniform way under the guidance of the Cabinet.

Article 135 The commissions and ministries of the Cabinet shall run committee meetings and cadre meetings respectively.

The committee meetings and cadre meetings of the commissions and ministries shall deliberate and decide on the measures for the implementation of the decisions and directives of the Cabinet and other important matters.

Article 136 The commissions and ministries shall issue directives.

Section 6 The Local People's Assembly

Article 137 The people's assembly of a province (or municipality directly under the central authority), city (or district) or county shall be the local organ of State power.

Article 138 The local people's assembly shall consist of deputies elected on the principle of universal, equal and direct suffrage by secret ballot.

Article 139 The term of office of the people's assembly of a province (or municipality directly under the central authority), city (or district) or county shall be four years.

A new local people's assembly shall be elected according to the decision of the local people's committee at the corresponding level prior to the expiration of the former's term of office.

When unavoidable circumstances render an election impossible, the term of office of the local people's assembly shall be prolonged until an election can be held.

Article 140 The local people's assembly shall have the following duties and authority to:

1. deliberate and approve the report on the development plan of local-level national economy and its implementation;
2. deliberate and approve the report on the local budget and its implementation;
3. adopt measures to enforce laws of the State in the corresponding local jurisdictions;

4. elect or recall the chairperson, vice-chairpersons, secretary general and members of the people's committee at the corresponding level;
5. elect or recall judges and people's assessors of the court at the corresponding local level; and
6. rescind unwarranted decisions and directives of the people's committee at the corresponding level and the people's assemblies and people's committees at lower levels.

Article 141 The local people's assembly convenes regular and extraordinary sessions.

Regular sessions shall be convened once or twice a year by the people's committee at the corresponding level.

Extraordinary sessions shall be convened when the people's committee at the corresponding level deems them necessary or at the request of one-third or more of the total number of deputies.

Article 142 The local people's assembly shall require a quorum of at two-thirds or more of the total number of deputies in order to meet.

Article 143 The local people's assembly shall elect its speaker.

The speaker shall preside over the sessions.

Article 144 The local people's assembly shall issue decisions.

Section 7 The Local People's Committee

Article 145 The people's committee of a province (or municipality directly under the central authority), city (or district) or county shall exercise the function of the local organ of State power when the people's assembly at the corresponding level is not in session, and of the administrative and executive organ of State power at the corresponding level.

Article 146 The local people's committee shall consist of the chairperson, vice-chairpersons, secretary and members.

The term of office of the local people's committee shall be the same as that of the corresponding people's assembly.

Article 147 The local people's committee shall have the following duties and authority to:

1. convene sessions of the people's assembly;
2. organize the election of deputies to the people's assembly;
3. work with the deputies to the people's assembly;
4. implement the orders of the Chairman of the State Affairs Commission of the Democratic People's Republic of Korea, the laws, ordinances and decisions of the Supreme People's Assembly, the decrees, decisions and directives of the State

Affairs Commission, the decrees, decisions and directives of the Presidium of the Supreme People's Assembly, the decisions and directives of the Cabinet and commissions and ministries of the Cabinet, the decisions and directives of the corresponding local people's assembly and the people's committees at higher levels;
5. organize and carry out all administrative affairs in the given local area;
6. make the local plan for development of the national economy and adopt the measures to implement it;
7. compile the local budget and adopt measures for its implementation;
8. adopt measures to maintain public order, protect the ownership and interests of the State and social, cooperative organizations and safeguard the rights of citizens in the given area;
9. inspect and control the establishment of order in State administration in the given area;
10. direct the work of the people's committees at lower levels; and
11. rescind unwarranted decisions and directives of the people's committees at lower levels, and suspend the implementation of unwarranted decisions of the people's assemblies at lower level.

Article 148 The local people's committee shall convene plenary meetings and meetings of the permanent committee.

The plenary meeting of the local people's committee shall consist of all its members and the meeting of the permanent committee shall consist of the chairperson, vice-chairpersons and secretary general.

Article 149 The plenary meeting of the local people's committee shall deliberate and decide on important matters arising from implementing its duties and exercising its authority.

The meeting of the permanent committee shall deliberate and decide on the matters entrusted to it by the plenary meeting.

Article 150 The people's committee shall issue decisions and directives.

Article 151 The local people's committee may have non-permanent sectoral committees to assist it in its work.

Article 152 The local people's committee shall be accountable to the corresponding people's assembly.

The local people's committee shall be subordinate to the people's committees at higher levels, the Cabinet and the Presidium of the Supreme People's Assembly.

Section 8 The Public Prosecutors Office and the Court

Article 153 Prosecutors work shall be conducted by the Central Public Prosecutor's Office, the public prosecutor's office of a province (or municipality directly under the central authority), city (or district) or county and the special public prosecutor's offices.

Article 154 The term of office of the Prosecutor General of the Central Public Prosecutor's Office shall be the same as that of the Supreme People's Assembly.

Article 155 Public prosecutors shall be appointed or removed by the Central Public Prosecutor's Office.

Article 156 The functions of the public prosecutor's office shall be to:

1. oversee if institutions, enterprises, organizations and citizens strictly observe State laws;
2. oversee if the decisions and directives of State bodies conform with the Constitution, the orders of the Chairman of the State Affairs Commission of the Democratic People's Republic of Korea, the laws, ordinances and decisions of the Supreme People's Assembly, the decrees, decisions and directives of the State Affairs Commission, the decrees, decisions and directives of the Presidium of the Supreme People's Assembly, and the decisions and directives of the Cabinet; and
3. protect, through identifying offenders of law including criminals and instituting legal proceedings, the State power of the Democratic People's Republic of Korea, the socialist system, the property of the State and social, cooperative organizations, personal right as guaranteed by the Constitution and the people's life and property.

Article 157 Prosecutors work shall be conducted under the unified direction of the Central Public Prosecutor's Office, and all public prosecutors' office shall be subordinate to their higher offices and the Central Prosecutor's Office.

Article 158 The Central Prosecutor's Office shall be accountable to the Supreme People's Assembly or to the Presidium of the Supreme People's Assembly when the Supreme People's Assembly is not in session.

Article 159 Justice shall be administered by the Central Court, the court of a province (or municipality directly under the central authority), the city (or district) or county people's courts, and the special courts.

Verdicts shall be delivered in the name of the Democratic People's Republic of Korea.

Article 160 The term of office of the President of the Central Court shall be the same as that of the Supreme People's Assembly.

The term of office of judges and people's assessors of the Central Court, the court of a province (or municipality directly under the central authority), city (or district) people's courts and county people's courts shall be the same as that of the people's assembly at the corresponding level.

Article 161 The presidents and judges of the special courts are appointed or removed by the Central Court.

The people's assessors of the special courts are elected by the military staff meeting concerned or by the employees' meeting concerned.

Article 162 The functions of the court shall be to:

1. protect through judicial activities the State power and the socialist system of the Democratic People's Republic of Korea, the property of the State and social, cooperative organizations, and constitutional rights and lives and property of the people;
2. ensure that all institutions, enterprises, organizations and citizens abide strictly by State laws and staunchly combat class enemies and all law-breakers; and
3. execute judgments and decisions with regard to property and conduct notarial work.

Article 163 The justice shall be administered by a court consisting of one judge and two people's assessors.

In special cases, there may be three judges.

Article 164 Court cases shall be heard in public and the accused shall be guaranteed the right of defense.

Hearings may be closed to the public as stipulated by law.

Article 165 Judicial proceedings shall be conducted in the Korean language.

Foreign citizens may use their own language during court proceedings.

Article 166 In administering justice, the court shall be independent, and judicial proceedings shall be carried out in strict accordance with the law.

Article 167 The Central Court shall be the highest judicial organ of the Democratic People's Republic of Korea.

The Central Court shall supervise the judicial activities of all the courts.

Article 168 The Central Court shall be accountable to the Supreme People's Assembly or to the Presidium of the Supreme People's Assembly when the Supreme People's Assembly is not in session.

Chapter 7 Emblem, Flag, Anthem and Capital

Article 169 The national emblem of the Democratic People's Republic of Korea shall bear the design of a grand hydroelectric power station under Mt. Paektu, the sacred mountain of the revolution, and the beaming light of a five-pointed red star, with ears of rice forming an oval frame, bound with a braided red ribbon bearing the inscription 《조선민주주의인민공화국 (The Democratic People's Republic of Korea)》.

Article 170 The national flag of the Democratic People's Republic of Korea shall consist of a central red panel, bordered with both above and below by a narrow white stripe and a broad blue stripe. The central red panel shall bear a five-pointed red star within a white circle near the hoist. The ration of the width to the length shall be 1:2.

Article 171 The national anthem of the Democratic People's Republic of Korea shall be 《애국가 (The Patriot Song)》.

Article 172 The capital of the Democratic People's Republic of Korea shall be Pyongyang.

[Source: *Joseon Minjujueui Inmin Gonghwaguk Sahoejueui Heonbeop* (Socialist Constitution of the Democratic People's Republic of Korea) as amended in September 2023 and taken from *Bukhan Beopryeongjip sang & ha* (Collection of Laws and Regulations of North Korea Vol. I & II, PDF), National Intelligence Service of the Republic of Korea, 2024, Seoul, *See* https://www.nis.go.kr/resources/synap/skin/doc.html?fn=NIS_FILE_1726189729836 (Last visited 01/30/2025)]

*The whole text of this Socialist Constitution is translated into English by the Author.

▪ LAW OF THE DEMOCRATIC PEOPLE'S REPUBLIC OF KOREA ON FOREIGN INVESTMENT

Adopted by Decision No. 17 of the Standing Committee of the Supreme People's Assembly on October 5, 1992, and amended by the Presidium of the Supreme People's Assembly on February 26, 1999, November 30, 2004, September 26, 2007, April 29, 2008, August 19, 2008, November 29, 2011, and March 1, 2022

Article 1 (Objective and status of this Law)

This Law is enacted for the purpose of encouraging foreign investment in the DPRK and protecting the legitimate rights and interests of the investors.

This Law is the basic law on foreign investment.

Article 2 (Definitions)

1. *Foreign investment* means an investment in the DPRK by a foreign investor of property, property rights or know-how for the purpose of carrying out economic activities;

2. *Foreign investor* means a corporate body or an individual of a foreign country that makes an investment in the territory of the DPRK;

3. *Foreign-invested businesses* mean foreign-invested enterprises and foreign enterprises;

4. *Foreign-invested enterprises* mean equity joint venture enterprises, contractual joint venture enterprises and wholly foreign-owned enterprises that are set up in the territory of the DPRK;

5. *A contractual joint venture* is an enterprise in which investors from the DPRK and a foreign country jointly invest, the management is undertaken by the partner from the host country and the share of the investment made by the foreign investor is redeemed or the profits are distributed according to the terms of the contract;

6. *An equity joint venture* is an enterprise in which investors from the DPRK and a foreign country jointly invest and operate the business, and the profits are distributed the investors proportionate to the shares of the investment;

7. *A wholly foreign-owned enterprise* is an enterprise in which a foreign investor makes an investment and undertakes management on his account;

8. *A foreign enterprise* is an enterprise of a foreign country that is registered with the investment management organ for conducting business activities;

9. *A foreign-invested bank* is a joint venture bank, wholly foreign-owned bank and branch of a foreign bank that are set up in the

territory of the DPRK; and

10. *Special economic zone* means an area where preferential treatment is accorded to business activities such as investment, production, trade and service pursuant to the laws and regulations enacted by the State for those purposes.

Article 3 (Establishment of foreign-invested enterprises and banks)

A foreign investor may establish and operate an enterprise or a bank in the territory of the DPRK. In this case approval thereof shall be obtained from the investment management organ.

The investment management organ shall include the competent central organ and the management organ of the special economic zones.

Article 4 (Protection of rights and interests of investors, provision of conditions)

The State shall protect the legal rights and interests of foreign investors and provide conditions for the operation of foreign-invested enterprises and foreign-invested banks.

Article 5 (Investors)

Foreign corporate bodies and individuals are free to make investment in the DPRK. Overseas Koreans may also make an investment in accordance with this Law.

Article 6 (Sectors and modes of investment)

Foreign investors may make investments of various modes in such sectors as industry, agriculture, construction, transportation, communications, science and technology, tourism, circulation and fiancé.

Article 7 (Priority sectors)

The State particularly encourages investments that are conducive to the introduction of high technologies and other state-of-the-art technology, manufacturing of internationally competitive goods, construction of infrastructure facilities, scientific research and development of technology.

Article 8 (Preferential treatment for priority sectors)

A foreign-invested enterprise that invests in the priority sector shall enjoy such benefits as preferential treatment in tax assessment, favourable conditions of land use and preferential bank loans.

Article 9 (Provision of preferential conditions for business in special economic zones)

The State shall ensure that foreign-invested businesses that are set up in the special economic zones are provided with preferential conditions for business activities in such areas as purchase, bringing-in and taking-out of materials, marketing of products, employment of labour, payment of taxes and land use.

Article 10 (Provision of conditions for immigration of foreign investors)

The State shall ensure that formation for entry and departure of foreigners making an investment in the DPRK are set in such a way as to suite their convenience.

Article 11 (Prohibition and restriction of investment)

Investment shall be prohibited or restricted on the following cases:

1. Projects that are detrimental to national security, pubic health and healthy social and moral life;
2. Projects for the purpose of exporting natural resources;
3. Projects that violate the environmental protection criteria;
4. Projects that are technically outdated; and
5. Projects with low economic efficiency

Article 12 (Investment property, property rights)

A foreign investor may invest in the form of currency, property in kind, industrial property right and property right. In this case the value of the assets and property rights invested shall be determined by agreement between the partners by reference to the prevailing world market price.

Article 13 (Establishment of branch, representative office or agency)

Foreign-invested enterprises, foreign-invested banks and wholly foreign-owned banks may open branched, representative offices or agencies in the DPRK or other countries. They may conduct joint operations with foreign companies.

Article 14 (Legal capacity)

Foreign-invested enterprises, foreign-invested banks and wholly foreign-owned banks shall be corporate bodies of the DPRK.

Branches, representative offices and agencies of foreign enterprises, and branches of foreign banks established in the DPRK shall not be corporate of the DPRK.

Article 15 (Term of land lease)

The State shall lease land to foreign investors, foreign-invested enterprises and foreign-invested banks for their establishment.

The Term of lease shall be 50 years at maximum.

Land so leased may be assigned or mortgaged during the term of lease subject to the approval of the land leasing institution.

Article 16 (Employment)

A foreign-invested enterprise and a foreign-invested bank shall employ the labour of the DPRK.

Some of the managerial personnel, and technicians and skilled workers for special jobs may be employed from abroad subject to the agreement of the investment management organ.

Article 17 (Taxation)

Foreign investors, foreign-invested enterprises, foreign enterprises and foreign-invested banks shall pay income tax, turnover tax and property tax according to the prescribed rates.

Article 18 (Reinvestment)

Foreign investors may reinvest the whole or part of their profits in the DPRK. In this case the whole or part of the income tax already paid on the reinvested amount shall be refunded.

Article 19 (Protection of investment property)

The State shall not nationalize or expropriate the properties of foreign-investors, foreign-invested enterprises and banks.

Should expropriation is required for public interests, notification thereof shall be made in advance and sufficient compensation for its value shall be made through legal procedures.

Article 20 (Remittance)

Legitimate profits and other income earned by a foreign investor from business or banking operations, and any money that remains after the liquidation of a business or bank may be remitted out of the territory of the DPRK without any restrictions.

Article 21 (Confidentiality)

The State shall protect by law the business secrets of foreign-invested enterprises and banks, and shall not disclose them without the consent of the foreign investor concerned.

Article 22 (Settlement of disputes)

Any disagreement concerning foreign investment shall be settled through consultation.

In case of failure in consultation, the disagreement shall be settled through mediation, arbitration or legal procedures.

[Source: (1) Laws and Regulations of the Democratic People's Republic of Korea Governing External Economic Matters, Legislation Press, Pyongyang, 2012; (2) *Bukhan Beopryeongjip sang & ha* (Collection of Laws and Regulations of North Korea Vol. I & II, PDF), National Intelligence Service of the Republic of Korea, Seoul, 2024]

*Amendments made after 2012 was translated into English by the Author..

▪ LAW OF THE DEMOCRATIC PEOPLE'S REPUBLIC OF KOREA ON WHOLLY FOREIGN-OWNED ENTERPRISES

Adopted by Decision No. 19 of the Standing Committee of the Supreme People's Assembly on October 5, 1992, and amended by the Presidium of the Supreme People's Assembly on February 26, 1999, November 30, 2004, May 17, 2005, May 23, 2006, September 26, 2007 and November 29, 2011

Chapter 1 Fundamentals

Article 1 (Objective)

This Law is enacted for the purpose of expanding and promoting economic cooperation and exchange with foreign countries through the establishment and operation of wholly foreign-owned enterprises.

Article 2 (Definition)

A wholly foreign-owned enterprise is a form of business whereby a foreigner invests the whole amount of capital required for the establishment and operation thereof and operates it independently.

Article 3 (Permitted sectors, prohibited sectors)

Foreign investors may establish and operate enterprises in the fields of electronics, automation, machine-building, food-processing, garment-processing, daily-necessities, transport, service and others.

Enterprises that are detrimental to national security or outdated from technical point of view shall not be established.

Article 4 (Protection of investment)

The State shall protect by law the capital invested by foreign investors and income from their business activities.

Article 5 (Observance by investors and law and regulations)

Foreign investors shall respect and strictly observe the laws and regulations of the DPRK and shall not commit any acts that may cause hindrance to the development of the national economy of the DPRK.

Article 6 (Applicability)

This Law shall be applicable to the wholly foreign-owned enterprises that are set up and operated in the designated areas.

Chapter 2 Establishment of Wholly Foreign-Owned Enterprises

Article 7 (Application)

A foreign investor who wishes to establish an enterprise shall submit to the investment management organ the documents of application to that effect.

The documents of application shall include an application stating the name, address, total amount of investment, registered capital, business category, number of employees and term of operation, a copy of the articles of association, a feasibility study report and the credit references of the investor.

Article 8 (Examination of application, date of establishment)

The investment management organ shall examine the application for the establishment of an enterprise within 30 days of receipt thereof and either approve or reject it.

A document of approval shall be issued in case of approval, or in case of rejection, a notice of rejection sent with the reason thereof stated.

Article 9 (Registration)

A foreign-investor shall, within 30 days of obtaining the approval, register the enterprise with the people's committee of the province (or municipality directly under the central authority) or management organ of the special economic zone.

Tax and customs registration shall be made within 20 days of registration with the people's committee of the province (or municipality directly under the central authority) or the management organ of the special economic zone.

Article 10 (Establishment of branches, representative offices and agencies)

A wholly foreign-owned enterprise may, subject to the approval of the investment management organ, establish branches, representative offices or agencies within or outside the territory of the DPRK.

Article 11 (Consignment)

A foreign investor may consign the construction work required for the establishment of the enterprise with a construction enterprise of the DPRK.

Article 12 (Term of investment)

A foreign investor shall make investment within the term prescribed in the document of approval of establishment of the enterprise.

Where it is impossible to make investment within the prescribed period due to unavoidable reasons, the term may be extended subject to the approval of the investment management organ.

Article 13 (Cancellation of approval)

Where a foreign investor fails to make investment within the prescribed term without any justifiable reasons, the investment management organ may cancel the approval for the establishment.

Chapter 3 Business Activities of Wholly Foreign-owned Enterprises

Article 14 (Alteration of business category)

A wholly foreign-owned enterprise shall carry on business within the approved limit of business category.

Where the business category is to be altered or extended, approval thereof shall be obtained from the investment management organ.

Article 15 (Submission of plan for production, export and import)

A wholly foreign-owned enterprise shall submit to the investment management organ its yearly and quarterly plans for production, import and export.

Article 16 (Import of materials for operation, marketing of products)

A wholly foreign-owned enterprise may, according to the prescribed procedures, purchase in the DPRK raw and other materials and equipment, or sell its products in the DPRK, which shall be conducted via the investment management organ.

Article 17 (Bank accounts)

A wholly foreign-owned enterprise shall open an account with a DPRK bank or a foreign-invested bank in the DPRK.

Account may (be)* opened with a bank in a foreign country subject to the approval of the foreign exchange control organ. *(be) is added by the author.

Article 18 (Accounting)

A wholly foreign-owned enterprise shall keep its financial statements in the area that it is located.

Financial management and accounting shall be conducted in accordance with the law and regulations on financial accounting of foreign-invested enterprises.

Article 19 (Employment)

A wholly foreign-owned enterprise shall employ the labour of the DPRK.

Some management personnel and technicians and skilled workers for special jobs may be employed from abroad, with the notification thereof made to the investment management organ.

Article 20 (Trade union)

Employees of a wholly foreign-owned enterprise may form a trade union.

The trade union shall protect the rights and interests of the employees, conclude a contract for the provision of working conditions with the wholly foreign-owned enterprise and supervise its implementation.

A wholly foreign-owned enterprise shall provide conditions for the activities of the trade union.

Article 21 (Reinvestment, remittance)

A wholly foreign-owned enterprise may reinvest legitimate profits made from its business activities or remit them abroad, in accordance (with)* the law and regulations on foreign exchange control. *(with) is added by the author.

Article 22 (Insurance)

Where a wholly foreign-owned enterprise wishes to be insured, it shall be take out the insurance policy of the DPRK.

Article 23 (Payment of tax)

A wholly foreign-owned enterprise shall pay prescribed tax.

A wholly foreign-owned enterprise in the priority sector shall benefit from reduction or exemption of income tax for a certain period of time.

Article 24 (Exemption from customs duties)

Where a wholly foreign-owned enterprise brings in materials for its production and management or exports its products, customs duties shall not be imposed thereon.

Article 25 (Registered capital)

A wholly foreign-owned enterprise may increase the registered capital.

Registered capital shall not be reduced during its term of operation.

Article 26 (Inspection of investment and tax payment)

The investment management organ and the financial institution concerned shall be empowered to examine the records of investment and tax payment of a wholly foreign-owned enterprise.

Chapter 4 Dissolution, Settlement of Dispute

Article 27 (Dissolution, extension of term of operation)

A wholly foreign-owned enterprise shall be dissolved upon expiry of its term of operation.

Where the enterprise is to be dissolved before the expiration of the term of operation or its term of operation extended, approval thereof shall be obtained from the investment management organ.

Article 28 (Sanction)

Any violation of this Law shall, depending on the seriousness of the offense, lead to such sanctions as fines, suspension of business operation or dissolution of business.

Article 29 (Registration of dissolution and bankruptcy, disposal of assets)

Should a wholly foreign-owned enterprise be dissolved or go bankrupt, application to that effect shall be filed with the investment management organ.

The assets of a wholly foreign-owned enterprise shall not be arbitrarily disposed of before the liquidation is completed.

Article 30 (Settlement of disputes)

Any dispute relating to a wholly foreign-owned enterprise shall be settled through consultation.

In case of failure in consultation, the dispute shall be settled by mediation, arbitration or legal procedures.

[Source: Laws and Regulations of the Democratic People's Republic of Korea Governing External Economic Matters, Legislation Press, Pyongyang, 2012]

- # LAW OF THE DEMOCRATIC PEOPLE'S REPUBLIC OF KOREA ON EQUITY JOINT VENTURE

Adopted by Decision No. 10 of the Standing Committee of the Supreme People's Assembly on September 8, 1984, amended by the same organ on January 20, 1994, and amended by the Presidium of the Supreme People's Assembly on February 26, 1999, May 17, 2001, November 30, 2004, May 23, 2006, September 26, 2007, August 19, 2008, November 29, 2011, and October 8, 2014

Chapter 1 Fundamentals

Article 1 (Objective)

This Law is enacted for the purpose of expanding and promoting economic and technical cooperation and exchange with foreign countries through equity joint venture.

Article 2 (Parties to investment)

Institutions, enterprises and organizations may establish equity joint-venture enterprises with foreign corporate bodies or individuals subject to the approval of the investment management organ.

The equity joint-venture enterprises shall be set up mainly in production sectors.

Article 3 (Joint-venture sectors, priority sectors)

Equity joint ventures may be set up in such sectors as machine building, electronics, information technology, science and technology, light industry, agriculture, forestry, fisheries, building materials, transport and finance.

The State encourages equity joint ventures in the introduction of high technology, scientific research and technological development, manufacturing of internationally competitive goods and construction of infrastructure facilities.

Article 4 (Prohibition, restriction)

The State shall prohibit or restrict equity joint ventures on businesses exceeding the environmental protection standard, businesses exporting natural resources, economically and technically out-of-dated businesses, businesses generating lower profits, and service businesses such as restaurants or stores.

Article 5 (Ownership, independence, limited liability)

An equity joint-venture enterprise shall have the ownership of the property and property rights contributed by its partners and carry on business independently.

An equity joint venture enterprise shall be liable for the debt incurred in the course of its operations with its registered capital.

Article 6 (Legal capacity)

An equity joint-venture enterprise shall be a corporate body of the DPRK from the date of its registration with the investment management organ.

The legitimate rights and interests of the equity joint-venture enterprises shall be protected by law.

Article 7 (Preferential treatment)

The State shall ensure that equity joint-venture enterprises in priority projects and those with overseas Koreans enjoy such preferential treatment as reduction of or exemption from tax, favourable conditions of land use and preferential bank loaning.

Article 8 (Applicability)

The establishment, operation, dissolution and liquidation of an equity joint-venture enterprise shall be conducted in accordance with this Law.

Matters not covered this Law shall be governed by the relevant laws and regulations.

Chapter 2 Establishment of an Equity Joint-Venture Enterprise

Article 9 (Application, date of establishment)

Partners to an equity joint venture shall, after concluding a joint-venture contract, submit to the investment management organ an application to that effect, accompanied by a copy of the contract, articles of association and feasibility study report.

The investment management organ shall review the application within 30 days of receipt thereof, and either issue a notice of approval to the applicant or send a notice of rejection with reasons thereof stated.

Article 10 (Registration)

An equity joint-venture enterprise shall, within 30 days of receiving a notice of approval, be registered with the people's committee of the province (or municipality directly under the central authority) where the enterprise is to be located or with management organ of the special economic zone.

Tax and customs registration shall be made within 20 days of registration with the people's committee of the province (or municipality directly under the central authority) or the management organ of the special economic zone.

Article 11 (Amount of investment, invested assets, property rights)

The amount of investment by each partner shall be determined by mutual agreement between the partners.

Partners may invest in the form of currency, property in kind, industrial property right, land use right, and right to exploit natural resources. In this case, the value of the property or property rights that have been invested shall be set by agreement between the partners by reference to the prevailing international market price.

Article 12 (Transfer of share of contribution)

A joint venture partner may transfer its share of contribution to a third party. In this case agreement of the other partner and approval of the investment management organ shall be obtained.

Article 13 (Establishment of branch, representative office or agency)

An equity joint-venture enterprise may, subject to the approval of the investment management organ, open its branch, representative office or agency in the DPRK territory, or in a foreign country.

Article 14 (Term of contribution, investment ratio of intellectual property right)

A joint-venture partner shall make contribution within the time limit prescribed in the notice of approval.

Should unavoidable circumstances so require, the term of contribution may be deferred subject to the approval of the investment management organ.

Investment in the form of intellectual property right such as patent, trademark right or industrial design right shall not exceed 20% of the registered capital.

Article 15 (Registered capital)

The registered capital of an equity joint-venture enterprise shall be over 30~50% of the total investment amount.

Where the registered capital is increased, particulars of the change shall be registered with the institution concerned.

The amount of registered capital shall not be decreased.

Chapter 3 Structure and Management of Equity Joint-Venture Enterprises

Article 16 (Status of board of directors)

An equity joint-venture enterprise shall have a board of directors.

The board of directors shall be the highest decision-making body of the enterprise.

Article 17 (Functions of board of directors)

The board of directors shall discuss and make decisions on such issues as amending the articles of association, formulating corporate strategy, increase of registered capital, plan for business activities, settlement of accounts, distribution, appointment and dismissal of the manager, assistant manager and auditor, and dissolution of the enterprise.

Article 18 (Managerial staff)

An equity joint-venture shall have the manager, assistant manager, accountant and other managerial staff as may be required.
The manager shall be accountable to the board of directors for his work.
Article 19 (Auditor)
An equity joint-venture enterprise may have an auditor, who shall not be a member of the managerial staff.
The auditor shall regularly conduct inspection of the financial situation of the enterprise and shall be accountable to the board of directors for his work.
Article 20 (Basis of management)
An equity joint-venture enterprise shall be managed according to the articles of association and the decisions made by the board of directors.
Article 21 (Date of commencement of operation)
An equity joint-venture enterprise shall commence its operation within the time limit prescribed in the notice of approval.
Where it is impossible to commence its operation within the prescribed period of time, the date of commencement of operation may be deferred subject to the approval of the investment management organ.
The enterprise that had the date of commencement of operation deferred shall pay prescribed arrears.
Article 22 (Business license, inaugural date)
An equity joint-venture enterprise shall obtain a license for business operation not later than the scheduled date of commencing operation.
The date of receipt of business license issued by the investment management organ shall be the date of inauguration of the enterprise concerned.
Article 23 (Purchase of materials for operation, marketing of products)
An equity joint-venture enterprise may, according to the prescribed rates, purchase raw and other materials and equipment or sell its products in the territory of the DPRK. In this case plans for the purchase of materials and marketing of its products shall be submitted to the investment management organ.
Article 24 (Customs duties)
Where an equity joint-venture enterprise brings in materials needed for its production and operation or takes out the goods it has produced, customs duties shall not be levied. Where an enterprise sells in the

DPRK territory the goods for which customs duties had been exempted, customs duties shall be payable.

Article 25 (Categories of business)

An equity joint-venture enterprise shall carry on business within the approved limit of the categories.

In case the category of business is to be increased or changed, approval thereof shall be obtained from the investment management organ.

Article 26 (Employment)

An equity joint-venture enterprise shall employ the labour of the DPRK.

Some of the managerial personnel, and technicians and skilled workers for special jobs may be employed from foreign countries subject to notification thereof to the investment management organ.

Article 27 (Management of labour)

An equity joint-venture enterprise shall manage its employees in accordance with the labour-related law and the regulations of the DPRK for foreign-invested enterprises.

Article 28 (Bank account)

An equity joint-venture enterprise shall open an account with a bank of the DPRK or a foreign-invested bank.

Where an account is to be opened with a bank in a foreign country, approval thereof shall be obtained from the foreign exchange control organ.

Article 29 (Loan)

An equity joint-venture enterprise may secure a loan for its business operation either from a DPRK bank or a foreign bank.

The Korean Won loaned and the one exchanged from foreign currency shall be used while being deposited in the designated bank.

Article 30 (Financial management, accounting)

An equity joint-venture enterprise shall conduct its financial management and accounting in accordance with the accounting regulations of the DPRK for foreign-invested enterprises.

Article 31 (Insurance)

An equity joint-venture enterprise that wishes to be insured shall take out the insurance policy of the DPRK.

Compulsory insurance shall be taken with the insurance company designated by the central insurance guidance organ.

Article 32 (Trade union)

The employees of an equity joint-venture enterprise may organize a trade union.
The joint-venture enterprise shall provide conditions for the activities of the union.

Chapter 4 Settlement of Accounts, Profit Distribution

Article 33 (Fiscal year)
The fiscal year of an equity joint-venture enterprise shall begin on January 1 and end on December 31.
Settlement of accounts for any fiscal year shall be completed by the end of February of the following year.
Article 34 (Mode of settlement of accounts)
The accounts of an equity joint-venture enterprise shall be settled in such a way as determining the profit by deducting from the gross revenue the costs of materials, fuel, power, and labour, depreciation, purchase expenses, maintenance costs of workshop and company, insurance premium, sales costs and the likes, and calculating the net profit by deducting from it the turnover tax or business tax and other expenses.
Article 35 (Reserve fund)
An equity joint-venture enterprise shall create reserve fund by laying aside 5% of its annual net profit until the reserve fund amounts to 25% of tis registered capital.
The reserve fund shall be used only for the purpose of covering the losses of the enterprise or increasing the registered capital.
Article 36 (Types of funds, creating thereof)
An equity joint-venture enterprise shall create funds for production expansion, technological development, bonus for employees, welfare and training.
The type, size, benefiting objects and scope of the funds shall be discussed and determined by the board of directors.
Article 37 (Profit distribution)
An equity joint-venture enterprise shall distribute profits after its document of account settlement has been examined by an auditor and endorsed by the board of directors.
The profits shall be distributed among the partners according to the proportion of their contribution after the payment of the income tax and deduction of the reserve fund and other necessary funds from the net profit.
Article 38 (Payment of tax, reduction or exemption)

An equity joint-venture enterprise shall pay tax according to the prescribed rates.
An enterprise in the priority sector shall be entitled to benefit from reduction or exemption of income tax for a certain period of time.
Article 39 (Compensation for loss in management)
An equity joint-venture enterprise may use its net profit of a given year to cover the loss incurred in the preceding year. In this case, the compensation period shall be limited to 4 successive years.
Article 40 (Settlement of accounts)
An equity joint-venture enterprise shall settle its accounts at a fixed period of time.
The documents of account settlement shall be submitted to the financial institution concerned within the prescribed period of time.
Article 41 (Reinvestment)
The foreign partner of an equity joint-venture enterprise may reinvest in the territory of the DPRK the whole or part of the profit that has been allotted to him. In this case, the income tax on the reinvested profit may be wholly or partially refunded from the total amount of income tax that has already been paid.
Article 42 (Remittance)
The foreign partner of an equity joint-venture enterprise may, without any restrictions, remit abroad the profits earned from business and other income, as well as money received after the liquidation of business.

Chapter 5 Dissolution, Settlement of Disputes

Article 43 (Terms of dissolution)
An equity joint-venture enterprise shall be dissolved when it is unable to continue its operation for such reasons as the termination of the term of operation, insolvency, default of the contractual obligations by either of the partners, continued operational loss or natural calamities.
Article 44 (Dissolution before expiry of term)
An equity joint-venture enterprise may, in case the circumstance demands the dissolution before the expiration of the term of operation, make decision on that matter at the board of directors and dissolve itself subject to the approval of the investment management organ. In this case a liquidation committee shall be organized by the board of directors.
The liquidation committee shall settle all the transactions and complete the liquidation of the enterprise and, within 10 days thereof, go through the formalities for the cancellation of the registration of the

enterprise. Where it is deemed in the course of liquidation that the enterprise deserves bankruptcy, application to that effect shall be filed with court of law.

Article 45 (Extension of term of operation)

An equity joint-venture may extend the term of operation. In this case the matter shall be discussed and decided at the board of directors 6 months before the termination of the term of operation and submitted to the investment management organ for approval.

The term of operation shall be counted from the date when the approval for the establishment of the enterprise was granted.

Article 46 (Settlement of disputes)

Any dispute concerning equity joint venture shall be settled through consultation.

In case of failure in consultation, the dispute shall be referred to mediation, arbitration or court.

[Sources: (1) Laws and Regulations of the Democratic People's Republic of Korea Governing External Economic Matters, Legislation Press, Pyongyang, 2012; (2) *Choesin Bukhan Beopryeongjip* published by *Bukhanbeop yeonguhoe* (Collection of Current Acts and Regulations of North Korea), Myung-Bong Chang (ed.), Seoul, 2018; and (3) *Bukhan Beopryeongjip sang & ha* (Collection of Laws and Regulations of North Korea Vol. I & II, PDF), National Intelligence Service of the Republic of Korea, Seoul, 2024]

*Any amendments made after December 21, 2012 are translated into English by the Author.

▪ LAW OF THE DEMOCRATIC PEOPLE'S REPUBLIC OF KOREA ON CONTRACTUAL JOINT VENTURE

Adopted by Decision No. 18 of the Standing Committee of the Supreme People's Assembly on October 5, 1992, and amended by the Presidium of the Supreme People's Assembly on February 26, 1999, November 30, 2004, May 23, 2006, September 26, 2007, April 29, 2008, August 19, 2008, November 29, 2011, and October 8, 2014

Article 1 (Objective)
This Law is enacted for the purpose of promoting and expanding economic and technical cooperation and exchange with foreign countries through contractual joint venture.

Article 2 (Parties to investment)
Institutions, enterprises and organizations may establish contractual joint ventures with foreign corporate bodies or individuals subject to the approval of the investment management organ.
Contractual joint ventures shall be set up mainly in the production sector.

Article 3 (Priority sectors)
The State encourages contractual joint ventures in the projects that introduce high technology or modern equipment, and in sectors that manufacture internationally competitive goods.

Article 4 (Prohibition, restriction)
Contractual joint ventures shall be prohibited or restricted in the projects that violate environmental protection criteria, export natural resources, and the projects that are economically and technically outdated or of low economic efficiency.

Article 5 (Preferential treatment)
The State shall grant preferential treatment such as reduction or exemption of tax, favourable conditions of land use and preferential bank loans to the contractual joint-venture enterprises in priority projects or those to which overseas Koreans are parties.

Article 6 (Application, approval)
An investor that wishes to set up a contractual joint venture shall, after concluding a joint-venture contract, submit to the investment management organ an application to that effect, accompanied by a copy of the contract, the articles of association and feasibility study report.
The investment management organ shall examine the application within 30 days of receipt thereof, and either issue a license or send a notice of rejection with the reasons thereof stated.

Article 7 (Registration)

The investor shall, within 30 days of obtaining the approval, be registered with the people's committee of the province (or municipality directly under the central authority) where the enterprise is to be located or the management organ of the special economic zone.

Registration for tax purposes and customs shall be made within 20 days of registration with the people's committee of the province (or municipality directly under the central authority) or the management organ of the special economic zone.

Article 8 (Business license, inaugural date)

A contractual joint-venture enterprise shall obtain a business license not later than scheduled inauguration date.

The date of receipt of a business license issued by the investment management organ shall be the inaugural date of the business concerned.

Article 9 (Business category)

A contractual joint venture enterprise shall carry on business within the limit of approved business category.

Where the business category is to be changed or extended, approval thereof shall be obtained from the investment management organ.

Article 10 (Transfer of share of contribution)

A joint-venture partner may transfer his share of contribution to a third party. In this case consent of the other partner and approval of the investment management organ shall be secured.

Article 11 (Employment)

A contractual joint-venture enterprise shall employ the labour of the DPRK.

Technicians and skilled workers for special jobs may be employed from foreign countries, with notification thereof made to the investment management organ.

Article 12 (Customs duties)

Where a contractual joint-venture enterprise imports materials for its production and business operation or exports the goods it has produced, customs duties shall not be imposed. Customs duties shall, however, be payable in case the goods for which customs duties were exempted are sold in the DPRK.

Article 13 (Insurance)

A contractual joint venture enterprise shall, if it so wishes, take out the insurance policy of an insurance company in the DPRK.

Compulsory insurance shall be taken with the company designated by the central insurance guidance organ.

Article 14 (Redemption of investment, profit distribution)

The redemption of investment to the foreign investor shall be made mainly in terms of the goods produced by the joint-venture enterprise. Profit shall be distributed in a manner agreed upon by the partners in the contract.

Article 15 (Preferential use of enterprise income)

Goods produced and revenues earned by the joint-venture enterprise may be used primarily for the repayment of the invested capital or distribution of profit according to the terms of the contract.

Article 16 (Remittance of profits and other income)

The foreign partner of a contractual joint-venture enterprise may remit abroad without any restrictions the profits earned from business and other income, as well as money received after the liquidation of business.

Article 17 (joint consultative board)

The partners to a joint venture may organize a joint consultative board, which shall be non-standing.

The board shall discuss such important matters as introduction of new technology, improvement of product quality, reinvestment and others concerning business operation of the enterprise.

Article 18 (Settlement of accounts)

A joint-venture enterprise shall settle the account at a fixed period.

The documents of account settlement shall be submitted to the financial institution concerned within the prescribed time limit.

Article 19 (Tax payment)

A contractual joint-venture shall pay tax according to the prescribed rates.

A contractual joint-venture enterprise in the priority sector may benefit from reduction or exemption of enterprise income tax for a certain period of time.

Article 20 (Dissolution)

Partners to a contractual joint venture may dissolve the enterprise by mutual agreement and subject to the approval of the investment management organ upon expiry of the term of operation, default of contractual obligation, continued operational loss or natural disasters.

Liability for any damage incurred from the dissolution of the enterprise shall be borne by the party responsible.

Article 21 (Formation of liquidation committee)

In the event of dissolution, partners to a contractual joint venture shall form a liquidation committee.
The liquidation committee shall cancel the registration of the enterprise within 10 days of winding up transactions of the enterprise and completion of liquidation.
Where it is deemed in the process of liquidation that the enterprise deserves bankruptcy, application thereof shall be made to the court of law.

Article 22 (Extension of term of operation)
A contractual joint venture may extend the term of operation. In this case approval thereof shall be obtained from the investment management organ 6 months prior to the expiry of the original term.
The term of operation shall run from the date of obtaining the license of the enterprise concerned.

Article 23 (Settlement of disputes)
Any dispute concerning the contractual joint venture shall be settled through consultation.
In case of failure in consultation, the dispute shall be settled by mediation, arbitration or legal procedures.

[Source: (1) Laws and Regulations of the Democratic People's Republic of Korea Governing External Economic Matters, Legislation Press, Pyongyang, 2012; (2) *Choesin Bukhan Beopryeongjip* published by *Bukhanbeop yeonguhoe* (Collection of Current Acts and Regulations of North Korea), Myung-Bong Chang (ed.), Seoul, 2018; and (3) *Bukhan Beopryeongjip sang & ha* (Collection of Laws and Regulations of North Korea Vol. I & II, PDF), National Intelligence Service of the Republic of Korea, Seoul, 2024);]
*Any amendments made after December 21, 2011 are translated into English by the Author.

▪ LAW OF THE DEMOCRATIC PEOPLE'S REPUBLIC OF KOREA ON THE RASON ECONOMIC AND TRADE ZONE

Adopted by decision No. 28 of the Standing Committee of the Supreme People's Assembly on January 31, 1993, and amended by the Presidium of the Supreme People's Assembly on February 26, 1999, November 7, 2002, April 19, 2005, September 26, 2007, January 27, 2010, and December 3, 2011

Chapter 1 Fundamentals

Article 1 (Objective)

This Law is enacted for the purpose of providing strict guidelines for the development and management of the Rason Economic and Trade Zone, thereby contributing to developing it into an area of international transit transport, trade, investment, finance, tourism and service.

Article 2 (Status of the Zone)

The Rason Economic Trade and Zone (the Zone) is a special economic zone of the Democratic People's Republic of Korea (the DPRK), where preferential policy is pursued in the economic sector.

Article 3 (Establishment of industrial parks)

The State shall ensure that industrial parks mainly of high-tech industry, international logistic business, equipment manufacturing, primary processing industry, light industry, service business and modern agriculture are established in the Zone according to plan.

Article 4 (Investors)

The Zone is open for investment by corporate bodies, individual persons and economic organizations of different countries.

Koreans residing outside the territory of the DPRK may also invest in the Zone in accordance with this Law.

Article 5 (Principle of provision of conditions for economic activities)

Investors may freely conduct economic activities in the Zone through the establishment of companies, branches, representative offices and the like.

The State shall ensure that investors are preferentially provided with conditions for their economic activities in such areas as land use, labour employment, payment of tax and access to markets.

Article 6 (Sectors of priority, prohibition, limitation)

The State particularly encourages investment in the sectors of infrastructure construction, state-of-the-art science and technology and production of internationally competitive goods.

Investments shall be prohibited or restricted in those projects that are detrimental to national sectary, public health, healthy social and moral life, protection of environment and growth of animals and plants, and projects that are economically and technically outdated.

Article 7 (Principle of protecting investors' property, interests and rights)

The property, legitimate income and invested rights of the investors in the Zone shall be protected by law.

The State shall not nationalize or expropriate the property of the investors.

Where an investor's property is, for unavoidable reasons, to be expropriated or used temporarily for public interest, notification thereof shall be made before going through prescribed legal procedures, and sufficient and effective compensation for its value shall be made without any discrimination.

Article 8 (Manager and operator of the Zone, principle of non-involvement in work of management committee)

Management and operation of the industrial parks and designated areas of the Zone shall be undertaken by the management committee under the guidance and assistance of the central guidance organ of the special economic zones and the Rason municipal people's committee.

Other institutions shall not get involved in the work of the management committee except in such cases as are prescribed in this Law.

Article 9 (Protection of personal safety and human rights, prohibition of illegal detention and arrest)

Personal safety and human rights of citizens in the Zone shall be protected by law.

No one shall be detained or arrested, nor his place of residence be searched without a legal warrant.

Any treaty concluded between the DPRK and a foreign country in respect of personal safety and criminal matters shall take precedence.

Article 10 (Applicable laws and regulations)

Applicable to the development and management of the Zone, business operation and other economic activities therein shall be this Law, and its implementing regulations, rules and general standards.

Where the laws and regulations governing the Zone provide otherwise than the conventions, memoranda of understanding and agreement concluded between the DPRK and a foreign country, the latter shall prevail. Where the laws and regulations for the Zone differ from those in effect outside thereof, the former shall take precedence.

Chapter 2 Development of the Zone

Article 11 (Principle of development)

The Zone shall be developed on the principle of:

1. Ensuring comparative advantage of the Zone over the surrounding areas in natural and geographical conditions, natural resources and requisites for production;
2. Making economic and rational use of land and resources;
3. Protecting the ecological environment of the Zone and the surrounding areas;
4. Raising international competitiveness of production and service;
5. Providing facilities for economic activities like trade and investment;
6. Guaranteeing public interests; and
7. Ensuring sustained and balanced economic development

Article 12 (Development plan, modification)

The Zone shall be developed in accordance with the approved development plan.

The development plan shall include the master plan, regional plan and detailed plan.

Approval for the modification of the development plan shall be granted by the organ that approved the plan concerned.

Article 13 (Mode of Development of Zone)

Development of the Zone may be conducted in various modes: an enterprise may comprehensively develop a certain area of land and operate it, an enterprise may be granted a special license to construct, manage and operate an infrastructure and public establishments and parties to development may agree upon a certain mode of development.

The developer enterprise may invite other enterprise(s) to participate in the construction of infrastructure facilities and public establishments.

Article 14 (Approval for developer enterprise)

Approval for the developer enterprise of the Zone shall be granted by the central guidance organ of the special economic zones by issuing to him a development license via the management committee or the Rason municipal people's committee.

Authorization of the developer enterprise and application for development license shall be undertaken by the management committee or the Rason municipal people's committee.

Article 15 (Land lease contract for comprehensive development and management of land)

The developer enterprise that wishes to conduct comprehensive development and management of land shall enter into a land lease contract with the land management institution.

The land lease contract shall specify the term of lease, area, compartment, purpose of use, term and method of payment of land rent and other necessary particulars.

The land management institution shall issue a land use certificate to the developer enterprise upon receipt of the land rent.

Article 16 (Term of land lease)

The term of land lease in the Zone shall be 50 years from the date of issuance of the land use certificate to the enterprise concerned.

Upon the expiry of the term of lease, the enterprise in the Zone shall re-rent into a contract for the continued use of the leased land.

Article 17 (Acquisition of real property, issuance of certificates)

An enterprise in the Zone may, according to the regulations, acquire the right to use land and ownership of building. In this case the competent institution shall issue a land use certificate or a building ownership registration certificate.

Article 18 (Assignment of right to use land and building, rental value)

The developer enterprise shall have the right to assign or lease the developed land and buildings as the infrastructure construction progresses in accordance with the development plan. In this case the value of assignment or lease shall be determined by the developer enterprise.

Article 19 (Changes in the right to use land and building ownership, registration thereof)

An enterprise in the Zone may, within the term of validity, assign, lease or mortgage the right to use land and building ownership through sale, exchange, donation or succession. In this case the particulars of change in the right to use land and building ownership shall be registered, and the certificate of land use and registration certificate of building ownership shall be re-issued.

Article 20 (Removal and location of buildings and attachments)

An institution or enterprise that is in charge of removal or relocation of public buildings, dwelling houses and attachments shall remove or relocate them and have the inhabitants moved to a different location so that the development process may not be interrupted.

Article 21 (Time for commencement of development process, development in planned manner)

The developer enterprise shall commence development upon completion of removal and relocation of buildings and attachments within the development area.

Article 22 (Development and use of farmland, forest land and hydric land)

The developer enterprise may, under contract system, develop and use the farmland, forest land and hydric land in the Zone. In this case a contract shall be concluded with the institution concerned.

Chapter 3 Management of the Zone

Article 23 (Principle of management)

The Zone shall be managed on the principle of:

1. Strictly observing and enforcing laws an regulations;
2. Ensuring autonomy of the management committee and enterprises;
3. Offering preferential treatment to trade and investment activities;
4. Complying with the objective laws of the economy and principles of market; and
5. Referring to international practices.

Article 24 (Establishment of a management committee, status)

A management committee shall be set up for the management and operation of the Zone.

The Committee is a local management organ that is in charge of the management and operation of the industrial parks and other designated areas.

Article 25 (Composition of management committee)

A management committee shall be composed of the chairperson, vice-chairperson(s), secretary and other members as may be required.

The management committee shall have such departments as are necessary for the development and management of the Zone.

Article 26 (Chief of the management committee)

The chief of the management committee shall be the chairperson.

The chairperson shall represent the management committee and be in charge of its work.

Article 27 (Functions of the management committee)

The management committee shall, within its competence, perform the following functions:

1. To prepare rules required for the development and management of the Zone;
2. To foster investment climate and attract investment;
3. To approve establishment of enterprises, register and grant license;
4. To make a public list of sectors of priority, limitation and prohibition;
5. To grant permission of specially-ordered construction projects and conduct completion inspection of construction of work;
6. To take custody of designs for ordered equipment;
7. To establish independent financial management system;
8. To register the rights to use land and building ownership;
9. To manage the property under its custody;
10. To render cooperation in the management of the enterprises;
11. To undertake supervision and render cooperation in the construction and management of infrastructure and public establishments;
12. To take measures for the environmental protection and fire-fighting in the area under control;
13. To render cooperation in the work concerning entry and exit of personnel, vehicles and goods;
14. To prepare articles of association of the management committee; and
15. To carry out other work in respect of the development and management of the Zone that are authorized by the central guidance organ of the special economic zones and the Rason municipal people's committee.

Article 28 (Setting up of office of management committee)

The management committee may, in case of need, set up an office and the like.

The office shall conduct work within the extent of its functions assigned by the management committee.

Article 29 (Submission of work program and statistics)

The management committee shall annually submit its work program and the statistics of the industrial parks and other designated areas to the central guidance organ of the special economic zones and the Rason municipal people's committee.

Article 30 (Functions of Rason municipal people's committee)

The Rason municipal people's committee shall perform the following functions for the development and management of the Zone:

1. To prepare implementing rules for the law and regulations of the Zone;
2. To provide workforce required for the development and business activities of the Zone; and
3. To carry out other work authorized by the central guidance organ of the special economic zones with regard to the development and management of the Zone.

Article 31 (Functions of central guidance organ of special economic zones)

The central guidance organ of the special economic zones shall:

1. Prepare development strategy for the Zone;
2. Contract local institutions for the development and construction of the Zone;
3. Cooperate and contact with foreign governments;
4. Approve screening criteria for the establishment of the enterprises;
5. Select local enterprises to make investment in the Zone; and
6. Render cooperation in the sale of the products of the Zone in local areas outside it.

Article 32 (Compilation and execution of budget)

The management committee shall compile and execute a budget. Documents concerning the compilation and execution of a budget shall be submitted to the central guidance organ of the special economic zones and the Rason municipal people's committee.

Article 33 (Cooperation in work of management committee)

The central guidance organ of the special economic zones and the Rason municipal people's committee shall render active cooperation in the work of the management committee.

Article 34 (Operation of advisory committee)

An advisory committee may be formed in the Zone for the purpose of consulting and coordinating problems arising in the development and management of the Zone and business operation.

The advisory committee shall be composed of the members concerned of the Rason municipal people's committee and the management committee, and the representatives of major enterprises.

Article 35 (Control of work concerning place of origin)
Work concerning the place of origin in the Zone shall be undertaken by the institution in charge of the control thereof.
The institution in charge of the work concerning the place of origin shall conduct its work in compliance with the laws and regulations of the Zone and the international practice.

Chapter 4 Establishment of Enterprises, Economic and Trade Activities

Article 36 (Streamlining of screening and approval procedures)
All forms of screening and approval procedures concerning economic and trade activities in the Zone shall be streamlined through the introduction of unified and concerning method of handling.
Article 37 (Application for business establishment)
An investor shall submit to the management committee an application for the establishment of an enterprise inside the industrial park, or to the Rason municipal people's committee if the enterprise is to be set up outside the industrial park.
The management committee or the Rason municipal people's committee shall either approve or reject the application within 10 days of receipt thereof, and notify the applicant of the result.
Article 38 (Registration of enterprise, incorporation)
An enterprise shall, upon obtaining approval for the establishment thereof, register its establishment, register with the customs office and taxation office within the prescribed period of time.
The enterprise so registered shall be a corporate body of the DPRK.
Article 39 (Establishment and registration of branches and offices)
Where a branch or an office is to be set up in the Zone, approval thereof shall be obtained according to the prescribed procedures from the Rason municipal people's committee or the management committee, and relevant registration shall be made.
Article 40 (Rights of enterprise)
Enterprise in the Zone shall have the rights to formulate at their discretion the rules for operation and management, to work out plans for production, sale and financial management and to determine the forms of employment, wage standard and form of payment, price of products and plan for profit distribution.
Illegal interference in the operation of business shall be prohibited and expenses and obligations that are not prescribed in the laws and regulations shall not be imposed.
Article 41 (Business category, approval for modification)

An enterprise shall conduct its business operation within the range of approval business category.

Where business category is to be extended or modified, approval thereof shall be obtained.

Article 42 (Fulfillment in good faith of contracts)

Enterprise shall give priority to implementing the contracts, abide by the terms of credit and fulfill the contracts in good faith.

Prices to the contracts shall adhere to the principle of equity and mutual benefit in concluding and fulfilling contracts.

Article 43 (Economic transactions with DPRK enterprises outside Zone)

Enterprises may, under contracts, purchase in the DPRK territory outside the Zone raw and other materials and supplies needed for their business operation or sell their products therein.

Processing of raw and other materials and components may be consigned to the institutions, enterprises and organizations of the DPRK.

Article 44 (Prices of commodities and services)

Prices of the commodities and services sold and bought between the enterprises in the Zone, and prices of the commodities sold and bought between enterprises in the Zone and the DPRK institutions, enterprises and organizations outside it shall be determined by the parties concerned by reference to the prevailing world market price.

Prices of basic consumer goods such as food and essential foodstuff and charges for public services shall be fixed by the Rason municipal people's committee. In this case monetary compensation shall be made for the losses caused to the enterprise concerned.

Article 45 (Trade)

Enterprises in the Zone may conduct various forms of trade such as processing, transit trade and barter trade.

Article 46 (Special license for operation)

Infrastructures and public establishments in the Zone may be given special operation license.

Where an enterprise that has a special operation license wishes to transfer it to or divide it among other enterprises, a contract shall be concluded and approval thereof shall be obtained from the competent institution.

Article 47 (Permission for exploitation of natural resources)

An enterprise in the Zone may, subject to the approval of the competent institution, exploit the natural resources in the Zone for the provision of raw materials and fuel for production.
Exploitation of natural resources outside the Zone shall be conducted via the central guidance organ of the special economic zones.

Article 48 (Purchase of products of Zone)
The DPRK institutions, enterprises and organizations outside the Zone may, under contract, purchase the goods produced or sold by the enterprises in the Zone.

Article 49 (Employment of labour)
Enterprise in the Zone shall primarily employ the labour of the DPRK.
Where foreigners are to be employed as circumstances so require, notification thereof shall be made to the Rason municipal people's committee or the management committee.

Article 50 (Minimum monthly wage)
Minimum monthly wages of employees of the enterprises in the Zone shall be determined by the Rason municipal people's committee through consultation with the management committee.

Article 51 (Advertising, approval for installation of outdoor advertisement)
Advertising business may be conducted and advertisements may be put in the Zone in accordance with the regulations.
Where advertisements are to be put outdoors, approval thereof shall be obtained from the competent institution.

Article 52 (Accounting of enterprises)
Enterprises in the Zone may apply internationally accepted accounting standards to their accounting and settlement of accounts.

Chapter 5 Customs Duties

Article 53 (Introduction of preferential tariff system)
Preferential tariff system shall be introduced in the Zone.

Article 54 (Duty-free articles)
The following articles shall be duty-free:

1. Materials needed for the development of the Zone;
2. Imports needed for the production and operation of enterprises, and export goods;
3. Materials brought into the Zone for processing , transit trade and barter trade;
4. Office articles and daily necessities for the investors;
5. Transit cargoes of other countries;

6. Donations of foreign governments, institutions, enterprises or organizations, or international organizations; and
7. Other designated articles

Article 55 (Levying of customs duties on duty-free articles)
Where the articles that are brought in duty-free, except for the goods of the duty-free shops, are sold in the Zone, customs duties shall be payable.

Article 56 (Levying of customs duties on imported raw and other materials and components)
Where goods produced in the Zone are not exported but sold to the DPRK institutions, enterprises or organizations in or outside the Zone, customs duties shall be levied on the imported raw and other materials, supplies and components used for the production of the goods,

Article 57 (Declaration of inward or outward materials)
Duty-free articles shall be brought into or taken out of the Zone subject to declaration.
Where duty-free articles are to be brought in or taken out, a declaration form shall be filled truthfully for submission to the customs concerned.

Article 58 (Retention of customs documents)
Enterprises shall retain for a period of 5 years the documents of customs duties payment, customs inspection, goods invoice and the like.

Chapter 6 Currency and Financial Matters

Article 59 (Circulating money, settlement currency)
Circulating money and settlement currency in the Zone shall be Korean Won or other designated currency.
Exchange rate of foreign currency for Korean Won shall be determined by the foreign exchange control institution of the Zone.

Article 60 (Establishment of banks)
Investors in the Zone may, in accordance with the regulations, set up banks or branches and conduct banking operations.

Article 61 (Accounts of enterprises)
Enterprises shall open accounts with the DPRK banks or foreign-invested banks set up in the Zone.
Where accounts are to be opened with foreign banks outside the territory of the DPRK, approval thereof shall be obtained according to the prescribed procedures from the foreign currency control institution of the Zone or the management committee.

Article 62 (Loaning)

Enterprises in the Zone may, for their economic and trade activities, obtain a loan from a DPRK bank or a foreign financial institution.
Korean Won so loaned or exchanged for foreign currency shall be used while being deposited at a bank designated by the Central Bank.
Article 63 (Establishment of insurance institution, insurance)
Investors in the Zone may set up and operate insurance companies, while foreign insurance companies may set up and operate branches or representative offices.
Enterprises and individuals in the Zone shall take out the policy of the insurance companies in the territory of the DPRK, and obligatory insurance shall be insured at a designated company.
Article 64 (Transaction of securities)
Foreign-invested enterprises and foreigners may, in accordance with the regulations, transact securities in the Zone.

Chapter 7 Incentives and Preferential Treatment

Article 65 (Remittance of income, taking-out invested property)
Such income as profits, interests, dividend, rentals, service charges and proceeds from property sale that are legitimately earned in the Zone may be remitted outside the territory of the DPRK without any restrictions.
Investors may take out of the Zone without any restrictions the property that had been brought therein or legitimately acquired therein.
Article 66 (Encouragement of export and import)
Enterprises or individual foreign businesspersons in the Zone may, under contracts with the enterprises in or outside the Zone, conduct transactions of commodities, services and technology, and conduct agent's business for export and import.
Article 67 (Rate of enterprise income tax)
Enterprise income tax in the Zone shall be 14% of the net profit.
Income tax for the enterprises in the priority sectors shall be 10% of the net profit.
Article 68 (Exemption or reduction of enterprise income tax)
Designated enterprises that operate in the Zone for more than 10 years shall be entitled to exemption or reduction of enterprise income tax.
The period and rate of exemption or reduction of enterprise income tax and the starting point of calculation shall be as stipulated in the relevant regulations.
Article 69 (Preferential treatment concerning use of land)

Land for the use of enterprises in the Zone shall be provided in consideration of the actual demand, and depending on the sector and the purpose of land use, different preferential treatment shall be accorded in respect of term of lease, rentals and mode of payment.
Enterprises investing in infrastructure construction, public establishments and top priority sectors shall be given a prior lien in selecting the location of land, with the land use rent exempted for a designated period of time.

Article 70 (Preferential treatment for developer enterprise)
The developer enterprise shall have a preferential right in obtaining the right of management of tourist business, hotel business and the like.
Tax shall not be levied on the property of the developer enterprise and infrastructure and public establishments that he operates.

Article 71 (Refund of income tax on reinvested amount)
Where dividends are reinvested in the Zone to increase the registered capital or to set up a new business for more than 5 years' operation, 50% of the enterprise income tax paid on the reinvented amount shall be refunded.
Where reinvestment is made in infrastructure construction, the whole of the enterprise income tax that had been paid on the reinvented amount shall be refunded.

Article 72 (Protection of intellectual property rights)
Intellectual property rights of the enterprises and individuals in the Zone shall be protected by law.
The Rason municipal people's committee shall establish a system for the administration of registration, use and protection of intellectual property rights.

Article 73 (Services for management work)
Services for managerial work such as banking, insurance, accounting, legal work and measuring may be provided in the Zone in accordance with the regulations.

Article 74 (Tourist business)
International tourism shall be extensively arranged in the Zone by developing favourable tourism resources such as seaside pine grove, sand beach, islets and other peculiar scenic beauty, and folk culture.
Investor may conduct tourist business in the Zone in accordance with the regulations.

Article 75 (Provision of facilities)

Mail, telephone, fax and other communications devices shall be freely used in the Zone.

Residents and visitors shall be provided with facilities in the area of education, culture, medical care and physical culture.

Article 76 (Free entry and exit of goods)

Goods may be freely brought into the Zone, which can be stored, processed, manufactured, sorted and packed to be taken out to other countries. Contrabands shall not be brought in or taken out.

Article 77 (Provision of conditions for entry or exit of persons, vehicles and goods)

Institutions of immigration inspection, customs, quarantine and others concerned shall streamline the procedures for the entry and exit of persons, vehicles and goods in order that development of the Zone and business activities may progress smoothly.

Article 78 (Entry and exit of foreign ships and seamen)

Foreign ships and seamen may enter or leave the Rajin Port, Sonbong Port and Ungsang Port of the Zone in accordance with the internationally accepted procedures for entry or exit of free trade ports.

Article 79 (Entry/exit, stay, and residence of foreigners)

Foreigners may enter, leave, stay or reside in the Zone and may, without visa, enter or leave the Zone through the designated route upon presentation of passport or other equivalent pass.

Procedures for entering the Zone from other areas of the DPRK shall be prescribed separately.

Chapter 8 Complaints, Settlement of Disputes

Article 80 (Complaints, settlement)

Enterprises and individuals in the Zone may lodge complaints with the management committee, the Rason municipal people's committee, central guidance organ of the special economic zones and other institutions concerned.

The institutions shall conduct investigation and settle the complaints within 30 days of receipt and notify the complainant of the result.

Article 81 (Settlement of dispute by mediation)

The management committee or the institution concerned may, upon request of the parties to a dispute, mediate a dispute. In this case mediation plan shall be worked out by reference to the opinions of the parties to the dispute.

The mediation plan shall take effect upon signature of the parties to the dispute.

Article 82 (Settlement of disputes by arbitration)
Parties to a dispute may, upon agreement, apply for arbitration to a DPRK or a foreign international arbitration institution established in the Zone.
Arbitration shall be conducted in accordance with the arbitration rules of the international arbitration committee concerned.
Article 83 (Settlement of disputes by court)
Parties to a dispute may bring an action to a competent court in the Zone.
Procedures for administrative action in the Zone shall be provided separately.

Appendix

Article 1 (Date of entry into force)
This Law shall enter into force as from the date of promulgation.
Article 2 (Right of interpretation)
Interpretation of this Law shall be provided by the Presidium of the Supreme People's Assembly.

[Source: (1) Laws and Regulations of the Democratic People's Republic of Korea Governing External Economic Matters, Legislation Press, Pyongyang, 2012; (2) *Choesin Bukhan Beopryeongjip* published by *Bukhanbeop yeonguhoe* (Collection of Current Acts and Regulations of North Korea), Myung-Bong Chang (ed.), Seoul, 2018; and (3) *Bukhan Beopryeongjip sang & ha* (Collection of Laws and Regulations of North Korea Vol. I & II, PDF), National Intelligence Service of the Republic of Korea, Seoul, 2024)]

▪ Defunct LAW OF THE DEMOCRATIC PEOPLE'S REPUBLIC OF KOREA ON THE MT. KUMGANG SPECIAL ZONE FOR INTERNATIONAL TOURISM

Adopted by Decree No. 1673 of the Presidium of the Supreme People's Assembly on May 31, 2011 and reportedly abolished this law in December 2023

Chapter 1 Fundamentals

Article 1 (Objective)

This Law is enacted for the purpose of contributing to turning Mt. Kumgang into a world-famous special tourist zone by providing strict guidelines for the development and management of the Mt. Kumgang Special Zone for International Tourism (the Special Zone for International Tourism).

Article 2 (Status of the Zone)

The Special Zone for International Tourism (SZIT) is the special area for tourism in the DPRK that is open for freely conducting tourism and economic activities related thereto.

SZIT shall include the Township of Kosong County, some area of Onjong-ri, Lagoon Samil, Sea Kumgang area, Inner Kumgang area of Kumgang County and some area of Thongchon County of Kangwon Province.

Article 3 (Principle for development of the SZIT)

It is the State policy to turn the world famous Mt. Kumgang into a special zone for international tourism.

The State shall ensure that tour of Mt. Kumgang is actively promoted by turning it into a comprehensive tourist zone that can serve various purposes of tour and play diverse functions.

Article 4 (Principle of encouraging investment providing conditions for economic activities) SZIT shall be open for investment by foreign corporate bodies, individuals and economic organizations.

South Koreans, overseas Koreans and institutions and organizations concerned of the DPRK may also make an investment in the SZIT.

The State shall actively encourage investment in the SZIT and provide preferential conditions for economic activities to the investors.

Article 5 (Principle of protecting property)

The State shall protect by law the investment property, legally earned income and vested rights of the investors.

Article 6 (Manager of the SZIT)

The management of the SZIT shall be undertaken by the management committee of the Mt. Kumgagn Special Zone for International Tourism (the SZIT management committee) under the unified guidance of the central guidance organ of the Mt. Kumgang Special Zone for International Tourism (the SZIT guidance organ).

Article 7 (International exchange and cooperation)

The State shall promote exchange and cooperation with international tourist organizations and foreign tourist bodies in respect of the administration of the SZIT.

Article 8 (Applicability)

Development and management of the SZIT, touring, tourist business and other economic activities shall be governed by this Law and its implementing regulations and rules.

Chapter 2 Management of the Special Zone for International Tourism

Article 9 (Status of guidance organ of the SZIT)

The SZIT guidance organ is a central organ that provides unified guidance for the development and management of the SZIT.

Article 10 (Functions and powers of the SZIT guidance organ)

The functions and powers of the SZIT guidance organ shall be as follows:

1. To provide guidance for the work of the SZIT management committee;
2. To formulate rules for the implementation of the laws and regulations for the SZIT;
3. To examine the master plan for the development of the SZIT;
4. To receive and take custody of copies of designs for the construction of ordered projects;
5. To administer tax affairs of the SZIT; and
6. To carry out other work entrusted by the State.

Article 11 (Status of the SZIT management committee)

The SZIT management committee is a local executive organ that conducts the management of the SZIT.

The Chief of the SZIT management committee shall be its chairperson.

Article 12 (Functions and powers of the SZIT management committee)

The functions and powers of the SZIT management committee shall be as follows:

1. To prepare and put into effect master plan for the development of the SZIT;

2. To conduct survey, development and management of tourism resources;

3. To conduct tourism promotion, attract tourists and organize tours;

4. To maintain law and order, protect personal safety and property in the SZIT;

5. To lease land and buildings;
6. To attract investment, screen and register establishment of business, and issue a license;
7. To register the right to use land, buildings and vehicles;
8. To provide labour needed for business operation;
9. To give permission for construction and conduct inspection of completion of construction works;
10. To maintain the infrastructure facilities of the SZIT;
11. To take measures for the environmental protection and fire-fighting in the SZIT;
12. To render cooperation in the work related to the entry and departure of persons, vehicles and goods; and
13. To carry out other work authorized by the SZIT guidance organ.

Article 13 (Organization and operation of joint consultative board)

A joint consultative board may be established in the SZIT, consisting of members of the management committee, investors and representatives of the enterprises.

The joint consultative board shall discuss and coordinate important issues arising in the development and management of the SZIT and the operation of business therein.

Article 14 (Immigration)

No visa shall be required to enter or leave the SZIT.

Persons and vehicles entering or leaving the SZIT form areas other than the territory of the DPRK shall, upon production of a passport or an equivalent pass, immigrate at the designated point without visa.

Procedures for entering or leaving the SZIT through other parts of the DPRK, and the procedures for entering or leaving other parts of the DPRK from SZIT shall be provided separately.

Article 15 (Inspection, quarantine)

Persons, animals, plants and vehicles entering or leaving the SZIT shall undergo immigration inspection, customs inspection, health and other quarantine.

The institutions of inspection and quarantine shall carry out their functions expeditiously and in a scientific and technological manner so that the safety of and immigration into the SZIT may be ensured.

Article 16 (Environment control)

No one shall cut down ornamental trees, cause damage to or destruction of such landscape as beauty spots, seaside pine groves, swimming beaches, rare rocks and cliffs, attractive and impressive physical features in mountainous areas and picturesque islands, destroy caverns, waterfalls, sites of old castles and other natural monuments, or construct buildings or facilities that are detrimental to the environmental protection. Such prescribed criteria for environmental protection as emission of pollutant, noise and vibration shall be observed.

Article 17 (Use of telecommunication devices)

Such telecommunication devices as mail, telephone, fax and internet shall be freely used in the SZIT.

Chapter 3 Touring and Service

Article 18 (Tourists)

The SZIT shall be open for tourism by foreigners.

Citizens of the DPRK, south Koreans and overseas Koreans may also tour the SZIT.

Article 19 (Forms of tourism)

Tourism shall be practiced in such forms and ways as mountain climbing, sightseeing, swimming, recreation, experiencing, amusement, sport and curative treatment.

Tourists may freely practise tourism in the SZIT.

Article 20 (Creation of environment and conditions for tourism)

The SZIT management committee shall create sufficient environment and provide conditions so that tourism may be practiced at a high level.

Article 21 (Service for tourists)

An investor may set up various forms of service facilities such as accommodations, restaurants, shops, casinos, golf course, nightclubs, curative treatment and amusement for tourists.

Article 22 (Hosting of international events)

The SZIT may host various types of events such as international meetings, expositions, exhibitions, symposiums, art performances and sports games.

Article 23 (Provision of traffic conditions)

The guidance organ and management committee of the SZIT shall build international airports, harbours, tourist railways and tourist highways to provide sufficient conditions for traveling of the tourists.

Chapter 4 Establishment, Registration and Operation of Businesses

Article 24 (Establishment of business)

Investors may, either on their own accounts or jointly with others, make an investment for the establishment of various forms of businesses such as construction of infrastructure facilities for the development of the SZIT, and businesses concerning travel, accommodation, restaurant, casino, golf, amusement and welfare service.

Article 25 (Compliance with master plan for development of the SZIT)

The SZIT shall be developed in accordance with the master plan for development.

Investors that wish to undertake the construction of infrastructure facilities or establish businesses in the SZIT shall comply with the requirements specified in the master plan.

Article 26 (Approval of establishment of business, registration thereof)

Investors that wish to establish and operate businesses in the SZIT shall obtain the approval thereof from the SZIT management committee.

An investor shall, upon obtaining the approval for the establishment of a business, shall register the business and carry out tax and customs registration within the prescribed period of time.

Article 27 (Approval for construction of infrastructure facilities)

Approval for the construction of infrastructure facilities for the development and management of the SZIT such as the airport, railway, road, harbour and power station shall be granted by the SZIT guidance organ.

Investment in the construction of the infrastructure facilities such as airport, railway, road, harbour and power station shall be particularly encouraged.

Article 28 (Establishment of branches, representative offices and agencies)

Branches, representative offices and agencies may be set up in the SZIT. In this case approval thereof shall be obtained from the SZIT management committee.

Article 29 (Opening of accounts)
Businesses and individuals may open accounts with a DPRK bank or a foreign bank established in the SZIT.
Article 30 (Transaction of securities denominated in foreign currency)
Businesses and individuals may, in the designated places of the SZIT, transact securities denominated in foreign currency.
Article 31 (Insurance)
Businesses and individuals may take out the insurance policy of a DPRK or a foreign insurance company established in the SZIT.
Article 32 (Disposal of wastes)
Businesses shall set up such environmental protection facilities and sanitation facilities as modern purifying stations, depositing basin and waste disposal sites so that wastes may be purified or disposed of in the interest of tourism and environmental protection.

Chapter 5 Provision of Conditions for Economic Activities

Article 33 (Employment of labour)
Businesses in the SZIT may employ the labour of the DPRK, as well as foreigners, South Koreans and overseas Koreans.
Article 34 (Circulating currency)
Circulating currency in the SZIT shall be convertible foreign currency.
The kinds of convertible foreign currency and the base currency shall be determined by the SZIT guidance organ through consultation with the institution concerned.
Article 35 (Bringing in and taking out foreign currency, remittance, taking out property)
Foreign currency shall be freely brought in or taken out of the SZIT and profits and income legally earned remitted.
Investors may, upon expiry of the term of operation, take out of the territory of the DPRK the property that was brought into the SZIT from a foreign country or legally acquired therein.
Article 36 (Taxation)
Businesses and individuals in the SZIT shall pay tax as prescribed in the relevant laws and regulations.
Businesses in the top priority sectors such as construction of airport, railway, road, harbour and power station shall benefit from exemption or reduction of tax.
Article 37 (Bringing in or taking out materials)

Materials needed for the operation of businesses shall be brought in or taken out freely with the exception of the designated contrabands.

Article 38 (Objects to be exempted from or payment of customs duties)

Preferential tariff system shall be enforced in the SZIT.

Customs duties shall not be payable for the materials brought in for the development of the SZIT and operation of business, and office articles and daily necessities of prescribed amount for the investors.

Customs duties shall be payable where duty-free articles are sold outside the SZIT or the materials controlled by the State are brought in to the SZIT.

Article 39 (Entry and exit of persons and vehicles, provision of conditions for inward and outward movement of materials)

The management committee of the SZIT and the institution concerned shall provide sufficient conditions for the entry and exit of persons, vehicles and materials so that no hindrance may be caused to the development of the SZIT and operation of business.

Airport dues shall not be levied in case of entering or leaving the SZIT at a designated airport.

Chapter 6 Sanction, Settlement of Disputes

Article 40 (Sanction)

Where hindrance is caused to the management of the SZIT and tourism or damage to a business or an individual through violation of this Law, the person concerned shall, depending on the seriousness of the act committed, be liable to restoration to original state, compensation or fines.

Where security of the DPRK is disturbed or public order seriously violated, administrative or penal liability shall be imposed in accordance with the relevant law.

Article 41 (Settlement of disputes)

Disputes concerning the development and management of the SZIT, and operation of business shall be resolved through consultation between the parties concerned.

In case of failure in consultation, the disputes shall be settled through the arbitration procedures agreed upon by the parties concerned or by the legal procedures of the DPRK.

[Source: Laws and Regulations of the Democratic People's Republic of Korea Governing External Economic Matters, Legislation Press, Pyongyang, 2012]

▪ LAW OF THE DEMOCRATIC PEOPLE'S REPUBLIC OF KOREA ON THE KAESONG INDUSTRIAL COMPLEX

Adopted by Decree No. 3430 of the Presidium of the Supreme People's Assembly on November 20, 2002, and amended on April 24, 2003

Chapter 1 Fundamentals

Article 1 (Objective)

The Kaesong Industrial Complex (the KIC) is an international industry, trade, commerce, finance and tourism zone managed and operated in accordance with the laws of the Democratic People's Republic of Korea (the DPRK).

The Law of the Democratic People's Republic of Korea on the Kaesong Industrial Complex shall provide strict guidelines for the development and management of the KIC, thereby contributing to the development of the national economy.

Article 2 (Mode of development, division)

The development of the KIC shall be made by the way for the developer to lease land, clear the sites of the land, construct infrastructure and attract investment.

The KIC shall be divided into the industrial area, commercial area, residential area and tourism area.

Article 3 (Principle of provision of conditions for economic activities)

South Koreans, overseas Koreans, foreign corporate bodies, foreign individuals and foreign economic organizations may invest in the KIC.

Investors may establish companies, branches, business offices and representative offices and freely conduct business activities in the KIC.

The State shall ensure in the KIC that investors are preferentially provided with conditions for their economic activities in such areas as labour employment, land use and payment of tax.

Article 4 (Sectors of prohibition, priority)

In the KIC, investment and business operation shall be prohibited in those projects that are detrimental to the security of society, sound development of national economy, public health and protection of environment, and projects that are economically and technically outdated.

It shall be particularly encouraged for the investment in the construction of infrastructure, light industry sectors, state-of-the-art science and technology sectors.

Article 5 (Guidance organ)
The unified guidance for the work of the KIC shall be provided by the central guidance organ of the industrial complex.
The central guidance organ of the industrial complex shall guide the work of the industrial complex through the management organ of the KIC.
Article 6 (Non-involvement in work of KIC)
Institutions, enterprises and organizations shall not get involved in the work of the KIC.
In case they need to get involved in the work of the KIC, they shall consult with the central guidance organ of the industrial complex.
Article 7 (Protection of investor's rights and interests)
In the KIC, investor's rights and interests shall be protected and inheritance rights to the invested properties shall be guaranteed.
Investor's property shall not be nationalized. Where an investor's property is, for unavoidable reasons, to be expropriated for public interests, prior consultation shall take place and compensation for the value of the expropriated property shall be made.
Article 8 (Detention, arrest, search and seizure, personal safety, agreement or treaty)
South Koreans, overseas Koreans and foreign nationals shall not be detained or arrested nor himself or his place of residence be searched without a legal warrant.
Any agreement concluded between North Korea and South Korea or any treaty concluded between the DPRK and a foreign country in respect of personal safety and criminal matters shall take precedence.
Article 9 (Applicable law, consultation)
Economic activities in the KIC shall be made in accordance with this Law and its implementing regulations.
Matters not stipulated in the law and regulations shall be handled in consultation between the central guidance organ of the industrial complex and the management organ of the KIC.

Chapter 2 Development of the KIC

Article 10 (Designation of developer)
Development of the KIC shall be made by the designated developer.
The central guidance organ of the industrial complex shall designate the developer.
Article 11 (Land lease contract and license)
A developer shall enter into a land lease contract with the central guidance organ of the industrial complex.

The central guidance organ of the industrial complex shall issue a land use certificate to the developer that has concluded a land lease contract.

Article 12 (Term of land lease)

The term of land lease in the KIC shall be 50 year from the date on which a land use certificate is issued.

Leased land may continuously be used even after the expiration of the term of land lease provided that the lease-holding enterprise files an application for it.

Article 13 (Preparation and screen of comprehensive development plan)

A developer shall accurately prepare a comprehensive development plan of the KIC and submit it to the central guidance organ of the industrial complex.

The central guidance organ of the industrial complex shall notify the developer of the screened result within 30 days from the date on which the comprehensive development plan is received.

Article 14 (Modification of comprehensive development plan)

Development of the KIC shall be made in accordance with the approved comprehensive development plan of the KIC.

Where wishing to modify the approved comprehensive development plan, an approval for modification shall be obtained by submitting an application to the central guidance organ of the industrial complex.

Article 15 (Removal and relocation of buildings and attachments, bearing costs)

The central guidance organ of the industrial complex shall remove or relocate buildings and attachments in a timely manner and relocate residents therein so that development shall not be hindered.

Expenses for removal and relocation of buildings and attachments as well as relocation of residents in the developing area of the KIC shall be borne by the developer.

Article 16 (Commencing development, stages)

A developer shall commence the development projects right after the completion of removal of buildings and attachments in the development area.

Development of the KIC may be made in stages.

Article 17 (Construction of infrastructure)

Construction of infrastructure in the KIC shall be made by the developer.

A developer may construct infrastructure facilities such as power supply, telecommunications and water reservoir jointly with other investors, or by way of transfer or assignment to them if necessary.

Article 18 (Designation of location, transfer of right to use land and building, sublease)

A developer shall designate locations of enterprises in accordance with the comprehensive development plan of the KIC right after the completion of infrastructure construction. In this case the developer may transfer or sublease to other enterprises the right to use land and buildings in the KIC.

Article 19 (Economic activities of developer)

A developer may engage in business activities in the KIC such as construction of dwelling houses, tourism and entertainment, and advertising.

Article 20 (Ensuring passage of persons and materials)

The central guidance organ of the industrial complex and relevant institutions shall ensure the conditions for both inward and outward passage of persons and materials so that development of the KIC shall not be hindered.

Chapter 3 Management of the KIC

Article 21 (Management organ)

The management organ of the KIC shall be the responsible authority to manage the KIC under the direction of the central guidance organ of the industrial complex.

The management organ of the KIC shall make a quarterly report on the management and operation of the KIC to the central guidance organ of the industrial complex.

Article 22 (Functions of central guidance organ)

The central guidance organ of the industrial complex shall:

1. Designate developers;
2. Direct the work of the management organ of the KIC;
3. Prepare implementing rules of the Law and regulations of the KIC;
4. Provide labour, water supply, and material resources as requested by enterprises;
5. Receive and take into custody of the projected construction design documents;
6. Take into action in the DPRK for the sales of products produced in the KIC;
7. Manage the tax affairs in the KIC; and

8. Conduct other businesses authorized by the State.

Article 23 (Consultation, cooperation)

The central guidance organ of the industrial complex shall consult matters arising from the management and operation of the KIC with relevant institutions in due course.

The relevant institutions shall fully cooperate with the work of the central guidance organ of the industrial complex.

Article 24 (Members of management organ)

The management organ of the KIC shall be comprised of members recommended by the developer.

An official sent by the central guidance organ of the industrial complex as requested by the management organ of the KIC may be a member of the management organ.

Article 25 (Functions of management organ)

The management organ shall:

1. Foster investment conditions and attract investment;
2. Approve establishment of enterprises, register and license them;
3. Grant permission of construction and conduct inspections of completion of construction;
4. Register the right to use land, buildings, and means of transportation;
5. Support business activities of the enterprises;
6. Manage infrastructure facilities;
7. Protect environment and take measures for fire-fighting of the KIC;
8. Issue entry and exit passes for persons and vehicles from South Korea to the KIC;
9. Prepare operating rules of the management organ of the KIC;
10. Carry out other works authorized by the central guidance organ of the industrial complex.

Article 26 (Chief of management organ)

The chief of the management organ of the KIC shall be the chairperson of it.

The chairperson shall organize and guide all works of the management organ of the KIC.

Article 27 (Operational fund of management organ)

The management organ of the KIC shall hold the operational funds.

The operational funds shall be appropriated from revenues such as fees.

Article 28 (Entry and exit of persons and vehicles)

South Koreans, overseas Koreans, foreigners and vehicles from South Korea may enter and leave, without visa, the KIC with an entry-exit pass issued by the management organ of the KIC through the designated point.

Procedures for entering into the KIC from other parts of the DPRK, and procedures for leaving the KIC for other parts of the DPRK shall be provided separately.

Article 29 (Provision of facilities)

In the KIC, South Koreans, overseas Koreans and foreigners may be provided with necessary facilities in the areas of culture, health, physical culture and education, and freely use the means of communication such as mail, telephone and fax.

Article 30 (Tourism in Kaesong and services)

South Koreans, overseas Koreans and foreigners who commute, reside or stay in the KIC may take a tour to historic sites of revolution, historic heritages, famous places and natural monuments in the City of Kaesong as arranged.

The People's Committee of Kaesong City shall take good care of tourism sites and facilities, preserve and manage them, and provide for necessary services.

Article 31 (Advertising, permission on outdoor advertising)

Advertising business in the KIC may be conducted without restriction on the location, types, contents, methods and duration. However, for the installation of outdoor advertising materials, permission shall be obtained from the management organ of the KIC.

Article 32 (Inward or outward materials)

Articles brought into or taken out of the KIC shall be subject to declaration.

A person wishing to bring in or take out an article shall accurately fill out a declaration form and submit it to the customs office located at the passage point of the article.

Article 33 (Duty free and levying duties)

Customs duties shall not be levied on articles brought in the KIC or taken out of the KIC to South Korea or other countries, as well as on articles brought in for consigned processing to an institution, enterprise and organization of the DPRK.

Where articles brought in the KIC from other countries are sold to other place of the DPRK, customs duty may be levied.

Article 34 (Inspection and quarantine)

Inspection and quarantine institutions shall, in a scientific-technical and expeditious manner, conduct inspections for immigration, customs, hygiene, and quarantine for animals and plants in the KIC so that safety and attraction of investment may not be hindered.

Chapter 4 Establishment of Enterprises in the KIC

Article 35 (Approval, rejection of establishment of enterprises)

An investor wishing to establish a business in the KIC shall file with the management organ an application for the establishment of an enterprise.

The management organ shall either approve or reject the application within 10 days from the date on which the application is filed and notify the applicant of the result.

Article 36 (Registrations of enterprise, customs, tax)

An investor whose application for establishment of an enterprise was approved shall invest designated amount of capital, register his enterprise with the management organ of the KIC, and, within 20 days thereafter, register customs and tax affairs with the institutions concerned. In this case prescribed documents shall be submitted.

Article 37 (Employment of labour)

An enterprise shall employ the labour force of the DPRK as its employees.

An enterprise may employ the labour force from South Korean or foreign countries for the positions of the members of management, specialty engineers and technicians after notifying the management organ of the KIC. In this case, the management organ shall report such employment to the central guidance organ of the industrial complex.

Article 38 (Business category, approval for modification)

An enterprise shall conduct its business operation within the range of approved category.

Where business category is extended or modified, approval thereof shall be obtained from the management organ of the KIC.

Article 39 (Purchase, sales of materials, processing)

Enterprises in the KIC may purchase materials necessary for their business operation from the other parts of territory of the DPRK or sell their products produced in the KIC to the other parts of territory of the DPRK.

They may consign the processing of raw materials, other materials and parts to the institutions, enterprises and organizations of the DPRK if necessary.

Article 40 (Prices of commodities, service fees)

Prices of commodities and service fees in the KIC and prices of commodities transacted between enterprises in the KIC and institutions, enterprises and organizations of the DPRK shall be determined by the parties in consultation by reference to the prevailing international market.

Article 41 (Circulating currency, base currency)

The circulating currency in the KIC shall be a convertible currency and a credit card and the like may be used.

The types of circulating currency and base currency shall be determined by the management organ of the KIC in consultation with the central guidance organ of the industrial complex.

Article 42 (Accounts of enterprises)

Enterprises shall open accounts with the banks established in the KIC. They may open accounts with the banks of South Korea or other countries located outside the KIC after notifying the management organ of the KIC.

Article 43 (Payment of tax, income tax rate)

Enterprises shall accurately conduct its accounting and pay taxes such as enterprise income tax, turnover tax, business tax and local tax in a timely manner.

The enterprise income tax rate in the KIC shall be 14% of the net profit and the same tax rate for the sectors of the construction of infrastructure, light industry and state-of-the-art science and technology shall be 10%.

Article 44 (Inward and outward movement of foreign currency, remittance)

Foreign currencies shall be freely brought into or taken out of the KIC. Investors may remit or take out of the KIC the profits earned from business activities and other incomes to South Korea or other countries without taxes.

Article 45 (Establishment and registration of branches, offices)

Where an enterprise wishes to set up a branch, business office or representative office in the KIC, it shall obtain approval from the management organ of the KIC after filing a relevant application with the organ.

The branches or business offices shall register themselves with the management organ of the KIC in order to conduct business activities.

Chapter 5 Settlement of Disputes

Article 46 (Settlement of disputes)

Any arising disagreement in relation to the development and management of the KIC or the business activities shall be settled through consultation among parties concerned.

If case of the failure in consultation, the dispute shall be settled through the procedure for commercial dispute settlement concluded between North Korea and South Korea, arbitration or by the legal procedure of the court of the DPRK.

Appendix

Article 1 (Date of entry into force)

This Law shall enter into force from the date of adoption.

Article 2 (Effect of agreement)

The contents of an agreement concluded between North Korea and South Korea in relation to the KIC shall have the same effect as this Law.

Article 3 (Authority to interpret law)

The Presidium of the Supreme People's Assembly shall be the authority to interpret this Law.

[Source: (1) *Bukhan Beopryeongjip sang & ha* (Collection of Laws and Regulations of North Korea Vol. I & II, PDF), National Intelligence Service, Seoul, 2024; and (2) *Choesin Bukhan Beopryeongjip* published by *Bukhanbeop yeonguhoe* (Collection of Current Acts and Regulations of North Korea), Myung-Bong Chang (ed.), Seoul, 2018]

*The whole text of this Law is translated into English by the Author keeping in mind North Korean fashion of legal translation.

▪ LAW OF THE DEMOCRATIC PEOPLE'S REPUBLIC OF KOREA ON THE HWANGGUMPHYONG AND WIHWADO ECONOMIC ZONE

Adopted by Decree No. 2006 of the Presidium of the Supreme People's Assembly on December 3, 2011

Chapter 1 Fundamentals

Article 1 (Objective)

This Law is enacted for the purpose of providing strict guidelines for the development and management of the Hwanggumphyong and Wihwado Economic Zone, thereby contributing to expanding and promoting external economic cooperation and exchange.

Article 2 (Status, location)

The Hwanggumphyong and Wihwado Economic Zone (the Zone) is a special economic zone of the Democratic People's Republic of Korea (the DPRK), where preferential policy is pursued in the economic sector.

The Zone shall include the Hwanggumphyong area and Wihwado area of the north Phyongan Province.

Article 3 (Development of the Zone, industries)

The Zone shall be developed by areas and stages.

The Hwanggumphyong area shall be developed with priority given to information technology, light industry, agriculture, commerce and tourism, while the Wihwado area (shall be developed)* according to the Wihwado development plan. * ( ) is added by the author.

Article 4 (Investors)

The Zone is open for investment by corporate bodies, individual persons and economic organizations of foreign countries.

Koreans residing outside the territory of the DPRK may also invest in the Zone in accordance with this Law.

Article 5 (Provision of conditions for economic activities)

Investors may freely conduct economic activities in the Zone through the establishment of companies, branches, representative offices and the like.

The State shall ensure that investors are preferentially provided with conditions for their economic activities in such areas as land use, labour employment, payment of tax and access to markets.

Article 6 (Sectors of priority, prohibition and limitation)

The State particularly encourages investment in the Zone for the construction of infrastructure facilities, state-of-the-art science and technology and production of internationally competitive goods.

Investments and business operation shall be prohibited or restricted in those projects that are detrimental to national security, public health, healthy social and moral life, protection of environment, and projects that are economically and technically outdated.

Article 7 (Manager and operator of the Zone, principle of non-involvement in work of management committee)

Management and operation of the Zone shall be undertaken by the management committee under the guidance and assistance of the central guidance organ of the special economic zones and the north Phyongan provincial people's committee.

Other institutions shall not get involved in the work of the management committee except in such cases as are prescribed by this Law.

Article 8 (Protection of investors' rights and interests)

The property, legitimate income and invested rights of investors in the Zone shall be protected by law.

The State shall not nationalize or expropriate the property of the investors.

Where an investor's property is, for unavoidable reasons, to be expropriated or used temporarily for public interests, notification thereof shall be made to him or her before going through the prescribed legal procedures, and sufficient and effective compensation for its value shall be made without any discrimination.

Article 9 (Protection of personal safety and human rights, prohibition of illegal detention and arrest)

Personal safety and human rights of the citizens in the Zone shall be protected by law.

No one shall be detained or arrested nor his place of residence be searched without a legal warrant.

Any treaty concluded between the DPRK and a foreign country in respect of personal safety and criminal matters shall take precedence.

Article 10 (Applicable laws and regulations)

The development and management of the Zone, business operation and other economic activities therein shall be governed by this Law and its implementing regulations, rules and general standards.

Where the laws and regulations governing the Zone provide otherwise than the treaties like conventions, memoranda of understanding or agreement concluded between the DPRK and a foreign country, the latter shall take precedence. Where the laws and regulations for the

Zone differ from those in effect outside the Zone, the former shall prevail.

Chapter 2 Development of the Zone

Article 11 (Principle of development)

The Zone shall be developed on the principle of:

1. Ensuring the comparative advantage of the Zone over the surrounding areas in natural and geographical conditions, natural resources and requisites for production;
2. Making economic and rational use of land and resources;
3. Protecting the ecological environment of the Zone and the surrounding areas;
4. Raising international competitiveness of the production and service;
5. Providing facilities for economic activities like trade and investment;
6. Guaranteeing public interests; and
7. Ensuring sustained and balanced economic development.

Article 12 (Development plan, modification)

The Zone shall be developed in accordance with the approved development plan.

Approval for modification of the development plan shall be granted by the organ that approved the plan concerned.

Article 13 (Mode of development of the Zone)

The Hwanggumphyong area of the Zone shall be developed by the developer enterprise, which shall lease the whole area of the land for comprehensive management and development.

The Wihwado area shall be developed in a mode agreed upon by the parties to the development.

Article 14 (Approval for developer enterprise)

Approval for the developer enterprise of the Zone shall be granted by the central guidance organ of the special economic zones by issuing to it a development license via the management committee.

Authorization of the developer enterprise and application for development license shall be undertaken by the management committee.

Article 15 (Land lease contract)

The developer enterprise shall, upon obtaining the development license, enter into a land lease contract with the land management institution.

The land lease contract shall specify the term of lease, area, compartment, purpose of use, term and method of payment of land rent and other necessary particulars.

The land management institution shall issue a land use certificate to the developer upon receipt of the land rent.

Article 16 (Term of land lease)

The term of land lease in the Zone shall be 50 years from the date of issuance of a land use certificate to the enterprise concerned.

Upon the expiry of the term of lease, the enterprise in the Zone may re-enter into a contract for the continued use of the leased land.

Article 17 (Removal and relocation of buildings and attachments)

An institution or enterprise that is in charge of removal or relocation of public buildings, dwelling houses and attachments shall remove or relocate them and have the inhabitants moved to a different location so that the development process may not be interrupted.

Article 18 (Time for commencement of development process)

The developer enterprise shall commence development upon completion of removal and relocation of buildings and attachments within the development area.

Article 19 (Construction of infrastructure and public facilities)

Construction of infrastructure and public facilities in the Zone shall be undertaken by the developer enterprise, which shall be given a special license to operate them.

The developer enterprise may invite other enterprise(s) to construct the infrastructure and public facilities.

Article 20 (Transfer of rights to use land and building, rental value)

The developer enterprise shall have the rights to transfer or lease the developed land and buildings as the construction of infrastructure facilities progresses in accordance with the development plan. In this case the value of transfer and lease shall be determined by the developer enterprise.

Article 21 (Modification of rights to use land and building ownership, registration thereof)

Enterprises in the Zone may, within term of validity, transfer, lease or mortgage the rights to use land and building ownership through sale, exchange, donation or succession. In this case particulars of modification of the rights to use land and building ownership shall be registered, and the certificate of land use and registration certificate of building ownership shall be re-issued.

Chapter 3 Management of the Zone

Article 22 (Principle of management)
The Zone shall be managed on the principle of:

1. Strictly observing and enforcing laws and regulations;
2. Ensuring autonomy of the management committee and the enterprises;
3. Offering preferential treatment to trade and investment activities;
4. Complying with objective laws of the economy and principles of market; and
5. Referring to international practices.

Article 23 (Establishment of management committee, status thereof)
A management committee shall be set up in the Zone for its management and operation.
The committee is a local management body that is in charge of the development, management and operation of the Zone.
Article 24 (Composition of management committee)
The management committee shall be composed of the chairperson, vice-chairperson, secretary and other members as may be required.
The management committee shall have such departments as are necessary for the development and management of the Zone.
Article 25 (Chief of management committee)
The chief of the management committee shall be its chairperson.
The chairperson shall represent the management committee and be in charge of its work.
Article 26 (Functions of management committee)
The management committee shall perform the following functions:

1. Preparing regulations required for the development and management of the Zone;
2. Fostering investment climate and attracting investment;
3. Approving establishment of enterprises, registering and licensing;
4. Making a list of sectors or priority, restriction and prohibition and announcing it;
5. Granting permission of specially-ordered construction projects and conducting inspection of completion of construction;
6. Taking custody of designs for ordered equipment;
7. Establishing independent financial management system;

8. Registering rights to use land and building ownership;
9. Managing property under its custody;
10. Rendering cooperation in the management of enterprises;
11. Undertaking supervision and cooperation with construction and management of infrastructure and public facilities;
12. Taking measures for environmental protection and fire-fighting in the area under control;
13. Rendering cooperation in the work concerning entry and exit personnel, vehicles and goods;
14. Preparing articles of association of the management committee; and
15. Carrying out other work assigned by the central guidance organ of the special economic zones and the north Phyongan provincial people's committee with regard to the development of the Zone.

Article 27 (Convening of meetings of chiefs of enterprises)
The management committee may convene a meeting of the representatives of the enterprises.
The meeting of the representatives of the enterprises shall discuss important matters concerning the development and management of the Zone and business operation.

Article 28 (Compilation and execution of budget)
The management committee shall compile and execute a budget. Documents concerning the compilation and execution of budget shall be submitted to the central guidance organ of the special economic zones and the north Phyongan provincial people's committee.

Article 29 (Functions of north Phyongan provincial people's committee)
The north Phyongan provincial people's committee shall perform the following functions for the development and management of the Zone:

1. Preparing implementing rules of the law and regulations of the zone;
2. Providing workforce required for the development and management of the Zone and business operation; and

3. Carrying out other assignments of the central guidance organ of the special economic zones with regard to the development and management of the Zone

Article 30 (Functions of the central guidance organ of the special economic zones)

The central guidance organ of the special economic zones shall:

1. Prepare development strategy for the Zone;
2. Contact local institutions for the development and construction of the Zone;
3. Cooperate and contact with the governments of foreign countries;
4. Approve screening criteria for establishment of enterprises;
5. Select local enterprises to make investment in the Zone; and
6. Render cooperation in the sale of the products of the Zone in local areas outside it.

Article 31 (Submission of work program and statistics)

The management committee shall annually submit its work program and the statistics of the Zone to the central guidance organ of the special economic zones and north Phyongan provincial people's committee.

Chapter 4 Establishment, Registration and Operation of Enterprises

Article 32 (Application for establishment)

An investor who wishes to establish an enterprise in the Zone shall submit an application to the management committee.

The management committee shall either approve or reject the application within 10 days of the receipt thereof, and notify the applicant of the result.

Article 33 (Registration of enterprise, incorporation)

An enterprise shall, upon obtaining approval for its establishment, register its establishment, and* make customs and tax registration within the prescribed period of time. * is added by the author.

The enterprise registered with the management committee shall be a corporate body of the DPRK.

Article 34 (rights of enterprises)

Enterprises in the Zone shall, at their discretion and in accordance with their articles of association, have the rights to lay down rules for operation and management, to work out plans for production, marketing and financial management and to determine the forms of employment, wage standard and form of its payment, price of products and plan for profit distribution.

Illegal interference in the operation of business shall be prohibited and expenses and obligations that are not prescribed in the laws and regulations shall not be imposed.

Article 35 (Business category, approval of modification)

An enterprise shall conduct its operational activities within the range of approved business category.

Where the business category is to be extended or modified, approval thereof shall be obtained.

Article 36 (Employment of labour)

Enterprise in the Zone shall primarily employ the labour of the DPRK. Where foreign labour is to be employed as circumstances so require, notification thereof shall be made to the management committee.

Article 37 (Minimum monthly wage)

Minimum monthly wages of employees of the enterprises in the Zone shall be determined by the north Phyongan provincial people's committee through consultation with the management committee.

Article 38 (Economic transactions with DPRK enterprises outside Zone)

Enterprises may, under contract, purchase in the DPRK territory outside the Zone raw and other materials and supplies required for their business operation or sell their products therein.

Processing of raw and other materials and components may be consigned to the institutions, enterprises and organizations of the DPRK.

Article 39 (Prices of commodities and services)

Prices of commodities and services sold and bought between the enterprises in the Zone, and the prices of the goods between enterprises in the Zone and the DPRK institutions, enterprises and organizations outside it shall be determined by the parties concerned by reference to the prevailing world market price.

Prices of basic consumer goods such as food and essential foodstuff and charges for public services shall be determined by the north Phyongan provincial people's committee. In this case, monetary compensation shall be made for the losses caused to the enterprise concerned.

Article 40 (Accounts of enterprises)

Enterprises shall open accounts with the DPRK banks or foreign-invested banks set up in the Zone.

Where accounts are to be opened with foreign banks outside the territory of the DPRK, approval thereof shall be obtained from the management committee.
Procedures for setting up banks or branches in the Zone shall be provided by regulations.

Article 41 (Insurance, establishment of insurance institution)
Enterprises and individuals in the Zone shall take out the policy of the insurance companies in the territory of the DPRK and compulsory insurance shall be taken with the designated insurance company.
Investors may set up insurance companies, and foreign insurance companies may set up and operate branches and offices in the Zone.

Article 42 (Accounting of enterprises)
Enterprises in the Zone may apply internationally accepted accounting standards to their accounting and settlement of accounts.

Article 43 (Obligation to payment of taxes, rate of enterprise income tax)
Enterprises in the Zone shall pay taxes according to the prescribed rates.
The rate of enterprise income tax shall be 14% of the net profit and the rate for enterprises in priority sectors shall be 10% of the net profit.

Article 44 (Establishment and registration of branches and representative offices)
Where a branch or a representative office is to set up in the Zone, approval thereof shall be obtained from the management committee and registration thereof shall be made as required.
The branches and representative offices shall be registered with the customs and tax offices within the prescribed time limit from the date of registration with the management committee.

Chapter 5 Provision of Conditions for Economic Activities

Article 45 (Streamlining of screening and approval procedures)
All forms of screening and approval procedures in respect of the economic activities in the Zone shall be streamlined through the unified and concentrated method of handling.

Article 46 (Circulating money, settlement currency)
Designated currency shall be circulated in the Zone.
Circulating money and settlement currency in the Zone shall be Korean Won or other designated currency.
Procedures for foreign exchange and the rate of exchange shall be provided by regulations.

Article 47 (Inward and outward of movement of foreign currency, profits and property)

Foreign currency shall be freely brought into or taken out of the Zone, and legitimate profits and other income may be remitted out of the Zone without any restrictions.

Investors may take out of the Zone without any restrictions the property that had been brought therein or legitimately acquired therein.

Article 48 (Protection of intellectual property rights)

Intellectual property rights of the enterprises and individuals in the Zone shall be protected by law.

The management committee shall establish a system for administration of the registration, use and protection of intellectual property rights in the Zone.

Article 49 (Control of work concerning place of origin)

Work concerning the place of origin in the Zone shall be undertaken by the institution in charge of the control thereof.

The institution in charge of the work concerning the place of origin shall conduct its work in compliance with the laws and regulations of the Zone and the international practice.

Article 50 (Special license for operation)

Special license may be granted for the operation of the infrastructure facilities and public establishments in the Zone.

Where an enterprise that has a special operation license wishes to transfer or distribute it to other enterprises, a contract shall be concluded and approval thereof shall be obtained from the management committee.

Article 51 (Purchase of products of Zone)

The DPRK institutions, enterprises and organizations outside the Zone may, under contract, purchase the goods produced or sold by the enterprises in the Zone.

Article 52 (Implementation in good faith of contracts)

Enterprises shall give priority to performing the contracts, abide by the terms of credit and fulfill the contracts in good faith.

Parties to the contracts shall adhere to the principle of equality and mutual benefit in concluding and carrying out contracts.

Article 53 (Services for managerial work)

Services for managerial work such as banking, insurance, accounting, legal work and measuring may be provided in the Zone in accordance with the regulations.

Article 54 (Advertising, approval for installation of outdoor advertisements)
Advertising business may be conducted and advertisements may be put in the Zone in accordance with the regulations.
Where advertisements are to be put outdoors, approval thereof shall be obtained from the management committee.
Article 55 (Construction standards, technical norms)
Advanced standards of design and building technique, and technical norms of foreign countries may be introduced to the construction design and building work in the Zone.
Article 56 (Tourist business)
International tourism shall be promoted in the Zone by developing tourism resources such as scenic beauty and folk culture.
Investors may conduct tourist business in the Zone in accordance with the regulations.
Article 57 (Use of communications devices)
Mail, telephone, fax and other communications devices may be freely used in the Zone.
Article 58 (Provision of conditions for entry/exit of persons, vehicles and goods)
Institutions of immigration control, customs, quarantine and others concerned shall streamlined the procedures for the entry and exit of persons, vehicles and goods in order that development of the Zone and business activities may progress without hindrance.
Article 59 (Transaction of securities)
Foreign-invested enterprises and foreigners may transact securities in the Zone in accordance with the regulations.

Chapter 6 Incentives and Preferential Treatment

Article 60 (Mode of investment)
Investors may invest in the Zone in such forms as direct investment, indirect investment and the like.
Article 61 (Encouragement of export and import)
Enterprises may, under contracts with the enterprises in or outside the Zone, conduct transactions of goods, technology and services, and conduct agent's business for export and import.
Article 62 (Exemption or reduction of enterprise income tax)
Designated enterprises operating in the Zone for more than 10 years shall be entitled to exemption or reduction of enterprise income tax.

The period and rate of exemption or reduction of enterprise income tax and the starting point of calculation shall be provided by the relevant regulations.

Article 63 (Preferential treatment concerning use of land)

Land for the use of enterprises in the Zone shall be provided in order of the actual demand presented, and depending on the sector and the purpose of land use, different preferential treatment shall be accorded in respect of term of lease, rentals and method of payment.

Enterprises in investing in infrastructure, public establishments and top priority sectors shall be given a priority in selecting the location of land, with the land use rent exempted for a designated period of time.

Article 64 (Refund of income tax on reinvested amount)

Where dividends are reinvested in the Zone to increase the registered capital or to set up a new business for more than 5 years' operation, 50% of the enterprise income tax paid on the reinvested amount shall be refunded.

Where reinvestment is made in the construction of infrastructure facilities, the whole of the enterprise income tax that had been paid on the reinvested amount shall be refunded.

Article 65 (Preferential treatment for developer enterprise)

The developer enterprise shall have a preferential right in obtaining the right of operation of tourist business, hotel business and the like.

Tax shall not be levied on the property of the developer enterprise and the infrastructure facilities and public establishments that it operates.

Article 66 (Preferential treatment for operations of specially licensed objects)

The management committee shall provide preferential treatment to operators of specially licensed objects so that he may make profits to his satisfaction.

Article 67 (Entry or exit from Zone)

Foreigners and vehicles may enter or leave the Zone through the designated route without visa upon presentation of passports or other equivalent pass.

Procedures for entering or leaving the Zone from other areas of the DPRK and the procedures for entering or leaving other areas of the DPRK from the Zone shall be provided separately.

Article 68 (Special tariff system, exemption from customs duties)

Preferential tariff system shall be introduced in the Zone.

Customs duties shall not be levied on materials brought into the Zone for processing, transit trade and barter trade, imports needed for the production and operation of the enterprises and exports produced, office articles and daily necessities for the investors, material needed for the construction of the Zone and other designated articles.

Article 69 (Declaration of inward or outward materials)

Materials shall be brought into or taken out of the Zone subject to declaration.

Where materials are to be brought in or taken out, enterprises or individuals concerned shall fill out the declaration form truthfully for submission to the customs concerned.

Article 70 (Provision of facilities for education, culture, medical are and physical culture)

Residents and visitors shall be provided with facilities in the area of education, culture, medical care and physical culture.

Chapter 7 Complaints, Settlements of Disputes

Article 71 (Complaints, settlement)

Enterprises and individuals may lodge complaints with the management committee, the north Phyongan provincial people's committee, central guidance organ of the special economic zones and other institutions concerned.

The institutions shall make inquires and settle the complaints within 30 days of receipt thereof and notify the complaint of the result.

Article 72 (Settlement of dispute by mediation)

The management committee or the institution concerned may, upon request of the parties to a dispute, mediate the dispute. In this case mediation plan shall be worked out by reference to the opinions of the parties to the dispute.

The mediation plan shall take effect upon signature of the parties to the dispute.

Article 73 (Settlement of disputes by arbitration)

Parties to a dispute may, upon agreement, apply for arbitration to a DPRK or a foreign international arbitration institution established in the Zone.

Arbitration shall be conducted in accordance with the arbitration rules of the international arbitration committee concerned.

Article 74 (Settlement of disputes by court)

Parties to a dispute may bring an action to a competent court in the Zone.

Procedures for administrative action in the Zone shall be provided separately.

Appendix

Article 1 (Date of entry into force)

This Law shall enter into force as from the date of promulgation.

Article 2 (Rights of interpretation)

Interpretation of this Law shall be provided by the Presidium of the Supreme People's Assembly.

[Source: Laws and Regulations of the Democratic People's Republic of Korea Governing External Economic Matters, Legislation Press, Pyongyang, 2012]

▪ LAW OF THE DEMOCRATIC PEOPLE'S REPUBLIC OF KOREA ON THE ECONOMIC DEVELOPMENT ZONES

Adopted by the Decision No. 3192 of the Presidium of the Supreme People's Assembly on May 29, 2013; amended by the same organ on August 10, 2016; on September 21, 2017; on October 24, 2019; and on November 2021

Chapter 1 Fundamentals

Article 1 (Objective)

The Law of the Democratic People's Republic of Korea on the Economic Development Zones shall contribute to establishing the system and order in the creation, development and management of the economic development zones (the EDZs), promoting the national economy through encouraging external economic cooperation and exchange, and improving the standard of people's life.

Article 2 (Definition and categories)

The EDZs shall be special economic zones whose preferential treatments are guaranteed for economic activities in accordance with the laws and regulations specially enacted by the State.

The EDZs shall encompass the development zones for economy, science and technology sectors such as industrial development zones, agricultural development zones, tourism development zones, export processing zones, high-technology development zones.

Article 3 (Categorization of zones)

The State shall categorize and manage the EDZs into provincial level zones or central level zones depending on the level of managing authority.

Article 4 (Non-standing Reviewing Committee of the State)

In relation to designation of an EDZ, securing beneficial environment and conditions for investment, and management and operation of EDZs, the State shall establish the Non-standing State Reviewing Committee under the Cabinet in order to review and respond to issues raised by the Committee, provinces and central organs.

Article 5 (Guidance organ of the zones)

The central organ of special economic zones under the direction of the Cabinet shall uniformly conduct state-wide control and guidance for the work of EDZs.

With regard to the creation, development and operation of the EDZs, the State shall designate the central organ of the special economic zones as the sole authority to handle any issues arising internally and externally.

Article 6 (Investors)
Corporate bodies, individual persons, economic organizations of foreign countries, and overseas Koreans may invest in the EDZs and they may freely conduct economic activities after establishing companies, branches, representative offices and the like.
Governmental bodies, enterprises and organizations of the DPRK may conduct economic activities by way of investing in the EDZs.
Article 7 (Sectors of priority, prohibition, restriction)
The State particularly shall encourage investment in the EDZs in the sectors of infrastructure construction, state-of-the-art science and technology, and production of internationally competitive goods.
It shall be prohibited or restricted that investments and economic activities which are detrimental to national security, public health, sound social and moral life and protection of environment or which are economically and technically outdated projects.
Article 8 (Protection of investors' rights and interests, guaranteeing preferential economic activities)
The State shall legally protect investors' rights and invested properties, and legitimate incomes, and guarantee such investors' preferential economic activities as in land use, labor employment, paying taxes.
The State shall not nationalize or expropriate properties of investors; however, where an investor's property is, due to unavoidable reasons, to be expropriated or used temporarily for public interests, notification thereof shall be made in advance, and sufficient compensation for its value shall be made in a timely manner.
Article 9 (Personal safety)
Personal safety in the EDZs shall be protected by laws of the Democratic People's Republic of Korea (DPRK).
No person shall be detained or arrested, nor shall his place of residence be searched except in accordance with law.
Any treaty, if any, concluded between the DPRK and a foreign country with respect to the personal safety shall take precedence.
Article 10 (Applicable laws and regulations)
This Law, its implementing regulations and rules shall be applied to the development and management of the EDZs, and economic activities such as operation of businesses.
Where contents of the Law of EDZs and of its regulations differ from other laws and regulations, the former shall take priority over the latter.

Chapter 2 Creation of Economic Development Zones

Article 11 (Basis of creation)
The creation of the EDZs shall be based on economic prospects in connection with the economic development of the State.
Article 12 (Principles of selecting location)
The principles of the selecting location of the EDZs shall be as follows:

1. It shall be advantageous to the cooperation with and the exchange of external economy:
2. It shall contribute to the development of economy, science and technology of the State;
3. It shall be somewhat remote from the local residents; and
4. It shall not encroach on the protective zones designated by the State.

Article 13 (Handling questions)
In case institutions, enterprises or organizations of the DPRK receive inquiries from foreign investors about the creation and development of the EDZs, they shall transfer in writing such questions to the central guidance organ of the special economic zones.
The central guidance organ of the special economic zones shall elaborately review and ascertain the inquiries and further deal with them.
Article 14 (Creation of provincial level EDZs)
An application for the creation of a provincial-level EDZ shall be filed with the central guidance organ of the special economic zones by the people's committee of the province (or municipality directly under the central authority) concerned. In this case a consultation document made with relevant institutions of the province (or municipality directly under the central authority) concerned shall be submitted together with the application above.
Article 15 (Creation of central level EDZs)
An application for the creation of a central level EDZ shall be filed with the central guidance organ of the special economic zones according to the stipulated procedures after the institution concerned prepares it. In this case a consultation document made with relevant institutions shall be submitted together with the application.
Article 16 (Agreement of relevant institutions)
The central guidance organ of the special economic zones shall sufficiently consult with relevant central institutions before it proposes a review of documents for the creation of an EDZ to the Non-standing Reviewing Committee of the State.

Article 17 (Approval of creation of EDZ)
The Non-standing Reviewing Committee shall have the authority to approve the creation of an EDZ.
Where the central guidance organ of the special economic zones proposes the review of documents for the creation of an EDZ, it shall submit the documents consulted with the relevant central institutions.
Article 18 (Promulgation of creation of EDZ)
The Presidium of the Supreme Peoples' Committee shall have the authority to promulgate the State's decision for the establishment of an EDZ.

Chapter 3 Development of EDZs

Article 19 (Principle of development)
The EDZs shall be developed on the principles of:

1. Developing phase by phase as planned;
2. Diversifying introduction of investments;
3. Protecting the ecosystem of the EDZs and their surrounding areas;
4. Using land and its resources in a reasonable manner;
5. Raising international competitiveness of production and service;
6. Ensuring both convenient economic activities and public interests;
7. Ensuring sustained and balanced development of the EDZs concerned.

Article 20 (Party of development)
A foreign investor may develop an EDZ solely or jointly upon approval.
An institution or enterprise of the DPRK may develop an EDZ upon approval.
Article 21 (Approval to developer enterprise)
Approval to the developer enterprise shall be made by the central guidance organ of the special economic zones.
The central guidance organ of the special economic zones shall register the developer enterprise with it and issue a development license.
Article 22 (Development plan and approval)
The development plan for EDZs shall be made into two categories - comprehensive development plan and detailed individual plan.
The institution or a developer enterprise concerned shall make the comprehensive development plan based on the regional

comprehensive construction plan of land, and the detailed individual plan based on the comprehensive development plan above.

The Cabinet shall have the authority to approve the development plan.

Article 23 (Mode of development)

The mode of development of the EDZs may be decided in the reasonable way that complies with characteristics and development conditions of the EDZs concerned and that contributes to the economic progress of the State.

Article 24 (Land lease contract)

An investor who wishes to lease land in an EDZ shall have a contract with the management institution of an EDZ concerned.

The land lease contract shall specify the term of lease, area, compartment, purpose of use, term and method of lease payment and other necessary particulars.

The land management institution shall issue a land use certificate to the investor who has paid a tax institution the land lease as stipulated in the contract.

Article 25 (Term of land use and extension)

The term of land lease in the EDZs shall be 50 years in maximum and the term shall be calculated from the date on which the land use certificate is issued.

An enterprise whose term is complete may re-enter into a contract for the continued use of the leased land.

Article 26 (Investment of right to use land as share)

In case institutions, enterprises or organizations establish a developer enterprise jointly with foreign investors, they may invest the right to use land in the form of equity as arranged.

Article 27 (Removal of building and attachment, bearing cost)

Expenses for removal and relocation of buildings and attachments as well as relocation of residents in the developing area of an EDZ shall be borne by the developer enterprise.

Article 28 (Construction of infrastructure and public facilities)

The developer enterprise shall take up construction of infrastructure and public facilities in the EDZs.

The developer enterprise may bring other enterprises into the construction of infrastructure and public facilities as arranged.

Article 29 (Sales of right to use land and building, sublease price)

Enterprises may mortgage or sublease the right to use land and building ownership, and transfer them by way of sales, exchange, gift or inheritance.

The price of the right to use land and a building shall be determined as agreed by the transacting parties..

Article 30 (Registration of right to use land and building ownership)

Where the developer enterprise obtains the right to use land or ownership of a building, it shall register it with the management institution and be issued the relevant certificate.

Where the right to use land or ownership of building has a change in its right, it shall be registered for the change with the institution and be re-issued the certificate of it..

Chapter 4 Management of the EDZs

Article 31 (Management institution)

The management institution of an EDZ shall have the authority to manage the EDZ under the guidance and auspices of the central guidance organ of the special economic zones and relevant organs of the peoples' committee of the provinces (or municipalities directly under the central authority) concerned.

Except otherwise stipulated in the laws and regulations about the EDZs, other institutions shall not take part in the works of the management institution of the EDZs.

The management institution of an EDZ as a State's organ to directly operate an EDZ concerned may organize the management committee or management office depending on circumstances of respective EDZs.

The Cabinet office shall organize the structure of the management institutions.

Article 32 (Principles of management)

The principles of management of the EDZs are:

1. Strictly observing and enforcing laws and regulations;
2. Ensuring independence of enterprises;
3. Offering preferential treatment in economic activities;
4. Considering international customs.

Article 33 (Functions of the central guidance organ of the special economic zones)

The central guidance organ of the special economic zones shall:

1. Prepare development strategies of the State in relation to the EDZs;
2. Cooperate with governments, non-governmental organizations and civic organizations of foreign countries in connection with the development and operation of the EDZs;

3. Maintain a contact with committees, provinces and central institutions that are related to the work of the EDZs;
4. Direct and facilitate the work of the management institutions;
5. Screen and approve the examining criteria for the establishment of enterprises in the EDZs;
6. Prepare and provide the rules and directives for enforcing laws and regulations of the EDZs; and
7. Perform other works authorized by the State.

Article 34 (Functions of provincial peoples' committees)

In relation to the EDZs located in its jurisdiction, the peoples' committee of a province (or municipality directly under the central authority) shall:

1. Organize the management institution and practice relevant works of it;
2. Prepare and direct management documents of the State in relation to works of the EDZs such as implementing rules of the EDZs Law and regulations;
3. Facilitate works of the management institution;
4. Secure labor force, electricity and water supply necessary to the management of the EDZs and operation of enterprises therein; and
5. Other works authorized by the State.

Article 35 (Composition of management institution)

The management institution shall be composed of necessary members in consideration of the situation and interests of the EDZ concerned, and the responsible person of the management institution shall be the chairperson of the management committee or the chief of the management office.

Article 36 (Functions of management institution)

The management institution shall perform following functions:

1. Preparing rules required for the development and management of the EDZ;
2. Fostering investment climate and attracting investment;
3. Approving establishment of enterprises, registering them and issuing a business license;
4. Granting a permission on projected constructions and inspecting completion of constructions;
5. Taking custody of projected architectural designs of constructions;

6. Registering the rights to use land and ownerships of buildings with it;
7. Rendering cooperation for the management of enterprises;
8. Undertaking supervision over and cooperation for the construction and management of infrastructure and public facilities therein;
9. Taking measures for protection of environment and for fire-fighting;
10. Preparing rules of the management institution;
11. Supervising and controlling on compliance of the EDZ Laws and regulations
12. Carrying out other works assigned by the central guidance organ of the special economic zones and the peoples' committee of the province (or municipality directly under the central organ).

Article 37 (Compilation and execution of budget)
The management institution shall compile and execute its own budget. Documents concerning the compilation and execution of the budget shall be submitted to the peoples' committee concerned or the central guidance organ of the special economic zones.

Chapter 5 Economic Activities in the EDZs

Article 38 (Creating and operating an enterprise)
An investor may establish and operate in the EDZs upon approval of the management institution.
In this case where other laws and regulations stipulate differently with regard to the creation and operation of the enterprises for specially-designated business category and domestic enterprises, such laws and regulations shall take precedence.
The central guiding organ of the special economic zones, provincial (or municipality directly under the central authority) peoples' committee, the management institutions and relevant institutions shall streamline the procedures for establishment and operation of enterprises in the EDZs.

Article 39 (Application for creation of enterprise)
An investor wishing to establish an enterprise in an EDZ shall submit an application for the establishment of an enterprise to the management institution.
The management institution shall approve or reject the establishment of an enterprise within 10 days from the date on which the application was filed, and notify the applicant of the result.

Article 40 (Registration of enterprise, incorporation)
An enterprise approved for creation shall register its corporate affairs, customs affairs, and tax affairs within the prescribed period of time.
The enterprise shall be a corporate body of the DPRK from the date on which its creation is registered with the management institution. However, a branch or representative office of an enterprise shall not be a corporate body of the DPRK.
Article 41 (Employment)
Enterprises in the EDZs shall preferentially recruit labor of the DPRK. In this case they shall submit an employment application to the labor administrative institution and be provided for the workforce.
Where they wish to necessarily employ a foreigner, it shall be agreed with the management institution.
Article 42 (Determination of minimum wage)
The monthly minimum wage of the employees in the EDZs shall be determined by the central guidance organ of the special economic zones. In this case the central guidance organ above shall consult with the management institution or people's committee of province (or municipality directly under the central authority) concerned.
Article 43 (Prices of commodities and service)
Prices of the commodities and services transacted between enterprises in an EDZ, and prices of the commodities transacted between enterprises in an EDZ and institutions, enterprises and organizations of the DPRK outside the EDZ shall be determined by the parties in accordance with the prevailing prices of international market.
Article 44 (Accounting of enterprises)
Accounting and settlement of enterprises in the EDZs shall conform to the relevant laws and regulations of finance and accounting of the DPRK applicable to the EDZs.
The internationally accepted accounting customs shall be applied to any matters not stipulated in the laws and regulations above.
Article 45 (Enterprise income tax rate)
Enterprise income tax rate in the EDZs shall be 14% of net profit, and the same tax for the enterprises in the priority sectors shall be 10% of net profit.
Article 46 (Circulating money, settlement currency)
Circulating money and settlement currency in the EDZs shall be Korean won or other designated currency.
Article 47 (Inward and outward movement of foreign currency, profits and property)

Foreign currency shall be freely brought into or taken out of the EDZs, and legitimate profits and other incomes may be remitted out of the EDZs without any restrictions.

Investors may take out of the EDZs the property that had been brought into and legitimately acquired therein.

Article 48 (Protection of intellectual property rights)

Intellectual property rights in the EDZs shall be protected by law.

Measures for the registration, use and protection of intellectual property rights shall be stipulated in the relevant laws and regulations.

Article 49 (Tourism)

International tourism shall be promoted in the EDZs by developing tourism resources matching with natural scenic beauty, environment and characteristics of the area concerned.

Investors may conduct tourism businesses in the EDZs in accordance with the relevant laws and regulations.

Article 50 (Entry or exit of persons, vehicles and goods)

Institutions of immigration inspection, customs, quarantine and other relevant institutions shall be committed to the smooth service for the entry and exit of persons, vehicles and goods in order to facilitate development and management of the EDZs as well as investors' economic activities.

Article 51 (Transaction of securities)

Foreign-invested enterprises and foreigners may trade securities in the EDZs in accordance with the laws and regulations.

Chapter 6 Incentives and Preferential Treatment

Article 52 (Preferential treatment in use of land)

Industrial lands in the EDZs shall be allocated based on actual needs, and differentiated preferential treatments shall be offered as to the terms of lease, rentals, and method of payment depending on the business field and the purpose of land use.

Enterprises investing in infrastructure, public facilities and priority sectors shall be given a priority in selecting a location of land, and rentals for land use may be exempted for a designated period of time.

Article 53 (Exemption or reduction of enterprise income tax)

Designated enterprises operating in the EDZs for more than 10 years shall be entitled to exemption or reduction of enterprise income tax.

The period of exemption or reduction and the rate reduction of enterprise income tax, and the starting point of calculation for them shall be stipulated in the relevant regulations.

Article 54 (Refund of income tax on reinvested amount)

Where an investor reinvests profits in the EDZs to increase the registered capital or operates a business for more than 5 years after setting up a new enterprise, 50% of the enterprise income tax paid on the reinvested portion shall be refunded.
Where reinvestment is made in the construction of infrastructure, the whole enterprise income tax paid on the reinvested amount shall be refunded.
Article 55 (Preferential treatment for developer enterprise)
The developer enterprise in the EDZs shall have a preferential right in acquisition of beneficial service-oriented businesses.
Tax shall not be levied on the property of the developer enterprise, and the operation of infrastructure facilities and public facilities.
Article 56 (Preferential tariff treatment and exemption from customs duties)
Preferential tariff treatment shall be taken into effect in the EDZs.
Custom duties shall not be levied on materials brought in for the construction of the EDZs, on materials for processing, transit trade and barter trade, on materials for production or management of enterprises, on commodities produced for export, on personal necessities for investors, and on other materials designated by the State.
Article 57 (Declaration of inward or outward materials)
Materials brought into or taken out of the EDZs shall be subject to declaration.
Where materials are to be brought into or taken out of the EDZs, a declaration form shall be filled out and submitted to the customs office concerned.
Article 58 (Provision of telecommunication)
Convenience shall be provided for the use of communication means such as postal mail, telephone and fax in the EDZs.

Chapter 7 Complaints, Settlement of Disputes

Article 59 (Complaints, settlement)
Enterprises and individuals in the EDZs may file complaints with the management institution, the central guidance organ of the special economic zones or other institutions concerned.
The institutions shall conduct fact-findings to sort it out within 30 days of receipt and notify the complainant of the result.
Article 60 (Dispute settlement by mediation)
Parties in the EDZs may settle disputes by mediation.

A plan of mediation process shall be made based on the opinions of the parties and it shall take into effect upon signature of the parties on it.

Article 61 (Dispute settlement by international arbitration)

Parties to a dispute may, upon agreement, file arbitration with international arbitration institutions in the DPRK or a foreign country in order to settle the dispute.

Arbitration procedures shall be conducted in accordance with the arbitration rules of the international arbitration committee concerned.

Article 62 (Dispute settlement by court)

Parties to a dispute may bring an action to a provincial court (or municipal court directly under the central authority) whose jurisdiction covers the EDZ concerned or the supreme court of the DPRK in order to settle the dispute.

Appendix

Article 1 (Date of entry into force)

This Law shall enter into force from the date of adoption.

Article 2 (Limit of application)

This Law shall not be applicable to the Rason Economic and Trade Zone, the Hawnggumphyong and Wihwado Economic Zone, the Kaesong Industrial Complex and the Mt. Kumgang Special Zone for International Tourism.

[Source: *Bukhan Beopryeongjip sang & ha* (Collection of Laws and Regulations of North Korea Vol. I & II, PDF), National Intelligence Service of the Republic of Korea, Seoul, 2024)]

*The whole text of this Law is translated into English by the Author.

▪ LAW OF THE DEMOCRATIC PEOPLE'S REPUBLIC OF KOREA ON FOREIGN CURRENCY CONTROL

Adopted by Decision No. 27 of the Standing Committee of the Supreme People's Assembly on January 31, 1993, amended by the Presidium of the Supreme People's Assembly on February 26, 1999, amended on February 21, 2002, amended on November 16, 2004, and amended on August 22, 2020

Chapter 1 Fundamentals

Article 1 (Objective)

This Law is enacted for the purpose of providing strict guidelines for earning, using, bringing in an taking out foreign currency, thereby contributing to controlling foreign currency in a unified way and using it rationally.

Article 2 (Definitions)

Foreign currency in this Law shall indicate convertible foreign currencies and such foreign currency securities as State bonds, debentures, bills, cheques, bank cards and negotiable certificates of deposit, gold, silver and platinum other than decorative articles, gold and silver coins traded on international financial market, and other precious metals.

Article 3 (Main principle of foreign currency control)

Unified control is an important principle in foreign currency control.

The State shall ensure that the central financial guidance organ establishes unified foreign currency control system, secures balance of foreign currency, controls it as planned, and improves works of foreign currency control to cope with fluctuating environment and given conditions.

Article 4 (Prohibition of circulation of foreign currency in cash)

Foreign currency in cash shall not be circulated in the territory of the DPRK.

Foreign currency shall be converted into Korean won to be used.

Article 5 (Protection of legally earned foreign currency)

The State shall protect the foreign currencies earned legally and ensure their inheritance by citizens.

Article 6 (Applicability)

This Law shall be applied to the institutions, enterprises, organizations (including external settlement banks) and citizens that earn or use foreign exchange.

This Law shall also be applicable to the representative offices of foreign countries and international organizations, foreign-invested businesses, foreign individuals and overseas Koreans that earn or use foreign currency in the territory of the DPRK.

The system of foreign currency control applicable to the special economic zones shall be established separately.

Chapter 2 Earning and Use of Foreign Currency

Article 7 (Rate of obligatory payment to the State)
The central financial guidance organ, in accordance with the State plan for foreign currency income and expenditure, shall fix the rate of obligatory payment of foreign currency to the State by the institutions, enterprises and organizations that earn foreign currency.

Article 8 (Foreign currency accounts)
Institutions, enterprises, organizations, foreign-invested enterprises, and representative offices of foreign countries and international organizations shall open their foreign currency account with an external settlement bank and use the foreign currency therefrom.

In case they wish to open their accounts with the banks outside the territory of the DPRK, consent thereon shall be sought from the central financial guidance organ.

Article 9 (Financial plan of foreign currency and registration)
Institutions, enterprises and organizations shall make a financial plan for foreign currency and register it with the central financial guidance organ.

The financial plan of foreign currency shall be categorized into the foreign currency earning and the foreign currency spending including foreign currency payment plan to the State.

Article 10 (Earning plan of foreign currency)
Institutions, enterprises and organizations shall make foreign currency in accordance with the registered earning plan of foreign currency.

Article 11 (Executing spending plan of foreign currency)
Institutions, enterprises and organizations shall use foreign currency in accordance with the spending plan of foreign currency as registered.

In case foreign currency is used differently from figures or items in the registered spending plan of foreign currency, an approval from the relevant institution shall be required.

Article 12 (Payment plan of foreign currency to the State)
Institutions, enterprises and organizations shall accurately execute the payment plan of foreign currency to the State.

Institutions, enterprises and organizations may use their own currency after fulfilling the payment plan of foreign currency to the State.

Article 13 (Settlement of foreign currency)

Institutions, enterprises and organizations shall report settlement of accounts on earning and spending of foreign currency, after having it verified by an audit office, to the central financial guidance organ.

Accounting periods and detailed procedures and methods in relation to the earning and spending of foreign currency shall be set by the central financial guidance organ.

Article 14 (Reviewing session)

Institutions, enterprises and organizations shall be obliged to be given *chonghwa** for the use of foreign currency fund according to the item, indicator and method as set by the central financial guidance organ.

The central financial guidance organ shall conduct the *chonghwa* for the use of foreign currency fund of the State.

*Author's translation note: *chonghwa* in the context of business is a sort of reviewing session peculiar to the North Korean work place among members of a unit, group, enterprise or other organization. In the session attending individual members are respectively allowed to criticize or review themselves or other members in order to improve their overall work.

Article 15 (Managing payments to the State)

The central financial guidance organ shall open its account with the Foreign Trade Bank and manage the foreign currency payments to the State.

Article 16 (Spending State's foreign currency)

The central financial guidance organ shall spend foreign currency as planned and upon approval of the Cabinet within the range of deposited foreign currency fund in the account of the State's foreign currency.

Article 17 (State's foreign currency earning, spending and balance)

The central financial guidance organ shall comprehensively handle earning, spending and balance of foreign currency of the State and use them for the work of State's foreign currency control.

Article 18 (Retaining, selling and saving of foreign currency by citizens)

Citizens of the DPRK may retain foreign currency earned legally.

In case they wish to sell or deposit it, they shall deal with an external settlement bank, not with a foreign-invested bank.

Article 19 (Savings and selling of foreign currency by foreigner)

A foreign individual may deposit foreign currency remitted from abroad or earned legally in an external settlement bank or sell it to that bank.

Article 20 (Scope of use)

Foreign currency may be used in the following transactions:

1. Payment under external economic contracts and payment agreements:
2. Payment in such non-trade transactions as payment of travel expenses, overheads and maintenance costs;
3. Buying or selling of Korean Won at a bank; and
4. Such transactions as depositing, trusting, loaning and debt guarantee.

Article 21 (Foreign currency loans)

An external settlement bank may grant a loan of foreign currency to the institutions, enterprises, organizations and foreign-invested businesses according to the laws and regulations concerned.

Article 22 (Loan from foreign countries and international organizations)

Institutions, enterprises and organizations may, for their management and operation, obtain a loan of foreign currency from a foreign country or an international organization. In this case, agreement thereon shall be sought from the central financial guidance organ and endorsement thereon obtained from the Cabinet.

Article 23 (Issuance of securities)

The institutions, enterprises and organizations that wish to issue securities denominated in foreign currency shall obtain the approval of the relevant organs.

Chapter 3 Bringing In and Taking Out Foreign Currency

Article 24 (Commission, tariff)

Foreign currency in cash, securities denominated in foreign currency and precious metals may be brought into the territory of the DPRK without any restrictions. In this case, commission or tariff shall not be payable.

Article 25 (Foreign currency in cash)

Foreign currency in cash may be taken out of the territory of the DPRK within the limit specified in the foreign currency exchange statement issued by a bank according to the formalities set by the central financial guidance organ or declared to the customs upon entry.

Citizens of the DPRK departing the territory may take out foreign currency upon declaration to the customs without the foreign currency exchange statement but within the limit specified by the central financial guidance organ.

Article 26 (Securities denominated in foreign currency)

Securities in foreign currency shall not be taken out of the territory of the DPRK without the consent of the central financial guidance organ and the approval of the institution concerned.

Securities in foreign currency declared to the customs upon entry may be taken out of the territory of the DPRK without permission being sought.

Article 27 (Precious metals)

Precious metals may be taken out of the territory of the DPRK subject to the approval of the Central Bank.

Precious metals brought into the territory of the DPRK shall be taken out within the limit declared to the customs upon entry.

Article 28 (Profit and other income of foreign investor)

A foreign investor shall be allowed to remit out of the territory of the DPRK tax-free the distributed profits earned from business operation.

Article 29 (Salary and other legally earned income of foreigners)

Foreigners may remit out of the territory of the DPRK salaries and legally earned foreign currency after paying relevant taxes.

Chapter 4 Guidance and Supervision of Foreign Currency Control

Article 30 (Guidance organ)

The work of foreign currency control shall be placed under guidance and control of the central financial guidance organ under the unified direction of the Cabinet.

The central financial guidance organ shall guide and control the institutions, enterprises and organizations in order for them to comply with the State's finance-related rules and orders in their use of foreign currency.

Article 31(Rules and directives of foreign exchange control, implementation)

The central financial guidance organ shall accurately make elaborate rules and directives in relation to the work of the financial control of foreign currency and accounting practice organs in compliance with the laws and regulations of foreign currency control, and direct them to others accordingly.

Relevant institutions, enterprises, organizations and foreign-invested businesses shall strictly comply with such rules and directives on the control of foreign currency.

Article 32 (Control of foreign currency by budget)

Management of foreign exchange holdings by institutions, enterprises and organizations under the central budget shall be placed under the direct guidance of the central financial guidance organ. Management of foreign currency holdings by the institutions, enterprises and organizations under the local budget shall be guided by the provincial people's committee.

Article 33 (Unified control of foreign exchange claims and debts)

The central financial guidance organ shall exercise unified supervision and management of the foreign currency claims and debts to foreign countries.

The relevant institutions, enterprises and organizations shall comply in time with the demands of the central financial guidance organ.

Article 34 (Salary, traveling expenses and fees paid in foreign currency)

The financial guidance organ shall define a correct standard of living allowances, travel expenses and fees to be paid in foreign currency, and ensure proper compliance therewith.

Article 35 (Control of external settlement banks)

The central financial guidance organ shall receive from the external settlement banks quarterly and yearly financial statements and other necessary statistical data concerning their business.

Article 36 (Inspection of foreign exchange management)

The central financial guidance organ may inspect the status of foreign currency management of the institutions, enterprises, organizations and the external settlement banks.

The relevant institutions, enterprises, organizations and the external settlement banks shall provide proper circumstances necessary for the inspection conducted by the central financial guidance organ.

Article 37 (Enforced payment)

Where foreign currency due to the State is not paid at the prescribed time and short of the required amount, it may be enforced to be paid by the bank in transaction.

Article 38 (Imposition of arrearage)

Where foreign currency due to the State is not paid at the prescribed time and short of the required amount, arrearage shall be charged.

Article 39 (Compensation)

Where losses are inflicted on the other party in the course of using foreign currency, the loss so caused shall be compensated.

Article 40 (Fines)

Where foreign currency is not deposited with a bank within the prescribed period of time or deposited with a different bank, fines shall be imposed.

Article 41 (Forfeiture)
Foreign currency in question shall be forfeited where one:
1. circulated foreign currency in cash within the territory of the DPRK;
2. did not use foreign currency for the prescribed usage;
3. used foreign currency beyond the prescribed limit;
4. used foreign currency outside the accounting/bookkeeping system;
5. embezzled foreign currency;
6. diverted foreign currency to foreign countries; and
7. transacted illegally foreign currency otherwise.

Article 42 (Administrative or penal liability)
In case the grave consequences in the management of foreign currency were caused by the violation of this Law, the responsible party shall be liable to administrative or penal liability depending on the gravity of the offense.

[Source: (1) Laws and Regulations of the Democratic People's Republic of Korea Governing External Economic Matters, Legislation Press, Pyongyang, 2012; (2) *Bukhan Beopryeongjip sang & ha* (Collection of Laws and Regulations of North Korea I & II, PDF), National Intelligence Service of the Republic of Korea, Seoul, 2024; and (3) *Choesin Bukhan Beopryeongjip* published by *Bukhanbeop yeonguhoe* (Collection of Current Acts and Regulations of North Korea), Myung-Bong Chang (ed.), Seoul, 2018]
*Amended portions on or after August 22, 2020 are translated into English by the Author.

▪ LAW OF THE DEMOCRATIC PEOPLE'S REPUBLIC OF KOREA ON FOREIGN-INVESTED BANKS

Adopted by Decision No. 42 of the Standing Committee of the Supreme People's Assembly on November 24, 1993, and amended by the Presidium of the Supreme People's Assembly on February 26, 1999; November 7, 2002; December 21, 2011; March 8, 2018; and June 19, 2020.

Chapter 1 Fundamentals

Article 1 (Objective)

This Law is enacted for the purpose of promoting and expanding cooperation with foreign countries in the area of finance.

Article 2 (Classification, definition)

Foreign-invested banks shall include joint-venture banks, wholly foreign-owned banks and branches of foreign banks.

Joint-venture banks are jointly established and operated by a party(ies) of the DPRK and a foreign investor(s) and distribute profits according to the proportion of their contribution.

Wholly foreign-owned banks are established and operated after an investment solely made by a foreign investor(s).

Branches of foreign banks are established by investments from foreign banks and operated by the headquarters of the foreign banks.

Article 3 (Location)

A foreign investor may establish and operate a bank within the territory of the DPRK.

Joint-venture banks may be established on the approved locations in the territory of the DPRK.

Wholly foreign-owned banks and branches of foreign banks may be established in the special economic zones.

Article 4 (Ownership and independent management)

Foreign-invested banks shall have the ownership of their banking property and be independent in their management.

Article 5 (Protection of rights and interests)

The State shall protect the legitimate rights and interests of foreign-invested banks established in the territory of the DPRK and ensure the priority in the business activities.

Article 6 (Governing law and regulations)

Foreign-invested banks shall be operated pursuant to the relevant laws and regulations.

Article 7 (Supervisory and control organ)

Foreign-invested banks shall be placed under the supervision and control of the Central Bank and the central tax guidance organ.

Article 8 (Scope)
This Law shall be applicable to foreign-invested banks established and operated in the territory of the DPRK.

Chapter 2 Establishment and Operation of Foreign-invested Banks

Article 9 (Application for the establishment of a foreign-invested bank)
An investor who wishes to establish a foreign-invested bank shall file an application with the Central Bank. In this case, the application shall be accompanied by relevant documents verified by the public notary institution.

Article 10 (Application for the establishment of a joint-venture bank)
The application for the establishment of a joint-venture bank shall be filed by the party of the DPRK.
A financial institution shall only be a qualified party of the DPRK of a joint-venture bank.
The application shall be accompanied by such documents as a copy of the joint-venture contract, the articles of association, feasibility study report, a copy of the investor's business license, investor's balance sheet for three years audited and verified at the foreign investor's country, and résumés of the foreign investor and the president of the bank.

Article 11 (Application for the establishment of wholly foreign-owned bank)
The application for the establishment of a wholly foreign-owned bank shall be filed by the foreign investor concerned.
The application shall be accompanied by such documents as the articles of association, feasibility study report, a copy of the investor's business license, investor's balance sheet for three years audited and verified at the foreign investor's country, and resumes of the foreign investor and the president of the bank.

Article 12 (Application for the establishment of a branch of a foreign bank)
The application for the establishment of a branch of a foreign bank shall be filed by the head office of the bank concerned.
The application shall be accompanied by such documents as the articles of association, annual reports, balance sheet, profit and loss account and a copy of the business license of the head office, written guarantee by the head office against the tax and debts of the branch, a feasibility study report of the branch, a copy of the approval notice for

foreign exchange transactions, and a resume of the president of the bank.

Article 13 (Approval or rejection of a foreign-invested bank)

The Central Bank having received an application for the establishment of a foreign-invested bank shall decide, after conducting an examination, whether to approve or reject it within 30 days of receipt thereof.

In case of approval, a notice of approval for establishing a bank in question shall be issued, and in case of rejection a notice shall be sent with the reasons thereof stated.

Article 14 (Business preparation)

A foreign-invested bank approved for establishment shall complete its preparation for operation before the first day of the term as indicated on the approval notice comes on.

In case a foreign-invested bank had not completed preparation for operation until the first day of the business term as indicated on the approval notice, the Central Bank shall cancel the approval of the establishment, retrieve the approval notice and notify relevant institutions of such measures taken by it.

Article 15 (List of work to be done during the prep period)

A foreign-invested bank shall complete following works during the preparation period:

1. To register address and tax purposes pursuant to the laws and regulations concerned;
2. To open an bank account for deposit with the bank designated by the Central Bank;
3. To hire, depending on the prescribed workforce quota, such workers of the bank as banking-experienced workers, banking specialists, and professionally trained staff;
4. To make official seal of the bank, nameplate, workers' personal seal and sign board;
5. To set up facilities such as vaults, communication means, security system and be ready for various documents, operation programs, and working systems for tellers;
6. To make internal guidance of work according to the business categories and have bank workers skilled on it;
7. To deposit the primary paid-up capital at least 50% of the registered capital on the bank designated by the Central Bank and have such a performance verified; and

8. To deposit the prescribed amount of bank reserves in the Central Bank.

Article 16 (Application for approval of operation of foreign-invested bank)

A foreign-invested bank having finished preparation shall file an application for approval of business operation with the Central Bank.

The application for approval of business operation shall be accompanied by such documents as the approval notice of the bank establishment, internal guidance of work, registration certificate of address, registration certificate of tax, verification report for performed investment, confirmation letter for opening a deposit account, deposit certificate of bank reserves and the like.

Article 17 (Business operation license)

The Central Bank having received an application for approval of business operation of a foreign-invested bank shall decide, after conducting an examination, whether to approve or reject the application based on on-the-spot inspection for the preparedness of business operation within 30 days of receipt thereof.

In case of approval, a banking business license shall be issued, and in case of rejection a notice shall be sent with the reasons thereof stated.

A foreign-invested bank shall be subject to *gyeongyu** of the license of banking business once a year.

*Author's note: '(be) *gyeongyu*' (경유 in Korean) shown on the Source (2) at the end of this Law in Korean is a unknown terminology even to the North Korea's largest volume of Korean dictionary. Considering the context, it may be guessed one of such terms as 'show', 'renewal', 'review' or 'inspection.'

Article 18 (Term of business and extension)

The business term of a foreign-invested bank shall be for 20 years.

Where a foreign-invested bank wishes to continue its banking business beyond its term, an application shall be submitted to the Central Bank for the approval of the extension of the term 6 months before the expiry of the original term.

Article 19 (Establishing bank offices)

Foreign-invested banks may, if necessary, open bank offices under their control to handle such businesses as economic survey, data collection or external affairs. In this case, an approval from the Central Bank shall be obtained.

A foreign-invested bank shall not open a branch or sub-branch office under it that offers banking services, nor allow a bank office to deal with business transactions.

Article 20 (Alteration of registered items)

Where a foreign-invested bank wishes to revise its articles of association, merge or divide the bank, make changes in the registered capital, the place of business and the categories of business, or replace the president or a vice-president of the bank, application for approval to that effect shall be filed with the Central Bank and the particulars of the change shall be registered upon approval.

Chapter 3 Capital and Reserve Funds of Foreign-invested Banks

Article 21 (Registered capital and payment due)

The registered capital of a foreign-invested bank as a monetary asset invested in substance to be used for banking operation shall be used for only banking business.

The payment of registered capital shall be made within 1 year from the time the payment of primary paid-up capital was deposited.

Article 22 (Amount of registered capital)

The amount of registered capital of a foreign-invested bank shall be set up by the Cabinet.

A foreign-invested bank may increase the prescribed amount of registered capital but shall not decrease the amount.

Article 23 (Reserve fund)

A foreign-invested bank shall deposit with the Central Bank the reserve fund whose amount was prescribed by the Central Bank

The reserve fund deposited with the Central Bank shall not generate interests and may be withdrawn only in the case of merger, separation or dissolution of a foreign-invested bank.

Article 24 (Contingency fund)

A foreign-invested bank shall set aside 5% of its annual profits each year as a contingency fund until it amounts to 25% of the registered capital.

The contingency fund shall be used for the capital increase or in the compensation for the operational loss.

Article 25 (Setting set-aside allowance and use)

A foreign-invested bank shall set enterprise's set-aside allowance within 15% of its annual profits.

The set-aside allowance may be used for bonus, culture and welfare, training employees, expanding production, R & D and the like.

Chapter 4 Transactions, Settlement and Dissolution of Accounts

Article 26 (Business categories)

A foreign-invested bank may conduct the following transactions with foreign-invested enterprises and foreigners:

1. Accepting foreign currency deposits;

2. Granting loans in foreign currencies and conducting investment business;
3. Foreign exchange transactions;
4. Conducting overdraft transactions and discounting foreign currency bills;
5. Guarantee on foreign currency liabilities and implementation of contractual obligations;
6. Remittance of foreign currency;
7. Clearing of the importer's and exporter's bills of exchange;
8. Credit check, confirmation and consultation;
9. Trust banking;
10. Issuing cards for customers; and
11. Conducting separately permitted transactions between non-residents.

Article 27 (Loans in foreign currency and works for investment)
A foreign-invested bank may grant a loan in foreign currency to and conduct an investment business with institutions, enterprises and organizations of the DPRK. In this case, the bank shall not conduct other businesses with such entities aside from the loan in foreign currency and the investment.

Article 28 (Limit of bank loan)
A foreign-invested bank shall not grant a loan of more than 25% of its registered capital exclusively to a single institution, enterprise or organization aside from a financial entity.

Article 29 (Standing reserves)
A foreign-invested bank shall keep reserves on hand at all times for the smooth payment to depositors. In this case, 30% of fund received from depositors shall be kept in cash.

Article 30 (Fiscal year)
The fiscal year of a foreign-invested bank shall begin on January 1 and end on December 31 each year.
Annual settlement of accounts shall be completed by not later than February of the following year.

Article 31 (Submitting annual settlement)
A foreign-invested bank shall submit a business report on annual settlement of accounts to the Central Bank by not later than March of the following year.
The business report on annual settlement of accounts shall be accompanied by verifying certificate on accounting and tax payment

certificate issued by the audit office and the tax institution respectively.

Article 32 (Submitting financial management and settlement documents)

A foreign-invested bank shall conduct its financial management in accordance with the laws and regulations on financial management of foreign-invested enterprises.

Documents of quarterly financial settlement shall be submitted within 15 days of the month following the end of the quarter and those of yearly financial settlement shall be submitted to the tax institution concerned not later than February of the following year.

Article 33 (Preferential treatment)

A foreign-invested bank shall be accorded the following preferential treatment:

1. No enterprise income tax shall be payable for the interest accruing from loans granted on favourable terms to the banks and enterprises of the DPRK;
2. In case having increased registered capital by reinvestment of profits, 50% of reinvested portion of enterprise income tax shall be returned; and
3. The income derived from the banking business and the residual fund after the liquidation of the bank may be remitted out of the territory of the DPRK without any restrictions.

Article 34 (Transfer of invested capital)

An investor in a foreign-invested bank may, subject to the approval of the Central Bank, transfer to a third party part or whole of the capital invested. In this case the transferring investor of an equity joint venture shall seek the consent of the other party.

Article 35 (Causes for dissolution)

A foreign-invested bank shall be dissolved in case of:

1. Expiry of term approved;
2. Merger of banks;
3. Transfer of bank's capital;
4. Insolvency;
5. Default of the contractual obligations;
6. Failure to deposit registered capital or reserves as prescribed;
7. Incurred natural disaster; or
8. Impossibility to continue business operation for other reasons.

Article 36 (Dissolution)

A foreign-invested bank wishing to dissolve shall file an application for dissolution with the Central Bank.

A foreign-invested bank whose dissolution was adjudged by a judicial institution or decided by the Central Bank shall not be required to file an application.

Article 37 (Liquidation)

The Central Bank upon receiving an application for dissolution shall, after an examination of it, organize a liquidation committee that consists of workers from the Central Bank, tax institution concerned, audit institution concerned and foreign-invested bank in question.

The liquidation committee shall, after completion of the liquidation, return to the Central Bank the approval notice of the foreign-invested bank and business license of the bank together with a reviewing report on the liquidation.

Article 38 (Approval of dissolution and revocation of registration)

The Central Bank shall approve the dissolution of the foreign-invested bank after examination of the reviewing report.

The foreign-invested bank whose dissolution was approved shall take steps for revocation of the registration with the institution for establishment and registration of banks.

Chapter 5 Sanction, Settlement of Disputes

Article 39 (Fines)

A foreign-invested bank shall be fined in cases where it:

1. Failed to keep the amounts of contingency fund and set-aside allowance as prescribed;
2. Grants a loan to an enterprise exceeding to the prescribed amount of registered capital; and
3. Fails to keep an amount of reserves on hand at all times as prescribed.

Article 40 (Suspension of business)

Business operation of a foreign-invested bank shall be suspended in case where it:

1. Changed the address or name of the bank without approval;
2. Engaged in transactions other than those approved;
3. Caused hindrance to or interfered with supervisory work; and
4. Failed to submit regular report within the prescribed time limit, or misrepresented it.

Article 41 (Administrative or penal liability)

Anyone who causes grave consequences in violation of this Law shall be liable to administrative or penal liability depending on the gravity of the offence.

Article 42 (Dispute settlement)

Any dispute concerning foreign-invested banking business shall be settled through consultation.

In case of failure in consultation, the dispute shall be settled through mediation, arbitration or legal procedures.

[Source: (1) Laws and Regulations of the Democratic People's Republic of Korea Governing External Economic Matters, Legislation Press, Pyongyang, 2012; and (2) *Bukhan Beopryeongjip sang & ha* (Collection of Laws and Regulations of North Korea I & II, PDF), National Intelligence Service of the Republic of Korea, Seoul, 2024]

*Amendments made after December 21, 2011 are translated into English by the Author.

▪ LABOUR LAW OF THE DEMOCRATIC PEOPLE'S REPUBLIC OF KOREA FOR FOREIGN-INVESTED ENTERPRISES

Adopted by Decree No. 3053 of the Presidium of the Supreme People's Assembly on January 21, 2009 and amended on December 21, 2011, and August 26, 2015

Chapter 1 Fundamentals

Article 1 (Objective)

This Law is enacted for the purpose of providing strict guidelines for the employment of labour, work and relaxation, payment of remuneration, labour protection, social insurance, social security and dismissal of employees, thereby ensuring the business activities of the enterprises and protecting the rights and interests of the employees thereof.

Article 2 (Principle of labour employment)

A foreign-invested enterprise shall mainly employ the labour of the DPRK. Managerial personnel or technicians and skilled workers for special jobs may, in case of need, be employed from abroad.

Minors under 16 years of age shall not be employed.

Article 3 (Principle of provision of working conditions)

A foreign-invested enterprise shall provide employees with safe, cultured and hygienic working conditions and protect their lives and health.

Article 4 (Principle of providing remuneration)

A foreign-invested enterprise shall accurately pay the employees the remuneration due to them and increase the amount systemically.

Employee shall be paid equal amount of remuneration for equal work without any distinction as to their sex and age.

Article 5 (Principle of social insurance and social security)

A foreign-invested enterprise shall ensure that the citizens of the DPRK under its employment benefit from social insurance and social security.

Article 6 (Prohibition from mobilization for irrelevant work)

The labour of a foreign-invested enterprise shall not be mobilized for purposes irrelevant to the production and management of the enterprise except in such unavoidable circumstances as the occurrence of natural calamities.

Article 7 (Guidance institution)

Labour management of a foreign-invested enterprise shall be placed under the unified control and guidance of the central labour administration guidance organ.

Article 8 (Applicability)
This Law shall be applicable to such foreign-invested enterprises as (equity)* joint venture and contractual joint venture enterprises, and wholly foreign-owned enterprises. * ( )was added by the author.
This Law shall also be applicable to the foreign-invested banks and foreign enterprises that wish to employ the labour of the DPRK.

Chapter 2 Employment of Labour and Conclusion of Labour Contract

Article 9 (Institution responsible for provision of labour)
Labour of a foreign-invested enterprise shall be provided by the labour administration institution in the seat of the enterprise concerned.
Institutions, enterprises and organizations other than the labour administration institution in the seat of a foreign-invested enterprise shall not be entitled to provide labour for a foreign-invested enterprise.
Article 10 (Application for provision of labour)
A foreign-invested enterprise shall file an application for provision of labour with the labour administration institution in the seat of its operation.
The application shall specify the required number of employees, their sex, age, type of jobs, technical skill, term of employment and amount of remuneration.
Article 11 (Recruitment and provision of labour)
The labour administration institution shall provide the requested labour within 30 days of receipt of an application to that effect.
Where the required labor is to be recruited from other area, agreement shall be sought from the labour administration institution in the area concerned.
Article 12 (Employment of labour)
A foreign-invested enterprise shall employ the labour provided by the labour administration institution concerned. It may, nevertheless, refuse to employ such persons that fail to satisfy the prescribed criteria.
Article 13 (Employment of foreigners)
Where a foreign-invested enterprise wishes to employ foreigners, application to that effect shall be filed with the investment management organ.
The application shall contain their name, sex, age, nationality, place of residence, education, technical qualification and occupation.
Article 14 (Conclusion and implementation of labour contract)

A foreign-invested enterprise shall enter into a labour contract with a trade union of the enterprise.
The labour contract shall specify such matters as working day, relaxation, provision of working and living conditions, labour protection, payment of remuneration, reward and punishment.

Article 15 (Validity of labour contract)

A foreign-invested enterprise and a trade union shall submit to the labour administration institution in the seat of its operation a labour contract concluded with the trade union.

The labour contract shall be valid from the date of its conclusion.

Article 16 (Alteration of labour contract)

Labour contract may be altered subject to the agreement of the parties concerned. In this case particulars of the change shall be notified to the labour administration institution in the seat of the enterprise.

Chapter 3 Work and Relaxation

Article 17 (Working day)

The working day shall be 8 hours a day, 48 hours a week.

A foreign-invested enterprise may set the working day shorter in consideration of the level of intensity of labour and special working conditions.

In the sectors influenced by seasonal limitations, the working day may be set flexible within the range of the total working hours of the year.

Article 18 (Observance of working day)

A foreign-invested enterprise shall work its employees within the limit of prescribed working day.

Where the working day is to be lengthened for unavoidable reasons, agreement thereon shall be reached with the trade union.

Employees shall strictly observe working day.

Article 19 (Sundays and legal holidays)

A foreign-invested enterprise shall give its employees rest on legal holidays and Sundays.

Where employees are made to work on a legal holiday or Sunday under unavoidable circumstances, they shall be given a compensatory day-off the following week.

Article 20 (Regular and additional holidays)

A foreign-invested enterprise shall give its employees 14 days of regular holidays, and 7~21 days of additional leave to those doing heavy or harmful work.

Article 21 (Maternity leave)

A foreign-invested enterprise shall, in addition to the regular and additional holidays, give pregnant employees a maternity leave of 60 days before and 180 days after childbirth.

Chapter 4 Remuneration

Article 22 (Categories of remuneration)

A foreign-invested enterprise shall pay its employees their remuneration accurately according to the prescribed standard.

Remuneration shall include wage, standard allowance, bounty and bonus.

Article 23 (Fixing of monthly minimum wages)

The minimum monthly wage of an employee working for a foreign-invested enterprise shall be fixed by the central labor administration guidance organ or investment management organ.

The minimum monthly wage shall be set on the principle of compensating for the physical and mental strength of employees used up in the course of their labour and fully guaranteeing their livelihood.

Article 24 (Raising of wage standard)

A foreign-invested enterprise shall gradually raise the rate of wage in line with the growth of production and in consideration of the improved technical qualifications of its employees and labour productivity.

Article 25 (Calculation and payment of holiday allowances)

A foreign-invested enterprise shall pay holiday allowances to its employees on regular, additional or maternity leave on the basis of the number of the days of leave.

Regular and additional holiday allowances shall be calculated by multiplying the average daily remuneration for actual working days during the 3 months immediately before the leave by the number of days of leave.

Amount and method of payment for maternity holiday allowances are decided by the central labour administration institution upon approval of the Cabinet.

Article 26 (Subsidy)

A foreign-invested enterprise shall pay its employees subsidy equivalent to at least 60% of daily or hourly wage for the days or hours when they were off work due to mismanagement of the enterprise or their training.

Article 27 (Allowances for work on holidays)

Where a foreign-invested enterprise has worked its employees on Sundays or legal holidays for unavoidable reasons but failed to give a compensatory day off, allowances equivalent to 100% of their daily or hourly wage for the days or hours of their extra work shall be paid to them.

Article 28 (Allowances for overtime or night work)

Where a foreign-invested enterprise has worked its employees overtime during the day or worked them on night shifts, allowances equivalent to 50% of their daily or hourly wage for the days or hours of their extra work shall be paid to them.

Where a foreign-invested enterprise has worked its employees overtime at night, allowances equivalent to 100% of their daily or hourly wage shall be paid to them.

Article 29 (Bonus)

A foreign-invested enterprise shall create a bonus fund out of its net profits and pay bonus to model employees.

Article 30 (Payment of remuneration)

A foreign-invested enterprise shall pay its employees a full amount of their wages in cash on the prescribed day.

Where an employee resigns or is dismissed before the payday, he shall be paid the remuneration after due procedures are over.

Chapter 5 Labour Protection

Article 31 (Labour safety, provision of industrial hygienic conditions)

A foreign-invested enterprise shall provide labour safety facilities, and industrial hygienic conditions such as good lighting, illumination and ventilation to keep off heat, gas and dust, and ensure that facilities and conditions are further perfected and improved so that labour accidents and vocational disease may be prevented and employees can work in a sound and clean environment.

Article 32 (Education in labour safety)

A foreign-invested enterprise shall give its employees education in labour safety before working them.

The term and contents of education shall be determined at the discretion of the enterprise in consideration of the category of business and occupation.

Article 33 (Elimination of danger)

A foreign-invested enterprise shall, prior to organizing production and giving work assignments, carry out comprehensive checks on working conditions and eliminate anything that is dangerous to the lives or detrimental to the health of the employees.

Where there is danger of an accident occurring in a production process, production must be stopped, and danger removed before resuming production.

Article 34 (Labour safety measures)

A foreign-invested enterprise shall ensure that such harmful elements as gas, dust, high temperature, humidity, radioactive rays, noise, vibration and electric field do not exceed the tolerance limits in the process of production.

Work places with dangerous elements shall have caution signals and be furnish with protective devices to cope with possible labour accidents.

Article 35 (Protection of female employees)

A foreign-invested shall provide adequate labour safety facilities to female employees.

Pregnant or nursing women shall not work overtime or on night shifts.

Article 36 (Operation of nurseries and kindergartens)

A foreign-invested enterprise may, in a way best suited to its actual conditions, build and operate nurseries and kindergartens for the bringing up of the children of the employees.

Article 37 (Provision of labour materials)

A foreign-invested enterprise shall regularly supply its employees with sufficient amount of labour materials such as protective tools, labour necessities, nutritional food stuff, protective medicine, detoxicants, skin protection materials and detergents.

Article 38 (Handling and investigation of accidents)

Where a serious industrial accident occurs resulting in death, injury or poisoning of its employee on the job, a foreign-invested enterprise shall take measures for medical treatment and promptly notify the matter to the labour administration institution in the seat of its operation.

The labour administration institution, foreign-invested enterprise and the institution concerned shall conduct an investigation of the accident, clarify the cause thereof and take relevant measures.

Chapter 6 Social Insurance and Social Security

Article 39 (Benefits of social insurance and social security)

The citizens of the DPRK employed by a foreign-invested enterprise shall be entitled to the benefits of social insurance and social security schemes in case they temporarily lose ability to work due to illness, injury or other reasons, or when they retire.

The benefits of social insurance and social security shall include subsidy, pension, recuperation, recreation and tour.

Article 40 (Calculation of pension and subsidy)

Subsidy and pension under social insurance and social security schemes shall be calculated in accordance with the relevant laws and regulations.

Article 41 (Creation of social insurance fund)

Benefits under social insurance and social security schemes shall be provided by the social insurance fund.

Social insurance fund shall be created with social insurance premium paid by the foreign-invested enterprise and their employees.

Article 42 (Payment of social insurance premium)

Foreign-invested enterprises and employees shall pay social insurance premium to the financial institution on a monthly basis.

The ratio of the social insurance premium shall be fixed by the central financial guidance institution.

Article 43 (Creation and use of cultural and welfare fund)

A foreign-invested enterprise may create cultural and welfare fund out of its after-tax profits.

The cultural and welfare fund shall be used for the improvement of technical and cultural standard of the employees and their cultural and sports events and operation of welfare facilities.

Chapter 7 Dismissal of Employees

Article 44 (Basic requirement of dismissal of employees)

A foreign-invested enterprise shall not, without any justifiable reasons, dismiss an employee before his term of employment expires or he reaches the retiring age.

Where an employee is to be dismissed, the trade union shall be consulted.

Article 45 (Reasons for dismissal of employee)

An employee shall be dismissed in cases where:

1. He cannot continue service in the present or other occupation because of disease or injury;
2. Workforce is redundant due to change in business operation or technical conditions;
3. He caused a serious accident through violation of labour discipline;
4. He is unable to perform work assignment for lack of technical qualification and skill; or
5. He caused serious damage to the property of the enterprise.

Article 46 (Agreement to and notification of dismissal of employee)
Where an employee is to be dismissed, a foreign-invested enterprise shall seek an agreement thereon of the trade union concerned and make a notification thereof to the person concerned and the labour administration institution in the seat of the enterprise concerned.
Article 47 (Reason for non-dismissal of employee)
An employee shall not be dismissed in cases where:

1. The period of medical treatment due to disease or injury is less than 1 year; or
2. She is on maternity leave or in the period of lactation.

Article 48 (Registration of employee)
An employee may apply for resignation in cases where:

1. He is unable to continue service due to disease or family problems;
2. He cannot perform work assignments due to lack of technical qualification or skill; or
3. He obtained admission to a university, college or vocational school

Chapter 8 Sanction, Settlement of Disputes

Article 49 (Fines, suspension of business)
Where an enterprise caused serious consequences through violation of this Law, fines shall be imposed or business operation suspended.
Article 50 (Complaints, settlement)
A foreign-invested enterprise may, if any, submit to the institution concerned complaints in connection with the enforcement of this Law. The institution concerned shall settle the complaints within 30 days of receipt thereof.
Article 51 (Settlement of disputes)
Any dispute concerning the implementation of this Law shall be settled through consultation between the parties concerned.
In case of failure in consultation, the dispute shall be settled through mediation, arbitration or legal procedures.

[Source: (1) Laws and Regulations of the Democratic People's Republic of Korea Governing External Economic Matters, Legislation Press, Pyongyang, 2012; (2) *Choesin Bukhan Beopryeongjip* published by *Bukhanbeop yeonguhoe* (Collection of Current Acts and Regulations of North Korea), Myung-Bong Chang (ed.), Seoul, Republic of Korea, 2018); and (3) *Bukhan Beopryeongjip sang & ha* (Collection of Laws and Regulations of North Korea I & II, PDF), National Intelligence Service of the Republic of Korea, Seoul, 2024]
*Any amendments made after December 21, 2011 are translated into English by the Author.

▪ TAXATION LAW OF THE DEMOCRATIC PEOPLE'S REPUBLIC OF KOREA FOR FOREIGN-INVESTED BUSINESSES AND FOREIGN INDIVIDUALS

Adopted by Decision No. 26 of the Standing Committee of the Supreme People's Assembly on January 31, 1993, amended by the Presidium of the Supreme People's Assembly on February 26, 1999, May 17, 2001, November 11, 2002, April 29, 2008, August 19, 2008, December 21, 2011, September 9, 2015 and October 8, 2020

Chapter 1 Fundamentals

Article 1 (Objective)

This Law is enacted for the purpose of ensuring impartiality in the imposition of tax on and accuracy in the payment of tax by foreign-invested businesses and foreign individuals.

Article 2 (Tax management organs)

Taxation of foreign-invested businesses and foreign individuals shall be placed under the administration of the central tax guidance organ and the tax institution concerned.

The central tax guidance organ and the tax institution concerned are supervisory and controlling organs that enforce laws and regulations on taxation.

Article 3 (Tax registration)

Foreign-invested businesses shall take steps for the registration of tax with the relevant tax institution and be issued the tax registration certificate pursuant to the prescribed procedures.

Where a foreign-invested business is merged, spun-off or dissolved, formalities shall be filed for alteration or revocation of the tax registration.

A foreign individual who earned an income while staying in the DPRK shall also file a tax registration.

Article 4 (Tax accounting, retention of documents)

The tax accounting of foreign-invested businesses shall be settled in accordance with the laws and regulations on the settlement of financial accounting of foreign-invested businesses.

Documents on financial accounting shall be retained for a prescribed period and important documents in financial accounting shall be retained until the last day of dissolution of the business.

Article 5 (Currency for tax payment, taxpayer)

Taxes to be paid by a foreign-invested business and a foreign individual shall be calculated in Korean won or prescribed currency, and they are paid directly by a taxpayer to the tax institution concerned or deducted and paid by a withholding entity.

Article 6 (Applicability)

This Law shall apply to the foreign-invested businesses (including foreign-invested banks), foreign individuals (including overseas Koreans) conducting business transactions or earning income in the territory of the DPRK.

Article 7 (Application of relevant treaty)

As to the taxation of foreign-invested businesses and foreign individuals, where any treaty concluded between the DPRK and a foreign country provides otherwise than this Law, the treaty shall prevail.

Chapter 2 Enterprise Income Tax

Article 8 (Obligation to pay business income tax)

Foreign-invested businesses shall pay on incomes earned from business activities in the DPRK and incomes from other sources.

Article 9 (Taxable objects)

Taxable objects shall be incomes derived from business activities such as income from sale of products, income from transfer of construction works, income from freight charges and fares, and other incomes such as those from interest, dividends, lease of fixed assets, sales proceeds of assets, royalties for intellectual property right and technical know-how, service provided in relation to business administration and gifts.

A foreign-invested business shall also pay tax on the income derived from its branches, representative offices and agencies established outside the territory of the DPRK.

Article 10 (Tax rates)

The income tax rate for foreign-invested businesses shall be 25% of the net profit.

Article 11 (Tax rate on other income)

Where a foreign enterprise earns other income such as income from dividends, interest, rental charge, patent royalties or other sources, such income shall be taxable at the rate of 20%.

Article 12 (Calculation)

Enterprise income tax shall be calculated from January 1 to December 31 of each year by applying the prescribed tax rate to the net profit, which remains after the deduction of turnover tax or business tax and other expenses from the gross profit, which shall be determined by deducting costs of materials, fuel, power and labour, depreciation, costs of goods purchased, expenses of enterprise management, insurance premium, sales cost and other expenses form the gross income.

Article 13 (Estimated payment)

An estimated enterprise income tax shall be paid each quarter. In this case estimated income tax returns shall be submitted to the tax institution concerned within 15 days from the end of each quarter.

Article 14 (Full payment)

A foreign-invested business shall determine its income tax after the annual settlement of the accounts, make a supplementary payment for any shortfall, and be refunded for the overpayment.

In the event of dissolution of an enterprise, the enterprise concerned shall create a security for tax payment in the relevant tax institution within 20 days of the official declaration of its dissolution and shall pay income tax within 15 days of settlement of accounts.

Should an enterprise be merged or broken up, the enterprise shall settle its income as of the date of such effect and pay income tax within 20 days of the declaration of the merger or break-up.

Article 15 (Tax payment on other income)

Tax on other income earned by a foreign enterprise shall be assessed and paid by the taxpayer, or deducted and paid by the withholding agency to the relevant tax institution within 15 days of earning such income.

Article 16 (Exemption, reduction)

Enterprise income tax shall be exempted or reduced in the following cases:

1. Enterprise income tax rates for a foreign-invested enterprise established in the special economic zones shall be 14% of the net profit, and in priority sectors such as high technology, infrastructure construction and scientific research shall be reduced to 10% of the net profit;
2. Where a foreign government or an international financial organization grants a loan to the DPRK, or a foreign bank grants a loan to a bank or enterprise of the DPRK on favourable terms, enterprise income tax shall not be payable to the interests accruing therefrom;
3. A foreign-invested enterprise having invested in a priority sector and operated business for more than 15years thereafter may be entitled to an exemption from enterprise income tax

for 3 years and to a reduction of up to 50% for the following 2 years;

4. A foreign-invested enterprise having invested in a production sector except for in restricted categories by the State and operated business for more than 10 years may be entitled to an exemption from enterprise income tax for 2 years.
5. A foreign-invested enterprise having invested in a designated service sector and operated for more than 10 years may be entitled to an exemption from enterprise income tax for 1 year.
6. A foreign-invested enterprise that increases registered capital by reinvesting the profits or establishes a new enterprise and thereafter operates business for more than 10 years shall be entitled to the refund for 50% of the income tax paid on the reinvested amount or for full amount of the income tax paid on the reinvested amount if the investment was made to the priority sector.

Article 17 (Exempted or reduced period)

Exempted or reduced period for enterprise income tax shall be counted from the next year of creation of the foreign-invested enterprise in question.

Article 18 (Application for reduction or exemption)

A foreign-invested enterprise wishing to get reduction or exemption shall submit to the relevant tax institution an application for reduction or exemption of enterprise income tax together with ascertaining documents for the period of business operation and the amount of reinvestment.

The application shall contain the name of the enterprise, date of creation, location, category of business, year that makes a profit, amount of total investment, transacting bank's name and account number.

Article 19 (Return of benefited enterprise income tax)

Where a foreign-invested enterprise that has been benefited by exemption or reduction of the enterprise income tax is dissolved, merged, spun-off or has withdrawn reinvestment during the benefited period, the State shall collect the exempted or reduced enterprise income tax or impose an additional tax.

Chapter 3 Individual Income Tax

Article 20 (Obligation of tax payment)

Any foreign individual who earns income while staying in long-term or residing in the territory of the DPRK shall pay individual income tax.
A foreign individual who stays for more than 1 year or resides in the territory of the DPRK shall pay individual income tax on earnings from outside the territory of the DPRK.
Article 21 (Taxable objects)
Individual income tax shall be levied on income from:

1. Remuneration for work;
2. Interest payments;
3. Dividends;
4. Lease of fixed property;
5. Proceeds from the sale of assets;
6. Royalties for intellectual property right and technical know-how;
7. Provision of management-related service; and
8. Gift.

Article 22 (Tax rates)
Individual income tax shall be charged at the following rates:

1. Individual income tax on labour remuneration shall be the prescribed rate within the range of 5~30% of the income;
2. Individual income tax rate shall be 20% of interest payments, dividends, income from lease of fixed assets, royalties for intellectual property right and technical know-how and income from provision of management-related service;
3. Tax rate on income from gift shall be the prescribed rate within the range of 2~15% of the income; and
4. Individual income tax rate on the income from the sale of assets shall be 25%.

Article 23 (Calculation of tax on labour remuneration)
Individual income tax on labour remuneration shall be calculated by applying the prescribed tax rate to the monthly income.
Article 24 (Calculation of tax on dividends and others)
Individual income tax on dividends, proceeds from the sale of assets, royalties for intellectual property right and technical know-how, income from provision of management-related service and donation shall be calculated by applying the prescribed rate to the income in question.
Article 25 (Calculation of tax on interest)

Individual income tax on interest shall be calculated by applying the prescribed rate to the interest earned from bank deposits.

Article 26 (Calculation of tax on income from lease of fixed assets)

Individual income tax on income from lease of fixed assets shall be calculated by applying the prescribed rate to the remaining amount of income after deducting 20% from the income such costs as labour, packing and commission.

Article 27 (Tax payment)

Period and method of payment of the individual income tax shall be as follows:

1. Individual income tax on labour remuneration shall be deducted by the withholding entity at the time of payment and be paid within 5 days, or paid by a payment recipient within 10 days;
2. Individual income tax on sales proceeds of assets and income from gift shall be assessed and paid by the taxpayer within 30 days from the date of earning; and
3. Individual income tax on interest, dividends, lease of fixed assets, royalties for intellectual property right and technical know-how, and income from provision of management-related service shall be deducted and paid by the withholding entity or assessed and paid by the taxpayer within 10 days from the end of each quarter.

Chapter 4 Property Tax

Article 28 (Obligation to pay property tax)

Foreign-invested businesses and foreign individuals shall pay property tax on the property owned in the territory of the DPRK.

Article 29 (Objects of taxation)

Objects of property tax shall be such properties as buildings, vessels, or aircrafts that are registered with the DPRK.

Article 30 (Registration of property)

A foreign individual shall register his property with the relevant tax institution as follows:

1. The property shall be registered at an assessed value within 20 days of acquisition thereof;
2. In case of change of the ownership or registered value of property, new registration shall be made within 20 days from the date of the change;
3. The value of property shall be assessed as of January 1 each year and re-registered by the end of each February; and

4. In case a property is scrapped, revocation of registration thereof shall be made within 20 days.

Article 31 (Taxable amount)
Property tax shall be levied on the value of the property registered with the relevant tax institution.

Article 32 (Tax rate)
The rate of property tax shall be 1~1.4% of the value of the registered property.

Article 33 (Calculation)
Property tax shall be calculated from the month following the registration of the property by applying the prescribed rate to the value registered with the relevant tax institution.

Article 34 (Payment)
Property tax shall be paid by the owner of the property to the relevant tax institution before the end of January each year.

Chapter 5 Inheritance Tax

Article 35 (Obligation of payment)
Where property in the territory of the DPRK is inherited by a foreign individual, inheritance tax shall be payable.
Where a foreign individual residing in the territory of the DPRK inherited a property that is outside the territory of the DPRK, inheritance tax shall also be payable.

Article 36 (Taxable objects)
Inheritance tax shall be levied on the remaining value of the inherited property after all outstanding debts relating to it are cleared.

Article 37 (Assessment of value of inherited property)
The value of the property inherited shall be priced in view of the value of the property at the time of inheritance.

Article 38 (Tax rate)
The rate of inheritance tax shall be 6~30% of the inherited value.

Article 39 (Calculation)
Inheritance tax shall be calculated by applying the prescribed tax rate to the amount to be taxed.

Article 40 (Payment)
Inheritance tax shall be assessed and paid by an inheritor within 3 months of the date of inheritance.
Where the tax payable for inherited property exceeds the prescribed amount, payment by installment shall be permitted.

Chapter 6 Turnover Tax

Article 41 (Obligation of payment)
A foreign-invested business in the production and construction sectors shall pay turnover tax.
Article 42 (Taxable objects)
Turnover tax shall be levied on incomes from sale of products and from transfer of construction works.
Article 43 (Tax rate)
The rate of turnover tax shall be 1~15% of the incomes from sale of products and from transfer of construction works.
The rate of turnover tax on luxury goods shall be 16~50 % of the income from sale of products.
Article 44 (Calculation)
Turnover tax shall be calculated by applying the prescribed rate to the income from sale of products or income from transfer of construction works.
In case a foreign-invested business is engaged both in production and service, turnover tax and business tax shall be calculated separately.
Article 45 (Payment)
Turnover tax shall be paid each time the incomes from sale of products or from transfer of construction works are earned.
Article 46 (Exemption)
Goods for export shall be exempted from turnover tax. Turnover tax shall, however, be payable for restricted goods for export according to the prescribed rate.

Chapter 7 Business Tax

Article 47 (Obligation of payment)
A foreign-invested business in the service sector shall pay business tax.
Article 48 (Taxable objects)
Business tax shall be levied on the income from service in such sectors as transport, power, commerce, trade, banking, insurance, tourism, advertising, hotel, public catering, recreation and welfare facilities.
Article 49 (Tax rate)
The rate of business tax shall be 2~10% of the income concerned. However, the rate of business tax for the specially designated categories may be up to 50% of the income.
Article 50 (Calculation)
Business tax shall be calculated by applying the prescribed rates to the income by categories of business.

Where a foreign-invested business is engaged in several categories of business, business tax shall be calculated by each category of business.

Article 51 (Payment)

Business tax shall be paid to the relevant tax institution each time the income from service is earned.

Article 52 (Preferential treatment)

Where a foreign-invested business invests or operates in infrastructure sectors such as road, railway, port, airport, sewage or waste disposal, business tax may be reduced or exempted for a prescribed period of time.

Business tax may be reduced up to 50% for a prescribed period of time for an enterprise engaged in the sectors of state-of-the art science, technology or service.

Chapter 8 Resource Tax

Article 53 (Obligation of payment, classification of resources)

Where a foreign-invested business exploits resources for the purpose of export, sale or self-consumption, resource tax shall be payable.

Resources shall include natural resources such as mineral resources, forest resources, animal and plant resources, marine resources and water resources.

Article 54 (Taxable objects)

Resource tax shall be levied on the income earned from export or sale of resources, or at the prescribed value.

Article 55 (Tax rate)

Rate of resource tax for different categories of resources shall be fixed by the Cabinet.

Article 56 (Calculation)

Resource tax shall be calculated by applying the prescribed rate to the income from export or sale of resources or to the prescribed value.

Where different kinds of resources are found in the course of exploitation, calculation shall be made separately according to the type of resources.

Article 57 (Payment)

Resource tax shall be paid to the relevant tax institution each time income is earned from the export or sale of resources, or resource concerned is used.

Article 58 (Exemption, reduction)

Resource tax shall be exempted or reduced in the following cases:

1. Enterprises that exploit such resources as oil or natural gas shall be entitled to exemption for 5~10 years;
2. Resource tax may be reduced where, instead of selling resources in natural state, quality processed goods that are made thereof through modern technical process are exported, or resources are sold to the institutions, enterprises or organizations of the DPRK according to the measures taken by the State; and
3. Resource tax on the groundwater used for production by a foreign-invested enterprise in the priority sector may be reduced.

Chapter 9 City Management Tax

Article 59 (Obligation of payment of city management tax)

A foreign-invested business and a foreign resident shall pay city management tax.

Article 60 (Taxable objects)

City management tax shall be levied on the total amount of wage and salary paid by a foreign-invested business or on the monthly income of a foreign resident.

Article 61 (Calculation, payment)

City management tax shall be calculated and paid as follows:

1. City management tax on a foreign-invested business shall be calculated each month at the rate of 1% of the total amount of wage and salary paid by the business and paid within 10 days after the end of each month; and
2. City management tax on a foreign resident shall be assessed each month at the rate of 1% of the monthly income and paid by himself or herself to the relevant tax institution within 10 days after the end of each month. If a circumstance so requires, it shall be deducted and paid by a withholding entity.

Chapter 10 Vehicle Tax

Article 62 (Obligation of payment of vehicle tax)

Foreign-invested businesses and foreign individuals shall pay vehicle tax for the use of vehicles.

Article 63 (Registration)

Foreign-invested businesses and foreign individuals shall register vehicles with the tax institution within 30 days of the acquisition thereof.

Required vehicles for registration shall include passenger's cars, buses, cargo trucks, specially equipped vehicles and motor cycles.

Article 64 (Amount of tax)

The amount of tax for different types of vehicles shall be fixed by the central tax guidance organ.

Article 65 (Payment)

Vehicle tax shall be paid by the user of the vehicle before the end of February of each year.

Vehicle tax may be exempted for the period during which the vehicle concerned is not used.

Chapter 11 Guidance and Control on Tax Administration

Article 66 (Basic requirement of guidance and control)

State's unified guidance on the tax administration shall be conducted by the central tax guidance organ.

The central tax guidance organ shall correctly take control and guidance over the work of the relevant tax institutions.

Article 67 (Supervision)

The central tax guidance organ and the tax institutions concerned shall conduct the work of tax registration, tax collection and tax audit in accordance with relevant laws and regulations and strengthen supervision and control in order to prevent foreign-invested businesses and foreign individuals from evading taxes and violating laws.

Article 68 (Imposition of arrearage)

Where a foreign-invested business or a foreign individual fails to pay tax within the prescribed period of time, the tax institution shall levy arrearage of 0.3% every day on the amount overdue, beginning the day after the deadline for the tax payment.

Article 69 (Suspension)

Business operation may be suspended where a tax payer fails to pay tax for more than 6 months after due date without justifiable grounds, pay a fine for more than a month after receiving a penalty notice, comply with the tax auditing as required by the relevant tax institution, or offer required documents to the institution concerned.

Article 70 (Confiscation)

The State shall confiscate the property concerned if intentional tax evasion is made.

Article 71 (Fine)

Fine shall be imposed in cases that:

1. A fine of US$110~US$5500 for a foreign-invested business or a fine of US$11~US$1100 for a foreign individual shall be imposed where, without justifying grounds, a taxpayer fails to file tax registration, property registration and vehicle registration within prescribed time, or submit tax documents such as tax return forms or annual statement of accounting within the prescribed time.
2. A fine up to twice of unpaid tax amount shall be imposed where a tax withholding entity takes smaller amount of tax than required or does not pay taken withholding tax to the relevant tax institution.
3. A fine of US$1100~US$110000 for a foreign-invested business or a fine of US$110~US$1100 for a foreign individual shall be imposed where, for unjustifiable purposes, a taxpayer records inconsistent facts on the account books and taxation data, revises them incorrectly, keeps a second set of books, or destroys accounting books.
4. A fine of US$110~US$5500 shall be imposed on a taxpayer depending on seriousness if the taxpayer intentionally interferes with tax officials' conducting inspection.
5. Five times of unpaid amount of tax shall be imposed on a taxpayer if the taxpayer does not pay tax intentionally, pay smaller amounts, conceal or hide property or income.

Article 72 (Administrative or penal liability)
Where a serious consequence is caused as result of violation of this Law, administrative or penal liability shall be imposed depending on the seriousness of the offense.

Article 73 (Complaints, settlement)
Foreign-invested businesses or foreign individuals may lodge with the central tax guidance organ or relevant tax institution any complaint in connection with tax payment.
The institution that has received complaint shall examine and settle the case within 30 days of receipt thereof.

[Source: (1) Laws and Regulations of the Democratic People's Republic of Korea Governing External Economic Matters, Legislation Press, Pyongyang, 2012; (2) *Bukhan Beopryeongjip sang & ha* (Collection of Laws and Regulations of North Korea Vol. I & II, PDF), National Intelligence Service of the Republic of Korea, Seoul, 2024; and (3) *Choesin Bukhan Beopryeongjip* published by *Bukhanbeop yeonguhoe* (Collection of Current Acts and Regulations of North Korea), Myung-Bong Chang (ed.), Seoul, 2018]

*Amendments made after December 21, 2011 are translated into English by the Author.

▪ CUSTOMS LAW OF THE DEMOCRATIC PEOPLE'S REPUBLIC OF KOREA

Adopted by Decision No. 7 of the Standing Committee of the Supreme People's Assembly on October 14, 1983, amended on May 17, 1990, November 17, 1993, and also amended by the Presidium of the Supreme People's Assembly on July 26, 2001, June 16, 2009, Aril 3, 2012, October 25, 2017, February 22, 2018, July 26, 2020 and November 30, 2021

Chapter 1 Fundamentals

Article 1 (Objective)

This Law is enacted for the purpose of providing strict guidelines for cross-border cargoes for export and import, goods temporarily brought in or taken out, transports, international postal matter, personal effects and other articles, thereby contributing to safeguarding national security, protecting the independent national economy and promoting external economic relations.

Article 2 (Definition of terms)

Definitions of terms are as follows:

1. 'Goods temporarily brought in or taken out' is an article whose customs duty is suspended or exempted as it is brought into the DPRK on the condition that it is taken out to another country.
   'Goods temporarily brought in or taken out' includes such articles as goods for transit trade, goods for re-export, goods for processing trade, imported goods for production and operation of a foreign-invested business and exporting goods produced by such a business entity, imported or exporting goods for the purpose of international trade fair or exhibition, goods in bond and rental goods.
2. 'Other articles' means items that do not have characteristics of commercial transaction or are for the purpose of self-consumption.
   'Other articles' includes such items as goods for aid, cooperation and donation, necessities brought in or taken out through customs by a DPRK representative office residing in a foreign country and a foreign country's or international organization's representative office residing in the DPRK and members of these representative offices, goods for management, food, trade samples, and baggage.
3. 'Duty-free goods' is an item whose customs duty is exempted for the sale of it to the limited customers concerned.

4. 'Contrabands' is the prohibited goods or merchandise to be brought into the DPRK from other country or taken out of the DPRK to other country according to the measures of the State.
5. 'Controlled goods' is restricted or controlled goods or merchandise to be brought into the DPRK from other country or to be taken out of the DPRK to other country for a certain period of time according to the measures taken by the State.
6. 'Customs controlled areas (CCA)' is a designated area for customs affairs where inspection and supervision is conducted over such cross-bordering articles as exporting and importing cargoes, goods temporarily brought in or taken out, transports, international postal matter, personal effects and other articles.
   CCA includes areas of border bridges, general trade marketplace, wharves of trade ports, customs premise, open-air storage yard and warehouse, premises of border railway station, designated areas for inspection, cargo storage and/or international postal matters in international airports and international post offices, marketplace on the sea, access passageways between domestic areas and special economic zones and other places or areas concerned.
7. 'Temporary customs controlled areas (TCCA)' is an area temporarily designated by the customs office to inspect and supervise cargoes for import and export, goods temporarily brought in or taken out and other relevant articles placed on the outside of CCA.
   TCCA includes the relevant areas for conducting on-site customs inspection and circuiting customs inspection over cargoes for import and export or the factories or warehouse for handling goods temporarily brought in or taken out.
8. 'Customs borderline' is a boundary where customs duties are imposed on cargoes and relevant articles of imports and exports that cross over State's borderlines.
   Customs borderline includes crossing points of international border, marketplaces on the sea and access passageways between domestic areas and special economic zones.

Article 3 (Status of customs, establishment)

The Customs is the supervising and controlling institution to inspect such cross-border articles as cargoes of import and export, goods temporarily brought in or taken out, means of transport, international postal matters, personal effects and other articles, impose customs duties or tonnage dues on them, oversee the use, storage and disposal of articles whose customs duties are suspended, and conduct investigations and crackdowns on smuggling activities.

The State shall set up customs offices at border bridges, border railway stations, trade ports, international airports, international post offices, special economic zones and other places as may be required.

Article 4 (Functions of customs)

The Customs shall perform the functions of:

1. Supervising and controlling all cargoes, commodities, means of transport that are brought into the territory of the DPRK;
2. Inspecting and supervising cross-border cargoes, commodities and means of transport;
3. Imposing customs duties and tonnage dues;
4. Supervising the use, storage and disposal of goods temporarily brought in or taken out while customs duties are exempted or suspended as well as duty-free articles;
5. Reviewing and examining conditions in relation to the storing, processing, assembling and exhibiting of bonded articles and operation of duty-free shops;
6. Taking measures of disposal for goods temporarily brought in or taken out within the prescribed time or such goods handled differently from the prescribed usage and duty-free articles;
7. Investigating and cracking downing smuggling activities;
8. Making customs statistics; and
9. Performing works authorized by the State.

Article 5 (Power of customs)

The Customs has powers:

1. To check all cross-border cargoes, goods, means of transport and, where smuggling is suspicious, conduct a physical search over a relevant area, means of transport, and an individual's body;
2. To demand relevant documents for customs clearance of cargoes and articles, and means of transport;
3. To crackdown illegal activities revealed in the course of customs inspection and supervision and take further actions to redress such activities thereof;
4. To examine or inspect relevant documents and ledgers on cargoes of export and import, goods temporarily brought in

and taken out, duty-free goods' use, storage and disposal, payment of customs duties, tonnage dues, customs fees; and

5. To withhold customs clearance on cargoes for export and import, goods temporarily brought in or taken out, means of transport, international postal matters, and personal effects, charge fines on such articles and goods, or detain, seize or confiscate them depending on the gravity of violation of law.

Article 6 (Principle of enforcement)

The State shall tighten its checking and control on prohibited goods to be brought in and taken out, controlled goods to be brought in or taken out, and cargoes, articles and means of transport whose customs is not cleared or whose quarantine is not declared at the border post.

Prohibited goods shall not be brought into and taken out of the territory of the DPRK and controlled goods shall only be brought in or taken out upon approval of the State.

Prohibited goods shall not be transited through the territory of the DPRK.

Article 7 (Principle of streamlined customs clearance)

The State shall ensure streamlined customs clearance procedures, modernize technical instrument and equipment for customs clearance, and make faster clearance procedures on cargoes and commodities, means of transport and persona effects.

Article 8 (Principle of imposition of customs duties)

The State shall, for the purpose of protecting the independent national economy, apply either zero or low tariffs on materials whose import and export are encouraged, and high tariffs on materials whose import and export are restricted.

Articles 9 (Prohibition of interfering or hindering customs work)

The State shall ensure that the functions and responsibilities of the customs and the institutions related thereto are clearly defined.

Acts of interfering or hindering the customs work shall not be committed.

Article 10 (Enhancing responsibilities and role of customs officers, training of experts)

The State shall ensure that the Customs are staffed with personnel with due qualifications, their responsibility and role further enhanced and competent experts trained in a planned manner

Customs officials shall be required to wear prescribed uniforms for official functions and those who are not customs officials shall not wear such uniforms.

Article 11 (Exchange and cooperation)
The State shall promote exchange and cooperation with foreign countries and international organizations in the area of customs administration.
Article 12 (Applicability)
This Law shall be applicable to the institutions, enterprises, organizations and individuals that bring in or take out cargoes for exports and imports, goods temporarily brought in or taken out, means of transport, international postal matter, personal effects and other articles across the border of the DPRK.
Institutions, enterprises, organizations and individuals shall include the foreign-invested businesses, foreign-invested banks, and the representative missions of foreign countries and international organizations, foreign corporate bodies and foreign individuals in the territory of the DPRK.
The customs procedures in the special economic zones shall be set separately

Chapter 2 Customs Registration and Formalities

Article 13 (Registration)
Institutions, enterprises and organizations that obtained the license for foreign trade shall register with the Customs.
Customs registration shall not be required for DPRK's institutions, enterprises and organizations which receive an aid, cooperation or donation from a foreign country, international organization or international entity, and for major international organizations and representative agencies of foreign countries.
Article 14 (Application for customs registration, approval thereof)
Institutions, enterprises and organizations that wish to register with the customs shall submit to the customs concerned a business license and other necessary documents together with an application for customs registration.
The customs shall responsibly examine the application and either register or reject it.
Article 15 (Alterations in customs registration)
Where contents of customs registration such as business type or business boundary have been altered, institutions, enterprises and organizations shall register the alteration with the relevant customs institution.
Where a foreign-invested business or foreign-invested bank has been dissolved or bankrupt, the investment management organ and judicial

organ concerned shall notify the customs institution concerned of the type of dissolution or bankruptcy in a timely manner.

Article 16 (Customs formalities)

Customs formalities shall be performed where export-import cargoes, goods temporarily brought in or taken out or other materials are brought into the territory of the DPRK or taken out to foreign countries.

Customs formalities shall be completed before the arrival of such articles as the export-import cargoes, goods temporarily brought in or taken out, and other materials at the cross-border boundary.

Article 17 (Parties of customs formalities)

Customs formalities shall be performed by the institutions, enterprises and organizations that bring export-import cargoes, goods temporarily brought in or taken out of or other materials into the territory of the DPRK or take them out of it.

An agent who is authorized by an institution, enterprise or organization may perform customs formalities.

Customs formalities for bringing in or taking out merchandize at the border crossing point shall be performed by an agency for an owner of export-import cargoes.

Article 18 (Submission of documents for customs formalities)

Documents for customs formalities shall be submitted to the central customs guidance organ through the electronic customs clearance system. In this case, required documents issued by State's planning organ and the central foreign trade guidance organ such as a plan of foreign trade, price, approved document for bringing in and out, contract for sale of commodities and monetary statement shall be attached.

Customs clearance documents for designated items otherwise may be submitted directly to the customs institution concerned.

Article 19 (Amendment of customs formalities)

Where declared contents such as the place of border crossing point, receiver of cargoes or destinations of commodities became to differ unavoidably from the filed customs formalities, an amendment shall be filed with the central customs guidance organ.

Article 20 (Transports transiting the DPRK)

Transports going to a foreign country via the DPRK shall be allowed to pass only when the required formalities are carried out. In this case the person performing the clearance procedures shall submit to the customs a document concerning the transports and a manifest.

Article 21 (Formalities for disposal of goods temporarily brought in and taken out)
Where institutions, enterprises and organizations unavoidably dispose goods temporarily brought in and taken out in the territory of the DPRK, they shall, after obtaining a permit from the Cabinet, take steps for customs formality to convert them into imported goods as prescribed in the Article 19.

Article 22 (Transit cargoes)
Customs formalities for the cargoes of foreign countries that transit the DPRK territory shall be carried out by the institution that is responsible for the transshipment thereof. In this case controlled goods shall be permitted to go through formalities subject to the approval of the competent institution.

Article 23 (Declaration of personal effects and other articles)
An individual, where he/she pass through a border crossing point or an access passageway between a domestic area and a special economic zone, shall declare to the customs personal effects, precious metals, jewelry, currencies, securities and luggage.

Chapter 3 Customs Inspection and Supervision

Article 24 (Object of customs inspection)
The customs inspection shall cover cargoes for export and import, goods temporarily brought in or taken out, means of transport, international postal matter, personal effects and other articles that are brought into or taken out of the DPRK.
Those which have not been subject to the customs inspection shall not be permitted to enter or leave the DPRK.

Article 25 (Exemption from customs inspection)
Customs inspection shall not be made on personal effects and luggage of members of party, state and governmental delegations, holders of diplomatic passports of the representative missions of foreign countries or international organizations accredited to the DPRK, those who are exempted from the customs inspection according to the consular convention concluded between the DPRK and a foreign country and their transport means, personal effects and luggage of officials who are specially designated as well as on diplomatic postal matter and correspondence. Notwithstanding the previous provision, customs inspection may be made on those items where there is evidence to believe that they contain controlled or contraband articles.

Article 26 (Place of customs inspection)

Customs inspection shall be conducted at border bridges, border railway stations, trade ports, international airports, marketplaces on the sea, international post offices and other designated places.

Inspection of personal effects and luggage of individuals may be performed on transports such as a train or a ship.

Article 27 (Declaration)

Upon arrival of cargoes for export and import, goods temporarily brought in or taken out, international postal matter and other articles at a border crossing point, owners of cargoes, responsible persons for the means of transport, border railway stations, international airport and postal institutions shall declare them and submit required documents to the customs.

Article 28 (Method of customs inspection)

Customs inspection shall be conducted by two customs workers with the observation of owners of cargoes or their agents. In this case, no other persons except for the owners or agents shall be allowed to enter the inspection site.

The customs may inspect cargoes and articles with machines or by having them unpacked.

The customs shall accurately grasp the numbers by checking customs documents with actual materials.

Article 29 (Inspection on transports)

The customs may inspect the cargo compartments, passenger compartments, crew's quarters and other places of the transports as may be required.

Where contrabands or controlled goods are reported being loaded in the means of transport of a foreign country, the customs may suspend the use thereof or put them in a cargo compartment and keep them under supervision, and shall confiscate them if they are not declared.

Article 30 (Loading, unloading and transports at the border crossing point)

Cargoes or means of transports arriving at the border crossing point may be loaded or unloaded, or cross the border only after they are inspected or approved by the customs.

Article 31 (Seal of customs)

The customs may, in case of need, put seals under its supervision on the cargoes or commodities, or the warehouses, containers or cargo compartments of the transports.

The seal shall not be broken without the consent of the customs.

Article 32 (Cooperation with other institutions)

Customs shall strengthen cooperation with such other relevant institutions at a border crossing point as immigration inspection institution, institution for inspection and quarantine of exports and imports and institution for inspection of export-import cargoes.

In case an object which is required for inspection, quarantine, examination or supervision is found in the course of customs inspection process, it shall be transferred to a relevant institution.

The relevant institution which receives the transferred object shall accurately inform the customs of the result of inspection, quarantine, examination or supervision on it.

Article 33 (Cargoes of wrong delivery)

Cargoes of a foreign country and international postal matter that are brought in as a result of wrong delivery and articles whose owner cannot be identified shall be disposed of subject to the consent of the customs.

Article 34 (Supervision of cargoes in custody of customs)

The customs shall regularly check the cargoes in the custody of border bridges, border railway stations, trade ports and international airports to ensure that they are not damaged or lost, or disposed of without consent.

Cargoes or commodities that are not collected within the specified period of time or for which no claim is made may be disposed of by the customs according to the relevant procedures.

Article 35 (Overseeing suspended or exempted customs duty articles)

The customs shall correctly oversee and control the use, storage and disposal of commodities temporarily brought in or taken out whose customs duty is suspended or exempted and duty free articles in the custody of factory, storage and duty-free shops.

Commodities for transit trade or intermediary trade shall not be kept out of border bridges, border railway stations or trade ports.

Articles 36 (Prohibition for handling goods temporarily brought in or taken out)

Goods temporarily brought in or taken out shall be used for only prescribed purpose.

It shall be prohibited, without authorization, to dispose goods temporarily brought in or taken out that did not take customs formalities for import or are not approved by the customs.

Article 37 (Handling of goods temporarily brought in)

Goods temporarily brought into the DPRK shall be taken out to a foreign country within the prescribed time.

Goods temporarily brought in but not taken out of the DPRK within the prescribed time shall be handled by the customs pursuant to the relevant procedures.

Article 38 (Submission of declaration materials)

Institutions, enterprises and organizations shall regularly and accurately submit customs declaration materials about the use, storage and disposal of goods temporarily brought in and taken out.

Article 39 (Roving customs inspection, transit cargo inspection)

The customs may conduct roving customs inspection or inspect cargoes of foreign countries transiting the territory of the DPRK.

Procedure for roving customs inspection and for cargoes transiting the territory of the DPRK shall be made by the Cabinet.

Article 40 (Requesting customs inspection and report)

The customs may request a relevant institution located in the arrival place of cargoes to conduct inspection on them where the inspection is not available at the border crossing point. In this case the owner of cargoes shall timely report details of arrival of cargoes to the relevant institution at the arrival place.

The institution requested for customs inspection shall conduct customs inspection on the cargoes with its responsibility and reply the result to the customs.

Article 41 (Transporting cargoes for customs inspection)

Cargoes requested for customs inspection shall be only transported by means of transport having equipped with surveillance system and under the supervision of the customs authority.

The institution concerned shall transport the requested cargoes with its responsibility and shall not unload the cargoes on its way or change the destination without consent of the customs.

Article 42 (Customs inspection and compliance)

Institutions, enterprises, organizations and individuals that are subject to customs inspection or those who transport, store, use, process or dispose cargoes under the customs supervision shall comply with customs' requirements and timely ensure necessary conditions in relation to the customs inspection or supervision.

Article 43 (Prohibitions in use of international postal matter)

Institutions, enterprises, organizations and individuals shall not enclose articles in the letters and publications, nor letters, currencies, securities, precious metals and jewelry in the parcels that come into or go out of the DPRK.

No one shall bring in or take out controlled goods and contrabands by enclosing them in international postal matter or bring in or take out things for the purpose of sale.

Article 44 (Personal effects and other things)

Individuals who travel across the border of the DPRK may carry with them personal effects necessary for business and life and other materials as prescribed.

Individuals whose job involves making a business trip across the border of the DPRK may take with them only office articles and daily necessaries.

Article 45 (Household goods, inherited property)

Household goods being removed and the inherited property may be brought into or taken out of the DPRK without permission being sought. Where any items of the household goods or inherited property fall under the category of contrabands, they shall not be permitted to cross the border, and controlled goods shall be permitted entry or exit only subject to the consent of the competent institution.

Chapter 4 Customs Duties, Tonnage Dues and Fees

Article 46 (Imposing customs duty and payment)

Customs duties shall be imposed on the cargoes of import and export and such articles.

Customs duties shall be imposed by the customs institution concerned. Institutions, enterprises, organizations and individuals shall pay customs duties in a timely manner.

Article 47 (Standard price for customs duties)

Standard price for imposing customs duties on cargoes for export and import shall be based on the contract price concluded with a foreign trade counterpart but within the price range as approved by the central foreign trade guidance organ.

Standard price for imposing customs duties on international postal matter and personal effects and belongings that exceed prescribed standards shall be based on the retail price.

Article 48 (Calculation of customs duties)

Customs duty shall be calculated in consideration of the price of the articles at the time of declaration to the customs, tariff rate and national standard foreign exchange rates.

Where the price of articles brought in or taken out differs from that of declared ones, the customs may assess these prices and impose customs duties according to the result of assessment.

Article 49 (Designation of objects for customs duties, fixing and announcing of tariff rates)
Designation of objects for imposing export-import duties shall be based on the tariff line.
A relevant non-standing review committee shall deliberate and determine the code of commodities in the customs tariff and rulemaking and adjustment of tariff rates.
The Cabinet shall announce the code of commodities for foreign trade and tariff rates.
Article 50 (Payment of customs duties beyond duty-free limit)
Customs duties shall be imposed on the international postal matter and personal effects and luggage which exceed the limit of duty-freed amount.
The rule of duty-free limit and duty rates shall be determined by the central customs guidance organ and implemented after approval of the Cabinet.
Article 51 (Application of preferential tariff)
Where a preferential treatment clause is prescribed in treaties, conventions or agreements concluded between the DPRK and foreign countries, it shall be complied with.
The preferential tariff shall be applied in the special economic zones (SEZs).
Article 52 (Application of tariff rate on commodities from SEZs)
Where a commodity brought into a special economic zone from a foreign country is taken out of the SEZ, tariff rate applied to it shall be the one after preferential tariff rate is deducted from the base tariff one for such a commodity.
Article 53 (Articles with no fixed tariff rate)
For an article or item for which the tariff rate has not been set, the tariff for another similar article or item shall be applied.
Article 54 (Time of paying customs duties)
Customs duties shall be paid immediately after customs inspections on the cargoes and articles concerned are conducted.
No cargoes and articles shall pass through the customs before the payment of customs duties.
Article 55 (Manner of payment of customs duties)
Customs duties shall be paid by the electronic payment system according to the customs duty payment statement.
Customs duties for the international postal matter or individual luggage exceeding the prescribed duty-exempted limit shall be paid to

the customs-designated bank according to the notice of customs duty payment within the prescribed time limit.

Article 56 (Exemption from customs duties)

Customs duties shall not be levied on the following items:

1. Materials brought in according to the measures taken by the State;
2. Designated duty-free or duty-reduced cargoes and articles according to the treaty, convention or agreement concluded between the DPRK and a foreign country;
3. Goods temporarily brought in or taken out, duty-free commodities or other items; and
4. International postal matter or individual luggage within the prescribed limit.

Article 57 (Imposition of customs duties on duty-free goods)

Article 56 of this Law shall not be applicable in cases where:

1. Controlled goods are included in the equipment and materials imported for production and business operation by a foreign-invested business or foreign-invested bank or such imported equipment and materials and produced materials therefrom are to be sold in the territory of the DPRK;
2. Duty-free goods are sold or disposed for other than purported use;
3. Goods temporarily brought in for the international trade fair or exhibition are sold in the territory of the DPRK;
4. Goods temporarily brought in or taken out are sold domestically in unavoidable circumstances;
5. An individual with a diplomatic passport, representative mission of a foreign country or an international organization residing in the DPRK or its staff bring in or take out goods or luggage in larger quantities than the prescribed amount; and
6. International postal matter or the luggage of an individual exceeds the prescribed limit.

Article 58 (Procedures for payment of customs duties for duty-free articles)

Where customs duties are to be paid in accordance with article 57 of this Law, the institutions, enterprises, organizations and citizens concerned shall make a declaration thereof to the customs and pay the required amount of customs duties.

Article 59 (Imposition of additional customs duties)

Where no customs duties was levied or the amount of customs duties that was levied is found to be less than the amount payable, additional customs duties may be imposed within 3 years of clearance of the goods concerned.

Where a foreign-invested enterprise or foreign-invested bank under dissolution or bankruptcy wishes to dispose in the DPRK 'goods temporarily brought in or taken out' which were brought in by itself, the customs shall calculate customs duties according to its value and claim the amount to the liquidation committee concerned.

Article 60 (Refund of customs duties)

Where an imported article was returned, an exported article was taken back, or customs duties were overpaid due to incorrect imposition or miscalculation, the customs shall refund customs duties in question.

Article 61 (Application of refund)

Where the cause stated in article 60 arises, the payer of customs duties may submit an application to the customs for the refund within 1 year from the payment of the customs duties.

The customs shall settle the raised matter within 30 days from the receipt of the application.

Article 62 (Establishment and operation of bonded area, bonded factory, bonded warehouse, bonded fair)

Bonded area, bonded factories, bonded warehouses and bonded fairs shall be established and operated in order to promote external economic exchange.

The guidelines for the establishment and operation of bonded area, bonded factories, bonded warehouses and bonded fairs shall be approved by the Cabinet after consultation of the central customs guidance organ.

Article 63 (Bonded period)

Imposition of customs duties shall be temporarily suspended on bonded materials during the bonded period.

The bonded period shall be 2 years for a bonded factory and bonded warehouse, and the period for bonded fair shall be set by the customs.

Article 64 (Extension of bonded period)

Where the owner of a cargo wishes to have the bonded period extended for unavoidable reasons, he shall submit to the customs a written application to that effect 10 days before the termination of the original period.

The customs may permit the extension of the bonded period by up to 6 months.

Article 65 (Security for taking out or bringing in of bonded materials)

Where the bonded materials are to be taken out of a bonded area for purpose of processing, packing and assembling, a security that is equivalent in value to the customs duties shall be put in the custody of the customs.

Where the materials are brought in within the prescribed time limit, the security shall be returned. In case of failure the security entrusted with customs may be used as a substitute for the customs duties.

The customs shall sell for disposal materials that are not taken out of the bonded area until lapse of the bonded period.

Article 66 (Establishment and operation of duty-free shop)

A duty-free shop may be established at a border crossing point or service area for foreign diplomats.

Duty-free shops shall be operated by the external service institution or diplomatic service institution as approved by the Cabinet.

Article 67 (Use of duty-free shop and sale of duty-free goods)

Duty-free shops may be used only by individuals travelling to and from a foreign country and privileged diplomats and their family members exempted from customs duties.

Sales limit of duty-free goods per person shall be fixed by the central customs guidance organ and implemented upon approval of the Cabinet.

Article 68 (Prohibitions at duty-free shops)

The external service institution or diplomatic service institution shall not, in the course of operation of duty-free shops, sell goods by exceeding fixed limits, sell goods to one who is not eligible to buy them or use goods for other purpose than prescribed.

Article 69 (Imposition of protective tariffs, anti-dumping duties, punitive tariffs)

Measures may be taken to impose special protective tariffs, anti-dumping duties and punitive tariffs for a certain period of time for the purpose of protecting the key industrial sectors and natural resources.

The objects, tariff rate and the term of imposing the special protective tariffs, anti-dumping duties and punitive tariffs shall be prescribed by the Cabinet.

Article 70 (Imposition of tonnage dues)

Tonnage dues shall be levied on foreign vessels entering or leaving the ports of the DPRK, DPRK-owned vessels with foreign nationalities and foreign-owned vessels with the DPRK nationality.

Tonnage dues shall be paid within the prescribed time by a foreign shipping agency, after collecting the dues from cargo owners, according to the payment notice for tonnage dues issued by the customs.

Article 71 (Reduction of tonnage dues)

20% of tonnage dues shall be reduced for vessels using the ports of the DPRK according to the regular liner contract.

Article 72 (Exemption from tonnage dues)

Tonnage dues shall not be imposed for the following vessels:

1. A vessel entering a tonnage due-exempted trade port;
2. A vessel of war, rescue vessel, training ship, exploration vessel or hospital ship;
3. A vessel for repair and a vessel entered due to marine accident or broken down;
4. A vessel temporarily entering a port to get the supply of fuel, drinking water, food or necessities and leaving the port within 48 hours;
5. A vessel entering a port in need of medical assistance for crew members or passengers;
6. A vessel whose tonnage dues are exempted pursuant to the treaty, convention or agreement concluded between the DPRK and a foreign country; and
7. A vessel entering a port with cargoes friendly contributed by international organizations or foreign countries to the DPRK.

Article 73 (Calculation of tonnage dues)

Tonnage dues shall be calculated based on vessel's net tonnage and dues per ton.

Amount of dues per ton shall be fixed by the central customs guidance organ upon approval of the Cabinet.

Article 74 (Payment of customs fees)

Institutions, enterprises, organizations and individuals shall pay the customs within the prescribed time customs fees after receiving the payment notice of customs fee.

Customs fees include fees for roving customs inspection, using charges for customs inspection facilities, charges for customs supervision and the like.

The customs fees shall be set by the price institution.

Article 75 (Border fees and charges)

The customs shall uniformly collect border fees and charges emanating from inspections made by specialized institutions, performing quarantine or examination in the customs controlled areas. The relevant institutions shall accurately calculate fees and charges and transfer them to the customs.

Article 76 (Payment currency for customs duties, tonnage dues and other charges and fees)

Customs duties, tonnage dues, customs fees and charges, border fees and charges shall be paid by the currency designated by the State.

Chapter 5 Guidance and Control of Customs Administration

Article 77 (Basic requirements of guidance and control)

Tightening guidance and control of the customs administration is an important guarantee for the proper implementation of the customs policy of the State.

The State shall ensure that a proper system for the guidance of the customs is established and control is tightened.

Article 78 (Guidance, obedience)

The customs shall be placed under the unified guidance and control of the central customs guidance organ.

The central customs guidance organ shall exercise regular and proper control and guidance of the branch customs.

The customs shall be obedient to the central customs guidance organ.

Article 79 (Matters arising out of customs affairs)

Matters arising out of the customs administration at a border crossing point shall be collectively and consultatively discussed and handled at the regular meeting of relevant officials from the customs, immigration inspection institution, institution for the inspection and quarantine of imports and exports and other relevant institutions.

The consultative meeting shall be chaired by the superintendent of the customs and agreed matters shall be handled under his direction.

Article 80 (Consent from the customs)

Where an institution, enterprise or organization wishes to reflect customs-related matters in a convention, agreement or contract with a counterpart of other country, it shall obtain consent from the central customs guidance organ prior to the conclusion of it.

Article 81 (Request for cooperation)

The customs may request cooperation to the relevant judicial organs, frontier guard bodies, specialized assessment institutions and science and research institutions while it is investigating and controlling smuggling, where the cargoes, commodities and transports under its custody are missing or it needs an expert opinion.

The requested institution shall render the required assistance in time.

Article 82 (Inspection and examination of the customs)

The customs may inspect documents of institutions, enterprises and organizations that obtained the license for foreign trade in relation to the payment of customs duties or examine use, storage and disposal of customs duty suspended, reduced or exempted goods temporarily brought in or taken out and duty free goods.

Article 83 (Customs statistics)

The customs shall accurately secure scientific characteristics, objectivity and accuracy in compiling statistics for export-import cargoes, goods temporarily brought in or taken out, means of transport, international postal matter, other inward and outward articles, types of individuals' crossing border.

Article 84 (Fines)

Fines of 100,000~1,500,000 won shall be charged to institutions, enterprises or organizations and of 1,000~5,000 won to individuals for the following cases:

1. Hindering the work of customs inspection by not complying with the required action in relation to the customs inspection;
2. Non-payment of customs duties, tonnage dues and customs fees within the prescribed time; and
3. Violation of the protection order of environment within the controlled customs area.

Article 85 (Suspension, detention, seizure and confiscation)

Where cargoes, means of transport, international postal matter and commodities are unlawfully brought in or taken out of the DPRK, the customs formalities may be suspended or such materials may be detained or seized.

Article 86 (Warning, strict warning, unpaid labor, indoctrination through labor, demotion, dismissal or removal)

A person liable to following cases shall be punished by warning, strict warning, or not more than 3 months' unpaid labor or indoctrination through labor:

1. Bringing into or taking out of the DPRK contrabands or controlled goods;
2. Unlawfully taking out or helping to take out to a foreign country foreign currencies, jewelry or treasures;
3. Sneaking articles that are not inspected by the customs;

4. Not transporting cargoes supposed to be transported to a designated destination under the supervision of the customs or stealing them in the course of transporting;
5. Unlawfully disposing goods temporarily brought in or taken out in the domestic market or evading customs duties; and
6. Not depositing customs duties, tonnage dues and customs fees in the bank designated by the customs.

In case committing misconduct described in 1~6 above is severe, it shall be punished by unpaid labor or indoctrination through labor for more than 3 months, or demotion, dismissal or removal from the post.

Article 87 (Penal liability)

Where an action in violation of this Law is tantamount to a crime, penal liability shall be imposed on the responsible person pursuant to the relevant clause of the penal code.

Article 88 (Complaints, term of settlement)

Any complaint in connection with the customs administration may be lodged with the central customs guidance organ or the relevant organ. Complaints shall be settled within 30 days of receipt thereof.

[Source: (1) Laws and Regulations of the Democratic People's Republic of Korea Governing External Economic Matters, Legislation Press, Pyongyang, 2012; and (2) *Bukhan Beopryeongjip sang & ha* (Collection of Laws and Regulations of North Korea Vol. I & II, PDF), National Intelligence Service of the Republic of Korea, Seoul, 2024]

*Amendments made after March 3, 2012 are translated into English by the Author.

▪ IMMIGRATION LAW OF THE DEMOCRATIC PEOPLE'S REPUBLIC OF KOREA

Adopted by Decision No. 68 of the Standing Committee of the Supreme People's Assembly on January 19, 1996, amended by the Presidium of the Supreme People's Assembly on January 28, 1999, April 10, 2012, and July 10, 2013

Chapter 1 Fundamentals

Article 1 (Objective)

This Law is enacted for the purpose of strengthening the immigration system and affording facilities for the citizens entering or leaving the DPRK and foreigners entering, leaving, staying, residing or touring in the DPRK.

Article 2 (Definitions)

In this Law the following terms shall be construed as follows:

1. *Citizen* means a person that has the nationality of the DPRK;
2. *Foreigner* means a person that has the nationality of a foreign country;
3. *Immigration Certificate* means a passport or other equivalent identification document or visa;
4. *Border crossing point* means a route such as a declared border bridge, border railway station, trade port, international airport and designated area; *Translated by the author.
5. *Transports* mean a vehicle, train, ship or airplane that crosses the border of the DPRK; *Translated by the author.
6. *Stay* means the remaining of a foreign for a certain period in the territory of the DPRK;
7. *Residence* means the registering of residence and living of a foreigner in the territory of the DPRK; and
8. *Travel* means going out of the place of stay or residence by a foreigner to travel to and from other parts of the territory of the DPRK

Article 3 (Border crossing points, establishment of inspecting institution)

Immigration shall be effected through designated border crossing points.

The State shall ensure that the border crossing points are designated as in view of the requirement of the developing external relations and that establish institutions for immigration inspection.

Article 4 (Requirement of holding immigration certificate)

Citizens and foreigners including the ones who stay, reside or travel in the DPRK are obliged to hold immigration certificate as required by the State.

Article 5 (Performing of formalities)

Formalities for exit, entry, stay, residence and travel shall be performed by the person concerned. In the case of exit, entry, stay or travel on official business, the institution concerned may preform the formalities.

Formalities for minors shall be carried out by the guardian.

Article 6 (Fees)

The State shall charge the citizens and foreigners concerned prescribed fees for the entry into or departure from the DPRK. Fees for foreigners' visa shall be charged on the principle of reciprocity.

Article 7 (Immigration institutions)

The administration of immigration shall be undertaken by the Ministry of Foreign Affairs and the immigration administration organ. The immigration administration shall also be undertaken by the diplomatic or consular representative offices and other organs concerned of the DPRK accredited to foreign countries.

Article 8 (Exchange and cooperation)

The State shall, on the principle of reciprocity, promote exchange and cooperation with foreign countries in the field of immigration administration.

Article 9 (Immigration procedures in special economic zones)

The procedures for the entry into and departure from the special economic zones shall be governed by the relevant laws and regulations.

Chapter 2 Exit and Entry of Citizens

Article 10 (Immigration certificate)

Citizens may enter or leave the DPRK on official or private business. A citizen wishing to depart from or enter the DPRK shall have an immigration certificate issued by the Ministry of Foreign Affairs, the immigration administration organ or the relevant organ.

Article 11 (Application for passport and visa)

An application for the issuance of a passport and visa of a citizen who wishes to immigrate on official business shall be submitted to the Ministry of Foreign Affairs by organ dispatching him.

An application for the passport and visa of a citizen who wishes to immigrate on private business shall be made by the person himself to the immigration organ in the place of his residence.

Article 12 (Validity of border area travel permit)
A citizen in possession of a border area travel permit issued by the immigration administration organ or the organ concerned may enter or leave the border area of the country concerned.
Article 13 (Application for border area travel permit)
An application for the border area travel permit of a citizen who wishes to immigrate on official business shall be submitted by the organ dispatching him to the immigration administration organ or the organ concerned.
An application for the border area travel permit by a citizen who wishes to travel on private business shall be filed by the person himself with the immigration administration organ in the area of his residence.
Article 14 (Extension of validity of immigration certificate)
A citizen shall, upon expiry of the term of validity of his immigration certificate, shall have the term extended or a new certificate issued.
Article 15 (Immigration by seaman's certificate)
Citizens may immigrate with a seaman's certificate issued by the central maritime supervisory organ.
Citizens holding a seaman's certificate shall obtain a visa in case they wish to exit the country through a border crossing point rather than through a trade port.
Article 16 (Immigration of overseas citizens)
Overseas citizens shall, for entry into or exit from the DPRK, have a passport and visa issued by the diplomatic or consular representative office or a relevant organ of the DPRK.
Article 17 (Re-issuance of immigration certificate)
Citizens whose immigration certificates are soiled or lost shall have them re-issued.
Article 18 (Citizens prohibited from entry or exit)
Citizens who do not hold an immigration certificate, hold an invalid immigration certificate or are prohibited from traveling by a law-enforcement organ shall be denied to exit the country.

Chapter 3 Entry and Exit of Foreigners

Article 19 (Exit or entry by visa)
Foreigners shall have a visa issued by the DPRK Ministry of Foreign Affairs, the immigration administration organ or the diplomatic or consular representative office in a foreign country to enter or leave the DPRK.

A foreigner who carries a passport or equivalent identification papers for which no visa is required under the agreement between the DPRK and the country concerned may immigrate without visa.

Article 20 (Application for visa)

Foreigners who wish to enter the DPRK shall apply for a visa to the diplomatic or consular representative office in the country concerned.

Depending on circumstances, the foreigner concerned may request the inviting organ of the DPRK or the diplomatic or consular representative office of his country or a representative office of an international organization in the DPRK to file the application for him.

In the case of entry on private business, the application for visa shall be accompanies by a document of agreement issued by the immigration administration organ.

Article 21 (Entry by crewman's certificate)

Foreigners bearing crewman's certificate may enter the DPRK at the designated port without visa.

Where a foreigner who has a crewman's certificate wishes to exit by an airplane, train, automobile or other vehicle, due formalities shall be carried out.

Article 22 (Entry or exit by certificate of border area travel)

Foreigners bearing a border area travel permit shall enter the designated area.

Where a foreigner wishes to go to another part of the DPRK from the border area, approval of the relevant immigration administration organ shall be obtained.

A foreigner residing in the DPRK may immigrate on private business with a border area travel permit issued by the immigration administration organ concerned.

Article 23 (Tourist certificate)

Foreigners who have obtained a tourist certificate of the DPRK may immigrate without visa.

Article 24 (Prohibited immigrants)

The following foreigners shall be denied entry into the DPRK:

1. Those who have encroached upon the sovereignty of the DPRK;
2. International terrorists;
3. Drug addicts and insane persons;
4. Those suffering from contagious disease or coming from an area where a contagious disease has broken out;

5. Those carrying identification documents that are forged or soiled beyond recognition; and
6. Those who are prohibited entry by the relevant organ.

Article 25 (Extension of validity of immigration certificate)
Foreigners shall enter or leave the DPRK within the term of validity of their immigration certificate.
The term of validity of an immigration certificate shall be extended upon expiry.

Article 26 (Cancellation of registration of stay or residence)
Foreigners who have stayed or resided in the DPRK should cancel their registration with relevant immigration administration organ before returning home. In this case the certificate of long-term stay or residence shall be surrendered.

Article 27 (Exit or entry of foreigners staying for a long term or residing)
Foreigners who have taken up residence or stay in the DPRK for a long period shall leave their certificate of long-term stay or certificate of residence registration with the relevant immigration administration organ in case they wish to trip outside the territory of the DPRK for a certain period of time.
The same shall be returned upon completion of the trip.

Article 28 (Immigration by vehicles)
Foreigners staying in the DPRK for a long period of time may immigrate by the vehicles for which they have obtained license. In this case a border crossing pass shall be obtained for the vehicle concerned.

Article 29 (Foreigners prohibited from exit)
Foreigners who do not hold an immigrate certificate, hold an invalid immigration certificate or are prohibited from exiting by a law-enforcement organ shall not leave the DPRK.

Chapter 4 Immigration Inspection

Article 30 (Obligation for immigration inspection)
Citizens, foreigners and means of transportation that enter or leave shall be inspected at the border crossing point.
No one shall enter or leave the DPRK without immigration inspection.

Article 31 (Duties and powers of immigration inspection organ)
Duties and powers of the immigration inspection organ are as follows:

1. Inspecting immigration certificate held by citizens and foreigners who enter or leave the DPRK;

2. Inspecting documents of transports that enter or leave the DPRK;
3. Conducting official duties for security and order of border crossing at the border crossing points.
4. Conducting security inspection by using necessary equipment to citizens and foreigners who enter or leave the DPRK;
5. Checking and handling confiscated contrabands and classified documents and materials;
6. Demanding, if necessary, institution concerned or citizens or foreigners who enter or leave the DPRK the documents and relevant materials necessary to inspecting immigration inspection;
7. Detaining, inspecting or searching those who violate the border crossing order or damage national security and transports;
8. Holding to cross border citizens or foreigners who break the border crossing order and their transports; and
9. Performing other duties as authorized by the State.

Article 32 (Inspecting immigration certificate and stamping)
Citizens or foreigners who enter or leave the DPRK shall obtain an entry or exit stamp on a page of the immigration certificate after submitting it with required forms and getting inspected.

Article 33 (Complying with border crossing points)
Citizens or foreigners shall enter or leave the DPRK only through the border crossing point designated on the immigration certificate.
If they wish to cross the border not designated point or be inspected outside of the border crossing point du to unavoidable circumstances, they shall inform the immigration inspection organ concerned of what they wish in advance.

Article 34 (Prohibited personal effects)
Citizens or foreigners who enter or leave the DPRK shall not bring in or out contrabands damaging national security and social order and classified documents or other materials.

Article 35 (Providing information about border crossing transports)
The transport institution and immigration organ concerned shall provide the immigration inspection organ concerned with information about the arriving and departing time, location, passengers and cargo of train, airplane or ship that enter or leave the DPRK before arrival and departure of such transports.

The responsible person of the airplane or ship or his agent shall provide the immigration inspection organ concerned with the list of crewmembers and passengers immediately after the transports' arrival or prior to the departure at the international airport or the trade port.

Article 36 (Duties of responsible person of transports)

The responsible person of the transports shall prohibit any persons from exiting or entering the transports concerned or loading or unloading cargo to and from the transports concerned until the immigration inspection is made for departure or arrival.

The responsible person of the transports shall not put on the transports anyone who is prohibited to enter or leave the DPRK and if he has realized that such person was on board, he shall immediately inform the immigration inspection organ of the fact.

Article 37 (Cross-border certificate for vehicle, business hours)

Where citizens or foreigners cross a border point by driving their own motor vehicle, they shall show the cross-border certificate for vehicle for the immigration officer's inspection.

Citizens or foreigners who cross a border bridge by vehicle or on foot shall be bound to the publicly noticed business hours of the immigration office.

Article 38 (Obligation of foreign ships to be inspected for entering, voyaging)

Foreign ships shall be inspected at the anchorage area by the immigration organ concerned prior to entering a trade port.

Foreign ships shall not go off designated seaways in the waters of the DPRK.

Article 39 (Landing of foreign seamen)

Where foreign seamen whose ship is anchored at a trade port wish to land, the captain of the ship or his agent shall obtain shore leave after filing an application with the immigration inspection organ concerned.

Seamen who landed with the granted shore leave shall return to their ship within the designated time.

Article 40 (Embarkation, *gyeopseon* order)

When citizens or foreigners embark on or disembark from a ship, their immigration certificate or approved document for immigration shall be inspected by the immigration inspecting organ.

Where a foreign ship and a DPRK ship wish to do *gyeopseon*, it shall submit the application for *gyeopseon* or embarkation and get approval from the immigration inspection organ concerned.* *Author's note -

gyeopseon is unknown vocabulary even by the most voluminous Korean dictionary published by the North Korean authority but it seems to be "tug or tugging."

Article 41 (Responsibility for rejected person)

The person in charge of transport or the owning organization of the transport bringing a prohibited person to enter the DPRK shall be responsible for taking him back as well as for the relevant expenses for returning.

Chapter 5 Stay, Residence and Tour of Foreigners

Article 42 (Registration, formalities)

Foreigners may stay, reside or tour in the DPRK depending on the purpose of their entry. In this case they shall go through due formalities within the prescribed period of time.

Article 43 (Classification of stay)

The stay of foreigners shall be divided into two categories: short-term and long-term.

Short-term stay shall be up to 90 days from the date of entry and long-term stay more than 91 days.

Article 44 (Registration of stay)

Foreigners who have entered the DPRK territory shall, within 48 hours of their arrival at their destination, have their stay registered and have the registration confirmed in the passport or separate visa.

Foreigners who have entered without a visa due to unavoidable reasons shall have their visa issued before registration of their stay.

Article 45 (Stay in place other than destination)

Where foreigners stay in a place other than their destination for more than 48 hours for unavoidable reasons, they shall have their stay registered with the local immigration administration organ.

Article 46 (Registration institutions)

The stay of foreigners who are on official business shall be registered with the central or provincial (or municipality directly under the central authority) immigration administration organ.

Depending on circumstances, registration may be made with municipal (or district) or county immigration administration organ of the border area concerned.

The stay of foreigners who are on private business shall be registered with the municipal (or district) or county immigration administration organ.

Article 47 (Issuance of certificate of long-term stay)

Foreigners who wish to stay for a long term shall obtain a certificate for long-term stay depending on the purpose of stay. In this case they shall carry out due formalities.

Article 48 (Exemption from registration)

The following foreigners shall be exempt from registration of their stay:

1. Members of parliament, government or other high-level delegations;
2. Members of diplomatic or consular representative offices of foreign countries or international organizations in the DPRK;
3. Foreigners who enter the DPRK to leave on the same day without lodging;
4. Crewmen of foreign ships, airplanes and railway trains that entered the trade port, airport or railway station; and
5. Foreigners designated by the competent organ.

Article 49 (Registration of stay of foreign crewmen)

Where crewmen of foreign ships, airplanes or railway trains are staying for more than 48 hours in a place other than the designated port, airport or railway station, they shall be registered with the relevant immigration administration organ.

Article 50 (Changes in registration of long-term stay, re-issuance of certificate of long-term stay)

Where any change is made in the particulars of long-term stay registration, the foreigner concerned shall, within 7 days of the occurrence thereof, register the particulars of change with the immigration administration organ and have a certificate re-issued.

Where a certificate of long-term stay is lost or seriously soiled, the foreigner concerned shall have it re-issued.

Article 51 (Foreigners' residence)

Foreigners who have taken up residence in the DPRK shall register their residence with the immigration administration organ concerned and have a certificate of residence issued.

In this case, a minor shall have a birth certificate issued.

A foreigner's residence registration certificate and a birth certificate shall be valid for 3 years.

Article 52 (Formalities for transfer of residence)

A foreigner who wishes to change the place of residence shall, within 25 days of removing the original registration, register the residence with the immigration administration organ in the area of their new residence.

Article 53 (Change in foreigner's residence registration, re-issuance of residence registration certificate or birth certificate)

Foreigners who have taken up residence shall, within 14 days of any change in the registration caused by birth, death, marriage, divorce, change of profession and the like, register the particulars of change with the immigration administration organ concerned and have a new certificate of residence registration or birth issued.

Article 54 (Foreigners' trip in the DPRK)

Foreigners who have taken up residence, who are staying on private business and who have a border area travel permit shall need a pass issued by the relevant immigration administration organ to make a trip in the DPRK territory.

Foreigners shall, upon their arrival at their destination, have their arrival and departure confirmed in the pass by the immigration administration organ in the area concerned.

The staff of the consular or diplomatic representative offices of foreign countries, and international organizations, and foreigners who are on official business shall not need a pass.

Chapter 5 Sanction

Article 55 (Sanction against a citizen)

A citizen who violates this Law shall be fined or prohibited from leaving or entering the DPRK.

Where the breach is serious, penal responsibility shall be imposed.

Article 56 (Sanction against foreigner)

Where a foreigner violates this Kaw, he shall be liable for a fine, his entry or exit prohibited and approval for his stay or travel cancelled.

Where the breach is serious, he shall be deported out of the territory of the DPRK or liable to penal responsibility.

Article 57 (Complaints)

Complaints about the sanction shall be lodged with the Ministry of Foreign Affairs, the relevant immigration administration or a judicial organ.

[Source: (1) Laws and Regulations of the Democratic People's Republic of Korea Governing External Economic Matters, Legislation Press, Pyongyang, 2012; (2) *Bukhan Beopryeongjip sang & ha* (Collection of Laws and Regulations of North Korea Vol. I & II, PDF), National Intelligence Service of the Republic of Korea, Seoul, 2024; and (3) *Choesin Bukhan Beopryeongjip* (Collection of Current Acts

and Regulations of North Korea) published by *Bukhanbeop yeonguhoe* (North Korean Law Research Group), Myung-Bong Chang (ed.), Seoul, 2018]
*Any amendments made after April 10, 2012 are translated into English by the Author.

▪ LAW OF THE DEMOCRATIC PEOPLE'S REPUBLIC OF KOREA ON LAND LEASE

Adopted by Decision No. 40 of the Standing Committee of the Supreme People's Assembly on October 27, 1993 and thirdly and lastly amended by Decree No. 1995 of the Presidium of the Supreme People's Assembly on November 29, 2011

Chapter 1 Fundamentals

Article 1 (Objective)

This Law is enacted for the purpose of providing strict guidelines for the leasing of land to and the use of the leased land by foreign investors and foreign-invested businesses.

Article 2 (Lessee)

Foreign corporate bodies or individuals may lease and use the land.

Article 3 (Limited land use right of lessee)

A lessee shall have the right to use the land leased.

Natural resources and deposits in the leased land shall not belong to the holder of the right to use the land.

Article 4 (Parties to land lease contract)

Land shall be leased subject to the approval of the central land and environmental protection guidance organ.

A contract of land lease shall be concluded by the land and environmental protection department of the people's committee of the province (or municipality directly under the central authority) concerned.

Article 5 (Contribution of land use right)

Institutions, enterprises and organizations of the DPRK may contribute land use right to an equity or contractual joint venture. In this case approval thereof shall be obtained from the people's committee of the province (or municipality directly under the central authority) concerned.

Article 6 (Term of lease)

The term of lease shall be determined by agreement between the contracting parties within the limit of 50 years.

Article 7 (Property right of lessee)

The right to use the leased land shall be the property right of the lessee.

Article 8 (Use of leased land)

The leased land shall be used in accordance with the land-related laws and regulations of the DPRK and the contract of land lease.

Chapter 2 Mode of Land Lease

Article 9 (Mode)

Land shall be leased through consultation.

Land may also be leased by tender or auction in the special economic zones.

Article 10 (Information to be furnished by lessor)

The lessor shall provide the lessee with the following information:

1. Location and area of the land and its topographical map;
2. Purpose of land use;
3. Building area and land development plan;
4. Term of construction and the minimum amount of investment required;
5. Requirements related to environmental protection, hygiene, anti-epidemics and fire service;
6. Term of land lease; and
7. State of land development.

Article 11 (Consultation)

Land shall be leased through consultation according to the following procedures:

1. A potential lessee shall study the supplied information concerning the land and submit to the lessor an application for the use of land, accompanied by a copy of a document approving the establishment of an enterprise or the residence;
2. The lessor shall notify the application of its approval or rejection within 20 days of receipt of the application.
3. The lessor and the potential lessee shall enter into a contract containing the area and purpose of the land use, purpose and term of the lease, total amount of investment, term of construction, rental charge and other relevant matters; and
4. The lessor shall, after receiving the charges for the transfer of the land use right as specified in the contract of land lease, issue a certificate of land use and register it.

Article 12 (Tender)

The procedure for leasing land by tender shall be as follows:

1. The lessor shall either make public the information concerning the land in question, place and date of the tender, opening date of the tender, procedures of tender and other relevant information, or forward a tender guide to the designated bidder;
2. The lessor shall sell the tender documents to the potential bidder;

3. The lessor shall provide consultation with regard to the tender;
4. The bidder shall pay the prescribed security for a tender and place a sealed tender document in the tender box;
5. The lessor shall form a jury consisting of experts from economic, legal and other relevant sectors;
6. The jury shall review the tender documents and decide the best offer by taking into account the conditions of land development, construction and the amount of rental charge offered;
7. The lessor shall issue a notice to the successful bidder after the jury has reached a decision;
8. The successful bidder shall conclude a contract of land lease with the lessor within 30 days of the receipt of the notice, pay the relevant charges for the right of land use, receive the certificate of land use and register it.

   Should it be necessary to defer the signing of the contract, an application for a deferment of at least 30 days shall be submitted to the lessor 10 days prior to the prescribed date;
9. The unsuccessful bidder shall be informed of the result within 5 days of the decision of the jury and the security shall be refunded. In this case no interest shall be payable for the security; and
10. Should the successful bidder fail to conclude a contract of land lease within the prescribed period of time, the tender shall be declared null and void and the security shall not be refunded.

Article 13 (Auction)

Leasing of land by auction shall be concluded as follows:

1. The lessor shall make public the information concerning the land in question, date, place and procedures of the auction, standard price of the land, and other information necessary for the auction;
2. The lessor shall put up land for auction based on the standard price which has been made public, and the bidder who offers the highest price shall be declared the successful bidder; and
3. The successful bidder shall conclude a contract of land lease with the lessor, obtain a certificate for use of the land and register it.

Article 14 (Use of leased land, supplementary contract)

The lessee shall use land in a manner consistent with the purpose prescribed in the contract of land lease.
A lessee who wishes to alter the purpose of land use shall conclude a supplementary contract in that regard with the lessor.

Chapter 3 Transfer or Mortgage of Right to Use Land

Article 15 (Term of transfer or mortgage)
The lessee shall, subject to the approval of the lessor, be entitled to transfer (by selling, re-leasing, donating or inheriting) or mortgage to a third party the right to use the whole or part of the leased land.
The term of the transfer or mortgage of the right to use land shall not exceed the remaining term of the lease prescribed in the contract.
Article 16 (Terms of transfer)
The lessee shall be entitled to sell, re-lease, donate or mortgage the right to use the leased land only when the total amount of charges for the transfer of the land use right is paid and the investment prescribed in the land lease contract is made.
Article 17 (Scope of transfer)
Where the land use right is to be transferred, the rights and obligations related to the use of the land, and the structures and the attachments shall also be transferred.
Article 18 (Sale of land use right)
The land use right shall be sold in accordance with the following procedures:

1. The seller and buyer of the land use right shall conclude a contract and have it notarized;
2. The seller shall submit to the lessor an application for the sale of the land use right, together with a copy of the contract; and
3. The seller and buyer shall register with the relevant lessor the changes concerning the land use right.

Article 19 (Prior lien on leased land)
Where a lessee sells the right to use the land, the lessor shall have a prior lien on buying it.
Article 20 (Re-lease of leased land)
The lessee may re-lease the land leased. In this case an application for the re-lease shall be filed with the lessor for approval, accompanied by a copy of the contract of land lease.
Article 21 (Mortgaging land use right)

A lessee may mortgage the land use right for the purpose of securing a loan from a bank or other financial institutions. In this case the structures and other attachments on the land shall also be mortgaged.

Article 22 (Mortgage contract)

Where the land use right is to be mortgaged, the mortgagor and the mortgagee shall conclude a contract on the basis of the terms of the contract of land lease. In this case the mortgagee may require the mortgagor to provide a copy of the contract of land lease or the transfer contract, a copy of the certificate of land use and other information relating to the current state of land.

Article 23 (Registration of mortgage)

Both the mortgagor and the mortgagee of the land use right shall register the mortgaged right with the lessor within 10 days of the conclusion of mortgage contract.

Article 24 (Disposal of mortgaged land)

Where the mortgagor fails to redeem debts by expiry of the mortgage, or where business is resolved or goes bankrupt during the term of the mortgage contract, the mortgagee may dispose of the land use right mortgaged by contract, as well as the structures and other attachments on the land in accordance with the mortgage contract.

Article 25 (Use of disposed mortgaged land)

The winner of the land use right, and the structures and other attachments disposed of by the mortgagee shall have them attested by a notary office, register the changed name of the right holder with the registration office and use the land in a manner consistent with the contract of land use.

Article 26 (Prohibition of re-mortgage or transfer)

The mortgagor shall not, without the consent of the mortgagee, be entitled to re-mortgage or transfer the land use right during the term of contract.

Article 27 (Withdrawal of registration of mortgage of land use right)

Should a mortgage contract be terminated due to the payment of debt or other reasons, the mortgagee and the mortgagor shall withdraw the registration of mortgage of the land use right within 10 days of the said termination.

Chapter 4 Land Rental Charge and Land Use Fee

Article 28 (Obligation to pay rental charge)

The lessee shall pay the rental charge according to the prescribed rates.

The rental charge shall be paid to the lessor.

Article 29 (Cost of land development)
Where the developed land is to be leased, the lessor shall receive from the lessee the rental charges plus the cost of land development.
The cost of land development shall include the costs of land realignment, road construction, water supply and drainage, electricity, telecommunications and heating systems.
Article 30 (Term of payment of rental charges)
The lessee shall pay the total amount of rental charges within 90 days of concluding the land lease contract.
Where a large area of land is leased in such case as the comprehensive development of land, the lessee may make payment by installment within period of time approved by the lessor.
Article 31 (Payment of guaranty money for fulfilment)
A lessee who leased land through consultation or by auction shall pay to the lessor guaranty money equivalent to 10% of the rental charges within 15 days of concluding the contract of land lease.
The guaranty money for fulfilment may be appropriated for the rental charges.
Article 32 (Arrearage)
Where the lessee fails to pay the rental charges within the prescribed period of time, the lessor shall demand additional payment equivalent to 0.05% of the overdue rent on a daily basis, starting from the first day of default.
Where arrears are not paid for more than 50 consecutive days, the contract of land lease may be cancelled.
Article 33 (Payment of land use fee)
Foreign-invested businesses and banks annually pay fee for the use of the land.
For the investors in priority sectors the fee may be reduced or exempted for up to 10 years.

Chapter 5 Return of the Land Use Right

Article 34 (Return of land use right, compensation for residual values)
The land use right shall automatically return to the lessor at the expiry of the term of lease prescribed in the contract. The structures and other attachments on the land shall also return without charges being paid.
In the case of land leased for more than 40 years, compensation may be made for the residual value of the buildings completed within 10 years before the expiry of the land lease.
Article 35 (Cancellation of registration)

Upon expiry of the term of the land lease the lessee shall return the certificate of land use to the issuing organ and cancel the registration of the land use right.

Article 36 (Extension of term of lease)

The lessee who wishes to extend the term of land lease shall file with the lessor an application to that effect 6 months before the expiry of the term. In this case another contract of land lease shall be concluded, necessary procedures followed and the certificate of land use reissued.

Article 37 (Expenses for removal and clearing of land)

Upon expiry of the term of the lease, the lessee shall, in compliance with the request of the lessor, remove the structures, facilities and other attachments at his own expense and clear the land.

Article 38 (withdrawal of land use right)

The land use right shall not be withdrawn during the term of the lease. Should unavoidable circumstances demand the withdrawal of the land use right during the term of lease, the lessor shall obtain consent from the lessee 6 months in advance and offer the lessee other land in the same conditions or pay appropriate indemnity.

Article 39 (Penalties)

Where a lessee illegally uses land without the certificate of land use, or changes the purpose of use of land or transfers or mortgages the land use right without approval, he shall be fined, have the facilities on the land confiscated or be required to restore the land to original state, and the contract of transfer or mortgage be declared null and void.

Article 40 (Withdrawal of land use right)

Where a lessee fails to make an investment equivalent to 50% of the total sum during the term prescribed in the contract of land lease, or to develop the land as specified in the contract, the land use right may be withdrawn.

Article 41 (Complaints)

Where the penalty imposed is not acceptable, a lessee may, within 20 days of the receipt of the notice of penalty, appeal to an institution higher to the one that has imposed sanctions.

The higher institution shall settle the complaints within 30 days of receipt thereof.

Article 42 (Settlement of disputes)

Disputes concerning the land lease shall be settled through consultation between the parties concerned.

In case of failure in consultation, the disputes shall be settled through mediation, arbitration or judicial procedures.

[Source: Laws and Regulations of the Democratic People's Republic of Korea Governing External Economic Matters, Legislation Press, Pyongyang, 2012]

Bibliography

- Arbitration Tribunal in the Matter of an Arbitration between the Government of the State of Kuwait and the American Independent Oil Company (AMINOIL), Int'l Legal Mat. 976 (1982)
- Banco Nacional de Cuba v. Chase Manhattan Bank, 658 F.2d 875, 888 – 890 (2d Cir. 1981).
- Banco Nacional de Cuba v. Sabbatino, 376 U.S. 398 (1964)
- Bang, Chan Young, *Bukjoseon-eui Daewoe Gaebang Gaehyeok Jeongchaek-gwa Haprijeok Daebuk Jeongchaek-eui Mosaek* (North Korea's Open and Reforming Policy and Seeking for Reasonable Policy on North Korea), Bakyeongsa Publishing Co. Seoul, Republic of Korea (ROK), 1996
- Black's Law Dictionary, West Publishing Co. St. Paul, MN, United States,1990
- Carter, Barry E. and Trimble, Philip R., International Law, Little, Brown and Company, Toronto, Canada, 991
- Chang, Myung-Bong (ed.) *Choesin Bukhan Beopryeongjip* (Collection of Current Acts and Regulations of North Korea), *Bukhanbeop yeonguhoe* (Korea Society of North Korean Law Studies), Seoul, ROK, 2018
- Comeaux, Paul and Stephan, Kinsella N., *Reducing Political Risk in Developing Countries: Bilateral Investment Treaties, Stabilization Clauses, and MIGA & OPIC Investment Insurance*, 15 N.Y.L. Sch. J. Int'l & Comp. L. 1, 1994.
- Choi, Dal Gon and Shin, Young Ho, *Bukhanbeop Ipmun* (Introduction to Law of North Korea), Sechang Publishing Co., Seoul, ROK, 1998
- Choi, Jong Ko, *Bukhanbeop* (Laws of North Korea), Bakyeongsa Publishing Co., Seoul, ROK, 1996
- Chorzow Factory decision, 1928 P.C.I.J. (Ser. A) No. 17
- Sahoe Anjeonbu Chulpansa (Press of the Ministry of Social Safety), *Minsabeop Sajeon* (Civil Law Dictionary),

Pyongyang, Democratic People's Republic of Korea (DPRK), 1997

- Code of Regulations, Title III – the President, 1949-1953 Compilation at 1043 published by the National Archives and Records Service, General Service Administration, Washington D.C., U.S.A., 1958
- Constitution of the Socialist Republic of Vietnam of 2013
- Convention establishing the Multilateral Investment Guarantee Agency 1985 as amended, International Bank for Reconstruction and Development, Washington D.C. U.S.A.
- Covenant of the Workers' Party of Korea, DPRK, 2021
- Convention on the Recognition and Enforcement of Foreign Arbitral Awards (New York Convention), the United Nations Commission on International Trade Law (UNCITRAL), New York, U.S.A., 1958
- Chun, Hong Tack and Oh, Gang Su, *Bukhan-eui Woegukin Tujajedo-wa Daebuktuja Chujinbangan* (North Korea's Foreign Investment Climate and Proposals for Investment in North Korea), Korea Development Institute, (KDI), Seoul, ROK, 1995
- Daehanminguk Gukgajeongbowon (National Intelligence Service of the Republic of Korea), *Bukhan Beopryeongjip sang & ha* (Collection of Laws and Regulations of North Korea Vol. I & II, PDF), Seoul, ROK, 2024, available at <https://www.nis.go.kr/CM/1_2_1/list.do?category=nlaw>
- Dixon, Martin, Textbook on International Law, Oxford University Press, Oxford, United Kingdom (1990)
- Executive Order 13382, United States, June 28, 2005 available at <https://ofac.treasury.gov/media/8581/download?inline>
- Executive Order 13466 of the United States - Continuing Certain Restrictions With Respect to North Korea and North Korean Nationals on June 26, 2008 available at <https://www.gpo.gov/fdsys/pkg/WCPD-2008-06-30/pdf/WCPD-2008-06-30-Pg912.pdf>
- Executive Order 13551 of the United States on August 30, 2010 on the Federal Register Vol. 75 No. 169 at 53837-9.

- Executive Order 13570 of the United States on April 18, 2011 on the Federal Register Vol 76 No. 76 at 22291-2.
- Executive Order 13687 of the United States on January 2, 2015 on Federal Register Vol. 80 No. 3 at 819-20.
- Executive Order 13694 of the United States on April 1, 2015 on Federal Register Vol. 80 No. 63 at 18077-9.
- Executive Order 13722 of the United States on March 15, 2016 on Federal Register Vol. 81 No. 53 at 14943-5
- Executive Order 13757 of the United States on December 28, 2016 on the Federal Register Vol. 82 No. 1 at 18077-9.
- Executive Order 13810 of the United States on September 25, 2017 on the Federal Register Vol. 82 No. 184 at 47705-9
- Federal Register vol. 15, number 126 of the United States on June 30, 1950 available at <https://www.govinfo.gov/content/pkg/FR-1995-06-30/html/95-16046.htm>
- Federal Register Vol. 60. No. 32 of the United States on February 16, 1995 available at <https://www.govinfo.gov/content/pkg/FR-1995-02-16/pdf/FR-1995-02-16.pdf>
- Federal Register Vol. 61, No. 114 of the United States on June 12, 1996 at 29785 available at <https://www.gpo.gov/fdsys/pkg/FR-1996-06-12/pdf/96-14826.pdf>
- Federal Register Vol. 63 No. 85 of the United States on May 4, 1998 at 24585 available at < https://www.govinfo.gov/content/pkg/FR-1998-05-04/pdf/98-11745.pdf>
- Federal Register Vol. 65 No. 118 of the United States on June 19, 2000 at 38165-6 available at <https://www.gpo.gov/fdsys/pkg/FR-2000-06-19/pdf/00-15390.pdf>
- Federal Register Vol. 71, No. 66 of the United States on April 6, 2006 at 17346 available at <https://ofac.treasury.gov/media/4746/download?inline>

- Federal Register Vol. 72, No. 9 of the United States on Tuesday, January 16, 2007 available at <https://www.govinfo.gov/content/pkg/FR-2007-01-16/pdf/07-133.pdf>
- Federal Register Vol. 72, No. 22 of the United States on February 2, 2007 at 4960 available at <https://www.govinfo.gov/content/pkg/FR-2007-02-02/pdf/E7-1702.pdf>
- Federal Register Vol. 73 No. 127 of the United States on Tuesday July 1, 2008 at 37351 available at <https://www.govinfo.gov/content/pkg/FR-2008-07-01/pdf/08-1404.pdf>
- Folsom, Ralph H. and Gordon, Michael W. International Business Transactions, Hornbook Series, West Publishing Co., St. Paul, MN, United States, 1995
- Frisch, David and Bhala, Raj, Global Business Law Principles and Practice, Carolina Academic Press, Durham, NC, U.S.A., 1999
- Haendel, Dan, Foreign Investment and the Management of Political Risk, Routledge, New York, U.S.A., 1979
- Harmonized Tariff Schedule of the United States Rev. 11 (2025) available at <file:///C:/Users/User/Downloads/General%20Note%203%20(2).pdf>
- Hughes, Christopher W., Tumen River Area Development Programme: Frustrated Micro-Regionalism as Microcosm of Political Rivalries 19, Centre for the Study of Globalisation and Regionalisation (CSGR), University of Warwick, Coventry, United Kingdom, 2000, available at <https://wrap.warwick.ac.uk/id/eprint/2068/1/WRAP_Hughes_wp5700.pdf>
- International Atomic Energy Agency (IAEA), Treaty on the Non-Proliferation of Nuclear Weapons (NPT), INFCIRC/140 of 1968, New York, United States, 1968
- International Labour Organization (ILO), Tripartite Declaration of Principles

- concerning Multinational Enterprises and Social Policy, Geneva, 2022 available at <file:///C:/Users/User/Downloads/wcms_094386.pdf>
- Je, Sung Ho, *Bookhan woeja yoochi bupryong-eui moonjejum* (Issues on North Korea's Foreign Investment Laws): Research Report 98 – 05, Korea Institute for National Unification (KINU), Seoul, ROK, 1998
- Jodice, David, A., Political Risk Assessment: an Annotated Bibliography, Greenwood Press, Westport, CT, U.S.A., 1985
- *Joseon Minjujuui Inmingonghwaguk Beopjeon* (Compilation of Laws of the Democratic People's Republic of Korea) of 2005, published by Beopyul Chulpansa, Pyongyang, DPRK, 2004
- Chun, Hong Tack and Oh, Kwang Soo, *Bukhan-eui Woegukin Tujajedo-wa Daebuktuja Chujinbangan* (North Korea's Foreign Investment Climate and Proposals for Investment in North Korea), Korea Development Institute, (KDI), Seoul, ROK, 1995
- Kalyuzhnova, Yelena and Andreff, Wladimir (editors), Privatisation and Structural Change on Transition Economies, Palgrave Macmillan, New York, United States, 2008
- Kennedy Jr., Charles R., Managing the International Business Environment: Cases in Political & Country Risk, Prentice Hall, Englewood Cliffs, NJ, U.S.A., 1991
- Kim Il Sung University Publishing House, Investment Climate Rajin-Sonbong Free Economic and Trade Zone, Pyongyang, DPRK, 1995
- Kim, Jong Il, *Juche sasang-eh daehayeo* (About Juche idea), Thesis presented by Kim Jong Il to the Juche idea forum held on the occasion of celebration of Kim Il Sung's 70th birthday in 1982), published in Dong-A Ilbo, Wonjaryo-ro bon Bukhan (North Korea seen through Original Sources), Seoul, ROK, 1989.
- Kim, Sung Chull, *Bukhan gwanryobupae yeongu* (Study on Government Officials' Corruption in North Korea): Research Report 94 – 01, Korea Institute for National Unification (KNIU), Seoul, ROK, 1994
- Korbin, Stephen J., Managing Political Risk Assessment: Strategic Response to Environmental Change, University of California Press, Berkeley, CA, U.S.A., 1982

- Korea Development Bank, *Bukhan-eui Saneop* I, PDF (Industry of North Korea vol. I, PDF), 2020, Information Portal of the Ministry of Unification of the Republic of Korea, available at <file:///C:/Users/User/Downloads/%E3%80%8E2020%20%EB%B6%81%ED%95%9C%EC%9D%98%20%EC%82%B0%EC%97%85%E3%80%8F%201%EA%B6%8C.pdf>
- Korea Trade Promotion Corporation (KOTRA), *Segye Gakkook gyongje Jungbo – Bookhan* (Economic Information on Individual Countries – North Korea), Seoul, ROK, 1999
- Law of the People's Republic of China on Chinese-Foreign Equity Joint Ventures of 2005
- Law on Investment in Vietnam of 2020
- Lax, Howard L., Political Risk in the International Oil and Gas Industry, Routledge, New York, U.S.A., 1983
- Lee, Sang Jik, Choi, Sin Lim and Lee Seok Gi, *Bukhan-ui Gieop – Gwanggongeop Bumun Gieop Pyeolam* (Enterprises of North Korea – Prospectus of Enterprises in the Mining and Industry Sectors), Korea Institute for Industrial Economics & Trade (KIET), Seoul. ROK, 1996
- Legal Institute Information, Cornell Law School of Cornell University, United States available at <https://www.law.cornell.edu/>
- Legislation Press, Laws and Regulations of the Democratic People's Republic of Korea Governing External Economic Matters, Pyongyang, DPRK, 2012
- Library of Congress, North Korea - A Country Study – The Role of Chuch'e available at <http://countrystudies.us/north-korea/60.htm>
- Minsabeop Sajeon (Civil Law Dictionary), Ministry of Social Safety of the Democratic People's Republic of Korea, Pyongyang, 1997
- Muchlinski, Peter, Multinational Enterprises and the Law (2nd ed.), Oxford University Press, Oxford, United Kingdom, 1999
- Investment Guarantee Agency (MIGA), Convention Establishing the Multilateral Investment Guarantee Agency, Washington D.C., United States, 1985, available at <https://www.miga.org/sites/default/files/archive/Documents/MIGA%20Convention%20February%202016.pdf>

- Naewoe Press, *Bukhan Yongeo 250 Seonjip* (Anthology of North Korea's Terminology 250), Seoul, ROK, 1992
- (The) New Encyclopedia Britannica, Macropædia, Vol. 22 (15th ed.), Encyclopædia Britannica Inc., Chicago, United States, 1989
- OECD, Declaration on International Investment and Multinational Enterprises, OECD/LEGAL/0144, Paris, France, 1976
- OECD, Declaration on International Investment and Multinational Enterprises, OECD/LEGAL/0144, Paris, France, 2023, available at <https://legalinstruments.oecd.org/en/instruments/OECD-LEGAL-0144>
- Oh, Seung Ryeol et al, *Bookhan-eui Gyeongjegaehyeok-gwa Nambuk Kyeonghyeop* (North Korea's Economic Reform and South-North Korea Economic Cooperation): Research Report 95 – 22, Korea Institute for National Unification (KINU), Seoul, 1995.
- Park, Pilho, *Bukhan, Tuja, Gyoyeok, Mirae* (North Korea, Investment, Trade and Future), Lets Book, Seoul, ROK, 2019
- Park, Young Ja et al., *Bukhan Giyeop-eui Wunyeongsiltae mit Jibaegujo* (Operation of North Korean Enterprises and their Governance), Research Report 16-11, Korea Institute for National Unification (KINU), Seoul, ROK, 2016
- Presidential Determination on Sanctions against North Korea for Detonation of a Nuclear Explosive Device (Presidential Determination No. 2007-7 of December 7, 2006) available at <https://www.govinfo.gov/content/pkg/FR-2007-01-16/pdf/07-133.pdf>
- Presidential Proclamation 2914 of the United States, December 16, 1950
- Presidential Proclamation 2935 of the United States, August 1, 1951
- Presidential Proclamation 8271 – Termination of the Exercise of Authorities Under the Trading With the Enemy Act With Respect to North Korea" on June 26, 2008 available at <https://www.gpo.gov/fdsys/pkg/WCPD-2008-06-30/pdf/WCPD-2008-06-30-Pg911-2.pdf>

- Randolph Jr., Patrick A. et al, Chinese Real Estate Law, Kluwer Law International, The Hague, Boston, 2000
- Rennack, Dianne E., North Korea: Legislative Basis for U.S. Economic Sanctions, Congressional Research Service (CRS), CRS Report R41438, Washington DC, United States, 2023, available at <https://sgp.fas.org/crs/row/R41438.pdf>
- Restatement (Third) of Foreign Relations Law of the United States, American Law Institute, 1987
- Siegwart, Hans, Caytas, Ivo G and Mahari, Jukian I., Global Political Risk: Dynamic Managerial Strategies (1989), American Journal of International Law, Vol. 85, Issue 3, 1991
- Sin Dong-A (ed.), *Dong-A Ilbo* (Dong-A Daily Newspaper Co.), *Wonjaryo-ro bon Bukhan 1945-1988* (North Korea seen through Primary Sources 1945-1988), Seoul, ROK, 1989
- Seon, Han-seung, *Nambookhan nodongjedo-eui bigyo-wa nodongjeongchaek yonkoo* (Comparative Study of Labor Systems of South-North Korea and Labor Policy), Policy Research 98-22, Korea Labor Institute, Seoul, ROK, 1998
- Tariff Schedule of the United States of 1963 available at <https://www.gpo.gov/fdsys/pkg/STATUTE-77/pdf/STATUTE-77A-PgI.pdf>
- Texas Overseas Petroleum Co/California Asiatic Oil Co. v. Government of Libyan Arab Republic, 17 Int'l Legal Mat. 3, 29 (1978)
- Thunell, Lars H., Political Risks in International Business Investment Behavior of Multinational Corporations, Praeger Publishers, New York, United States, 1977
- United Nations Resolution 3281 on the Charter of Economic Rights and Duties of States (1975).
- United Nations Security Council Resolution 1695 (S/RES/1695 (2006))
- United Nations Security Council Resolution 1718 (S/RES/1718 (2006))
- United Nations Security Council Resolution 1874 ((S/RES/1874 (2009))
- United Nations Security Council Resolution 2087 (S/RES/2087 (2013))

- United Nations Security Council Resolution 2094 (S/RES/2094 (2013))
- United Nations Security Council Resolution 2270 (S/RES/2270 (2016))
- United Nations Security Council Resolution 2321 (S/RES/2321 (2016))
- United Nations Security Council Resolution 2356 (S/RES/2346 (2017))
- United Nations Security Council Resolution 2371 (S/RES/2371 (2017))
- United Nations Security Council Resolution 2375 (S/RES/2375 (2017))
- United Nations Security Council Resolution 2397 (S/RES/2397 (2017))
- United States-Mexico-Canada Agreement (USMCA), United States Trade Representative (2020)
- 2012 U.S. Model Bilateral Investment Treaty, United States Trade Representative
- Wang, Guiguo and Mo, John, Chinese Law, Kluwer Law International, Hague-London-Boston, 1999
- Woo, Wing Thy, Parker, Stephen and Sachs, Jeffery D., Economies in Transition: Comparing Asia and Eastern Europe, The MIT Press, Cambridge, Massachusetts and London, England, 1997
- Yoon, Yeon-ok (ed.), Bukhan-eui Juyo Tonggyeojipyo (Major Statistics of North Korea), Statistics Korea of the Republic of Korea, Seoul, ROK, 2017
- Zink, Dolph Warren, The Political Risks for Multinational Enterprise in Developing Countries: with a Case Study of Peru, Praeger, New York, United States, 1973

About the Author

Pilho Park is an Attorney at Law in the State of New York, United States. He was a foreign-service officer of the Republic of Korea, Administrative Officer of WHO, Director of the International Institute for Central Asian Studies (IICAS-UNESCO) and an Invited Professor of Dankook University, lectured in law, cultural heritage and international relations mainly at South Korean universities, conducted academic work across these fields in South Korea and Eurasian countries (most of them were economies-in-transition), and practiced law in New York City and the surrounding area. He studied law in South Korea (KNOU), South Africa (UNISA), the Philippines (UST) and United States (IUB and UW-Madison) and earned a Doctor of Juridical Science (S.J.D.).

www.ingramcontent.com/pod-product-compliance
Lightning Source LLC
LaVergne TN
LVHW052025200926
848481LV00005B/1591
* 9 7 9 8 9 5 0 0 1 1 0 3 0 *